The First

American Frontier

The First American Frontier

Advisory Editor: Dale Van Every

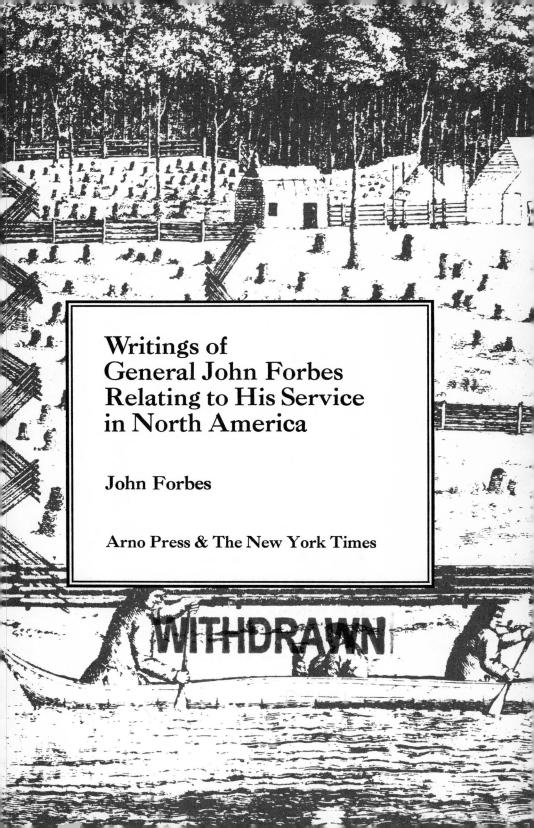

Writings of
General John Forbes
Relating to His Service
in North America

John Forbes

Arno Press & The New York Times

Reprint Edition 1971 by Arno Press Inc.

Reprinted from a copy in
The Pennsylvania State Library

LC #   78-106091
ISBN 0-405-02849-0

The First American Frontier
ISBN for complete set: 0-405-02820-2

See last pages of this volume for titles.

Manufactured in the United States of America

Writings of General John Forbes

Portrait of Brigadier General John Forbes presented to the Royal Greys Regiment by Colonel T. S. G. H. Robertson-Aikman, a collateral descendant. Reproduced through the courtesy of Mr. Henry King Siebeneck.

WRITINGS
of
GENERAL JOHN FORBES

Relating to his Service in North America

Compiled and Edited by
ALFRED PROCTER JAMES, Ph.D.
Professor of History, University of Pittsburgh

for

THE ALLEGHENY COUNTY COMMITTEE
of
THE PENNSYLVANIA SOCIETY
of the
COLONIAL DAMES
of America

THE COLLEGIATE PRESS · MENASHA, WISCONSIN
MDCCCCXXXVIII

Foreword

IN 1927 the *Letters of General John Forbes, relating to the Expedition Against Fort Duquesne in 1758,* was "Compiled from Books in the Carnegie Library of Pittsburgh, *for the* Allegheny County Committee Pennsylvania Society of the Colonial Dames of America" by Irene Stewart, Reference Librarian, Carnegie Library of Pittsburgh. To this publication was added a "list of References on the Expedition." A foreword by Helen H. Pearson, Chairman of the Allegheny County Committee, states,

> The Allegheny County Committee feels that in placing these letters before the public they are rendering a service peculiarly fitting to the people of Pennsylvania. Around Fort Duquesne centered the struggle between the French and the English for supremacy in the country west of the Alleghanies. This struggle ended in the victory of General John Forbes, who wrested Fort Duquesne from the French, and gave to it the name of Pittsburgh, in honor of William Pitt.

In an Introduction, presumably written by Miss Stewart, the statement is made,

> The letters here reproduced are those which are available in the Carnegie Library of Pittsburgh. Though but a small part of Forbes's correspondence, these letters, chiefly to William Pitt, Governor Denny of Pennsylvania and Governor Sharpe of Maryland, form a valuable history of this difficult and important campaign. A very few letters not by General Forbes have been included because of their relevancy and for the sake of continuity.

This small volume of eighty-eight pages put out in 1927 was of much use to students of the history of that period. It has saved many students hours of time in libraries. Much credit for its publication is due both its sponsors and its compiler. But, as hinted in the Introduction, the volume included only "a small part of Forbes's correspondence." About forty Forbes documents were found, available in print, in the Carnegie Library of Pittsburgh. No effort was made to locate manuscript materials widely scattered in archival and manuscript depositories. This was beyond the scope and plan of the praiseworthy enterprise.

Research carried on by the Western Pennsylvania Historical Survey under the sponsorship of the Buhl Foundation of Pittsburgh, the University of Pittsburgh and the Historical Society of Western Pennsylvania, 1931-

1936, revealed in time much of the additional manuscript Forbes material. When this was known to Miss Stewart and to the sponsors of the 1927 volume the project of printing a more complete edition of the writings of General Forbes was taken up with keen interest. Active effort in promoting the enterprise was made by Irene Stewart, compiler of the first edition, Helen H. Pearson, Chairman of the Allegheny Committee, Mary Updike Ely, Chairman of the Committee on Historical Research, and others, and the proposition to undertake more extended publication was, on presentation to the Allegheny County Committee in formal session, graciously received and heartily supported.

This relatively small group of women, concerned to do something of wide public and historical value, agreed to raise the funds necessary to underwrite publication of the more complete edition. Their courage was rewarded with success, no small accomplishment in the trying economic and financial circumstances of the decade.

The agreeable but difficult and responsible task of compiling and editing this more complete edition was assigned to the writer by reason of his service as Research Associate of the Western Pennsylvania Historical Survey in which connection he had the opportunity to canvass manuscript material in many of the larger manuscript depositories of the United States, Canada, England and France. Only those who have attempted to collect and edit so large a collection can justly conceive the difficulty and responsibility involved.

The sponsors and the compiler and editor are under many obligations to others for aid and assistance. In point of time the first obligation is to the sponsors and compilers of the earlier edition mentioned above. Then chronologically, they are indebted to the sponsors and staff of the Western Pennsylvania Historical Survey. Their support and interest made possible a year spent in research and travel by the editor, and, on request, they secured the use of photostatic reproductions of many important documents, in many cases furnishing carefully collated transcripts, now accessible to the public. In fact this publication may be credited in part to the already considerable results of the Western Pennsylvania Historical Survey. In turn great obligation is due to the Library of Congress and its staff, particularly in the Division of Manuscripts. Much use was made of the library, which deserves particular thanks for sending whole volumes of photostats to be used at leisure in the Historical Society of Western Pennsylvania. Among these volumes those of greatest importance were the Bouquet Papers from the British Museum, listed as B. M., Add. MSS. 21630-21660, and the Amherst Papers, found in the British Public Record Office, listed as P. R. O. W. O.

34:44. To the Library of Congress we are indebted also for transcripts of the documents listed as P.R.O.C.O. as well as transcripts from sundry other divisions of the Public Record Office. In particular in the Division of Manuscripts of the Library of Congress the editor secured help beyond her official duties from Miss Grace Gardiner Griffin, the well known compiler of *Writings in American History*. Special obligation is also due to Mr. Henry King Siebeneck of Pittsburgh, Pennsylvania. Greatly interested in General Forbes, Mr. Siebeneck made a trip to Scotland in search of data. Through his courtesy were obtained the portrait of Forbes used as a frontispiece and four letters from manuscripts in the possession of Colonel T. S. G. H. Robertson-Aikman, The Ross, Hamilton, Lanarkshire, Scotland. Appropriate and deserved, also, is mention of the inspiration, services and endurance under strain, of M. W. J. and W. A. J., the wife and son of the compiler and editor.

In search of documents, the editor sought assistance widely from librarians and archivists, whose uniform attention to solicitations in person or in writing was most gratifying, though too often unable to furnish any material whatever. Among the depositories furnishing valuable materials as well as great courtesy may be listed the Maryland Historical Society, The Hall of Records of Maryland, the New York Public Library, the Historical Society of Massachusetts, the Dominion Archives of Canada, the British Museum and the Public Record Office of Great Britain.

In the course of research, information was gleaned that some Forbes material could be found only in the Huntington Library and Art Gallery of San Marino, California. On investigation it was eventually found that no publication of the writings of General Forbes would be more than fractional without the use of the numerous manuscripts in the Loudoun Papers and Abercromby Papers of the Huntington Library and Art Gallery. A survey of the location of the documents herein published, reveals not only the wealth of that manuscript collection, but also the heavy indebtedness of this volume to the Huntington Library and Art Gallery and its staff. Of the one hundred and ninety-nine documents obtained, fifty-eight, or thirty percent, could be found only in the Huntington Library and Art Gallery. In addition about fourteen, also available elsewhere, were found in the Loudoun Papers and Abercromby Papers.

The unreliability of transcripts of manuscripts is well known and hardly calls for comment. To mention examples would be needlessly invidious. More significant is the unfortunate fact that printed editions prove too often unreliable. Editors have exercised great liberty in omissions and changes. Where the original manuscript of a printed document can be located the necessary corrections can be made. Where the manuscript cannot be found, the printed edition with all its defects must be used. In this connection it is a pleasure to mention the uniformly excellent edition of manuscripts found in the *Pennsylvania Magazine of Biography and History* and in the *Maryland Archives*.

A complete statistical statement of the American Writings of General John Forbes would be easy, but is hardly necessary in so small a number of documents. Most of them come from the papers of Loudoun, Abercromby, Bouquet, Sharpe, Washington, and Amherst, located in various depositories. So far as the office copies of Forbes himself are concerned, they have not been located. They may have been turned over to his cousin and executor, Governor James Glen of South Carolina and, according to the archivist of South Carolina, may have been destroyed in the burning of Columbia, South Carolina, during the Civil War. But there are Forbes papers in Scotland in the possession of relatives, whether or not manuscripts written in America, it has been impossible to ascertain. Should they be made available to the public later, it is at least hoped that while they may contain additional documents, they will not invalidate greatly the items of this edition.

Forbes letters are rarely offered for sale in the public auction of manuscripts. A number of documents mentioned in letters available, cannot be located and seemingly have perished. Some notice of such letters is given here in appropriate footnotes. Unless additional manuscripts are found in Scotland, it is highly improbable that the present list will be later greatly enlarged. Requests for information about additional documents, made in the *American Historical Review* and the *Mississippi Valley Historical Review* brought no response whatever. It has seemed advisable in this larger edition to omit many valuable documents throwing light on the Expedition of Forbes. But several documents obviously emanating from the headquarters of Forbes and therefore indirectly Forbes documents, although written by assistants or amanuenses, have been purposely included. In such procedure it is, however, difficult to know what to include and what exclude and some materials of the kind may easily have escaped detection altogether. Under all the circumstances, in this as well as in other matters, it has seemed impossible to go beyond the present publication.

ALFRED P. JAMES

Biographical Sketch of Forbes

AS Francis Parkman has so well told, the French and Indian War began in Western Pennsylvania. Domination of the upper Ohio Valley was the original aim in the conflict. At no time from 1749 to 1760 was this objective lost sight of. Plans of campaign by Dinwiddie and Washington, by Braddock, by Shirley, by Abercromby, by Loudoun; and by the authorities in England invariably involved securing possession of the forks of the Ohio. Under William Pitt, as His Majesty's principal Secretary of State, the plan was carried to success under the command of Brigadier General John Forbes. The biography and the personality of Forbes, his writings and a critical study of his expedition are vital features of Pennsylvania history. The final critical history of Forbes' expedition remains to be written. An effort is made in this volume to present to the public the surviving writings of General Forbes. A brief treatment of the biography and personality of Forbes is an essential introduction.

In his obituary, included as the last document in this volume, and in biographical sketches in the *Dictionary of National Biography* and the *Dictionary of American Biography* it is stated that Brigadier General John Forbes was born in 1710. But in the Historical Society of Pennsylvania is a photostat of the birth certificate, duly attested, of General John Forbes, "Extracted from the Register of Births and Baptisms for the Parish of Edinburgh in the County of Edinburgh," which reads: "Edn. 5th Septr. 1707. The Deceased Lieut. Coll. John Forbes of Pittencrief and Eliz. Graham his relict A. S. N. John." According to this certificate, Brigadier General John Forbes was a posthumous son, and thereby the youngest child and could not have been born as late as 1710.

Residents of Allegheny County, Pennsylvania, in particular, but of the world in general should be interested in the fact that the father of the General was Laird of Pittencrief, Dunfermline, Fifeshire, Scotland. In Dunfermline, a little more than a century after the birth of General Forbes, was born Andrew Carnegie, who in his *Autobiography* mentions Pittencrief and its lairds, how they impressed him in his early boyhood and how one of his life's satisfactions was that of purchasing Pittencrief and thereby becoming in late life the Laird of Pittencrief.

Papers still in the possession of the descendents of the relatives of General Forbes may contain valuable information on his early life, but there is at present in print an almost complete lack of documentary material.

As indicated in his letters and noted in his obituary, young John Forbes was "bred to the profession of physic." In other words he studied medicine, possibly at the University of Edinburgh. But like so many younger sons of good British stock he turned to a military career. His obituary and biographical sketches state that he was "early ambitious of the military character."

He appears to have purchased in 1735 a cornetcy in the 2nd Royal North British Dragoons, the Scots Greys, in which by additional purchases and faithful services, he rose to the rank of lieutenant-colonel in 1750. In the war of the Austrian Succession, the Scots Greys saw several years of service on the continent, and Forbes won for himself high honor, continuous promotion and appointment to important staff positions. On the continent he came into intimate contact with Sir James Campbell, Sir Francis Campbell, the Earl of Stair, the Duke of Bedford, Lord Ligonier and even with the Royal Duke of Cumberland. He performed noteworthy services as aide-de-camp to important commanders and eventually, as indicated in his writings, rose to the important staff position of Deputy Quartermaster General. In fact he became so affiliated with high command in the British Army that biographers of William Pitt have classified Forbes as a member of the old school of officers, many of whom were shelved by William Pitt in 1758.

In the British Museum there is a noteworthy relic of Forbes in the period of his rapid promotion. Imbedded in a plush holder is a small coin, a farthing, bearing the indentation of a bullet. The coin is said to have saved the life of Forbes at the battle of Culloden, April 16, 1746. It serves as an indication that Forbes was among the troops called back from Flanders in the autumn to suppress the attempt of Charles Stuart, the young pretender, to recover the throne.

As indicated in the second document of this volume, Forbes was given the colonelcy of the 17th Foot in the early part of 1757, and ordered to America with Lord Loudoun, the recently appointed Commander-in-Chief of His Majesty's Forces in North America. On good terms with the Campbells he became adjutant general to Lord Loudoun, a position which he filled with much insight and skill until March 1758. The correspondence and other documents of the winter of 1757-1758, clearly reveal Forbes as the confidant and in the same degree the mentor of Lord Loudoun. His military capacity is as much demonstrated at this point as in later events of his own command of the expedition against Fort Duquesne. His good sense and excellent spirit are well revealed.

In the revolutionary changes which were made, in December 1757, by

William Pitt, in which Abercromby replaced Loudoun as Commander-in-Chief, and Amherst and Wolfe were sent against Louisburg, Colonel John Forbes was appointed Brigadier General in America and assigned to command of the expedition against Fort Duquesne.

News of his appointment reached Forbes at his headquarters as Adjutant-General in New York, about the middle of March. For nearly a month he remained there making preparations for his campaign. But in the middle of April he was ordered to Philadelphia by Abercromby. For ten weeks he remained in Philadelphia gathering troops, supplies and money. His difficulties with regulars, volunteers, provincials, commissary supplies, quartermaster supplies, the Colonial legislatures and the Indians are revealed in his writings. In spite of enormous difficulties of circumstances and personnel, he managed to push forward 1400 of Montgomery's Highlanders, 400 of the Royal American Regiment, 40 artillery men and about 5,000 provincials, mainly Pennsylvanians and Virginians, but with scattered companies of Marylanders and North Carolinians. As is evident from his writings his main aid came from Colonel Henry Bouquet, sent forward in advance, but Colonels John Armstrong and James Burd of the Pennsylvania Forces and Colonels George Washington and William Byrd III of the Virginia Troops gave valuable service, while Colonel Archibald Montgomery and Major James Grant were available for consultation and use.

Leaving Philadelphia the last of June, Forbes reached Carlisle about July 4, 1758, where he remained for more than five weeks engaged in collecting and forwarding supplies, while Bouquet, in advance, was opening a new road over the Alleghenies. On August 12th Forbes reached Shippensburgh, where he remained until the end of the first week in September. After a stop of ten days at Fort Loudoun, Pennsylvania, he reached Raystown about the middle of September, from which place after a six weeks' halt he reached Loyal Hannon in the first days of November. The location of the route, the construction of the new road and the provision of adequate supplies demanded his continuous attention and effort, from Philadelphia in April to Loyal Hannon in November.

During most of these months General Forbes was painfully and dangerously ill. It is little short of a marvel that he was able to carry on in his command. An elaborate medical diagnosis would be necessary to indicate the complication of diseases from which he suffered. It is not necessary to add to the indications revealed in the writing of one "bred to the profession of physic." There are few more heroic cases of success in the face of adversity than that of General Forbes in his expedition of 1758.

As revealed in his writings, but more clearly demonstrated in other documents, General Forbes was at a standstill at Loyal Hannon in the second week of November. Heavy rains had ruined the road. Winter was coming on rapidly. He was not aware of the French weakness at Fort Duquesne. The failure of his expedition seemed destined to follow Grant's defeat at Fort Duquesne in September and the defense of Loyal Hannon against the French assault in October. But the clouds soon cleared away. In a final skirmish, a French prisoner, taken near Loyal Hannon, revealed the fatal weakness of the French. A hurried advance of his overwhelming forces put Forbes, in ten days, in possession of the historic point. Too ill for further stay and responsibility General Forbes returned after one week's stay in Pittsburgh. His trip in midwinter, on which he was carried in a litter between horses, consumed more than six weeks. For nearly a month, though bedridden and slowly dying, he tried to continue his command. His end came on March 11, 1759. He was buried in Christ Church with an imposing military service. The best estimation of the man and his work, and one which from writings seems eminently just, is that found in his obituary.

A. P. J.

Table of Contents

Table of Abbreviations

AB	Abercomby Papers, Huntington Library and Art Gallery
A. C.	Autograph Copy
Add. MSS.	Additional Manuscripts. British Museum Classification
A. C. S.	Autograph Copy Signed
A. Df.	Autograph Draft
A. D. S.	Autograph Draft Signed
Aikman MSS	Manuscripts in the possession of Colonel T. S. G. H. Robertson-Aikman
A. L. S.	Autograph Letter Signed
A. N. S.	Autograph Note Signed
B. M.	British Museum
C. O.	Colonial Office Papers
D. A. B.	*Dictionary of American Biography*
D. N. B.	*Dictionary of National Biography*
Df.	Draft
H. S. P.	Historical Society of Pennsylvania
L. C.	Library of Congress
LO.	Loudoun Papers, Huntington Library and Art Gallery
L. S.	Letter Signed
Md. Arch.	*Archives of Maryland*
Md. H. S.	Maryland Historical Society
N. B. G.	*Nouvelle Biographie Generale*
N. C. Col. Recs.	*Colonial Records of North Carolina*
N. J. Arch.	*Archives of the State of New Jersey*
N. Y. C. D.	*Documents Relative to the Colonial History of the State of New York*
N. Y. P. L.	New York Public Library
Pa. Arch.	*Pennsylvania Archives*
Pa. Col. Recs.	*Pennsylvania "Colonial Records"*
Pa. Mag.	*Pennsylvania Magazine of Biography and History*
Pa. MSS.	Manuscripts in the Department of Archives, Harrisburg, Pennsylvania
P. R. O.	Public Record Office, London
T.	Treasury Papers, London
W. O.	War Office Papers, London

Writings of General Forbes

John Forbes, to Hugh Forbes[1]
[AIKMAN MSS.]

Manchester, 19th October. [1754]

My Dear Hughie

I gott only to this place day before yesterday, and have had my hands full ever since. This day I had yours of the 10th with Geo: Ross's and have likewise seen yours to Iock[2]—All I can say I had anticipate all you Intelligence, for before I left Scotland. I sent my offers to Service to go to America as Q^r Mr Gen^r, with particular restrictions and provisoo's—to which I have not had any answer, But find by the news papers Sir John Stclair[3] has been named to it. but whether true or false God knows—Had my offers been accepted off—My friend Iock would have been furthwith putt in action but as they may probably have been refused. and that I must drudge on here. I shall by to morrows post write to Sir peter Halkett[4] Ld Sandwich[5] &c and in short all my friends, that can have any interest to gett what can be gott for him, and after our review which is thursday next, If I find I can be of any wise serviceable to him I will go with him to London directly, for he is a very fine boy, and without relation I think I would go a great way on foot to do him Service.

I am hurry'd at present and so big with thought that I could burst, If Sir john stclair has had the fortune to be named, to what I really thought was showing Spirit in me, and serving of the Government in offering my service, but a post or two determines it, I find I shall be extreamly hurt, but patience—I know the other a Mad sort of Fool.

---

[1] An advocate, or lawyer, of Edinburgh, the brother and joint heir of John Forbes.

[2] Not identified, but from the context, a young relative.

[3] Lieutenant-colonel in the 60th regiment and deputy quarter-master general, well known for his career in America, 1755-1767.

[4] Colonel of a regiment under Braddock, killed at the Battle of the Monongahela, July 9, 1755.

[5] John Montague, fourth Earl of Sandwich (1718-1792), British political figure, involved in grave private and public scandal. Consult the *D. N. B.*

I am weary and tyred with a long day of exercise, so pray tell peggy[6] I am most faithfully hers and am no less yours.

Jo: fforbes.

I am heartily sorry for Mamy fforbes[7] and do in my heart pity Little Willy,[8] who I know has and is, sensible of passions.

*   *   *   *   *

Forbes to Loudoun[9]
[LO 3006 A.L.S.]

Portsmouth March 10th [1757]

My dear Lord

A Week ago Richbell dyed and his Majesty gave me his regiment so that here I am wt out almost any thing in order to join the Regt at Cork when wee proceed with the six others to join you, where I shall be extreamly happy If I can render my service Agreeable to you or any way or in any shape Contribute to the worsting the ennemy and gaining you renown.

As I shall want a place to putt my head in upon my arrivall, as also perhaps a horse or two, or perhaps a Cart or waggon, If your Lordship therefore would compassionate ane old friend, and allow any of your aid de Camps or men employed about you, to take some care of me, I shall be most thankfull at meeting.

Wee have had bad luck last year God send us better this, but the Defference and dissentions of our ministry, are terrible things for any Expedition— I am affraid the two new raised Regts of Highlanders, will not be ready to go wt us. Wee sail for Cork Sunday morning and hope for a Speedy and prosperous voyage.

Admiral Holburn[10] Commands, wt 12 Line of battle Ships and some

---

[6] Probably the sister of Forbes.

[7] Probably, Elizabeth Graham Forbes, mother of General Forbes.

[8] Not identified.

[9] John Campbell, fourth Earl of Loudoun (1702-1782), prominent in the Stuart rebellion of 1745; governor-in-chief of Virginia, February 17, 1756; commander-in-chief of the British forces in North America, March 20, 1756. Having accomplished little in the campaigns of 1757, Loudoun was replaced by General James Abercromby and recalled to England. Consult the *D. N. B.* and Pargellis, *Lord Loudoun in America.*

[10] Francis Holburne (1704-1771), admiral in naval service 1720-1770; present at Louisburg in 1755 and again, in 1757, in command of the fleet, his last service in America. Consult the *D. N. B.*

Frigates, I wish to God wee gett to your seas before the French—

As Mr Campbell[11] our Chieff Engineer is just going off I cou'd not help writing you this scrawl.

Mr Pownall[12] is this day examined before the house of Commons about your Contracts, As the Contractor Mr Baker is attacked, Mr Pownall joins us to morrow and sails w^t us

Service to John Young & all

God bless you
Adeu—Y^{rs} &c &c
Jo: fforbes.

[*Addressed:*] To the Right Hono^{ble} The Earl of Loudoun Command^r in Chieff in North America
by Capt. Dugall Campbell

[*Endorsed:*] Col John Forbes Portsmouth
Mar. 10th 1757 R. June 30th

*   *   *   *   *

John Forbes to Hugh Forbes
[AIKMAN Mss.]

St. Helens road just sailing
March 17th 1757.

My Dr Hughie

I this moment received yours of the 8th of march, and have just time to tell you that wee are under sail 12 Sail of the Line Battele 4 frigates, 3 Bomb vessells and 60 or 70 transports. So the Confusion, hurry, and even danger is immense by the Ships running eternally on board. But all that apart, what wee are about is a secret as yet, and hope the first news you will hear will be success.

I must own My Dear Hughie that the parting Jock two days ago hurt me, extreamly as you may believe, my tenderness for him, grew and augmented, with his years, I said as much to him as to his future conduct, as I possibly could think off, and told him to sell his, Adjutancy whenever it had paid itself, because I could probably have ane opportunity of taking him into

---

[11] Dugal Campbell, who died at sea in 1757.

[12] Thomas Pownall (1722-1805), secretary in 1753 to Governor Osburn of New York; friend of many prominent American colonials; lieutenant governor of New Jersey, 1755-1757; governor of Massachusetts, 1757-1760; famous commentator on the American Colonies. Consult the *D. N. B.* and the *D. A. B.*

my own Reg^t I have done everything to recommend him to Preston,[18] but no mortall can influence a bad heart, however Jock must make the best of it. If I live he must come on, as I believe No person of my rank, has gone with more eclat to N° America than I have done—so patience.

Tell Peggy to pardon my not having time to write her but I shall from Cork where I expect to hear from her and you My Dr Hugh. God bless you and the family and in writing my eyes shows the sincerity and tenderness of at least an honest heart

Adieu   Y^rs   Jo fforbes

[*Addressed*:] To
<blockquote>
Mr Hugh Forbes advocate
at his home in the Land Markett
Edinburgh

N° 2
Home
Seal
</blockquote>

John Forbes to Hugh Forbes
[Aikman Mss.]

Portsmouth Aprile. [1757]

Dear Hugh.

I wrote you a short letter the other day f^m London acquainting you of the tripp I am to take to North America and in what Situation, The time that I had to prepare my equipage for such ane affair joined to my present lameness, has created me infinite hurry and confusion, however we must look forward.

The Situation of Arthurs[14] affairs of which he wrote me a detail has perplexed me, and should be sorry to think he was beton to pieces by Law, Arrestm^ts &c So proposed to Hugh Forbes to advance so much money and become principall creditor, but he plainly showed me that he had it not in his power, altho he had never so good Inclination—I than spoke to George Ross, who told me, that he would make Ronald Craufurd enquire into the State of Affairs, and would do every thing in his power to contribute to the making Arthur easy but I dont think y^t by any means Mr Forbes ought to be disoblidged, only I think Arthur ought to accept of money at 4 p cent in place of five, that he pays which, no body ought

---

[18] Not identified.
[14] Arthur Forbes, brother of General Forbes and joint heir of the latter's estate.

to take amiss—As Arthur expatiates upon his own frugality and all for the good of your family, I really think you ought to leave no stone unturned, of convincing him, and the world that you have them at heart as much as he or any one can have, I need not point out the method as your know the taking care of your own health is the foundation to the whole. And I am astonished that two Brothers can not contrive to live together in one family, when there views & scope tend to the same purpose.

As to Jock He is in a fair way to go through the world & I hope by the time I gett home to be able to serve him most essentially, as he is now left to himself if he can abstain from Company for a year or two untill he becomes more steady. I doubt nothing of his succeeding.

As to me Dr Hugh. I am now going to beginn a very active life, when perhaps my time of life intiteled me to ease and retreat. but there is no help for it, wee must make a tryal of what has but a bad aspect in every ones eyes, our Success will be glorious, our failing must be regreated.

As

New York October 20th

Looking over some papers the other day I found the above part of a letter, which makes me think that I had been so hurryed at Portsmouth as not to have had time to finish it and as I am at present in one constant confusion I send it you now as it is.

Adieu   Y^{rs} Jo fforbes

[*Endorsed in another hand:*]
Mr. Hugh Forbes principall Clerke

John Forbes to Hugh Forbes
[AIKMAN Mss.]

Cork Aprile 27th [1757]

My Dear Hughie,

I have receivd severall of your letters,[15] to which I should have given regular returns, but I have been most miserable aboard a ship these five weeks, in order to gett here where we arrived yesterday after ten days sail from St Helen's road, But figure to yourself my misery, Lame & Sick neither able to eat, drink write or think, so you may easily find I could not well tell you what was going on.

Wee are here all in hurry and confusion and I have only time to tell

---

[15] Not found.

you, you shall have a long letter next post, and pray tell peggy that I designed writing her from St Helens road, for which reason I went aboard ship to be quiet and free from the hurry of Portsmouth, but there I lay a fortnight at Anchor in one continued hurry of wind.

As we shall probably be here these ten days I shall have both leisure & health, particularly as my leg is now better, So least I lose the post I shall cutt this short without any remarks but of wishing all well. Adieu My Dr Hughie

Y^{rs} Jo fforbes.

My friend Jock is
ane Idle Dog for
he promised me to write
to his mother every step of
what passed at Portsmouth,
but find he has not done it.

Forbes to Peregrine Hopson[16]
[LO 3949 L.S.]

[Halifax, July 15, 1757]

Sir

As you know the Situation of the seven Regiments lately come from Ireland under your Command, and the great Expences they have unavoidably been put to, I must beg you will be pleased to move his Excellency Lord Loudoun in behalf of his Majesty's seventeenth Regim^t of Foot, that they may be put on the same footing with the other Regim^{ts} on their Establishment, in regard to Batt Baggage and Forrage money.

I am   Sir
Your most Obedient humble Servant
Jo fforbes Col^o of the 17th Reg^t

July 15th 1757.

[*Addressed:*] The Honble Major Genl Hopson

*   *   *   *   *

---

[16] Peregrine Thomas Hopson, Colonel of the 40th regiment.

Forbes to Loudoun
[LO 4096 L.S.]

Halifax 6ᵗ, August 1757.—

My Lord,

In Obedience to Your Lordship's Orders, I waited upon Major General Lord Charles Hay, in Company with Captain Cunningham[17] your Lordship's Aid de Camp; And Signified to him, that Upon the report I had made to Your Lordship, of his Answer to Your Orders of this day, that thereupon I had receiv'd Your Lordship's Commands to Order him into Arrest; Whereupon Lord Charles demanded those Orders in writing; either from your Lordship, from me or to be given out to the Line in Publick Orders; and said, he would remain in his Quarters till Nine o'Clock tomorrow morning, when he should Expect to receive those Orders in Writing.

I must further add, that notwithstanding I produced Your Lordship's signed Order to me, for putting Lord Charles Hay in Arrest, His Lordship still insisted to have Orders in writing tomorrow morning.

I am with the greatest regard.

My Lord. Yʳ Lordships. most obedᵗ & most humˡᵉ Servᵗ Jo: fforbes

The Right Honᵇˡᵉ, The Earl of Loudoun.

[*Endorsed:*] Report of Colonel Forbes and Capᵗ. Cunningham after delivering Lord Loudoun's orders of Arrestment to Lord Chas Hay 6ᵗʰ Aug. 1757

* * * * *

Forbes to Hay[18]
[LO 4097 A.L.S.; P.R.O. C.O. 5:48 (Copy) L. of C. transcript, p. 483]

[Halifax, August 6, 1757]

My Lord.

I am order'd by the Earl of Loudoun, to acquaint your Lordship, that he does not think himself impowerd to comply with the Request your Lordship made this forenoon, for His Leave of Your Returning to Great Britain. And I am further directed to acquaint your Lordsp, that the Hawke or Jamaica sloops of war, whichever you are pleased to make choice off shall

---

[17] Captain James Cunningham of the 45th regiment.

[18] Lord Charles Hay (d. 1760), soldier by profession; in 1752 colonel of the 33rd regiment; in 1757 major-general. Sent back to England as a result of this quarrel. He died before the final adjudication of the case. Consult the *D. N. B.*

have orders to receive Your Lordship & Equipage on board, in order to proceed to sea along with Lord Loudoun, and the troops.

I am with the greatest regard & esteem

My Lord, Y^r Lordships
most ob^t & most humb^{le} Servt

Jo fforbes.
Adjutant Gen^{li}

Hallifax Augst : 6th 1757
Ld Chas Hay—
[*Addressed:*] To The R^t Honb^{le}. Lord Chas Hay, Maj^r Gen^{ll} of His Maj^{ties} Forces—

Hallifax

[*Endorsed:*] Col. Forbes Letter to Lord Charles Hay w^t Lord Chas Answer to Lord Loudouns Message
6th Augt. 1757

*   *   *   *   *

Forbes to Loudoun
[LO 4097 A.L.S.; P.R.O. C.O. 5:48 (Copy) L. of C. transcript, p. 484]
Lord Charles Hay's Answer as taken from His
Mouth by Colonel Forbes—

[Halifax, August 6, 1757]

Sir,

Lord Loudoun has given me leave, & I have taken his Leave, and I am going what His Lordship has more to say he must send in writing=

My Lord—

I deliver'd your Lordships message by word of Mouth to Lord Chas Hay, & least I had not explained myself properly, I offer'd to read him the letter on the other page of paper—which his Lordship declined having read to him, and gave me for Answer the four lines at the Head of this page, which I wrote down in presence of Capt: Ourrie[19] of the Success Man of Warr & Capt Monypenny[20] his Lordship's Aid de Camp.

I am Y^r Lordships
ob^t & most humb^{le} Servt

To The Earl of Loudoun   Jo: fforbes.

---

[19] Captain Paul Henry Ourrie [Ourry] of the Royal Navy.
[20] Captain Alexander Monypenny of the 22d regiment.

Forbes to Lord Charles Hay
[LO 4126 A.L.S.]

[Halifax, August 7, 1757]
My Lord

The Answer that your Lordship gave me to Lord Loudouns message, and which I wrote down in your Lordship's Capt Ourries & Monypennys presence and read to you was.

Sir

Lord Loudoun has given me leave and I have taken Leave—And I am going, What his Lordship has more to say, He must send in writing.

This is the report I made to the Earl of Loudoun

I am Y[r] Lordships
most ob[t] and most hum[ble] Serv[t]
Jo fforbes Adj[t] Gen[l]

Hallifax Aug[st] 7th. 1757
[*Endorsed:*] Col: Forbes's Answer to L[d] C: Hays second Letter
7th Aug[t]. 1757

* * * * *

Forbes to Lord Charles Hay
[LO 4127 A.L.S.]

[Halifax, August 7, 1757]
My Lord

Underneath I send your Lordship a Copy of the Earl of Loudoun's orders to me Dated at Hallifax Aug[st] 6th, 1757—

Sir

Upon your Report of Maj[r] Gen[ll] Lord Charles Hays answer to my orders of this date. I do hereby require and Direct you, As Adjutant General to return to His Lordship and signifye to him that He is under Arrest

Sign'd Loudoun
a true Copy signed Jo fforbes
Adj[t] Gen[ll]

Hallifax, Augst 7th. 1757
To The R^t Honble
The Lord Chas Hay
Maj^r Gen^{ll} &cc
[*Endorsed:*] Col. Forbes's ans^r to Ld Chas Hays First Letter
6 Augt. 1757

*   *   *   *   *

Forbes to the Justices & Inhabitants of Newark in the Jerseys
[LO 4452 A.Df.S.]

New York Sept. 12th. 1757.—

Gentlemen.

I am Commanded by His Excell^{cy} The Earl of Loudoun to return you his thanks for the kind care you took of the sick belonging to the Army last spring, and his Lordship making no doubt of your continuing the same care to the poor sick Soldiers now amongst you, He therefore desires me to assure you, that your zeal for the publick service shall not be forgott, and he will take the first and properest method of letting His Majesty know of it.

As the provisions for the Army are furnished by a Treasury contract, Mr Kilby[21] the Contractor Agrees to pay the five Shillings and six pence a week new York Currency demanded by you in Y^r petition. Upon Condition that the Officer Commanding and the Surgeons attending the party are made the judges of what shall be furnished to the sick from time to time.

The Intention [ing]† of this being to secure to the sick, laboring under Infirmitys of Different kinds not only proper food but all [& care]† the attendance and Care that their unhappy Circumstances may require. So you will be so good as show this to the Commanding Officers and Surgeons attending the sick in your District or in any other who will give their Complyances—
I am gentleme^n

Y^r most ob^t & most hum^{le} Servt

Jo fforbes Adju^t Gen^{ll}

To the Justices & Inhabitants of Newark in the Jerseys
[*Endorsed:*] Answer to the Petition about the sick from the Jerseys
New York Sepr. 11, 1757

*   *   *   *   *

---

[21] Christopher Kilby of London, of the firm of Baker, Kilby, and Baker, contractors for provisions 1757-1758.
† Stricken out.

Forbes to Simon Fraser[22]
[LO 4478 Contem. Copy]

New York, Septr. 16th. 1757.—

Sir,

I am commanded by the Earl of Loudoun, to acquaint you, that as your Regiment is ordered directly to New York, that you will order Returns to be made out, to be deliver'd in upon your Arrival there.

1st A General Return of the Battalion, with the Numbers of your Supernumeraries.—

2^d A Copy of your Recruiting Accounts, stating the Time from whence the Pay of the Battalion commenced; the Sum allowed by Government for the inlisting each Man; With a true State of the Sums paid for Recruiting and Subsisting each Man. As also the Number that the Regiment consisted of, from the 24th of December last, and so forward weekly to the 24th. of June.—

You are likewise to give an Account to what Time the Pay of the Regiment has been issued from the Pay Office into your Agent's Hands; and to what Time the Regiment has received Money for their Subsistence; and what Provision is made for supporting the Regiment that his Lordship may give Orders accordingly.—

In Case that His Lordship be gone from hence, before your Arrival, You are to take the Earliest Opportunity of transmitting the above to his Lordship, wherever he may chance to be. And in His Absence, you will find Orders left here with the Commanding Officer, How you are further to proceed. I am

Sir,

Your most ob^t Humble Servant.
Jno. Forbes.—

L^t. Col^o. Fraser—

Copy

[*Endorsed:*] Copy. A Letter from Colonel John Forbes Adj^t Gen^{ll} to Lieu^t Colonel Fraser New York Sept. 16th 1757

*   *   *   *   *

[22] Lieutenant Colonel Simon Fraser (1726-1782), master of Lovat, colonel of the 71st regiment, Fraser's Highlanders, which he raised and which served in America five years; late in life a lieutenant-general. Consult the *D. N. B.*

Forbes to John Donaldson[23]
[LO 4924 A.Df.]

[New York, October 13, 1757]

Sir

Your are hereby ordered to make a Detachment of one Capt 2 Lieuts 2 Ens^{gns} 6 Serj^{ts} 4 Drummers and one hundred men of the 55th Reg^t under your Command to pass to new Windsor from thence One Lieu^t one Ensign Serj^{ts} Drums & c and fifty rank & file are to march by the most convenient route to Brunswick alias Shawungun—The Capt and the other party is to march from new Windsor to Goshen. Those partys are ordered for the protection & Defence of the Country against the Insults of the Indians, and the Lt Govr Delancey[24] has sent his directions and orders to the Col^{ols} and Commanding officers in those Districts to send a proper number of their militia along with any of our partys that may have occasion to march out of which you will acquaint the Different Officers—

As Capt West[25] is march'd to Rochester you will order this last [party to]† Detachment to putt themselves under his command of which he is to be acquainted, & that as he is at present in that Country, he will make choice of the properest place for himself to reside in, and to have communication w^t those under his Command [and]† as also with the Earl of Loudoun—

As your numbers will now be diminished the Sloops that you can spare, are to be directly discharged with proper Certificates to the Dep^{ty} Q^r Mr Gen^{ll} for their paym^t. You are to [acquaint]† order those Detachments that they are to take provisions, and afterwards provide themselves according to the orders sent to the last Detachment—that went with Capt West—

[Capt West and all]† those partys are to remain in those parts; untill further orders. Notwithstanding the orders given formerly = that the first party was to march and join the reg^t upon Cap^l Thodys[26] relieving

---

[23] Lieutenant Colonel John Donaldson, of the 55th regiment of Lord Howe.

[24] James De Lancey (1703-1760), chief justice and lieutenant-governor of New York, 1753-1755 and 1757-1760, a stormy petrel in New York politics. Consult the D. A. B.

[25] Captain Hon. George West of the 55th regiment. Cf. West to Forbes, October 14, 1757, from Rochester, LO 4634 A.L.S.

† Stricken out.

[26] Probably Captain Michael Thodey. Francis Thodey was also a captain in the New York militia.

him w^t his Company of which you will be so good as let the Commanding officer know—

To Col. Donnaldson

[*Endorsed:*] Col. Forbes's letter to Lieu^t. Col. Donnaldson to Detach 1 Capt. 2 L^{ts}. 2 Ens: 100 Men

*   *   *   *   *

Forbes to Captain West
[LO 4639 Contem. Copy]

New York 14th October 1757

To Capt. West
Sir

My Lord Loudoun having had intelligence that the Indians threaten to be very troublesome in that Country where your Detachm^t is Posted, His Lordship therefore order by last nights Post, that Colonel Donnaldson should Detach 1 Capt 2 Lieu^{ts} 2 Ensigns & 100 Men of the 55th Regim^t to march into that Country, the Captain with one half of the Men is to March from New Windsor to Goshen, the Eldest Lieut with the other half of the Men is to march to Brunswic^k alias Shewungun the whole of these Parties are to be under your Command, therefore you will order them to Report to you Regularly, as you will likewise to the Earl of Loudoun through me

His Lordship likewise Commands me to tell you, that as those hundred men are Detach'd to Reinforce you, upon information that the Seneka and Delaware Indians were resolvd to fall upon the back Settlements, he therefore thinks that you ought to make choice of a Centricall place for your own Residence, for the sake of communication, and to make such a disposition of the Officers & 150 Men under your Comm^d as you from the best information shall judge most proper for fulfilling the service you are ordered upon

And notwithstanding of former orders, upon the arrival of Capt Thodys Comp^y of the New York Regiment that you was to leave these parts, and join your Regiment, you'r now hereby directed to take the Command of Capt Thodys Company and dispose of them likewise to the best advantage for the good of the Service, and you, & the whole are to Remain upon this duty till further orders from the Earl of Loudoun.

           I am Sir

                Your Most humble Servant

                      Jo: florbes Adj^t Genl

P S—

My Lord Loudoun desires that you will make enquiry of what number of Troops can be conveniently Quartered this Winter at your Posts, and in their neighbourhood.

*   *   *   *   *

Orders Left For Colonel Simon Fraser On His Arrival at New York
[LO 4665 A.Df.]

[October 18, 1757]

Sir

I am Commanded by His Excel^cy^ The Earl of Loudoun, to Signifye to you. That upon your Arrivall here, It is expected that you will wait upon the Lt Governour Delancey And acquaint him thereoff—

You will than find in the hands of Murray of your Battalion a March route which carries you and your Supernumerarys to Conecticutt. where the quarters will be ready for you.

As you may gett Sloops for the transporting of y^r people to come along side of the transports you will therefore make them go on board of the Sloops without Allowing them, to disembark. Mr Oliver Delancey will be assisting to you in procuring the Sloops as he is to victuall them in proportion to the number each Sloop carries

There is ane order for taking all the mens bedding from the transports, for which Murray has the Dep: Q^r Mr Gen^lls orders to the Agent of the transports [*Illegible*] by which you will be directed—

Mr Murray will likewise furnish you with the regulations how the Contractors are oblidged to furnish the men, to which you are to order all your Officers to conform.

Upon Y^r Arrivall you are immediately to acquaint me, [as also]†　with the State of your Batt^n and Supernumerarys, and upon your Arrivall in your Quarters in Connecticut, you are to send me a report of your Quarters with a Controull of them, as also the monthly return of your reg^t. with a W:B. of the Supernumerarys at the bottom, In order that I lay the same before My Lord.

In Regard to the Deserters belonging to the different Regiments up the Country you will Embark them on board of a Sloop under a proper Officers Guard for Albany and these Men whoes crimes are not very no-

† Stricken out.

torious my Lord intend to pardon, but thoes who are flagrant he will [have]† Reserve the tryal of them to his own discretion by this information you may give a greater liberty to the most innocent as your number is great

[*Endorsed in Halkett's handwriting:*] Orders left for Lieut. Col: Fraser upon his arrival at New York.
18 October 1757

* * * * *

Forbes to Loudoun
[LO 4780 A.L.S.]

Albany Novr. 7th [1757]

My Dr Lord.

There is nothing new. Gen^{ll} Abercromby[27] and I returnd from the Ferry, by the other road wch wanting a good deal of repair Gen^{ll} Abercromby orderd one hundred men of offarells to work upon it.

I send your Lordship a letter from Parson Brooks[28] to me to be communicate to Yr Lordsp—if you judge his request reasonable and if this reach before y^t you leave the Fort, two words to Col: Haviland[29] will settle it.

I am told that the river up from this to the fort might easily be made passable & at a Small expence by cutting a passage through the riffs, which would be a great saving to the Government, So your Lordship may cause enquiry to be made, whether this is so or not.

Col: Donaldson has a letter from New York telling him that the Duke[30] came to London in Sepr last—I do not believe it.

The Quarters of the 17th reg^t is farr from being Settled, but suppose

---

† Stricken out.

[27] James Abercromby (1706-1781), second in command under Loudoun in 1756 and 1757, as colonel of the 44th regiment and major-general, and Loudoun's successor as commander-in-chief in North America in 1758. His disastrous defeat at Ticonderoga in 1758 resulted in his recall to England and replacement by Amherst. Consult the *D. N. B.*

[28] John Brooke of Albany. Cf. Brooke to Forbes, November 6, 1757, LO 4773.

[29] Lieutenant Colonel William Haviland of the 27th regiment of William Lord Blakeney.

[30] Common army terminology of the period for the Duke of Cumberland, younger son of George II.

it will soon [So]† I beg my Complim^ts to M^r. Webb^31 & Col° Young^32 and believe me most Sincerely

My Dr Lord Y^rs &c

Jo: fforbes

The Masachusets province sloop is taken and carryed in to Louisburgh. and by a Cartell Ship come in to Hallifax, it is said 200 Men of the Tilbury were saved and carried in to Louisburgh and that the French Fleet had receivd no Dammage—

[*Endorsed:*] Col. John Forbes Albany Novem 7th 1757 R. Novr 10th

*   *   *   *   *

Forbes to Loudoun
[LO 4803 A.L.S.]

Albany Novr. 10th [1757]

My Lord.

M^r. Christie^33 who had survey'd the houses in Nestiguna, has now fixed the quarters of the 17th Reg^t viz 100 Men at Half moon and fifty at the ferry where they must Hutt, upon the sides of Hudsons River two Companys and the rest of the Reg^t amounting to about 450 are to be putt up in the Suburbs of this place, And According to this disposition I have wrote to Colonel Morris.^34

The 44th and forty eight Reg^ts will be all embarked this day and will be gone by tomorrow morning.

We have no Accounts of Frazers^35 Battalion, and the News from Germany is not the most comfortable in this damn'd rainy foggy day, Keep warm and return soon, and let us know your day that the Chariot may meet you I am My Dr Lord

most sincerely y^rs

Jo fforbes.

[*Addressed:*] To the R^t. Honb^le The Earl of Loudoun &c &c &c
[*Endorsed:*] Col. John Forbes Albany Novr 10th 1757 R Novr 10th

---

† Stricken out.
^31 Colonel Daniel Webb of the 48th regiment. Note that Forbes, December 2, 1758, *post* p. x, calls him General Webb.
^32 Lieutenant Colonel John Young of the 60th regiment.
^83 Captain Gabriel Christie of the 48th regiment.
^34 Lieutenant Colonel Arthur Morris of the 17th regiment.
^35 Probably the 78th regiment of Lieutenant Colonel Simon Fraser.

Forbes to Major Fletcher[36]
[LO 4917 A.Df.]

New York Novr. 30th. 1757.—

Sir.

By a Letter I have just receiv'd from Capt Shaw[37] of the New Jersey Reg^t [I find]† dated from Philadelphia Novr 24. I find he is arrived there with some of the forces taken at the Affair of Fort William Henry

You will therefore receive from him Nine of the Independents which you are to send to Maryland to join their respective Companys, now in quarters there.

The 34 men of the Jersey Reg^t are to be sent home directly, and the three men of the York Reg^t, are to be sent here.

The Sawyer I suppose is a Philadelphia man. and may therefore be [turned about his Business]† Dismissed

Capt Shaw likewise tells me that Capt Faesch[38] of the Royall Americans, had embarked on board the Dutchess of Hamilton transport at Hallifax and bound to Philadelphia but not Arrived, you are therefore to order Capt Faesch upon his Arrival at philadelphia to sett out directly for this place [and that he is to order the men he may have under his command to go to their different destinations]† with the Soldiers he may have with him belonging to the 3^d Battalion of the Roy^{ll} Americans and leaving those of the 35th with you, to be joined to their Companys. And what provincialls he may have, are to be sent to their Different provinces.

I am S^{ir}

[*Endorsed:*] To Maj^r Fletcher, or the Officer Commanding the Troops at Philadelphia
New York Novr. 30th 1757

* * * * *

---

[36] Major George Fletcher of the 35th regiment.

[37] Captain Thomas Shaw, who served in the campaigns of 1757 and 1758 in upper New York and was wounded at Ticonderoga. Consult *N. J. Arch.*, IX, 185; *Pa. Arch.*, III, 203, *N. Y. C. D.*, X, 732.

† Stricken out.

[38] Rudolph Faesch or John Faesch, both captains in the 60th regiment.

Scroll of Instructions For Lord Howe[39]
[LO 5171 A.Df.]

[New York, December 1757]

As the present State of the Garrison of Crown point, and of Tunderoga are represented (from the best Informations) to be but weak as to numbers and mutinous as to Dispositions And as the present season will very greatly facilitate any attempts y^t may be made to reduce those fortresses. And as the Success of all such attempts depends greatly upon the ability, Activity and vigour of the Commandg officer

In consequence of these Considerations, And as I repose especiall trust & Confidence in your Lordships Abilities and Activity, Have therefore thought proper to Appoint Your Lordship to take the Command of a Sufficient Detachment of his Maj^{ties} Forces under my Command—to be conducted and directed by your Lordsp in order to reduce [these]† either [one]† or both of these two Fortresses, And as there is no time to be lost in the execution of such projects, Your Lordship will with all diligence proceed to Albany, Where Major Generall Abercrombie will order this detachment of the forces to Assemble;* [*Marginal note:* *if either it be thought convenient to go on w^t the Expedition, or Albany a proper place to [assemble at]† collect the troops, from the Intelligence that you may receive.] [if thought convenient]† and where he will give you all the Aid and Assistance depending upon him, and providing you with all and Sundry that you may have a Demand for, or that he may think necessary for carrying this Intended reduction (with all the expedition possible) into Execution.

I have not specifyed the number of troops that I should think necessary to employed upon this Service, leaving that to Major Gen^{ll} Abercrombie and your Lordship to Settle at Albany, where from further Intelligence, you might be oblidged to make changes in what I might order upon that head.

Nor do I lay down any rules or Directions about Artillery Stores or provisions not at all Doubting But Major Gen^{ll} Abercrombie and your Lordship will Direct all for the good of [the]† His Maj^{ties} Service.

[I need not recommend]†

---

[39] George Augustus, Third Viscount Howe (1724-1758), colonel of the 55th regiment. Having entered the army in 1745, his birth and talents brought rapid promotion. His untimely death at Ticonderoga in 1758, as brigadier-general and second in command in the expedition under Abercromby, was a great British disaster. Consult the *D. N. B.* and the *D. A. B.*

† Stricken out.

You are to take care to have able body'd men capable of enduring fatigue, and before leaving of Fort Edward if any of them should be sick or not able to proceed you are to leave them there taking others in their place, from the Reg^t in Garrison there

In case of Success against one or both of the forts, you are utterly to Burn and blow up Crown point—[And if upon thorough examination of Tunderoga it be found y^t wee can keep and defend it against the Ennemy. In that case You will putt every thing in the best order, leaving a proper Garrison for its defence, As it]†

And likewise destroy Tunderoga, taking care to bring away with you all the Cannon &c that you can with any conveniency carry, and bursting and destroying the remainder of all kinds of Stores and Ammunition—

[As Circumstances may make great changes in a few days. And as it often happens that wise retreat is preferable to a rash and precipitate attempt for Success I therefore intirely leave it to your Lordships Judgment and disposition to dispose of the troops, as you shall think most proper for H. M. Service and according to the Different Intelligence that your Lordship may receive from time to time—]†

[In case Your Lordship from a new Intelligence, find that ane attempt upon these forts]†

As in all such expeditions Numberless Accidents, must produce many changes. I must therefore leave to your Lord^ps judgment and discretion, to make what alterations as you shall think proper from time to time for the good of his Majes^tys Service

* * * * *

General Orders to Lieut. Col. Bouquet[40]
[LO 4936 Contem. Copy]

New York, 2^d. December 1757—

Sir

General Orders.

Major General Webb being appointed to Command at New York it is Lord Loudoun's Orders, that you send all your Returns to New York, and

---

† Stricken out.

[40] Colonel Henry Bouquet (1719-1765), Swiss born soldier of fortune, second only to Forbes in importance in the campaign in Pennsylvania in 1758. His papers in the British Museum are of great value. His untimely death in Florida, in 1765, cut short a possibly brilliant military career. Consult the *D. A. B.* and Mary C. Darlington, *Colonel Henry Bouquet.*

that you make Duplicates to General Webb, during his Command this Winter, writing upon the Back of the Cover.—

Returns.—

Albany 26th. Novr.—1757.

Whereas Lord Loudoun's several Orders, given out at different Times, with Regard to Officers not receiving Money in Lieu of Provisions has not produced the desired Effect of making a Saving to the Crown, Lord Loudoun therefore orders, that all those Rations that are not taken in Kind from the Contractors, are to be paid in Money from the Contingent Account, at the Rate of four Pence Sterling pr Ration, as the Recruiting, and out Parties are paid at Present, by which there will be a Saving to the Crown of two Pence Sterling Pr, Ration

Each Regiment is to keep regular Accounts of their Rations received in Kind, from the Contractor, that they may be enabled to make a just Demand of their four Pences from the Quarter Master General, according to their Effectives, and the Number of Rations appropriated to each Person. And it is the Earl of Loudoun's further Orders, that no Contractor or any of his Deputies do issue any provisions whatever but according to His Lordship's general Orders, or according to the Orders that may be given by the Commanding Officer of any Body of Troops detached from him.

This Regulation to take Place from the 26th. Novr. 1757. & to have no Retrospect.—

Lord Loudoun Orders that all Officers either in Camp, or Quarters, upon Duty or not, do constantly appear in their Regimentals, or uniforms; Commanding Officers of Corps to be answerable that this Order is punctually complied with.

I am   Sir
Your most humble Servant.
John Forbes Adjt. Gen.—

To Lieut. Colonel Bouquet[41]
or Officer Commanding at
Charles Town.—

Be so good as to give out those Orders to the Troops in Carolina

Jo: Forbes—

Copy

[*Endorsed:*] General Orders for Lieut. Colonel Bouquet

*   *   *   *   *

---

[41] Consult Bouquet to Forbes, December 25, 1757, B.M., Add. MSS. 21632, f. 26.

Forbes to Loudoun
[LO 4165 A.L.S.]

New York Decr. 4th 1757.

My Lord.

I had the honour to represent to your Lordship by Letter[42] upon the arrivall of the 17th Reg^t at Hallifax, the State of the Arms and Accoutrements of that Reg^t, under my Command.

As I have now been able to examine into the Cloathing sent over for the Reg^t, and find great Deficiencys, I think it my duty to acquaint your Lordship that you may give your orders for a proper enquiry, that regular demands may be made for the replaceing what is due to the Reg^t, out of the moneys sett apart by order, for that purpose—

I have the honor to be w^t Great respect & esteem
My Lord   Y^r Lords^{ps} most ob^t
& most humb^{le} Servt

Jo fforbes. Colonel of the
17th Reg^t of Foot

To His Excell^{cy} The E of Loudoun.

[*Endorsed:*] A Letter from Col° Forbes to Lord Loudoun New York, Decr. 4th 1757

*   *   *   *   *

Forbes to Loudoun
[LO 4992 A.L.S.]

[New York, December 10, 1757]

My Lord

As I have been, and am still very much out of order it is therefore impossible for me (without augmenting my complaints) to wait upon you.

But as Major Halkett[43] could not distinctly tell me what you would have to be done with the returns or with what view, I am therefore affraid, you will have bungling work unless better explained to him

At present As I conceive, it is to have the just number ascertained of what men each reg^t wants to Compleat to the Allowance, exclusive of

---

[42] Not found, but consult Forbes to Hopson, July 15, 1757, ante, p. 6.

[43] Brigade Major Francis Halkett, the constant attendant and often the secretary of General Forbes in 1758. He was a son of Sir Peter Halkett the regimental commander under Braddock.

Chelsea men,[44] Prisoners, or Capitulation men, In order to Compleat the whole out of the Draughts and Supernumerarys. And this done to putt the Chelsea Men, Prisoners, Capitulation men and the remainder of the Draughts, into a Contingent account.

If this is the Case, I think it but fair to remind your Lordship of some particulars upon the breaking up of the Blanford Encampment last year, We were told that Application had been made for more troops to America, In order to enable you, both to go and attack the Ennemy, and to leave Sufficient strength to defend our own Frontiers—This measure was approved off by the whole nation, and ten of the best British reg[ts] were ordered to the Seaports in order to embark early in the year to America.

The present minister[45] came into play some time after this, and adopted the same measure, but found both Numbers of Reg[ts] lessen'd, and the quality of the troops infinitely Inferior, to what was before destined to have gone off this He and all that party complained highly; upon which Perrys reg[t][46] was joined to the six Irish. But than not thought Sufficient, and the Consequence has since shown, For I see that M[r]. Pitt[47] has the moment that he gott the Duke[48] over to Germany given orders for those draughts and the nine Highland Companys to go for to strengthen you, and to make up the numbers that he thought defective, of what was at first agreed to, which was seven or eight thousand men.

These being Facts, I must beg that your Lordship will consider that they have your Monthly returns at home. which always tells them your Numbers. that they have likewise access to know your publick orders, where they will see that* [Marginal note: *in latter end of July—] at Hallifax you ordered all men unfitt for service or recommended to be sent home in the returned transports. and they will find the same orders att New York in Octob[r] thereafter—From whence, they can not possibly suppose you have people to be turned away the latter end of Nov[r] or beginning of Dec[r]— when neither battle or laborious marching, nor Distemper has interfer'd.

---

[44] Badly and possibly permanently disabled soldiers, destined to be sent to the hospital and disabled soldiers' home at Chelsea in England.

[45] A reference to William Pitt, whose influence in the ministry became dominant in 1757.

[46] Colonel Perry's Regiment, raised in 1758, the 55th regiment, generally identified with Lord Howe.

[47] William Pitt (1708-1778), the Great Commoner, for whom Pittsburgh was named by General Forbes. As "His Majestys Principal Secretary of State" he dominated British policy from 1757 to 1761, with astonishing success. His most detailed biography is by Basil Williams.

[48] The Duke of Cumberland.

From these reasonings I should think that allowing of any to be discharged, and to replace them from the Draughts a step to be taken with great circumspection. For surely the middle of a warr is not a time to beautify Reg^{ts} and if any size is taken in England that can carry a muskett, there can be no reason for refusing them here, where from behind a tree a pigmy may kill a Polyphemus, nor would I be very quick in sending home all the Draughts that may not please, for I am told and have always heard the strength of Armies reckoned from the numbers of Fire arms, and Not the height and strength of mankind, that being only a Secondary Consideration. There is nothing to hinder your Complaining of the badness of the men they have sent you, but pray give them no handle to complain, that proper use was not made of the numbers they sent.

Your Lordship would probably ask me, whence all this precaution and foresight, but I can give no wiser reason than the above considerations and to endeavor to make your Lordship reflect sometimes upon things that would escape the most clearsighted without Information; I think is my duty?

If I had either Spirits or Feet to tread upon I could give your Lordship severall Arguments for the Above reasonings, but if you follow your own councill—refuse nobody's advice, as that, you can either take, or let alone.

Adieu My Dr Lord from

Lazarus   Jo fforbes.

Saturday 5 o'clock
My letter is damned long but I can neither read it over nor Correct it.

[*Addressed:*] For The R^t. Honb^{le} The Earl of Loudoun &c. &c.
[*Endorsed:*] Col. John Forbes New York Decr. 10th 1757 R Decr. 10th

*   *   *   *   *

Forbes to Loudoun
[LO 5029 A.L.S.]

[New York, December 17, 1757]

My Dear Lord.

I have just receiv'd the two Enclosed letters[49] from Albany, which your Lordship must give me directions how to answer when I have the pleasure of seeing you.

I hope your Draughts are now settled and disposed off, I fancy Capt

---

[49] Not identified.

Cosnan[50] and ane officer from each of the Nova Scotia reg^{ts} now at Boston ought to be sent for, & officers ordered to take their Draughts under Charge untill they arrive.

officers must likewise be ordered to take charge of any Draughts and de-serters that are to go up the Country—Major Halkett can acquaint your Lordship off any Officers that are in town that belong to the reg^{ts} above.

I am affraid I shall not be able, at least it would not be prudent for me to go abroad tomorrow, But if you venture out I should be glad to kiss your hands.

I am &c &c &c.
Jo :fforbes

Saturday night.

[*Addressed:*] For The Earl of Loudoun &c. &c.
[*Endorsed:*] Col. John Forbes New York
Decr. 17th 1757 R Decr. 17th

*   *   *   *   *

Memorandum Concerning Patrols
[LO 5035 A.Df.]

[New York, December 18, 1757]

As not only the health of troops, is to be Carefuly [for]† looked after but also those troops who are strangers to those Climates, and Countries, ought to be enured to the one, and endeavour to gett a knowledge of the other, In order to be Capable of doing a reall service when called upon, either in the defence of our own Settlements, or of Marching and attacking the Ennemy in theirs, And as the Indians who have it is Supposed very good Intelligence of all our motions, may be Invited during the Winter to make some descent upon our back Settlements, upon finding the troops are kept closs in their quarters—It is therefore thought proper (both for Intelligence and to Intimidate the French or Indians from making any attempts either of attacking the back Settlements or endeavouring to pierce down the Country, where a few Indians may cause a very great allarm) to cause the troops make regular patroniles during the winter and to dispose of the troops so, that those patroniles will rather be wholesome Exercise than any fatigue.

The troops to be regularly cantooned at 12 fourteen or 16 miles distance, not only along the Mohawk river but all along the Hudsons river from

---
[50] Captain John Cosnan of the 45th regiment.
† Stricken out.

Fort Edward down to new York. That each of those posts do send out two patroniles, one to go upwards and the other Downwards untill that they meet the patroniles from the next Stations to them, and for which meeting a Centricall place from each station may be agreed upon where they may communicate either their Intelligence or orders. and than return to their quarters to report what they have learned—

They may likewise fix the time for meeting, and this to take place only when the weather will permitt.

The patroniles must learn to march in Snow shoes.

*   *   *   *   *

Forbes to Loudoun
[LO 5045 A.L.S.]

[New York, December 19, 1757]
nine at night

My Dear Lord.

I have sent you the Different reports and returns from the recruiting partys in New England, Your Lordship will see that some give Billetts according to their Late act of Assembly, and that some of the Conjunct Colonies, give the order for quartering they taking proper measures to make up the Demands upon the troops; for the same,

I have wrote Letters[51] this night to L^t McKinnen[52] of the Royall to repair here immediately, in order to take the Charge of the men belonging to [the]† Nova Scotia But as they are too numerous for one officer and as Cosnan is a Clever fellow. I shall write to him if you think proper to sett out Immediatly with any other officer within his reach; in order to join them and take the Command of them untill you give further orders—I should think were they marched to the Castle at Boston and kept there untill ane Opportunity offerd of transporting them to Hallifax, no bad Scheme; and that a Certain Allowance might be made to the Officers, who must have great plague & trouble would not be money ill bestowed—but this I submitt.

I find I can not well reconcile the regimentall returns of the 35th Reg^t. with the Gen^{ll} returns—given in by Gen^{ll} Webb., so I have wrote to Major Fletcher to send [to send]† me distinct Reg^{ll} returns (accounting for everything) for Septr Nov^r. & Dec^r—Maj^r Halket will explain this

---

[51] Not found.
[52] Lieutenant Robert McKinnon of the 60th regiment.
† Stricken out.

You will see a few people recruited in New England, and Accordingly will I suppose give orders how they are to proceed—

This is necessary else where. I

Your two[53] Lieu^t Col^os dined with me, but I plainly saw, I was not of their secret; altho upon my word, they were very forthy, upon severall Subjects—but It was as I might foolishly imagine—Catch that Catch could so you may believe, my words were weighd by Grains and Scruples—

Adieu My Dr Lord—

I will see you tomorrow—

Y^rs J: ff.

[*Addressed:*] For The Earl of Loudoun
[*Endorsed:*] Colonel John Forbes New York
Decr. 19th 1757 R Decr. 19th

*   *   *   *   *

Forbes to Simon Fraser
[LO 5050 Contem. Copy]

New York Decr. 20th, 1757—

Sir,

I am order'd by the Earl of Loudoun to acquaint you,—

That you are to chuse out from your whole Numbers of Men that are along with you, five Hundred including Corporals who are to be set apart for your own Regiment.

The whole remaining Men are then to be properly sized and drawn up into Front, Center, & Rear Ranks; then according to the Number of Supernumeraries to be drafted, You will settle, according to the Numbers, and draw for them, by Files as they stand, which is to prevent the Appearance of taking any Advantage.

I am, Sir,

Your most obedient, humble Servant.

Jo: Forbes, Adj^t. Gen:—

P. S. You are to allow the Men drafted from you, to carry [their]† their present Cloathing along with them, to Elizabeth Town in the Jerseys from whence the Officer of Otway's[54] Reg^t will have them properly packed up, and

---

[53] Probably Lieutenant Colonels Simon Fraser and John Donaldson.

† Stricken out.

[54] The 35th regiment of Colonel Charles Otway.

sent back to you, where you please to direct them, and this at the Charge of Otway's Reg^t.—

To Lieut. Col^o. Fraser—

Copy

[*Endorsed:*] Copy A Letter from Col^o. Forbes to L^t. Col^o. Fraser New York Decr. 20th 1757

*   *   *   *   *

Forbes to Loudoun
[LO 5056 A.L.S.]

[New York, December 21, 1757]

My Lord.

The Cards are not sent nor should it ever have enterd into my head to have sent them but four or five days ago some folks dining with me hinted that S^{ir} Charles Hardy [55] made himself popular in the place, by making M^{rs}. Barnes[56] give a Sort of Card Assembly, which had a very good effect amongst the towns people. And that was the reason that I took upon me to make out those Cards, which was intirely to take every trouble and Embarras off your hands.

My Legs and thighs are struck out again, there must be some devilry in this Air, that has such ane effect upon me. So I must again keep the house for a day or two. So you may tell M^{c}adam[57] to let any of those people know that saw the Cards wrote, that my falling sick again prevented my sending any Cards or Invitations and that the things must be delayed to a more proper opportunity—

I am My Lord y^r ob^t &c

J: fforbes.

Decr. 21st.

[*Addressed:*] For The Earl of Loudoun

[*Endorsed:*] Col. John Forbes New York Decr. 21st 1757 aboot the Card Playing R Decr. 21st

*   *   *   *   *

---

[55] Sir Charles Hardy (1716-1780), naval officer, governor of New York, 1755-1756, present at the capture of Louisburg in 1758. Consult the *D. N. B.*

[56] Mrs. Phoebe Barnes, wife of a Thomas Barnes, wealthy New York merchant and skipper. She died June 13, 1788. *Daily Advertiser,* June 16, 1788.

[57] Possibly Lieutenant Gilbert McAdam of the 60th regiment, aid de camp to Loudoun and son-in-law of Christopher Kilby.

Forbes to Captain Cosnan
[LO 5120 Contem. Copy]

New York, Dec.[r] 27th. 1757.—

Sir,

I have the Favour of Yours[58] of the 18th last Night, and as You do not mention my Letter[59] of the 21st suppose it had not come to Your Hands. As it was to desire You to set out immediately for this place in order to take the Command of the Drafts for the Nova Scotia Regiments, but as Lieut. Mackinnen of the Royal is in this Neighborhood, he is order'd here for that Purpose, so if this Reaches You in Time, there will be no Necessity for your Leaving Boston, as he will conduct them there, and by him You will receive L[d] Loudoun's further Orders.

As I wrote you that each Officer was to keep a distinct Account of whatever Monies he was obliged to lay out over the four Pence Sterling for either Men's Diet or Quarters, His Lordship therefore Orders, that you shou'd write to all the Nova Scotia Recruiting Parties to immediately make up those Accounts from their first Out Setting to the 1st. of Jan[ry]. 1758. and to send those Accounts to Me, under Cover to Loudoun, in Order that His Lordship may be enabled to make a Demand for the Superplus over the four Pence Stg. from the different Provinces.

Let Ensign West[60] of the 47th. know that if he recruits any Men in Jail, he must discharge their Debts altho under ten Pound.

I have not taken any Notice of the Drafts to any of the Recruiting Parties, lest it shou'd relax the Zeal but have sent You the Numbers for each Reg[t] by which You will be able to judge when it will be necessary for me to give Orders to stop the Recruiters.

I am Si[r]
Your most hum[ble]. Serv[t].
Jo: Forbes Adj[t] Gen—

Return of the Number of Drafts & Deserters belonging to the Nova Scotia Regiments—

---

[58] Not found.
[59] Not found.
[60] Probably Ensign Milborne West, of the 47th regiment.

	drafts	Deserters
Royal	18........	3.
28th. Braggs	1........	3.
40. Hopsons	24........	1.
43. Kennedys	—	12.
45th. Warburtons	23........	—.
47th. Lasselles	3........	—.
	Total 69........	19

[*Endorsed:*] Col. Forbes Letter to Capt. Cosnan Countermanding his coming to New York. 27 Decr. 1757

*   *   *   *   *

Forbes to Simon Fraser
[LO 5129 A.L.]

New York, Decr. 28th 1757

Sir

Notwithstanding the orders of Decr 20th about the Draughting your Regiment you are now hereby directed, To choose from your whole Numbers five hundred men including Corporalls which you are to keep for your own Battalion.

You are after this to have all the other mens names wrote down on different pieces of paper, And from which the Officer of the 35th Reg^t is to draw 90 Men. and the remainder makes up the rest of your Battalion.

You are to allow the Men draughted from you, to carry their present Cloathing along with them to Elizabeth Town in the Jerseys, From whence the Officer of otways reg^t will have them properly packed up and sent back to you, where you please to direct them, and this at the Charge of Otways Reg^t I am S^ir

y^r most ob^t Servt

[*Endorsed:*] Col. Forbes to Col. Fraser Regulating the Draft.
28 December 1757

*   *   *   *   *

Extract of Orders to Col. Prevost[61]
[LO 5156 A.Df.]

[New York, December 30, 1757]

Col°—Prevosts is [to give a reason]† explain his reasons why that Jn°
Kelly and Donald M^cdonalds pay have not been drawn for in former war-
rants and why that the pay of the Cadet philip Du perron and James
Dunstar stands in the same Situation.

A Return likewise to be given in of the Recruits from Germany that
were prisoners in France: and delivered over to the 4th Batt^n—R:A: specifying their names and the Day they embarked from England, with ane account
of the pay due to them to the 24th Decr in order that they may be cleared
after making the proper Stoppages—That Serj^t Frederick Hamback be
charged in this acco^tt as a private man, and that the Difference to compleat his pay to Serj^ts pay be charged upon a Separate paper.

That in all returns for payment of money that the Days of Commencement and ending be particularly specifyed—

A Return to be given in Immediatly of the number of Draughts receivd by the 4th Battalion at Hallifax, with the names of the Reg^ts—they
were drawn from and the day they commenced upon the pay of the Batt^n—w^t
ane Account of what money is due to them.
[*Endorsed:*] Col: Forbes to
         Col: Prevost—
         30 December 1757

*   *   *   *   *

Forbes to Loudoun
[LO 5342 A.L.S.]

[New York, January 5, 1758]
My Lord.

A Mistake of a Serjeant of mine who Imagined he had been Sent for
by the Major[62], occasioned a little Altercation, which was immediatly
settled upon my writing him and explaining the trifling nonsense by ane
officer————

Att present the Sloop going up the Country with the Deserters, has

---

[61] James Prevost, colonel commandant of the second battalion of the 60th regiment.
† Stricken out.
[62] Not identified.

only one person on board, who at the same time wants to gett on shore—
And to leave her—without a Kettle or any other kind of vessel for containing
water or Cooking their provisions—

   If Your Lordship therefore approves of the Inclosed letter[63] to the
Major you will be so good as forward it

                                        I am My Dr Lord &c &c &c
                                                Jo. fforbes.

New York Jany 5th 9 at night .
E: of Loudoun

[*Addressed:*] For His Excellency The Earl of Loudoun
[*Endorsed:*] Col. John Forbes New York January 5th 1758. The People
        of the Sloope for Albany are Deserted wants to have Men
        Pressed to Navigate her R January 5th

                    *   *   *   *   *

              Plan of Instructions to Capt. John Bradstreet[64]
                        [LO 5460 A.Df.]

                              [New York, January 25, 1758]

   As a Diversion to the Ennemy on the Western Boundaries, might take
off their attention to those Places betwixt and the River of St Laurence.
And as nothing promises more success than a Descent upon the Fort and
river of Cataraqui, which if prosecute with Secrecy Vigour and Activity
can scarcely fail, by which wee not only make ourselves Masters of the
Lake and cutt off the communication with the western Indians, but likewise
gett possession of the Cannon and vessells taken at Oswego—by which
means all provisions or Succours sent to Niagara and the forts upon the
Ohio, will be Stopt and the Ennemy reduced to extream difficulty for
Subsisting

   Upon these Considerations & foreseeing the many advantages that would
occur upon a Successful attempt of this kind, In carrying on this necessary
Warr for the Support of His Maj^{ties} Dominions in North America

   And as I repose especiall trust in your Secrecy, Diligence, and activity
and in your knowledge of that Country. I do therefore Constitute and ap-

---

   [63] Not found.
   [64] John Bradstreet (*c.* 1711-1774), British and colonial officer, who rose to the rank
of Major-general. His capture of Fort Frontenac, in August 1758, a noteworthy con-
tribution. In regard to this plan, consult Forbes to Abercromby, August 3, 1758, *post,*
p. 167. On Bradstreet's career, consult the *D. A. B.*

point you to the Command of such a Number of Officers and men as shall
be judged necessary of carrying this Expedition into execution

[For which purpose you are forthwith to engage [for in to the Serv-
ice]† Such a Number of officers sufficient to command a body of 800 men
∧[*Marginal note:* Consisting of 1 Capt at 8 Sh. 1 Lᵗ at 6 Sh and forty
privates divided into Compʸˢ—] Who are to be ingaged into the Service
at the rate of three Shillings currency P day [*Marginal note:* upon your
own pay] to commence the day of their rendezvous at Skenectady or where
else they may be appointed to assemble, and they are to be obligded to
serve not only upon this expedition, but likewise upon any other Service that
I may have occasion to employ them hereafter. You are therefore to take
particular care that they be able body'd active men, capable of enduring
fatigue and the Inclemency of the Weather.]†

[And as it will be impossible yᵗ such a body can subsist without that
provisions is provided for them, They shall therefore have provisions deliverd them by the Contractors in the same manner as the other troops are
Subsisted.]†

As ten or twelve Battoes, and 100 Whale Boats will be necessary upon
the lake and for the transport of Cannon Ammunition & provision You are
therefore hereby impowered to direct the building of such a number by
such people as are Capable of furnishing them at a limited time; and according to the directions that you give them. [*Marginal note:* The present
whale boats are improper for Lake George, but will serve upon this occasion
wᵗ 10 Additional Battoes—]

You are to take 4 piece of Cannon with proper Ammunition as likewise
some Scaling Ladders, for which you shall have my orders. [*Marginal
note:* 1 Officer Serjᵗ & 12 of the train] [*Marginal note:* 12 £ders if Brass
9 if Iron]

You are to order the above Officers and men to Assemble at Chenectady
the 1ˢᵗ week of March next with proper Arms [and Ammunition]† and
ready to sett out upon the first order.

You are from time to time or as often as you can to ∨ [*Marginal note:*
∨ give me Intelligence of your Situation &] [let me know of]† your Success.
and in case you fail of seizing the Fort you are to do your utmost to get
possession of the vessells, which if from want of sails or any other good
reason you can not bring away with you, you are than to destroy them.

[You are to manage the Indians that you may pass, according as you
find them disposed to be our friends or Foes. And if you Succeed in the

---

† Stricken out.

attack of the Fort Cataracqui, you are seriously to weigh whether y^t you might not fall down the River to La Galette and destroy it if possible.]†

*   *   *   *   *

Plan of Operations on the Mississippi, Ohio & Ca
[LO 5515 A.Df.]

[New York, February 1, 1758]

It is needless to sett forth the necessity that there is, to examine the Strength, nature, and Genius of [a]† any people, that you wage warr with, but it is also absolutely necessary for a Commander in Chief, to have a perfect knowledge of that country where the warr is most likely to be carryed on, in order to avail himself of that knowledge, and consequently to distress his Ennemy either in the Offensive, or Defensive Warr [which]† in the different managment of either the many combined circumstances, must be seriously Consider'd, and from thence a Generall Plan of Operations formed, Liable to de deviate from, or prosecute, as Accidents or thousands of different occurrences that present themselves dayly, would easily make a Commandg officer foresee, and consequently remedy by a Change of measures.

In prosecuting any Argument of what is proper now to be done in carrying on this necessary warr in America, I shall enter into no discussion How that the French have these severall years by past, outwitted us with our Indian Neighbors, have Baffled all our projects of Compelling them to do us justice, nay have almost every where had the advantage over us, both in politicall and military Genius, to our great loss, and I may say reproach—

For if it is a truth that the British Colonies Extend pretty near from the same Degrees of Latitude from North to South. × [*Marginal note:* x as the french do] That the British Colonies are a rich flourishing Commercant nation Supplyed by; and supplying, most Countries with every necessarys of Life, abounding with ten times the number of Inhabitants of that, of their Ennemys, With numberless good towns, Harbours, and at all times free sailing to all parts of the Globe. If

If on the Contrary the French Settlem^{ts} are narrow and badly Inhabited, altho of great length, If they must be supplyed with the Common necessarys, all from France, and that but at certain seasons. If their Climate is so rigorous, as almost to revolt nature during a long period of seven or 8 months of a winter—

If they are in such distress the latter end of Winter, for want of pro-

---

† Stricken out.

visions, as not to be able to take the field or assemble any body of troops, untill their ships arrive from Europe, If these are facts One may easily see where the advantage lyes, if time and opportunity be properly made use off.

I shall not pretend to show the Strength of the french Settlements either in defending themselves or of attacking of us.

But at present shall only show, what Strength wee have, and how and where wee may not only attack them, but be oblidging them to divide their force, render them weak and of easy conquest to a Zealous, vigorous & Active people—

Nova Scotia

Wee have now 5400 Regular troops in Nova Scotia besides 200 Rangers —And in case that it should be thought necessary to attack the Ennemy in that quarter. The New England Colonies may give 3000 Men or 3400 by which you are enabled to leave a Sufficient Garrison at Beau Sejour, the only inlett where the Ennemy could attack you. As your Superiority at sea prevents any attempts either upon Hallifax or upon Annapolis.

If then by leaving 1000 men at Beau Sejour, you shall attempt any thing w^t the remaining 8000. I should most certainly advise the attacking of Louisburgh. and that the first week that the season would permitt, and before that the Ennemy could receive any succours of men, or provisions from Europe, or elsewhere—For with your 8 Line of Battleships and 2 Frigates now in [Louis]† Hallifax Harbour and 8 thousand Forces, I do maintain that you have twenty to one a better chance of success, than when this project was thought proper to be attempted last Autumn, with only 10000 Men and ane Inferiour Fleet to y^t of the Ennemy. At present you have not one Single ship of the Ennemys to oppose your navall operations —nor can you expect any before that you have struck your Blow.

Last autumn the Garrison was numerous and in plenty—At present the Garrison may be supposed to be in want & sickly as the able men were taken to carry their Fleet home, And the Invalides and Garrison left, have been all winter destroyed and infeebled by the black fever, & Salt provisions.

If this should be looked upon as too Hazardous ane effort, with the Assistance of the above Fleet, a part of the above Army may be transported to St Johns river in bay of Fundy, where by remounting that river and destroying the French Forts and Settlements. The Ennemy would be most effectually distressed as in all the French memorialls they acknowledge that by this river only it is that Quebec & Canada have any Communication with France or the Isle royall, during seven long winter months.

† Stricken out.

South Carolina

I make a jump from one extremity of the Continent to the other, on purpose to leave the Centricall places together as they are more Connected in their Operations.

In this province I would propose to have the whole 1ˢᵗ Battalion of the R: A. of 1000 Men. 3 Independent Companies 300 Men. And from the North & South Carolinas a body of 1500 or 2000 provinciall troops. which are certainly troops [in]† enough for the protection of those provinces.

But if it be judged necessary to anoy the Ennemy in those parts. after gaining the Chicasaw, and Cherokee Indians by any means, to attack the Ennemy on the Missisippi.

A body of 2000 men may be imbarked at Charlestown, who under Convoy of the Ships of warr in those parts and some privateers, might proceed to the River Missisippi, where by a Sudden descent, they might easily make themselves masters of New Orleans, and that gained, the Mobile would fall likewise. As at the same time their attention for the Defence of those two places would be diverted by the attack of their Settlements up the Country by our Indians.

If any such scheme as this should be attempted, the troops in those provinces might be strengthened by marching the Virginia Regᵗ into them.

Operations on The Ohio

As whatever can be done in those parts to harrass and drive the Ennemy from their Settlements, is of the utmost consequence to them, by cutting off in a great measure the Communication between Canada & Lousiana, by which the one or the Country must fall, so the advantage that any Success wee may have there is most evident.

Therefore while their Indians are out upon their hunting and their defence at home small; one is naturally led to believe, that any attempt made upon Fort de Casne and [*Marginal note:* the oyʳ Settlemᵗˢ—] might be attended with success.

And for that purpose would assemble early at Fort Cumberland—the 2ᵈ Battⁿ of the R: A: & the 1ˢᵗ Highland Battⁿ—which make 2000 Men who joined with the Virginia, Maryland and Pensilvania provinciall will make a body Stronger than any thing that the Ennemy can collect to [head]† make head against them, so there is no Doubt of their Success; which will secure the whole tribe of Seneca Indians to our Interest, and intirely destroy the French trade and communications in those parts.

---

† Stricken out.

Operations on Lakes Champlain, George & Ontario—

As the back parts of the Colony of New York and the Hudsons River seems to be the place where the Ennemy ought to make their strong push for Conquest and Settlement, And as it is evident that it is by Lake Champlain, that wee can ever penetrate to the St. Laurence river to any good purpose. of reducing the Ennemy to reason.

As therefore a Strong body of troops will be necessary in those parts. I am of opinion that the following[65] will answer all purposes and be a greater body than can ever act together or be brought to engage the Ennemy at any one place or time.

Forbe's ⎫		Whitmores ⎫	
Blakeneys ⎪ 2800		Highlanders ⎪	
Murrays ⎬		Abercrombys ⎪	
Perrys. ⎭		Webbs ⎬ 7000.	
		Provosts ⎪	
4 Independᵗ Comp:	400	Howes ⎪	
Rangers.	1000	2ᵈ Highland B. ⎭	
Gage	500		6000
Rogers	500		———
Bradstreet	800	Totall—	13,000
	———		
	6000		

Exclusive of our train of Artillery, and of The Jersey and New York Regiments with this great Force it is to be hoped wee shall not only be able to secure all our own frontiers, but by rendering ourselves masters of Carillon and Crown point, be able to penetrate to Canada. and drive the Ennemy to yʳ Capitall.

Or if thought more eligible by a bold stroke upon Fort Frontenac to gett possession of it and the vessells and Cannon taken at Oswego. by which

---

[65] This combination of imperial and colonial troops embodied the following: the 17th regiment of Colonel John Forbes; the 27th regiment Lord William Blakeney, Colonel; the 46th regiment of Colonel Thomas Murray; the 55th regiment of Colonel Perry; the 4 Independent Companies of New York; the Rangers of New York; the forces under Colonel Thomas Gage; the well known rangers of Robert Rogers; the forces of Captain John Bradstreet; the 22nd regiment of Colonel Edward Wentmore; the 78th regiment of Colonel Simon Fraser; the 44th regiment of Colonel James Abercromby; the 48th regiment of Colonel Daniel Webb; the battalions of the 60th regiment under Colonel James Prevost; the 55th regiment under Colonel Howe; and the 2nd Highland Battalion.

wee become Masters of the Lake ontario and cutt of the Communication of the western Ind

* * * * *

Forbes to Loudoun
[LO 5534 A.L.S.]

[New York, February 3, 1758]

My Dear Lord.

My Infirmitys are really no joke, nor are they to be played the fool with, Both legs and thighs being ane absolute sight, and the soals of my feet Blistered, so it was impossible for me to gett abroad—

I just receivd the enclosed[66] from Gen^{ll} Abercrombie, if it contained any Intelligence about the project now on hands. should be glad to know it if Interesting—

I am My Dr Lord Y^{rs} most
sincerely Jo: fforbes.

Fryday

[*Addressed:*] For the Earl of Loudoun
[*Endorsed:*] Col. John Forbes New York Feb^r. 3^d 1758 Inclosing a letter
from M. G. Abercromby R Feb^r 3^d 1758

* * * * *

Forbes to Loudoun
[LO 5539 A.L.S.]

[New York, February 4, 1758]

My Dear Lord.

The more one thinks upon the Situation of our publick Affairs on this Continent the more one sees the necessity of employing all our force in their different destinations, & that the sooner one setts about the necessary preparations (for whatever shall be thought proper to be execute) the better. because our great advantage lies in our being capable of acting before the Ennemy can be prepared for defence.

As the present attempt to be made on the french forts may be attended with Success, and as Bradstreets may succeed likewise, no doubt the Ennemy will be greatly perplexed and will no doubt assemble all their force at Montreall & Quebec, In which case it will be difficult for them to send Succours to Louisburgh or strengthen themselves on the Ohio, If than your

---

[66] Probably Abercromby to Loudoun, January 27, 1758, LO 5480.

Lordship Should think it expedient to attack one, or both of those; the moment the season permits—I submitt to you whether it would not be absolutely necessary to send me Express to Hallifax, to desire a meeting with Lord Colvill[67] and any other of his Sea Officers, and w^t Gen^ll Hopson and Laurence[68] at Boston. there to fix upon what is proper to be done in case that Louisburgh shall be thought practicable.

If in case you design any attack upon the Ohio—which indeed has the flattering Air of Success, as you may send two thousand regulars, besides the provinciall troops which I am assured will be readily granted for this Expedition, and Mr Bird[69] assures me that he could easily bring 500 Cherokees but there is not time for those—But as it is, our force would be greatly superiour to Braddocks, who had scarce 2000 Men.

In this case it will be absolutely necessary to send some Sensible discreet Officer to pensylvania & Virginia with proper Instructions, to settle the plan of Operations, and really I can see no person so fitt for this purpose as Major Robertson.[70] who in a Short time might be quite master of what can be done, and of the most likely method of Success—and than you could judge accordingly—In short my Lord you have stuff enough and power enough, had you only some good heads, which appears to be ye great want in your Army. I am affraid that you likewise will want Cannon—

As your Lordship has a good opinion of Col° Gages and Col°. Burtons[71] military Capacitys, I fancy you will hear what they say on this Subject—I am told the road from Fort Cumberland to the Monongehela, is still very practicable except a few bridges.

I have desired Mr Jamet[72] to sett out to morrow morning with the new petard, and have told him to be at your levée this morning and that your Lordship would Satisfye him as to the Commission, & order him some money —Mr Holland[73] may go w^t him in the same Slea.

I have likewise told M^r De ruine[74] the Miner to hold himself ready to go for Albany when orderd.

---

[67] Lord Alexander Colvill (Colville), of Culrose, captain in the Royal Navy, commander of the vessels at Halifax in the winter of 1757-1758.

[68] Charles Lawrence (d. 1760), soldier and politician, long governor of Nova Scotia and at this date a brigadier-general. Consult the *D. N. B.*

[69] William Byrd III, third in line of the Byrds of Westover, Virginia. Less distinguished than his father, he is best known for his military services in the French and Indian War. He left behind a minimum of papers for one of such high position.

[70] Probably Major James Robertson of the 60th regiment.

[71] Probably Lieutenant Colonel Ralph Burton of the 48th regiment.

[72] Probably Ensign John Jamet of the 60th regiment.

[73] Mr. Holland, probably a New York colonial.

[74] De ruine [De Ruyine], not in British army lists.

Your Lordship will see the design of this letter is to remind you, that if you want any people from Hallifax to meet you at Boston, y^t the sooner they are sent for the better. I dare not stirr abroad this day—as my leggs mend by ease.

> I am My Dr Lord
> Y^r most ob^t &c &c
> Jo: fforbes.

Saturday morning—

[*Addressed:*] For the Earl of Loudoun
[*Endorsed:*] Col. John Forbes New York Feb^r. 4th 1758. Memorandum
    R. Feb^r. 4th 1758

*　　*　　*　　*　　*

Forbes to Loudoun
[LO 5544 A.L.S.]

                                  [New York, February 5, 1758]

My Dear Lord.

My Epistolary Correspondence, may perhaps seem both troublesome and impertinent, but I hear so many things necessary for you, to know, that you would never hear off that I must proceed—

1st From what Gen^{ll} Abercrombie writes,[75] it will be necessary to putt a Stop to the recruiting officers going up the Country, as he says there are still a great many men wanting and many in the hospital good for nothing.

2^d Capt Reid[76] of the Highlanders is really in so bad a State of health, that the very going to Albany would kill him, which I dare say you have more humanity than to desire.

3^d Lieu^t Allaz[77] of the 4th Batt^n is now properly in Arrest upon your orders, as he was not relieved by you when he was reported.

The Generall opinion of every one is that he was unjustly confined by Col: prevost. so y^t he neither ought to ask M^r prevost pardon or make any Concession, and that M^r prevost ought to be reprimanded for daring to assume your power.

As to the secondary complaint, which they afterwards made ane originall one viz: of Changing his guard—M^r prevost in the opinion of the Officers

---

[75] Probably in Abercromby to Loudoun, January 27, 1758, Lo 5480.

[76] Probably Captain Alexander Reid of the 77th regiment.

[77] Lieutenant James Allaz of the 62nd regiment.

had as little to do with that, as that was [likew]† a fault against generall orders and only cognizable by you, and that if you was satisfyed with the Officers generall Character and his submissions, no person under your command, had any power to confine him—From these your Lordship may easily see the world blames prevost, nor is he justifyed by any but one person, and the people about him—

4th Mr Dice[78] who has the Charge of sending up the Carpenters, Nails &c is I am affraid very dilatory, having only asked for Sleas for tuesday next, when he should have been gone before this, so if you think proper to send and quicken him.

My damn'd legs have fallen down to my toes and soles of my feet, so hope by tomorrow it will fly off—but at present can not walk.

Will you be so good as Give your orders this Day about the recruiters and Capt Reid and let me know by Halkett.

I am My Dr Lord your most
devoted humle Servt
Jo fforbes

Feby 5th

Wou'd not the Air in the Chariot this afternoon do you good.

[Addressed:] For The Earl of Loudoun
[Endorsed:] Col. John Forbes New York Febr. 5th 1758 Memorandum R. Febr. 5th 1758

*   *   *   *   *

Forbes to Loudoun
[LO 6913 A.L.S.]

[New York, February 6, 1758]

My Lord.

Be so good as peruse the Enclosed[79] and send me your orders by Halkett You will please to observe that the Draughts do not sail for Hallifax these ten days from the date of the letter, so that if you have any orders to send to Hallifax, this opportunity will be both the safest and best, In case you order any body to meet you, from that place they can return with that vessell. And as it is now the sixth of Feby—I do not think yt they can well be at Boston before ye 2d of march, Nor can your Lordship be much sooner there if you propose sending off a packett before you sett out. And altho you are

---

† Stricken out.
[78] Not otherwise identified.
[79] Not identified.

some days at Boston before the meeting of the assembly, I fancy you will make things easy w^t the Commissioners of the several Counties—

I am etc.

Jo fforbes.

Monday morn^g

[*Endorsed:*] Col. John Forbes Jany [*sic*] 1758

*   *   *   *   *

Forbes to Lyttelton[80]
[LO 5568 Df.]

New York 12th February 1758

Sir

This will be deliver'd to you by my very good friend Mr Byrd of Virginia whoes views, and designs make it unnecessary for me to Rècommend him to your favour, & protection.

He Had the management of a suckcessfull Treaty Two Years ago with the Chirokie Indians, and by his treatment of, & bounty to them, acquir'd the friendship of some of their great men, & the esteem of their Nation in general.

As he is desirous of turning this influence to the publick advantage, & to emprove the present favourable disposition of the Chirokies, he proposes to go into their Country, & to Engage a body of their nation to join those Troops that I intend to employ upon the Ohio this ensuing Campaign.

I have wrote to Mr. Atkins[81] upon this Subject, & if his health does not permit him to make such a journey, that he would [aid]† be so good, to aid, & assist Mr Byrd, with all the lights, & [Accom]† Recommendations he [could]† can possibly give;

I hope that Mr Byrd's design to consult with, and be aided by Mr Atkins will give no kind of jelousie to the latter to the prejudice of the service, Mr Byrds disposition and manner of treating Mr Atkins I hope will prevent

[80] William Henry Lyttleton (1724-1808), governor of South Carolina (1756-1760) and of Jamaica (1760-1766). In South Carolina his main problems were the Acadians and the Cherokees. Consult the *D. N. B.* and the *D. A. B.*

[81] Edmond Atkin (*c.* 1700-1761), of North Carolina, Superintendent of Indian Affairs in the Southern Provinces, 1755-1763, later replaced by John Stuart.

† Stricken out.

this, but if notwithstanding appearences, any thing of this sort should happen, I must entreat that by your management, it may not be allow'd to obstruct this service, which I consider as of the greatest importance to the success of the next Campaign.

I shall not take up any more of your time upon this Subject, as Mr Byrd will be able to detail it more at large to you, when he arrives at Charles Town

To Governor Littleton

[*Endorsed:*] Col. Forbes Plan off a letter to Govr Littelton in Relation to Engaging the Cherokee Indians. Received Feb. 13th 1758. Rejected because he has mistaken the Plan and Mr. Mr. [*sic*] Bird the Principal altho the Other has the King's Commission. R. Feb^r. 13th 1758

* * * * *

Forbes to Loudoun
[LO 5590 A.L.S.]

[New York, February 14, 1758]

My Lord.

I send you enclosed the order[82] to Col° Bouquet for his Comming here, with ye 5 Companys.

Capt Hales letter[83] must be from yourself but in case he be out upon a Cruize. or not refitted what is Col: Bouquet to do in that case.

I shall write to Archie Montgomery[84] and acquaint him of your orders.

As I find that the Directions and Instructions[85] to be sent Gen^ll Hopson, must be not only pretty peremptory, but likewise worded with caution so it will require somewhat more circumspection than my loose thoughts putt down upon paper, So I can send them after you to Hartford or Boston, But send me up my loose thoughts. upon the Generall plan of operations, as I have neither Scketch nor remembrance of my Ideas at that time now.

I should be glad to have a reading of your letter[86] to the minister again,

---

[82] Of February 14, 1758, *post*, p. 43.

[82] Loudoun to Captain John Hale [Hales], February 16, 1758, LO 5612.

[84] Lieutenant Colonel Archibold Montgomery of the 77th regiment, prominent in the campaign of Forbes. No such letter by Forbes was found. Consult the *D. N. B.*

[85] *Post*, p. 50, of date, February 27, 1758.

[86] Loudoun to Pitt, February 14, 1758, printed in Kimball, *Correspondence of William Pitt . . .* I, 183.

for I can not help thinking you make too great ane affair of the German Flatts, which to us at Albany was really a Trifle of 24 hours, and forgott in twice y^t time, nor does it sound well, that wee knew nothing of this, untill they had struck their stroke and were absolutely gone. for Ld Howe upon post horses could neither see nor hear them, and of Consequence sent to Countermand the troops, who could be of no service by following him.

Mr Byrd has been with me this morning, and thinks he ought to have some sort of Authority from you for acting, and directing him in his proceedings, As with out that, he may have the Air of Adventurer, or of one acting from his own whims, which might be of prejudice to the service, in passing through the Different Colonys—

Mr Steuart[87] was with me last night and gave me the inclosed[88] estimate of the expence of some light Horse men, which I think may be brought down much cheaper by knocking the foolish Chimera of Horse out of Doors, and having them upon the same footing as our Guides in Flanders This is all I think of at present, only I am sorry to hear that four foot of Snow stops them from proceedings from Albany, In Switzerland and the Alps, when the snow is from ten to 16 feet Deep two or 3 flatt bottom'd sleighs push'd forward by some men in the front. makes the best roads in the world, and this is the method through muscovy—I am My Dr Lord

Y^{rs} &c J: ff:

Tuesday 12 oClock.—

[*Addressed:*] For The Earl of Loudoun &c &c &c
[*Endorsed:*] Col. John Forbes New York Feb^r 14, 1758 R. Feb^r. 14th 1758

*   *   *   *   *

Forbes to Bouquet[89]
[B.M., Add. MSS. 21640, f. 241. L.S.]

New York February [14, 1758]

(duplicate)
Sir

It is His Excellency The Earl of Loudouns Orders. That you do forthwith Cause the Five Companys of The First Battalion of Royal Americans

---

[87] Probably Captain Robert Stewart, of Virginia, later in the year in command of a Virginia Light Horse troop.
[88] Not found.
[89] Bouquet's reply, March 10, 1758 is in B.M., Add, MSS. 21632, f. 35.

under your Command, to Embark at Charles-Town, on Board of those Transports, now Lying there, that brought over the Highland Battalion, and proceed with them directly to New York.

My Lord has wrote to Captain Hales[90] of His Majesty's Ship the Winchelsea, to take the Transports under His Convoy, and to proceed to Sea with you directly.

And that there may be no loss of time, and the Transports are wanted here immediat[ely.] Mr. Kilby has sent orders to his Commission[ers] to have the Transports victuall'd.

My Lord desires that you will leave—your Instructions with all the money both for pay and Contingencies with Lieu^t Colonel Montgomery and that you will likewise leave him your Surgeons mate for His Battalion, as Mr Napier the director[91] can supply you, with another mate up[on] your arrival here, and if you have any men taken Sick at Sea, you will apply to Captain Hales of the Man of War, for the assistance of His Surgeon.

Wishing you a good and Speedy Voyage.

I am with great Regard

Sir   Your most Obedient Humble Servant

·Jo: Forbes, Adjnt. Gen^{ll}

[*Addressed:*] To Lieut. Col^o Boquet
[O]fficer commanding the
[Fi]ve Companys of the 1st Battalion
[of Royal American]ns at Charlestown

*   *   *   *   *

Forbes to Loudoun
[LO 5603 L.S.]

[New York, February 15, 1758]

My Lord,

I take the Liberty to trouble you with Maj^r Genl Abercrombie's Report[92] of the State of the Arms & Acouttrements of the 17th. Reg^t signed by himself, which I engaged my word and Honour to produce to Mr. Appy,[93] which would have saved this Trouble, had he been so good as to accept of it.

---

[90] Cf. Forbes to Loudoun, February 14, 1758, *ante,* p. 42, fn. 83.
[91] Doctor James Napier, Director of Hospitals.
[92] Not found.
[93] John Appy, Judge Advocate of the forces in America, and later secretary of Abercromby and Amherst. There are three letters of Appy to Forbes in the Abercromby Papers.

Perhaps he was in the Right in refusing, but there are agreeable and disagreeable ways of doings Things. I beg your Lordship would order me a
true Copy signed, that I may transmit it to London, to my Agent, if you
think that is a proper Way to apply. I beg to know when your Lordship
goes away, or whether I may flatter myself with the Hopes of seeing you,
being now lame of both Legs and Hands, which makes me employ another
Pen.

I send you a Letter inclosed for Colonel Montgomery,[94] to go by Colonel
Bird, if you approve of it.

I am, My Lord,

Your Lordships Most obedient and most humble Servt. Jo: fforbes.

Wednesday.
7 o'clock in the Evening—

[*Addressed:*] To His Excellency The Earl of Loudoun &c &c.
[*Endorsed:*] Col. John Forbes New York Feb^r. 15th 1758.
R. Feb^r. 15th 1758

*   *   *   *   *

Forbes to Loudoun
[LO 5628 A.L.S.]

[New York, February 19, 1758]
My Dear Lord.

The Albany post is this moment arrived and by Generall Abercrombies
Letter[95] to me with the enclosed from Himself, and Lord Howe to y^r Lordship[96] I thought it necessary to send them forward by express, as the Generall
says Lord Howe would be impatient for ane answer.

I see the Depth of Snow and the want of Snow Shoes, creates great
uneasiness, and I must suppose reasonably; therefore how to remedy those
complaints I must say I am at a loss to give ane opinion; but at no loss to see
that if 100 French can march to Fort Edward & back again; tht some 200, or
2000 British, might execute it liksewise, altho (do not mistake me) I am
against showing my teeth, where I can not bite. But sure, My Lord, in any
thing not only of this kind, which is ane entire *Coup de main* every delay

---

[94] Letter not found.
[95] Not found.
[96] Howe and Abercromby to Loudoun, February 14, 1758, LO 5584, and 5596.

weakens you and strengthens your Ennemy. And this damn'd party being surprized at Fort Edward. will certainly allarm them, but if wee cannot attack them, they can not send relieff to those Forts. and 3000 men going upon a Scout, is nothing, if they find no probability of success they return, and if they see ane opening, they may try.

I send you enclosed Major Masseys letter[97] to me, w^t the Account of Blakeneys party, in case that you had not gott such a Circumstantiall ane Account

I must take notice of another thing to Your Lordship, that I have two letters[98] upon [upon]† what follows which is that it is given out at Albany that Abercrombies reg^t are to have the Advanced guard, and Gen^ll Webbs the rear guard upon this detachment, and all this is said to be by your Lordships orders, which I see gives immense umbrage to the Officers of older Corps, So if your Lordship thinks it proper. to prevent such distinctions, by a hint to Lord Howe or Gen^ll Abercrombie, it will at least be agreable to the Army, whatever it is to particulars.—

There is no news, worth sending you, only wee have seven or eight of Col° prevosts Battalion taken up—since last night for house breaking robbery &c, which I ventured to assure the world that you would by no means either protect or give countenance to but to let the law of the Country take place. I shall be very glad to receive your Commands. and any orders that you think necessary, I shall write to morrow by the post so till than I am My Dr Lord.

Y^r Lordships most devoted
humb^le Servt Jo fforbes.

New York 19th Sunday
8 at night—
Complim^ts to Govr,[99] Kilby[100] &c &c &c
I am so well within these 2 Days I wish heartily I was with you—

[*Endorsed:*] Col. John Forbes New York Feb. 19th 1758 Albany Post Snow Shoes French Scout What we can do Advance & Rear Guard Prevost's House Breaker. R. Feb^r. 22^d 1758

* * * * *

---

[97] Eyre Massy, first baron Clarina, to Forbes, February 14, 1758, LO 5596 A.L.S.
[98] Not identified.
† Stricken out.
[99] Thomas Pownall, Governor of Massachusetts.
[100] Christopher Kilby of London, the contractor for provisions, 1757f., a member of the firm of Baker, Kilby, and Baker.

Forbes to Loudoun
[LO 5305 A.L.S.]

[New York, February 21, 1758]

My Lord.

There was no news by the Pensilvania post, nor nothing extraordinary since last night. Complim^{ts} to y^r Company and if Govr Pownall is with you, do me the honour to present my service to him—

I begin to mend and shall use exercise to please Huck.[1] and am with great Sincerity

My Dr Lord.
Y^r most ob^t Slave
Jo fforbes.

I wish Tom Morgan[2] could pick me up a light seasoned Beast, with good goings, not above 14 hands and one Inch. Gelding or mare, but steady.

[*Endorsed:*] Col. John Forbes New York Feb^r. 1758. R. Feb^r. 24th 1758

*   *   *   *   *

Forbes to Loudoun
[LO 5674 A.L.S.]

New York. Feby. 27th. '58

My Lord.

I had the honour of your 2 letters of the 23^d [3] and 24th [4] this morning, but forgive me to tell you that Doctor Hucks letter[5] with his News papers, was infinitely more Agreeable. In your Lordships a faint attempt to gett something to make the blood Circulate, whereas Dr Huck animates you at once., A Prince of the Blood and ane Austrian Marshall, with 30,000 Men prisoners is most Certainly a receipt to Cure the last throbbs of a decayed Constitution, either in body Corporeal or politick, but I have neither sett the Bells ringing nor made a Bonfire, altho as I had the news first, I threw it out and it has returned to me, as I expected, twice as big as I gave it.—

---

[1] Doctor Richard Huck, a physician to the general hospital, sometimes known as Huck-Saunders.
[2] Not identified.
[3] Not found.
[4] Not found.
[5] Not found.

I am glad your Northern Gentrys judgements are not froze like their rivers, and y^t the good of the Whole warms them Cordially. I hope they will agree to all you propose, As they can not suppose you to have any view but the publick welfare.

I thank your Lordship for your good opinion of my Intellects, but can not say you flatter me in judging of either what I have to do, or of employing my time, [*six and a half lines completely blotted out so as to be illegible. Seemingly done by Forbes.*]

I have just a Message from the Lt Governour[6] who is arrived and says you was well Saturday[7]—

I shall say nothing of our Tunderoga Expedition nor off the snow Shoes, nor Scaling Ladders, nor of all the field officers that go; not off their stay, nor of any *Coup d'Essai* that wants every one thing to putt them in motion. But the Lowest rascall here, thinks one can go when another comes,

I shall not enter upon the Descent of the Indians and Canadians upon the German Flatts. but Gen^{ll} Webb says it was very well known it was to happen when they came last. in which opinion severall oy^{rs} agree, However the Generall has of late, that is three days ago, asked me twice to dinner and has been otherwise very forthy.

I have deliverd your message to him about the 9 Companys of Highlanders, and have sent off your Dispatches[8] for Virginia.

In short I have done everything you wanted but taking care of my self, and by following Hucks advice am now a Down right Leopard. Struck out all over but neither sick nor Sorry, . . . I wish to God Huck was back again for out of Joke to earnest I am farr, nay very farr from being as I should be. altho I have tryed his damned Exercise, which has quite thrown me back again—

I hope the German news is true; you can not conceive how happy I am at present and how miserable a Contradiction would make me—

Pray, My Lord if things are to go on as now laid down, let the Engineer Gordon[9] be sent for down the country and let some of the Train come down Immediately to regulate their Stores, which will take time and De-Ruyine and the Miners ought to be here, likewise, which you will see I mention to Hopson [*Half a line crossed out*] and allow me to say I think he may be

---

[6] Lieutenant-Governor James De Lancey. The message was not found. It may not have been in writing.
[7] De Lancey may have seen Loudoun in person.
[8] Contents, doubtless a letter to John Blair, not found.
[9] Lieutenant Harry Gordon of the 60th regiment, the engineer who in the autumn. of 1759, constructed Fort Pitt, under the supervision of General John Stanwix.

most serviceable—It is now the first of march and no time to be lost—

Excuse all nonsense and blunders and may my Complim[ts] to His Excellency, but pray dont mistake and call him His Honor.

My fingers are sore and stiff and yet must write 3 lines to Huck—Adieu My D[r] Lord and believe me most sincerely

Y[r] most ob[t] & most

devoted hum[le] Serv[t]

Jo fforbes.

I should in decency write this letter over again but my fingers are both stiff and sore, and for the same reason have sent you my Brouillon of M[r] Hopson's Instructions,[10] which contain all that I thought it was necessary for to touch upon., but you may cutt and Carve as you think proper.[11] I desire that you would alter your Opinion of my Laziness or Indifference, when any business or that you are Concerned for those same Instructions now before you were finished the day or two after you left this—And I shall have the Ohio ones[12] Cutt & dry for you at your return or shall send them to you But pray be so good as write us often as you have time, And by all I see if wee go on this Campaign as wee beginn, twenty or 30 fellows on Horseback will be absolutely necessary to carry orders and Letters which will be a saving of money paid to Expresses. So I think wee may beginn by getting 20 directly and your Lordship may bring some from New England with you. But let me have your directions about this.

M[r] Appy has wrote to Gov[r] Fitch[13] and has sent him a Copy of two paragraphs in your letter to Gover[r] Pownalls of Jan[y] 9th [14] with regard to the 10 pences over charged by the provinces, which is what wee imagined your Lordship desired to be done—

Wednesday morn[g]

Feb[y] 28th

J: ff:

Your Lordship sees what Major Murray[15] and Col[o] Monckton[16] writes

---

[10] *Post*, p. 50, of February 27, 1758.

[11] Note that Forbes formulates Loudoun's instructions to others.

[12] *Ante*, p. 23, of February 1, 1758.

[13] Letter not found.

[14] Loudoun to Pownell, January 9, 1758, LO 5372.

[15] Major Alexander Murray to Forbes, January 10, 1758, LO 5388, A.L.S.

[16] Letter of Colonel Robert Monckton to Forbes not found. Robert Monckton (1726-1782), professional soldier who served in America 1752 to 1763; in command of affairs in Pennsylvania in 1760. He rose to the rank of Lieutenant general. Consult the *D. N. B.*

me. I wish you would give the Ensigncy to McQueen[17] that I spoke to you off.

E: of Loudoun

[*Endorsed:*] Col. John Forbes New York Feb. 27 and March 1st 1758
        R Mar. 5th 1758

*   *   *   *   *

Plan of Instructions of Maj. Gen. Hopson
[LO 5705 A.Df.]

[New York, February 27, 1758]

As the Honour and Dignity of His Majesties Dominions and Arms, and the Growth and Increase of these American Colonies depends greatly upon the success + [*Marginal note:* + of this ensuing campaign.] [of his Majestys Arms in support of both, during this Campaign]†

And as our + [*Marginal note:* + flattering] Superiority in numbers of regular, as well as provinciall troops + [*Marginal note:* + promises a happy issue to our Enterprises if properly conducted.] [properly made use of; may contribute greatly to bring our Ennemys to reason]† I have therefore after maturely considering how wee may avail ourselves of the many advantages wee seemingly have over the Ennemy though it proper and expedient for the publick good to order a proper Number of His Majties Forces under my Command conjoined with the Squadn of his Majestys Ships now in those seas, to cooperate together, & very early this Spring to proceed to Louisburgh. in order to render themselves Masters of that Fortress.

As the Importance of this Expedition is of the utmost consequence to the publick. [And as your known zeal for the publick service]† And as your present Command in Nova Scotia and known abilities & zeal for the publick Service very luckily coincide at this criticall time.

You are therefor hereby required and directed to take upon you the Command & Conduct of all his Majestys land Forces destined for carrying the above attempt into execution.

I shall not [pretend in]† take upon me in those my Directions to you, to point out any rules or orders that circumstances and the difference of time may not make it necessary for you either to change or make alterations in, as you shall see necessary for the good of his Majestys Service. As I only intend

---

[17] Not identified.
† Stricken out.

to communicate my Ideas of the best and most proper method of attacking the place with a probable view of success.

You will have under your Command [4900]† 5400 Men of the Regular troops with the two Companys of Rangers and a body of 3400 Men of the best, of the New Eng^ld people. The whole Ammounting to Nine thousand Men. If you leave one thousand of those in Nova Scotia, I fancy that will be enough of Regular troops to defend y^t Colony, as there is no danger = [*Marginal note:* = of any attack] from the Sea, And the only place Attackable by Land is Beau Sejour, to Garrison which I would send six hundred of the most active and most healthy of the 1000 Men. = [*Marginal note:* = left] I should think that this thousand men ought to be = [*Marginal note:* = made] by a Detachment from the whole six regiments by which you will gett ridd of many men, very capable of Garrison duty, but unfitt to carry on a Siege—If the 1000 Men should be thought too few, [The town of Hallifax may be Garrisoned by Some of the New England people, or some of them may be mixed with the regular troops]† [*Marginal note:* There may be a detachment of New England people left to act along with the regular troops either at Annapolis Hallifax or Disiquid. but I can scarce think they can be wanted, as Hallifax can not be insulted, while wee remain Masters at sea.]

As the passage from Hallifax to Louisburgh is so very short that a few transport vessells will serve to [convey]† carry—the troops, particularly as the men of warr, may take so many of them on board. I should therefore think that the sooner the troops and transports are assembled at Hallifax the better in order to profitt of the very first change of the season.

But as the Ennemy notwithstanding all your precautions and Secrecy, may discover your Intentions, and may probably oppose your landing in Chapeau rouge+ ∧[*Marginal note:* + ∧or Gabarouse] Bay. which for your Artillery and provisions would certainly be the nearest & most convenient place. You will therefore consider whether [that]† what follows, may not be putt in practice.

If you find that Gabarouse Bay is possessed or Fortifyed by the Ennemy; to proceed with those ships that have the troops on board to the Great and Little Sorembeck, And there to Land four thousand men with some artillery and Hobitzers. to march from thence directly to the Lighthouse and take possession of the ennemys Battery there and than march round the head of Louisburgh Bay, by the back of the Grand Battery (which is min'd) and so push forward with all diligence to the high grounds that overlook the west

---

† Stricken out.

134319

part of the town. by which means the Ennemy at Gabarouse bay may either be cutt off, or oblidged to retire. [*Marginal note:* with precipitation] into the town, and leave the bay open to the landing of the Artillery and Stores. which I suppose will be done with all diligence, taking care to throw up a proper Intrenchment round them for their defence in case of Accidents [and to this]† There must be no time lost in getting up the Hobitzers×∧ [*Marginal note:*+Royalls—] and 12 pounders of which I would instantly erect two Batterys as nigh the Coverd way as I possibly could approach. Nor can I make the least doubt of your knowledge of the Environs×∧[*Marginal note:* +of Louisburgh] so Consequently shall not venture upon giving my opinion, where you should endeavour to make a Breach.

our Information leads us to believe that they have a Battery upon Cape noir carried on by a Ditch and Fascinage to preserve the Communication with the Town. If this could be forced it would be of great consequence as wee are informed, it commands all the ground down to White house point in Gabarouse bay, and consequently the roads leading from thence to the Town or to your Camp.

As the making of a Breach is a principle *point de veu,* I dare say that will be your first attention altho from Accounts of the Garrison having been left weak, × [*Marginal note:*×2000 Men, one half in the Hospitall.] and Sickly and nothing but salt provisions, there is all the Encouragem^t to begin assault by escalade, altho I must think that would be more likely to succeed, were a breach made, because your different attempts might divert the Ennemys precautions, from where you design your reall push. I have therefore sent Capt de Ruyine and some miners, As he has served at several sieges I hope he may be of great utility, and by his miners may sooner facilitate a breach y^n by the Battering train.

As Distances by water are deceitfull I dare not presume to say what service you can expect from any Batterys you may erect at the Light house opposite to the Island Battery nor can I judge of what use may be made of the Green Island, but by the Distance laid down from either of those, they are within reach of Cannon altho not point Blank. But as the Island Battery has but 2 or three Gunns upon its right flank facing the entrance into the Harbour, if a Ship of Warr Could be brought to lay her Broadside to that Flank [*Blotted out*] ×∧[*Marginal note:*×∧she would effectually] enfilade[s]† the whole Battery and render it useless. They report that they have executed another Battery upon the low ground that runs out from the town towards the Island. This Battery has the Appearance of being danger-

---

† Stricken out.

ous for any of the Ships that may endeavour to push into the Harbour to Cannonade the town, but still I should think it was possible in spite of the shallow water, rocks &c to find some place where to land a body of men who might in the night surprize y^t Battery from behind, where I am given to understand it is open and exposed, all their gunns bearing = [*Marginal note:* = only] upon the Harbour.

I make no doubt but conjoined w^t Lord Colvill, all possible care will not only be taken of the Gulf of Canso, but likewise of St Johns and the Bay Cost by proper vessells being sent to prevent any succours of Indians or provisions being thrown into the Island, + [*Marginal note:* ✕ who might keep you in perpetual allarms] [and who would alarm you] † unless there be a very exact and diligent look out and that at some distance from your Camp, for which purpose and as these are almost the only places they can be succoured from, I should think sending a proper force to take possession of Fort St. Pierre upon the Isthmus at the upper end of Labrador would be of Consequence, and your Rangers going along the sides of that lake might attack any small vessell and prevent their landing. ✕ [*Marginal note:* ✕ from the other side]

Thus far Sir I have enumerate every thing that at present [that] † occurs to me, but as my Informations may be wrong, and as Circumstances and things may have quite a different aspect upon being examined more narrowly and upon the Spot, I therefore make not the least doubt of your acting to the best of your power for the honour of his Majestys Arms and the good of the service, I therefore need not recommended Diligence, Activity and vigour to you, but hope you will [recommend and] † encourage$_\wedge$ = [*Marginal note:* = and inculcate] them with all your address to every one under your Command, And as your recommendations of those Gentlem^n who distinguish themselves upon this criticall occasion + $_\wedge$ [*Marginal note:* + will go a great length] I do promise to second any who you think deserve it with all the Interest I have with his Majesty—

I come now to the last and the most disagreeable Circumstances attending those Expeditions, which is that of a retreat which altho the last action ought with all prudence to be very early provided for. I make therefore no doubt but you will make choice of the best spott of ground with the Advice of Ld Colvill either for landing, or for Embarking your Artillery, stores &c This piece of Ground I would intrench with small Bastions at proper distances. and I think it ought to be so large as to be able to contain [your whole numbers] † the one half of your Numbers and so Situate that the ships of

† Stricken out.

Warr might be able to facilitate either your landing or embarking with y^r Cannon.

I must beg you to send me as often as possible Intelligence of your proceedings, by the way of Boston, from whence they can be forwarded to me by express. For this purpose I would have you keep one or two light good Sailing sloops. I have not mentioned the Artillery, Stores or Ingineers or the Detachment of the train, though necessary, as that will come to you by those officers, who will = [*Marginal note:* = be sent to you But you will cause] survey the Fascines and Gabions left on George's Island. and which you may order to be [looked over and]† made serviceable in the meantime, as likewise the large boats.

[Given]†

built at Hallifax by Mr Campbell the Engineer[18] for the landing of the troops—

Given at New York

*   *   *   *   *

Forbes to Loudoun
[LO 5692 A.L.S.]

New ·York March the 4th [1758]

My Dear Lord

I shall not trouble you with any of our transactions or Situations here, as probably I shall have the honor and pleasure of seeing you soon.

The Squirrell Man of War came into this port about 12 this forenoon. and in a very short time I had the News brought me of your being recaled and Gen^{ll} Abercrombie appointed Commander in Chieff,[19] in your place— I shall not say how I found my self, nor how I find my self yet. But I see well who are pleased or displeased and I am happy to find you have a number of Friends, who show that the Change is no ways agreeable to them. and particularly the De Lanceys, who came and waited upon me this afternoon. and I must say showed the friends rather than the Courtiers.

All the Despatches from Government, were addressed to Generall Abercromby and are accordingly I believe sent to him by express, As it is said that there is a new plann of Operations[20] laid down, I fancy that your Lordship

† Stricken out.

[18] Doubtless Mr. Dugal Campbell, mentioned in Forbes to Loudoun, March 10, 1757, *ante,* p. 3, as "our Chieff Engineer." He died at sea in 1757.

[19] The information, Pitt's letters of December 30, 1757, printed in Kimball *Correspondence of William Pitt,* I, 133f.

[20] Found, *ibid.,* 133-154.

will drop your attention with regard to your future Operations with the Govern[r] and the New England Folks. and suppose will come here directly, to settle with M[r] Abercromby.

The news is but with what truth I know not, that L[d] George Sackville[21] who is L[t] Gen[ll] of the Ordnance, comes out w[t] 12,000 to Hallifax and is to command, That Admiral Boscawen[22] and S[ir] Charles Hardy are to bring 19 Line of Battle ships besides Frigates, but I need not entertain you with idle nonsense as you may believe there is a great deal said to very little purpose—

The plann of Operations sent by the Governm[t] no body pretends to know. so I fancy I shall not expect you long here. I assure you my D[r] Lord I wish the Government well, and that all their Servants may with the same zeal and assiduity be their humble servants is my reall wish, But I can say nothing upon a Subject that if you believe there is faith in Mankind, you must know is distressing to me to the outmost, but God be thanked I hope to laugh and eat Collops with you at Loudoun—Spite of all this treatment. I am quite impatient to see you. So God bless you. My Complim[ts] to Pownall &c. Commodore Durell[23] is expected in here in a day or two who is to Command the Fleet untill the Admiralls come—Believe me as ever nay more sincerely if possible. My D[r] Lord Y[r] most ob[t] & most devoted hum[le] Serv[t]

Jo: fforbes.

Bradstreet is made a Deputy Q[r] M[r] Gen[ll]
w[t] L[t] Col[o] Rank and Stanwix,[24] Forbes, Howe, Whitmore
and Laurence—Brigad[r] Gen[lls]—
10 Blank Colonels commissions come—
but Gage, Bouquet and Montgomery already made and
Monckton the 2[d] Batt[r] R Americans
L[d] Loudoun

[Endorsed:] Col. John Forbes New York Mar. 4th 1758
R March 10th 1758

*   *   *   *   *

[21] Viscount George Sackville (1716-1785), later known as Lord George Germain. On his tempestuous military and political career, consult the *D. N. B.*

[22] Edward Boscawen (1690-1766), entered the navy in 1706; in American waters as rear-admiral in 1755 and as admiral in 1758. Consult the *D. N. B.*

[23] Philip Durell, later admiral in the British Navy.

[24] John Stanwix (1690-1766), professional soldier. Entering the army 1706, he came to America in 1756 as colonel commandant of the 1st battalion of the Royal American Regiment. Builder of Fort Stanwix and Fort Pitt, he was in command in Pennsylvania in 1757 and again 1759. Consult the *D. N. B.*

Forbes to Loudoun
[LO 5714 A.L.S.]

[New York, March 6, 1758]

My Dear Lord.

As I fancy you will not stay long at [Alba]† Boston, after receiving my express I have therefore told Appy to keep any letters that comes for your Lordship—

A thousand foolish Clatters and nonsense goes forward but they must keep cold untill meeting

      I ever am

My Dr Lord Y^{rs}

Jo fforbes.

N: York March 6th

[*Endorsed:*] Brigadier John Forbes New York March 6th 1758. R March 28th 1758

*   *   *   *   *

Forbes to Loudoun
[LO 5717 A.L.S.]

N: York. March 7th [1758]

My Lord.

Commodore Durell came here last night in the Diana Frigate, and as he had a Duplicate of Mr Pitts Letter to your Lordship.[25] I thought it best tò keep it here untill your Lordship comes here. as it was more than probable that you would be sett out from Boston before that the express arrived there, and the chance of missing of you, upon the road and the letter in that Case falling into bad hands.

For I have no notion that you would stay longer at Boston after the receiving my express, than to write to those you expected from Hallifax, where they were now to apply for orders.

Durell says as I am told that Mr Shirley[26] is now a great man and is to

---

† Stricken out.

[25] Pitt to Loudoun, December 30, 1758, printed in Kimball, *Correspondence of William Pitt,* I, 133.

[26] Major-General William Shirley (1694-1771), English born American colonial figure. Coming to Massachusetts in 1731 he became governor in 1741; known for the capture of Louisburg in 1745, association with Braddock in 1756 and as commander-in-chief in 1756. Consult the *D. N. B.*

Facsimile of an autograph letter signed by Brigadier General John Forbes.

come out in a Shining Character—That Kilbys contract is to be found fault with, and numberless other things, that perhaps are not true or have any Foundation.

God Bless you my Dr Lord and believe me ever most sincerely

Y^r affectionate Friend
and most ob^t hum^le Servt

Jo: fforbes

[*Endorsed:*] Col. John Forbes New York March 7th 1758 Commodore Durel arived Shirley a Great Man Kilby's Contract to be found fault with. R March 12th 1758

*   *   *   *   *

Forbes to Loudoun
[LO 5726 A.L.S.]

[New York, March 8, 1758]

My Dear Lord.

As the packett came in last night and there are severall letters[27] for y^r Lordship—I thought it best to send ane Express with them, and has directed him to make particular Enquiry for you, upon the Road for fear of Missing of you, In which case he is to return with them directly.

Wee know nothing of the new plan of operations, but by what is given out wee are to be most formidable both by sea & land—You must be upon your journey before this reaches you. So pray send us forward ane Express, to let us know when wee should expect you.

I am My Dr Lord.

Y^r most devoted hum^le ser^t

Jo: fforbes

N: York. Wednesday
morn^g. March. 8th
Earl of Loudoun

[*Endorsed:*] Col. John Forbes New York March 8th 1758 The Packet arived last night we to be most Formidable R March 12th 1758

*   *   *   *   *

---

[27] Among others, probably a duplicate of Pitt to Loudoun, December 30, 1758. Kimball, *op. cit.,* I, 133.

*Forbes to Denny**[28]
[N. Y. P. L. Em. 6248. A.L.S.]

[New York, March 20, 1758]

Sir:

I have the favour of yours[29] of the 17th and make no manner of doubt of your doing, of every thing in your power in forwarding His Majesty's Service. And therefore must beg that the Officers and Soldiers raised in Pennsylvania for the Service are able body'd good Men, capable of Enduring Fatigue, and that their Arms be the best that can be found in the Province; As Carpenters and Axe Men are Absolutely Necessary upon many Occasions, I must recommend the sending as many of those as can be conveniently gott into the Troops.

And likewise that the Province will raise fifty good Men well mounted upon light serviceable horses, and every way Accoutred, to serve in Conjunction with those to be furnished by the other provinces, as a Body of light horse, from whom I expect very Important Service.

As the Roads from Lancaster to Williams Ferry[30] upon the Potowmack may want considerable repairs, and widening of them for the Carriages of Cannon, &c I have therefore wrote[31] to the Governour of Maryland for that purpose, In order that those roads may be repaired by the Inhabitants of the 2 provinces of pennsylvania and Maryland, living near those parts.

As I propose assembling the Regular troops and those of pennsylvania at+ Conegocheegue about the 20th of April, You will therefore give orders for all manner of diligence to be used in raising the numbers that your province is to send. Who shall be pay'd at the rate of 4 pence Sterling P diem, in lieu of provisions from the time they beginn their March untill that they are furnished with provisions from the King's Stores. [*Note in another hand:*] road from Phil[a]. to Conegochegue repaired.

I am informed that the Inhabitants upon the Frontiers of your Province, being much used to hunting in the Woods, would consequently make good Rangers. In which Case I am to beg you will give your direction for forming

---

* Printed, *Pa. Col. Recs.* VIII, 59, and Stewart, *Letters of General John Forbes,* p. 8.

[28] William Denny (1718-1762), deputy governor of Pennsylvania, 1756-1759, whose administration was ruined by conflict between the wishes of the Assembly and the proprietor in England.

[29] Not found.

[30] Williamsport of later times.

[31] Forbes to Sharpe, March 21, 1758, *post,* p. 61.

some of your properest men into Companys of Rangers, with good Officers who are well Acquainted with the Country to Command them.

If it could possibly be Contrived to find some Intelligent person who would venture up to the Ohio, either as a Merchant or a Deserter, and would bring us Intelligence, what was going on in those parts, I should certainly reward him handsomely, perhaps such a one might be found in some of your provinciall Companys up at Fort Loudoun, &c^a &c^a.

I should be obliged to you if you will give orders to send me ane Account of what provinciall troops you have now on foot, and where they are for the present, as likewise what Numbers (in the whole) your province is to raise for the Service of the present year.

I must beg the favour that you will order your Secretary to send the Enclosed packett by ane Express to Virginia[32]—And I have the honour to be with great regard, Sir,

Your most obed^t & most humb^le Servt

Jo: fforbes.

New York, March 20th, 1758.
P:S: I have this moment ane Express from Fort Edward[33] acquainting me of one of our Scouting partys of 180 Men, having been attacked by a thousand of the Ennemy's Indians, Canadians, &c^a., near Tunderoga, in which we have lost 130 Men, the party behaved most Gallantly, but were overpowered by Numbers—
Govr. Denny

*　　*　　*　　*　　*

Forbes to Dobbs*[34]
[*N. C. Col. Recs.* V, 926.]

New York, 21st March 1758.

Sir,

His Excellency Maj^r Genl Abercromby having pursuant to his Majesty's Directions been appointed unto the Command of the Kings regular Forces and Provincial troops, who are to be employed jointly in the operations to

---

[32] Contents not found, though letters of this period are mentioned in the *Jnls. of the House of Burgesses 1756-1758*, p. 301, under date April 5, 1758.
[33] Letter not found.
* Printed in Stewart, *Letters of General John Forbes*, p. 9.
[34] Arthur Dobbs (1689-1765), British born colonial governor of North Carolina. Consult the *D. N. B.*

be carried on this ensuing Campaign to the southward of Pensylvania included,

And as a great part of this force is to consist of the Southern Provincial troops of Pensilvania, Maryland, Virginia and North Carolina, I make no manner of doubt but these Provinces from their known Zeal for the publick service will most chearfully and unanimously join in Raising with the greatest dispatch the Body of Men expected from them for the Defence of their own Colonies and the Honour and support of his Majesty's Dominions in N° America,

I must therefore beg that officers and men employed for this Service be able bodied good men, capable of enduring fatigue, and that their arms be the best that can be found in the Province.

As I am given to understand and have great reason to expect that a Body of Cherokee Indians are to come and join us this Spring on the back Frontiers of Virginia and Pensilvania, and as their Rout leads them through your Province of North Carolina, I must therefore beg that you will be so good as to give orders that they meet with all kind of good usage in their passing, and hope that Mr. Atkins who has the Charge of Indian Affairs has taken Care of their being supplied with Provisions &c. upon their March. As I am a Stranger to the Southern Provinces, and therefore can make no guess of the Distance that the N° Carolina troops will have to march in order to join the Army at Wills⁵ Creek upon the Potowmack by the first of May, you will therefore be so good as to regulate their march, and order them to set out so as they may join me by that time. And as Provisions cannot Possibly be delivered to them upon their march, each effective mañ that joins the Army shall be paid four pence sterling in lieu of Provisions from the time he begins his march, until that he receives Provisions from the Stores.

I must beg Sir that you will give your orders that none but those men who are good and that can be depended upon may be sent, as people either inclined to mutiny or desert woᵈ prove an immense Detriment to the service at so intricate a Time, and that you will give orders to send me an account of the men you have at present in pay, and what numbers I may expect you are to send me, with the route they are to take in order to join me, and the time they will be ready to sett out, and you will order the officer that commands them to correspond with me directed for me at Philadelphia.

I have the honour to be with great regard
Your most obedient, &c.,

Jo Forbes.

*   *   *   *   *

Forbes to Sharpe * [35]
[Md. H.S. Port Folio 4. Papers and Letters No. 36, A.L.S.]

[New York,] March 21, 1758

Sir

His Excellency Major General Abercromby having (pursuant to His Majestys Directions) appointed me to the Command of the Kings Regular Forces and provincial Troops, who are to be employ'd jointly in the opperations to be carryed on this ensuing Campaign to the Southard of Pensilvania included.

And as a great part of this Force is to consist of the Southern provincial Troops of Pensilvania, Maryland, Virginia, and North Carolina, I make no manner of doubt, but these Provinces from their zeal for the publick service, will most chearfully and unanimously join, in Raising with the greatest dispatch, the body of men expected from them for the defence of their own Colonies & the Honour and support of His Majestys Dominions in North America. I must therefore beg that the officers, and Soldiers employ'd for this Service, be able bodied good men, capable of endureing Fatigue, & that there Arms, be the best that can be found in the Province.

As Carpenters, and Axe men, are absolutely necessary in the back Country, I must beg leave to Recommend to you, that a number of those men be sent & like wise that the Province will send twenty, or thirty men, mounted upon light servisable Horses, & every way Accouter'd, to serve in conjunction with those furnish'd by the other Provinces, as a body of light Horse, from which I expect very important service.

I am given to understand that the Inhabitants upon the Confines, being much used to Woods, and Hunting would consiquently make good Rangers, in which case, I am to beg, you will give Directions for the forming your properest men, into such a Company, with good officers, who know the Country to conduct them, As the Roads from Lancaster in Pensilvania to Williams's Ferry upon the Potowmack, may want considerable Repairs, & Widening for the Carriages of Cannon &c

I have therefore wrote[36] to the Governor of Pensilvania for that purpose, in order that these Roads may be Repaired by the Inhabitants of Pensilvania and Maryland, And you will be so good to give your orders, about the Road

---

* Printed *Md. Arch.* IX, 157.
[35] Horatio Sharpe (1718-1790) colonial governor of Maryland, 1753-1769. He returned to England in 1773. Consult the *D. N. B.*
[36] Forbes to Denny, March 21, 1758, *ante,* p. 58.

leading from Williams's Ferry, to Fort Cumberland, espetialy the road from Colonel Cressops to Fort Cumberland, which may be mended in some measure by your people now at that Fort.

Sr John St Clair[37] informs me,[38] that you have a body of Cherokee Indians at Fort Fredrick upon the Potowmack, which I must beg you will be so good as order to be taken care of, untill we can assemble our people which I hope may be done by the 20th April, and as I propose Canegocheeque for a Rendevouze for the Pensilvania Troops, and Regulars from Philadelphia, I beg you will order the Maryland People, to Fredrick town in Maryland by that time, where if they cannot have provisions delivered to them by our Contractors, I will allow of four pence sterling p^r day, to each Effective man in lieu of provisions.

As there is some times a great deal of time lost in Cloathing, and furnishing out Provintial Troops, I should think therefore that whatever time is lost in that sort of Equipment, is a real loss, as a good man in any Cloaths, and a Blanket, may well answer the purposes required of him.

As there will be a great deal of Forrage wanted for the support of Waggon & Baggage horses, I therefore beg that you will order as much Hay, Indian Corn, and oats, to be laid up at Canogocheeque as the Country can afford, & I will send and officer there to Receive, & Pay for it, according to the Current price of the Country.

If it could possibly be contrived [to send] some Intelligent person up to the Ohio, and Fort Duquesne, to get some Intelligence of the Enemys situation in those parts, I should make it very well worth his while perhaps Capt Dagworthy[39] at Fort Cumberland, might find some such person to send. Who likewise, as well as all your out posts, might have orders to send out frequent Scouting partys to keep the Enemy at a distance, & prevent their prying into our preparations.

They say there is one Fraser[40] at Will's Creek who knows all the Ohio Indians perfectly well.

I shall be extreamly proud of the pleasure of your acquaintance, but it would be too great presumption in me, to wish to see you at Philadelphia, where I must remain untill I can get every thing sent away, however, your zeal & warmth for His Majestys Service, and the good of these Colonies,

---

[37] Lieutenant-colonel in the 60th regiment and deputy quarter master-general.

[38] No such letter found. The statement may have been oral.

[39] Captain John Dagworthy of the Maryland militia, a local notable in frontier warfare.

[40] Evidently John Fraser, the famous Indian trader of Venango, Turtle Cneek, etc.

makes me flatter myself with the hopes of your assistance, in the Conduct of the ensuing Campaign.

I must beg the favour, that you order a Return of your Troops as they now stand, to be sent me
they are disposed and
what means your province has to Raise   for the
service of the present year & what
you have of Compleating them
for me at Philadelphia
I am with very great regard

Your most obedient &
most Hum^{ble} Servt
Jo: fforbes.

Governor Sharp.

*   *   *   *   *

*Forbes to Denny**
[N.Y.P.L. Em. F.B. A.L.S.]

[New York, March 23^d, (1758)]

Sir.

As there will be a Number of Waggons and Carriages wanted in the Province of Pennsylvania, and as the Inhabitants may be backward in furnishing of them, altho to be payed for them with ready money. I therefore take this opportunity of letting you know that press warrants will be necessary all over the province In order that if you are not vested with power to grant such warrants. that you will apply to the Assembly to grant theirs, & fix prices upon the Different Carriages and horses. I have the honour to be Sir

Y^r most ob^t and mos^t hum^{le} Servt

Jo: fforbes.

New York, March 23^d.
Govr. Denny

*   *   *   *   *

---

* Printed *Pa. Col. Recs.*, VIII, 60, and Stewart, *Letters of General John Forbes*, p. 10.

*Forbes to Sharpe**
[Md. H.S. Port Folio 4. Papers and Letters No. 36. Copy.]

[New York, April 4, 1758]

Sir

I Have the Honour of Yours of the 27ᵗʰ of March,⁴¹ the Contents of which I Communicated to General Abercromby, who Allows me to tell you, that he thinks himself Bound to make good the Obligation that the Earl of Loudoun Entered into, with regard to the Maryland Troops Garrisoned at Fort Cumberland,⁴² and cannot Imagine that the Province of Maryland, will, at this Critical time, Allow that Fort to be Abandoned. And makes no doubt but from your prudence & Zeal for the publick Service, that you will be able to persuade the Province, not only to Continue those Troops there, but with all Diligence to second His Majesty's Intentions, in Raising as many more Troops as the Necessity of the present Circumstances and the Strength of the Province will Admit of.

I am Extreamly obliged to you, for the Care you have taken to Repair the Roads, and for your orders about providing of Forrage at Conegocheugue, &c.

Sir John Sᵗ Clair who left this two days ago, will soon be up in those parts, & has money to Satisfye & pay for what will be Necessary.

I should be glad that any of the Scouting partys were so lucky as to bring a Prisoner from Fort Duquesne, as by that means something might be Learned, & hope the Encouragement you give the Cherokees will keep them alert, & make them Exert themselves in this Service.

As soon as the Troops Destined for the Service in the West Arrives at Philadelphia, I have General Abercromby's orders to Send proper Detachments up to Fort Cumberland. I hope soon to set out to Philadelphia, & shall be very happy in paying my Respects to you in Maryland, being with great Regard,

Sir, Yʳ most Humᵇˡᵉ and most Obᵗ Servᵗ

Jo: fforbes

New York, Aprile 4ᵗʰ 1758

Governʳ Sharp
[*Endorsed:*] Copy. Letter from Brig Genl Forbes to Governor Sharpe. Dated New York 4ᵗʰ April 1758

*   *   *   *   *

---

* Printed *Md. Arch.* IX, 167, and Stewart, *Letters of General John Forbes*, p. 10.
⁴¹ Not found.
⁴² Loudoun to Sharpe, November 3, 1758, *Md. Arch.* IX, 98.

Forbes to Abercromby
[AB 175 A.L.S.]

New York Aprile 20th 1758
[Philadelphia]

Sir.

I arrived here tuesday evening and Immediatly waited upon Governour Denny, who I found disposed to do every thing in his power for the good of the service, and was pleased to hear that the assembly had more favorable dispositions to pass the money bill, than what they had hitherto shown, however there is nothing as yet done, altho I should think that the necessity of the times would quicken their resolves the Indians having now come down the Country to Marsh Creek which lyes upon the road between Lancaster and Conegocheek. by which our Communication is intirely cutt off untill we can send some troops that way.

The Cherokees are at Winchester, but in want of everything, I have made a demand here of three hundred light Fuzees to send them (in the mean time) with some ammunition , and I see that I shall be oblidged to provide them in all their necessarys and presents which will not admitt either of delay or of temporizing, as I find they begin to show some uneasiness in not having things ready provided for them. I shall send S^{ir} John S^t clair towards that Country immediatly and persuade Govr Sharp to meet him at Winchester. in order to sett the Cherokees to work, they are about 600 in number, which if rightly looked after may be of infinite service. I send you inclosed a letter from the lower Cherokees to the Mohawks,[43] that you'l please to forward to S^{ir} William Johnston.[44] I send you likewise the enclosed Copy of it.

As my letters are but just come in from New York I send them to you for your perusall by which you will learn the state of affairs in the back country[45]. better than my writing, but must beg you will return them to me having no body to Copy for me and not having time myself.

I beg you would be so good as to send Mr Gordon the Engineer this way with any others that are to serve under him as there is plenty of business for them, and if you design to send ane Assistant to S^{ir} John I wish that he

---

[43] Not found.

[44] Sir William Johnson (1715-1774), baronet, major-general, but most famous as Superintendent of Indian Affairs. Consult the *D. A. B.* and various biographies by Stone, Pound, and others.

[45] Cf. Robert Stewart to Forbes, April 7, 1758, AB 123, copy.

was here, as also whoever Mr Napier appoints for the hospital having bodily need of their present advice.

You will see that Capt Steuart[46] wants very much to have the Commission given him, that S^{ir} john tells me he had spoke off to you, and had recommended it with great sincerity. He says it was a Lieut^{cy} in order that he might not be left without bread, upon a peace —

I am just now told that Col^o Bouquet is at Sandy Hook, and that there is no Intelligence of Col^o Montgomerys Battalion, If so you will be so good as send your orders to them, or let me know your directions that I may proceed accordingly—

I am afraid the animositys here have been carried on with too great heat, to cool soon, or produce any real good to the publick, but I shall leave no stone unturned on my part, to palliate Circumstances on both sides— I am D^r S^{ir} Y^r most obed^t and

most hum^{le} Servt

Jo fforbes.

I have this moment heard that the Assembly sent up their new money bill to the Governour, and shall in my next let you know the Event, but I fancy the Governour will pass it.

Gen^{ll} Abercromby

[*Endorsed:*] Brig. Genl Forbes Philadelphia 20th April 1758 R. the 22^d by Lieu^t Brown Ans^d the 24th by post

*   *   *   *   *

*Forbes to Denny**
[*Pa. Col. Recs.* VIII, 79.]

Philadelphia, April 20th, 1758.

Sir:

As the Situation of these Provinces is such at this Critical Juncture as requires all possible Means to be exerted to clear this Province of the Enemy who have at this Time invaded it, and as there is a great Scarcity of Arms for that purpose, I am under the necessity of requiring of your Honour that

---

[46] Captain Robert Stewart of the Virginia militia, who later obtained a commission in a British regiment. His voluminous correspondence with Washington and Bouquet can be easily located.

* Also printed, Stewart, *Letters of General John Forbes,* p. 11.

you will give orders[47] for delivering to me Two Hundred and Eighteen Light Fuzees, which are in your Store, as likewise as many of the 165 Arms as are found to be serviceable after they are Surveyed.

There will remain in your Store more Arms than will Compleat the Forces proposed to be raised by this Province, besides 2,000 Arms, which I have an Account of being embarked for the Service of this Expedition. I am, with the greatest regard,

Your Honour's most Obedient and most Humble Servant,

Jo. fforbes.

*   *   *   *   *

Forbes to Denny*
[*Pa. Col. Recs.* VIII, 83.]

Philadelphia, April 21st, 1758.

Sir :

I am extremely sorry that any just request of mine to you, as first Majestrate, should met with obstructions that I neither could foresee nor suppose; particularly as I had signed a receipt for the Arms I had demanded, according to your desire; and by which receipt of mine, I certainly showed the Necessity that I was under for such an application, in order to support His Majesty's Measures for the general welfare of North America, and for the immediate protection of this Province in Particular. Such a refusal of what is the Undoubted Right of the King to demand, or the Officer Commanding his Majesty's Subjects under Arms in the Province, is what I am astonished at; and as the Service is pressing, and will admit of no delay, I must beg, Sir, you will send me an answer in writing, as soon as possible, whether you are to deliver to my orders the Fuzees demanded or not.

I have the Honour to be, with the greatest regard,

Sir, Your most obedient and most hum. Servant,

Jo. Forbes.

*   *   *   *   *

---

[47] Cf. Denny to Janvier, April 20, 1758, *Pa. Arch.* 4th series, II, 925.
* Also printed, Stewart, *Letters of General John Forbes,* p. 12.

Forbes to Abercromby
[AB 185 A.L.S.]

[Philadelphia, April 22 (1758)]

Sir:

Last night I receiv'd the enclosed Proposal[48] and have letters[49] to the same purport from Mr Bosomworth, to whom I shall give no answer untill I receive your directions.

I think the Cherokees of such Consequence that I have done everything in my power to provide them in their necessarys, and shall send away to morrow Blanketts, Matchcoats, Deer Skins Vermilion &c all which I have been oblidged to buy for them here,[50] and must still buy a great deal more, as what I now send, is only to please them in the Interim. The 218 light Fuzees for the use of the Indians that I asked and gott ane order for, from the Governour upon my receipt—were last night stopt by two of the Commissioners, I acquainted the Governour of this by letter,[51] and he called his Councill to ascertain whether the King had a right to make use of the arms of the province in its own defence, This incited fresh altercations, but by reasoning cooly with some of the Commissioners, they have dropt it and I am to have the arms.

The money Bill is crammed down the Governor's throat by the Assembly,[52] and rather as lose any more time he is to pass it this day, although in so doing he is oblidged to sign and avow two Notorious falsehoods. In short I never saw such a sett of people, obstinate, & perverse to the last degree, nor do I conceive any way can be fallen upon to make them agree to anything proposed by Mr Denny. so I shall have a thousand little obstacles to gett the better off.

I have a letter[53] from Mr Blair[54] of the 9th of Aprile, Wherin he tells me that their Assembly have framed a Bill[55] to augment their forces to Two Regiments of 1000 Each. and to Garrison their Forts with their Militia

---

[48] Not identified.

[49] Not found. Abraham Bosomworth was a captain in the 60th regiment, the Royal Americans.

[50] Cf. the list, *post,* p. 70.

[51] Forbes to Denny, April 21, 1758, *ante,* p. 67.

[52] *Pa. Col. Recs.,* VIII, 80-83.

[53] Not found.

[54] John Blair (1687-1771), Virginia politician, deputy auditor-general, councilor, and acting governor, January-June 1758 and March-October, 1768. Only his official papers have survived. Consult the *D. A. B.*

[55] *Journals of the House of Burgesses of Virginia, 1756-1758,* 499-502.

WRITINGS OF GENERAL JOHN FORBES

which with their Rangers he hopes may guard their Frontiers in the Absence of the 2 Regiments. Col° Washington is to make the Campaign, and will soon have 900 Men ready to join me, and the rest are to be raised as soon as proper measures can be fallen upon.

The sick of Montgomerys 3 comp^ys are come in and I expect the three companies themselves to night, but must march then directly to Lancaster and Carlile where they are scalping every day and have broke up all the settlements in that neighborhood.

Montgomerys sick will amount to fifty besides some left behind of Otways, So be so good as order Mr Napier to send us people.

I should be glad to know what engagements was entered into with regard to the Cherokees, as I forsee I must not only make those good, but provide everything that can keep them steady to our Interest, as there is not the least trust to be putt in the dilatory measures of the provinces:

S^ir John tells me that we shall be in want of more money soon. so you will make Mr Mortier[56] write me how I am to come by it.

The money bill is this moment passed, and the Governour has sent me the 218 Fuzees as he has taken the Keys of the Province Magazines into his own hands. I am S^ir

Y^r most obed^t & most hum^le Servt

Jo: fforbes.

Philadelphia, Aprile 22^d

Mr Blair writes me that the Virginians will want a <u>1000</u> Arms and begs my Assistance—

I have just now seen yours of the 20th to Govr Denny.[57] & therefore am to remind you, that S^ir William Johnston can have nothing to do with the Cherokee Indians as they are all entirely in Mr Atkins and his Deputy, Mr Gists[58] Department. And for my own part I should think it bad policy to run any risque of losing the certainty of 1000 Cherokees, for the distant uncertainty of 40 or 50 Shawanes and delawares so untill I receive orders I shall continue sending the things to Winchester a list of which I send you.— Gen^ll Abercromby

[*Endorsed:*] Brig^r. Gen^ll Forbes Phila^a April 22^d 1758 Rd. 24th D° per Express

---

[56] Abraham Mortier, deputy paymaster general at New York.
[57] Loudoun to Denny, April 20, 1758, *Pa. Arch.* 1st series, III, 380.
[58] Christopher Gist (*c.* 1706-1759), famous explorer and frontiersman, whose life is much too little known by the general public. Consult Orrill, "Christopher Gist and His Sons," *W. Pa. Hist. Mag.* XV (1932), 191.

Lists of Indian Goods
[AB 219 Contem. Copy]

[Philadelphia, April 22, 1758]

List of things sent to the Indians at Winchester

60 light·Fuzees at p 32 Shillings
 2 pieces of Matchcoats £50 each
   Silver Georgets, Armbands & Bracelets, with Broaches

   To be sent from Philadelphia
218 light Fuzees— ⎫
300 Dressed Deer skins— ⎬ amounting to 20..12..0.
   Strouds & halfthicks ⎭
104 Kettles—
 50 lb Vermillion
50,000 Wampum
 500 powder horns—

*   *   *   *   *

Forbes to Loudoun
[LO 5813 A.L.S.]

Philad. Aprile 23ᵈ [1758]

My Dear Lord

I sent an Express this day to Genˡˡ Abercromby[59] and altho I had time to have wrote you, did not choose it to prevent nonsensicall jealousys—

I must confess the Situation of Denny here, is most miserable, and you will see by his remonstrance[60] to the house of Assembly that he has been oblidged to swallow a very bitter peel, for the public good, which most certainly must (by all right men) be judged a wise measure. I confess I spoke Italian to him half ane hour on the subject, which I am afraid was not rigidly honest, but it has answered ane honest purpose.

I hope you have almost gott your bottoms wind up. and are in a fair way to go where I hope you you [*sic*] will find more real friendship than I think you have mett with in America, altho in the highest Situation, Think a little of my Dʳ Lord how I am to proceed or succeed, I am here these six days by my self alone, having no mortall but Halkett. In short necessity will turn me a Cherokee, and dont be surprised if I take F: dυ

---

[59] Forbes to Abercromby, April 22, 1758, *ante,* p. 68.
[60] *Pa. Col. Recs.* VIII, 80-83.

Quesne at the head of them; and them only, For to this day I have no orders to command any troops nor has any troops orders to receive my Commands, that I know off. however the service shall not suffer, and I shall go on, but by Jove, it is hard. I can have no officer allowed me capable of writing three words of military business—which makes me write in place of thinking— The Express is just going which makes me cutt short my Grievances, but shall write you amply So God bless you.

Adieu Jo fforbes

[N: York]† Philad: Aprile 23ᵈ
      Pardon all this nonsense.—

[*Addressed:*] To The Rᵗ. Honᵇˡᵉ The Earl of Loudoun Lieuᵗ. Generall of His Majᵗⁱᵉˢ Forces &c &c &c New York
[*Endorsed:*] Brigadier John Forbes Philadelphia April 23ᵈ 1758 Situation of things there. R April 24ᵗʰ 1758

*   *   *   *   *

Forbes to Abercromby
[AB 198 A.L.S.]

Philadelphia Aprile 24ᵗʰ 1758

Sir.

I Receiv'd your Express[61] last night, and have sent off Governour Little-tons letter[62] by express this morning, I have likewise execute Mʳ Pitts private orders[63]. which was no more than to order ane officer of Colonel Mongomerys to repair immediately to Hallifax. So as he enjoins silence and secrecy I do not say one word.

Your taking it for granted that I am solely to Correspond with the southern provinces, would no doubt save a great deal of time in the executing of things when you may be in the back country, and I shall most certainly endeavour at giving' you as little trouble as possible, but when I see you are difficulted with regard to the money demands, not only of the Maryland Forces for the time past, but also for what may happen. As likewise how also those Indians and Savages are to be provided with all necessarys; in case I

---

† Stricken out.
[61] This express may not have contained a letter to Forbes, as no letter to Forbes between April 13th and April 24th, 1758, has been found.
[62] Letter, Abercromby to Lyttelton, not found.
[63] Pitt to Forbes, January 27, 1758, Kimball, *Correspondence of William Pitt,* I, 171.

find that they are either neglected, or that wee from some such mistake may runn a risque of loosing them. and as the present demands from South Carolina appear higher than those from Maryland. and for uses and purposes very precarious, you see the necessity there is that I have your opinion and direction upon those Subjects, being totaly a Stranger to the engagements entered unto upon those heads, or how farr bound, to fulfill them.

I thank you most heartily for appointing my Q^r M^r & Mr Christopher[64] Ensigns in my Reg^t. as I had a previous agreement with the first of which Col° Morris tell me he has acquainted you.

I sent Governour Denny the Extract[65] from S^{ir} William Johnstons letter.[66] which he was immediatly to Communicate to his Councill. but the plain matter of Fact is, that there are some leading folks here who would rather your whole expedition should go to the Devill, [rather]† than not please the Delaware Indians, because really that some of their rascally estates lyes at the mercy of those savages; who by the by when all collected together, would not make a breakfast to the Cherokees. So I am very clear of giving those last the preference in everything.

I am to thank you for allowing Serg^t Morton[67] of the 48th to go with me as they say he or some such was absolutely necessary. for the roads &c— but I wish you could send me either a Secretary or a Clerk or any thing, for I have not time to dine or Supp for this terrible writing, In short I can not mind the business of a Soldier, if I am to be so much a Clerk, and I really do not see from whom I can draw any assistance. For you well know that Major Halkett altho honest & willing is rather slow.

There is a letter from Mr Blair[68] this morning still wanting arms, I have wrote[69] to him and Govr Sharp[70] to encourage the provincialls to bring their own arms, and that some allowance should be made them for the use of them.

Sir John has had a letter[71] from Mr Hunter[72] with regard to money matters which I have desired him to forward to Mr Mortier that he may lay it before you.

[64] Ensign John Christopher of the 17th regiment.
[65] Printed, *Pa. Col. Recs.,* VIII, 97.
[66] Johnson to Abercromby, April 13, 1758, *Papers of Sir William Johnson,* II, 187.
† Stricken out.
[67] Not otherwise identified.
[68] Not found.
[69] Not found.
[70] March 21, 1758, *ante,* p. 61.
[71] Not found.
[72] John Hunter of Virginia, agent of Thomlinson and Hanbury of London.

I shall be much oblidged to you when you have any news, if you will make some of your Mirmidons let us hear it.

They say there are letters[78] in this town of the 12th from Charles town, and that Montgomerys Batn were quiet and tranquile, and had not than receiv'd any order of march.

> I am Sir Yr most obt
> & most humle Servt
> Jo: fforbes.

What is to be done about Camp necessarys for the provincials—I have persuaded the province to gett them ready in the mean time.—

I hope some body has orders to scrape together the necessarys from the train destined to those parts.

[*Endorsed:*] Brigr. Genll Forbes Phila. April the 24th 1758. Rd. the 26th Do. Ansd. the 27th by post

* * * * *

Forbes to Loudoun
[LO 5818 A.L.S.]

[Philadelphia, April 27, 1758]

My Dear Lord.

I design'd to have wrote you a long letter as also to have sent letters to have gone home with you, but I am wore out in writing, as I am here entirely alone, without any Assistance.

I will absolutely take the morrow to my self and send you a letter by express. but if you are gone God bless you. only pray let me know if this catches you, the Engagements you think your self bound in to the Cherokees, &c &c—

This is a damned troublesome place, So hope by behaving well some time or other to kiss your hands.

> Adieu My Dr Lord.
> God bless you yrs
> Jo fforbes

Aprile 27th

[*Addressed:*] To the Rt Honoble The Earl of Loudoun Lieut. Genll of His Majties Forces at New York
[*Endorsed:*] Brig: John Forbes 24 April 1758

* * * * *

---

[78] Not found.

*Forbes to Denny**
[H.S.P. Gratz Collection. A.L.S.]

[Philadelphia, April 28, 1758]

Sir,

Accident presented a particular thing to my view this day that had really escaped me, and therefore beg your Advice.

As your troops are immediately under my direction, and as the different demands of money from them is perhaps what neither you nor I can either determine or forsee, And as there may be severall Contingent expences accruing dayly that I can not have your advice or assistance in, I must therefore represent to you that it will be necessary that you have a provinciall treasurer or paymaster to attend me, In order to issue such summs of money for the provinciall service as I shall judge necessary to give orders for. It is needless to explain or to enter into the detail of what those demands may be, because every person must easily forsee a number of trifling demands, that at present I can not ascertain, but hope you will fall upon a method to give me such powers that no stop may be putt to the service, as I shall think myself accountable to you and the province for any moneys that may by my orders be laid out.

I am, Sir,
with great regard,
Y^r most ob^t & most humbel Servant,
Jo. fforbes.

Philadelphia, Aprile 28th.
[*Addressed*] The Honb^{le} Gov Denny &c
[*Endorsed:*] 28, April 1758
General Forbes.

*   *   *   *   *

Forbes to Abercromby
[AB 221 A.L.S.; P.R.O. W.O. :34:44 f. 297, Copy.]

Philadelphia, May 1st 1758

Sir.

Captain Bosomworth arrived here from Winchester two days ago and has had a Conversation with the Cherokees who he says at present are in

---

* Printed, *Pa. Arch.* 1st series, III, 383, and Stewart, *Letters of General John Forbes*, p. 12.

tollerable humour, altho impatient to see our Army, Artillery, and their own presents—Their numbers are above 600, four hundred of them I have gott pretty well equipt, and they are gone out in several party's both above and below Fort du Quesne What to do or how to provide the rest with arms &c I do not yet know. And Mr Gist has sent a list of things[74] wanted to Compleat a thousand Indians in every thing, the amount of which, would be near £8000—which is a great deal of money, and as there may be near a thousand (above the 400 equipt already) [I should]† that we may expect sooner or latter I should be glad of your directions and advice, how I am to proceed.

I have this moment receiv'd the enclosed letter[75] from Governour Sharp. As I can not meddle with the embargo without your authority I have given no Answer. to that part of his letter. And as I still kept your proposall to Capt Dagworthy untill I should know the resolution of the province, I think this proposall of Govr Sharp's a good expedient in the mean time, and we can make the proposal to Capt Dagworthy afterwards. or as this Virginia proposall is likely to take place So shall write[76] to Mr Sharp to know Mr Blairs Intentions before I communicate your proposall which I am afraid would not succeed as their present pay is much above your offers. I am S^{ir}

W^t great regard

Yr most ob^t & most hum^{le} Servt
Jo. fforbes.

Philadelphia, May 1, 1758

[*Endorsed:*] Brig^r Genl Forbes Philadelphia 1st May 1758 R the 3^d by post Ans. 4 by d°.

[*Endorsed:*] The General order about the issue of provisions in the field. [*Note:*] Close with Govr Sharps proposal by incorporating & Listing the Marylanders amongst the Virginians—

*   *   *   *   *

---

[74] Not found.
† Stricken out.
[75] Sharpe to Forbes, April 27, 1758, *Md. Arch.* IX, 173. The copy here mentioned is in AB 205.
[76] May 2, 1758, *post*, p. 79.

*Forbes to Pitt**
[P.R.O. C.O. 5:50, (L.C. trans.) p. 565-570.]

Philadelphia. May 1ˢᵗ. 1758.

Sir

By a Letter[77] that I have just received from Major General Abercromby, I am directed to Correspond with you, and impart to His Majesty's
Ministers the Steps that I take, and the Events following thereon, in prosecu-
tion to the Command entrusted to my Care, that no Time may be lost in
informing His Majesty of the progress of His Affairs in the Southern
Collonys.

I received General Abercromby's Commands[78] upon the fourteenth of
last Month, ordering me to repair from New York to Philadelphia, and
there to endeavour to reconceal Matters between the Governour and Assembly, in order to the passing of a Bill[79] of one hundred thousand pounds
for His Majesty's use, and Service of this Campaign. The Bill after various
Altercations was at last agreed to, and passed upon the 26ᵗʰ of last Month;
and the Provincial Troops were order'r to be augmented to two thousand
seven hundred Men. They have just now began to raise their Men by naming their Officers &cᵃ.; a few days will show what Success the Recruiting
Officers meet with; But everything except fresh Disputes which arise every
day, goes on very slowly, but I have and shall do everything in my power
to quell them.

The three lower Countys are raising three hundred Men, which I have
reason to expect will be soon compleated.

The Province of Maryland have been extremely dilatory in their proceedings, nor do I yet find, that they have come to any Resolution about
granting Supplys. At the end of last Year they voted their Troops (consisting of three hundred Men) shou'd be disbanded, by which Fort Cumberland and that back Country must have fallen into the Enemy's Hands.
But the Earl of Loudoun gave assurances[80] to Governour Sharpe, that rather
than these Men shou'd be disbanded his Lordᵖ wou'd make good the Expences of keeping them up. In this Situation these Troops have been these
four or five Months; and as General Abercromby seems averse at present

---

* Printed, Kimball, *Correspondence of William Pitt,* I, 235, and Stewart, *Letters
of General John Forbes,* p. 13.
⁷⁷ Abercromby to Forbes, April 24, 1758, AB 189, copy.
⁷⁸ Abercromby to Forbes, April 13, 1758 AB 163, copy.
⁷⁹ *Pa. Col. Recs.* VIII, 86 f.
⁸⁰ Loudoun to Sharpe, November 3, 1757, *Md. Arch.* IX, 98.

to have that Expence fall upon the Crown, I can have but very little dependence of Maryland doing any Good for the Service; even altho' they grant Eighty thousand Pounds for his Majesty's Use, twenty five or thirty thousand Pounds of which will be appropriated for their long Sessions of Assembly, and great part of the Remainder consumed in the pay and Arrears due to their Troops.

The Province of Virginia have voted to augment their Troops to two thousand Men, and are to garrison their forts and Frontiers with their Militia. But I doubt much if that Province will be able to raise that Number of Men, altho' they give ten pounds enlisting money. The Regiment that they have on foot amounts at present to eight hundred Men, but I may venture to say, that they will not be able to raise four hundred Men more, and if they shou'd draft their Militia to compleat the two thousand Men, these Men will not stay eight days with us. There is nothing expected from the Carolinas, It was impossible to bring the three Independent Companies of South Carolina this way; as they are stationed at the Forts in the Indian Country at the back of Georgia.

The Regular Forces destined for the Operations upon the frontiers of the Southern Provinces and the Ohio, are thirteen Companys of Montgomery's Highlanders, and four Companys of the first Battalion of the Royal American Regiment. The ten Companys of the former are not yet arrived from South Carolina. The three additional Companys who are in this Province, have one third sick, and the remainder have not yet recovered strength enough for Service, occasioned by their long passage from Britain. The four Companies of the first Battalion of Americans are got to this place, they are sickly, being just arrived from South Carolina, and they want fifty Men to compleat them, which will be impracticable to fill up, as the Provinces are giving so high Bountys for raising the Men they are to furnish during this Campaign. This is the Situation of the Military State of the Southern Provinces, and regular troops; by which you will see what may be expected from; more particularly when you will please to consider that the Artillery, Arms, Tents, and the other things necessary for carrying on the Service I am entrusted with the care of are not as yet arrived. The Cherokee and Catauba Indians have been fully as good as their Promise, in coming in at different times from their own Country for these two or three Months by past, to Winchester in Virginia, the place of their Rendez-vous. Their Numbers already come, are Six hundred and fifty two, and several more are expected, and are actually upon their March. As they are almost naked, and without Arms, I have left no Means untryed to provide them in both and have so far succeeded that I have now scouting Partys to the

Amount of four hundred of them (all equipt for War) who are gone upon the Ohio, above and below Fort Duquesne, in order to annoy the Enemy, gett Intelligence, and bring away some Prisoners if possible. As fast as the rest can be equipt they shall go out upon the same Errand. For as our greatest Dependance is upon them, and they capable of being led away upon any Caprice or whime that seizes them, I am obliged by every Artifice to amuse them from returning home, they being rather offended at not seeing our Army and Artillery assembled, which I am afraid they had reason to expect. However, I propose getting Governour Sharpe and an officer from this to go amongst them to keep up their Spirits, by constant Employment, altho' that may be difficult to do, without equiping them for War; which equipment for one thousand Indians amounts to the Value of Eight Thousand Pounds, and many of the things not to be gott in America, especially light arms.

In the mean time until the Troops arrive from South Carolina, the Artillery and Stores from England, and that the Provincial Forces are raised and collected at their different Rendez-vous: I shall be preparing the Magazines, and moving them up fifty or sixty Miles beyond the inhabited parts of this Province, that no Stop may be made for want of that Material Article provision. The carriage of which is so difficult and Expensive on this Continent but more particularly in the back parts of these Provinces, where there is no Water Carriage. I had the Honour of your Letter (dated at Whitehall Jan^{ry}. the 27th [81]) the 24th of last Month, with a Letter[82] for Governour Lyttleton. I executed the Orders it contained by writing[83] directly to Colonel Montgomery, and sent the Letters by Express over land to South Carolina, where if my Letter miss of Colonel Montgomery, I shall take care that he is immediately acquainted with its contents upon his arrival here. I beg pardon for having taken up so much of your time but thought it my indispensable Duty to say so much, lest the unavoidable delays that occur hourly in executing the Trust His Majesty has honor'd me with, might in some measure seem to lie at my Door. When I beg leave to assure you that no dilligence or application of mine shall ever be wanting to help forward the Service to the utmost of my Power.

> I am Sir, with the greatest Regard and Respect
> Your most obedient and most humble Servant
>
> Jo: Forbes

---

[81] Kimball, *Correspondence of William Pitt,* I, 171.
[82] *Ibid.,* 170.
[83] Letter not found.

[*Addressed:*] To the Right hon'ble William Pitt Esq[r] &c[a]
[*Endorsed:*] Philadelphia May 1st 1758/
Brigad[r] Gen[l] Forbes /R[e] July 3[d]

* * * * *

Forbes to Sharpe*
[Md. H. S. Port Folio 4. Papers and Letters No. 36 A.L.S.]

Philadelphia, May 2d 1758

Private

Sir,

In case your Assembly are mad enough to do Nothing, I like the proposal for the Virginians taking your Troops into their pay extremely, and as I was sending an Express to M[r] Blair,[84] I hinted to him that in Case such a proposal was made to him by you, that he ought to Jump at it Directly.

But in case he thinks they will be able to Raise their own men, rather than let your Troops be Disbanded, I will take them into the pay of the Crown, upon the Footing of Rangers. And that no time may be lost in Adjusting & Settling those & other measures, I have sent Sir John S[t] Clair to Lancaster, & from thence he is to repair to Winchester in Virginia, where I have Desired M[r] Blair, or some Person, with full powers, to meet him on the 18th of this month, and where also I must beg (if it any way suits your Conveniency) that you will be likewise, as by such a meeting numberless Difficultys may Easily be Removed.

I am, with the greatest Sincerity
Sir
Your most obedient and
most Humb[le] Serv[t]
Jo: fforbes

[*Addressed:*] The Hon[ble] Horatio Sharpe Esq &Ca
[*Endorsed:*] Copy. Private Letter from Brig Gen Forbes to Gov[r] Sharpe Dated Philad: 2[d] May 1758.

* * * * *

---

* Printed, *Md. Arch.* IX, 174, and Stewart, *Letters of General John Forbes*, p. 15.
[84] Not found.

*Forbes to Sharpe**
[Md.H.S. Port Folio 4, Papers & Letters No. 36. L.S.]

Sir   Philadelphia May 2ᵈ 1758

I have the Honour of yours of the 27ᵗʰ of April[85] yesterday morning, but as I could not by any means interfere with the Embargo: I sent your Letter with the Memorial[86] to General Abercromby by an Express, and make no doubt, but by the Return of the Express I shall have the Pleasure to acquaint you, of the Embargo being taken off; as I hear that all our Troops and Transports are sailed from New York.

I am extremely sorry that the annimositys betwixt your upper and lower House shou'd prove of so fatal a consequence, as to obstruct the Kings measures at this so critical a time for the whole Continent of North America. Can the Gentlemen that compose these Houses, imagine that His majesty and the whole people of Great Britain will be blind to their Behaviour upon this so urgent and pressing an occasion. And can they imagine that a great nation drained to the last in the protection and Defence of those Provinces and Collonys will forgive and forgett the being abandoned by any of them, in this critical time of publick Calamity and distress: If every individual was honestly to examine his own Heart, I am perswaded he wou'd be stung with a just and laudable Spirit of resentment, at the proceedings of the collected Representatives of the People of Maryland. For my own part I shall be very much difficulted, how I ought to behave my self, if the Province of Maryland does not (in consequence of His Majestys Pleasure communicated to them in the strongest manner by Mʳ Pitt His Majestys Principal Secretary of State[87]) come to a speedy determination, as one days delay is of infinite consequence. I shall be sorry to let it enter my thoughts, that they are not, to act as good and Loyall Subjects ought to do, because it wou'd grieve me much to think we had ever cherished and protected concealed Ennemys, infinitely more dangerous than the most open and declared ones.

I must beg you will let me know, as soon as possible the Resolutions concluded upon, that I may govern myself accordingly, and believe me to be with great Regard

                                              Sir
                              Your most obedient and
                                most humble Servant
                                        Jo. fforbes.

---

* Printed, *Md. Arch.* IX, 175, and Stewart, *Letters of General John Forbes,* p. 16.
[85] Sharpe to Forbes, April 27, 1758, AB 205 copy. Printed, *Md. Arch.* IX, 173.
[86] Not found, but mentioned as petition against the embargo, in Sharpe to Forbes, April 27, 1758, *Md. Arch.* IX, 173.   [87] Note William Pitt's official title.

[*Addressed:*] To the Honble Horatio Sharpe Esqr. Govr of Maryland
[*Endorsed:*] From Genl Forbes
2^d May 1758

* * * * *

*Forbes to Denny**
[*Pa. Col. Recs.* VIII, 110.]

[Philadelphia, May 3^d, 1758]

Sir:

Finding that the Storeship with the Tents, Arms, &c^a., has not arrived from England with the Transports, I applied[88] to General Abercrombie, to know how I was to proceed with regard to Camp Necessaries, and his answer[89] is:

"With regard to Camp necessaries for the Provincials, they must be furnish'd by the different Provinces; those to the Northward have agreed to it, and their Troops are to come provided with them at their Expence." I must therefore beg leave to Know the Resolution of the Province upon this Subject directly."

Upon your Application, I promised to send an Hundred of the Royal Americans up toward Reading, but as these Companies are very Sickly, coming from Carolina, and very much want some Days of Rest and Refreshment, I must, therefore, beg you will excuse me from my Promise, and in their Room you may send some of the new raised Provincials, which will answer every purpose fully as well.

I should be glad to know your Opinion of the Party of Cherokees at Carlisle, whether they should be allowed to proceed, or turned another Way. I should likewise want to know how far the Province thinks themselves Obliged to take Care of those Indians by Presents, Cloathing, etc^a.

I beg, Sir, that the Orders about the Light Horse may be given as soon as possible; and that you will likewise be so good as to order the Horses to be placed, for the Conveying Intelligence thro' your Counties, according to the plan given to you by the Quartermaster General.

I realy think Teedyuscung's Demands[90] ought to be agreed with, as he

---

* Original not found. Printed also, Stewart, *Letters of General John Forbes,* p. 16.
[88] Forbes to Abercromby, April 24, 1758, *ante,* p. 71.
[89] Not found, unless in Abercromby to Forbes, April 24, 1758, AB 189, which may have been posted after delay.
[90] Teedyuscung, Delaware Indian leader from north central Pennsylvania, whose demands and negotiations clutter the records of this period.

has the Publick Faith for the making such a Settlement, altho' I would parry off all Convoy of Troops, as Axmen and Carpenters will Answer all his purposes, and I think that he and his Tribes ought to be our Guards for those Back Settlements this Summer, as we shall want all the Troops somewhere else.

I am Sir, with great Regard, Your Most Obedient & most Hum. Servt.

John Forbes.

Philadelphia, May 3d, 1758

*   *   *   *   *

Forbes to Johnson
[AB 231 Contem. Copy.]

[Philadelphia, May 4, 1758.]

Sir/

The Situation of the Publick with regard to the Indians you are too well acquainted with for me to give you further information, then what you have already had from Gen^{ll} Abercromby.[91]

I was given to understand[92] by his Excellency that you design'd sending your Deputy here—Immediately, to adjust matters. I wish he may arrive in Time to be of any Service, for all those affairs have some how been cruelly neglected, and are at Present in the Greatest Confusion,

There is one Mr Wade[93] who has been some Days in this Town, buying up Goods for the Indians. and says it was by your orders, altho he had Persuaded some Merchants to let him have some Indian Goods that had been previously bespoke by the Q^r Mr Gen^{ll} and others employed to Provide those Necessarys for the Cherokees, yet I was willing to let him carry them off in Part. But the pressing demands of about 800 Cherokees now present with us, obliged me to lay an Embargo on every thing of that kind, that I could find in this City, the whole being but scarcely sufficient to keep those people together and to Prevent their returning home,

I thought it proper to acquaint you of this, that you may provide what you may want at New York or Boston, and I am with great Regard

Sir

Your Most Obed^t Humble Servant.

Jo: fforbes

---

[91] Abercromby to Johnson, April 14, 1758, *Papers of Sir William Johnson*, II, 812; April 10, 1758, *ibid.*, 815.
[92] Consult, Abercromby to Forbes, April 13, 1758, AB 150, and April 24, 1758, AB 153.   [93] Not otherwise identified.

Philadelphia May 4th
Sir Willm Johnston

[*Endorsed:*] Copy of a Letter from Brig^r Genl Forbes to Sir William Johnson. Philadelphia 4th May 1758 Enclosed in the Brig^{r,s} of the same day.

*   *   *   *   *

*Halkett to Washington**
[L.C. MSS Papers of Washington, VII, A.L.S.]

Philadelphia 4th May 1758

Dear Sir,—

General Forbes having information,[94] that a party of our Cataubas are just return'd to Winchester, from a Scout to the Ohio, and have brought in with them several Prisoners, and Scalps—as the General is extreamly desirous of Knowing the condition of Fort Duquesne, & the situation of the Enemys strength in these parts, he has ordered me to acquaint you, that if the Intilligence the Prisoners give is so distink, and of such consiquence, as to be of service to the General, that you will take the first opportunity to send them to Philadelphia—and to facilitate their convayance, you will send and open letter[95] to the Commanding Officers at the different Posts upon their Route, that they are to forward them with an Escort, from post, to Post You will at the same time be pleas'd to send the General any information[96] that you have taken from the Prisoners.

Their is a Treaty on foot just now between the Shawne's, the Delawares and the people of this province, and he is very sorry to learn, that several of the Cherokees have taken into their heads to ramble this way, that several of them are to Carlisle, and he is just now inform'd that some of them are coming in to this Town, the General therefore desires, that you will be at particular pains, to prevent any more of them coming this way, and that they may be employ'd as much as possible in Scouting parties, to cover our Posts, and Magazines, & keep the Frontiers of the Country quite, & as the most effectual Route for that purpose, he would recommend to you, the sending of them out by <u>Rays Town</u>, & <u>Franks Town</u>, to <u>long Island</u> in the West branch of the Susquhana, and examine all the Paths leading towards the Ohio.

---

* Printed in Hamilton, *Letters to Washington*, II, 284.
[94] Source of information not located.
[95] Not found.   [96] Not found.

The General is very much allarmd with a letter[97] which he has this moment Receiv'd, with an account that the Raven, (a Cherokee Captain) and 30 of his Men having returnd to their own Country, much displeas'd with the English, he therefore must press it in the warmest manner, that the utmost attention be paid by every body under your Command, towards keeping the Indians in a good disposition, & that all meens be used, in bringing back the Raven, & those Indians who have Return home.

The General is just now employd, in buying all the Strouds, and goods that will be necessary to make in presents to the Indians, and has laid an Embago upon everything in this Town, that will be of service in that way.

Provided that the Catawbas are not dispos'd to part with their Prisoners, you are not to send them, but if they can procur'd without giving umbrage, the General will be very desirous of seeing them. I am with great regard Dear Washington your most obedient & most humble Servant.

Francis Halkett

Col: Washington

P. S.—You will please for the future, to send all your Returns to me at Philadelphia, that I may make up a general State of the Whole to be laid before General Forbes at the different times as they shall offer.

*   *   *   *   *

Forbes to Abercromby
[AB 230 A.L.S.]

[Philadelphia, May 4, 1758.]

Sir

Our noble assembly broke up yesterday and took leave of the Governor with a short Epistle of 30 pages.[98] Containing they say more scurrility than ever.

They have left a sett of Commissioners or manadgers, who have gott their lesson by heart, and seem as if they would not forgett one word of it, with regard to the Governour.

With those jarring partys, spite of Coxing, Bullying and even double dealing, have I been kept of, till Yesterday morning before y^t I could gett them to issue the money. So we are now fairly begunn. And I hope will go on, for I am given to understand that what I desire shall be done provided it does not come through the Governour, And I have given them to under-

---

[97] Not found.   [98] Found in *Pa. Col. Recs.* VIII, 102-110.

stand that altho in decency I must apply to the Governour yet I shall look upon the despatch given to publick affairs, as ane obligation done me by them.

By Letters from Carlisle[99] there are 70 or 80 Cherokees arrived in that neighborhood, with a design I suppose of falling upon the Delawares &c who are now here solliciting a peace. I have therefore sent to stop and divert their process[100] untill wee see how matters turn out. with Tediuscung and the settlement that this province promised to make these tribes at Wioming. I am sorry to say and think that S[ir] William Johnston or his deputies has intirely neglected and disappointed every step that ought to have been taken, and to putt ane intire stop to the Cherokees likewise, he sent one Wade[1] here about 8 Days ago who in ane underhand way was engaging all the Indian Goods in this place severalls of which had previously been bespoke for the use of the Cherokees [before]† So I have been oblidged to putt a stop to that by laying ane embargo on all the Indian goods in this place. and the whole is not half enough to keep the Cherokees in humour, untill more Indian goods arrive from Europe. There having already a Cap[t] (Called the Raven) and 30 men gone away home disgusted, for want of the necessary Supplies promised them, and I wish I may be able to prevent this discontent from Spreading, for which purpose I think of sending old Conrad Weiser[2] with all that I can pick up of Indian things, up amongst them, to make a parsimonious distribution among them from time to time.

There is a party of Cherokees and Catawbas just arrived from a Scout upon the Ohio, where they scalped seven, and have brought in five prisoners. without any of ours kill'd, altho four or five are wounded. I can not tell what the prisoners say but have sent for them down to Lancaster provided they will part with them, but I foresee an immensity of trouble to managde the Indians. Nor will they be pleased untill they see some thing of ane Army and great guns, for which reason I must march the provinciall reg[ts] of Pensylvania, and Virginia up to Forts Littleton[3] & Loudoun,[4] but then I leave Fort Augusta exposed.

---

[99] Not found.

[100] Halkett to Washington, May 4, 1758, *ante*, p. 83.

[1] Mr. Wade, mentioned, Forbes to Johnson, May 4, 1758, *ante*, p. 82.

† Stricken out.

[2] Conrad Weiser (1696-1760), famous figure in Pennsylvania Indian affairs. Consult Walton, *Conrad Weiser*.

[3] Fort Littleton, west of Carlisle, Pennsylvania, and on the route of Forbes' march.

[4] Presumably Fort Loudoun, Pennsylvania, west of Carlisle, but there was another Fort Loudoun near Winchester, Virginia.

I send you some extracts of Intelligence[5] by wch you will see how necessary it is to preserve the Cherokees even for our own defense. I think S^{ir} Wm Johnston ought to have a Copy of the Mohawks advice to the Cherokees[6] sent him. signed by the Interpreter Ric^d Smith.

I am this moment informed that there are 6 or 8 Cherokees arrived here and that they are to be followed by 60 or 70 this afternoon. Poor Tediuscung is in a terrible pannick nor do I well know what to do with him, or how to dispose of them. You hereby see how necessary S^{ir} William Johnston or some of his deputies, would be in this place. So if you think proper to quicken him once more either to come or to send, for as you, yourself appeared to be cautious of giving any directions in those perplexed Indian Affairs without his participation, how much more so, ought I to be—[*Marginal note:* Since writing &c I am told there are but 3 Cherokees come in and no more Coming]

I should be glad to hear of Montgomerys Batt^n, and to know how they are to be pay'd Forrage, Batt, and Baggage money.

I have been oblidged to keep the four Companys of the first Bat^n here to recruit a little, as my letters and Acco^{tts} from Lancaster does no way correspond with what you told me. There being no kind of Spring or any kind of Garden Stuff as yet in those back parts, and S^{ir} Allen M^c lean[7] complains much of the severity of the Cold and the bad change made in leaving the Jerseys and this place—

I am S^{ir} with great regard.

> Y^r most ob^t & most hum^{le} Servt
> Jo fforbes.

Philadelphia, May 4th
I send you enclosed a letter[8] to Sir Wm Johnston which I must beg the favor you will make Mr Appy putt under Cover and send it if you think it proper, as I do not know his address.
G. Abercromby

[*Endorsed:*] Brig^r Forbes Philadelphia 4th May 1758. R the . . . 6th by post Ans. the 7th by d^o

*   *   *   *   *

[5] Not identified, but possibly that found in Washington to St. Clair, May 4, 1758, in *Writings* (Fitzpatrick, ed.), II, 91.

[6] Not found.

[7] Allan McLean (1725-1784), in 1758 a lieutenant in the 60th regiment, later the hero of Canadian defense in 1775-1776 and of high rank in the British Army. The full story of his life remains to be written, but consult the *D. N. B.*

[8] Forbes to Johnson, May 4, 1758, *ante,* p. 82.

Forbes to Abercromby
[AB 237 A.L.S.]

[Philadelphia, May 7th (1758)]

Sir.

I was yesterday very agreeably surprized with the Arrivall of ane Officer of Col: Montgomerys from Carolina, who having a Short passage makes me hope the Batt^n may be as lucky; and that in 3 weeks wee may expect to see them here. I shall endeavour to provide them (in the mean time [of]† with what they may have demands for upon their Arrival, that no stop may be attribute to the regulars. but what shall wee do for tents, for the provincialls who if any way tardy, will avail themselves. and retort upon us they were sooner ready than wee. So I really think wee may venture to bespeak—half of the tents necessary, which one may temporise with for some time, that is to say, 200 tents for the Pensylvanian's that must now march up to Cover the Convoys of Provisions, clear the roads, and build a pallisaded Deposit, for the same at Rays town:[9]

Your advice about the Maryland troops[10] I think has a great deal of weight, so shall be cautious how I proceed, but your thinking that the Virginians will gett their numbers [*Marginal note:* which is only 2000] is more than what they expect themselves, For both Mr Blair and Mr Robinson[11] their leading men, doubts that they will gett any men without draughting the militia which draughts will not stay 8 Days with us, & Col. Washington writes me[12] that he will have great Difficultys to Compleat his reg^t. Now if this prove true, and that the greatest part of the new raised Pensylvania Forces must garrison their back forts upon the Delaware and Susquehanah rivers, you will then find the 5000 provincialls that you mention reduced to less than 2000, So in this case it would be a pity to lose those 300 Maryland troops, who I am told are good rangers, nor can I as yet make any Complaint of the Marylanders disobeying His Majestys orders, as they have not yet come to a final resolution. I wrote Mr Sharp a publick letter[13]

---

† Stricken out.

[9] This seems to be the earliest indication of the intention of Forbes to go by way of the Pennsylvania route.

[10] Note Abercromby's endorsement on the letter of Forbes of May 1, 1758, *ante*, p. 75.

[11] John Robinson (1704-1766), Speaker of the House of Burgesses and Treasurer of Virginia, unfavourably known for his involved finances. Consult the *D. A. B.*

[12] April 23, 1758, *Writings* (Fitzpatrick, ed.), II, 182.

[13] May 2, 1758, p. 80.

the other day pressing their determination and representing their present behaviour to them in the strongest words that I could conceive.

I have return'd you Capt Dagworthys letter[14] According to your desire. The Embargo[15] I suppose will continue untill you send orders for taking it off.

You may be sure every means must be used to keep the Cherokees in humour, and I have therefore seized all the Indian Goods I could find in those provinces for that purpose. and I shall fall upon ways to keep them constantly employed.

In obedience to your directions[16] I shall for the future acquaint the ministry from time to time of our proceedings in these provinces. At present I have not time to write as you desire my letters so soon, but shall by the next packett.

I beg you will send the enclosed[17] to Ld Ligonier[18] and believe me to be with great regard.

> Your most ob^t and
> most hum^le Servt
> Jo: fforbes.

Philadelphia May 7th

P.S. I wish you would be so good as make your Aide de Camp enquire, if there be any Wampum to be bought at New York, and to let me know. G. Abercromby.

[*Endorsed:*] Brig^r Forbes Philadelphia 7th May 1758 R the.....14 by Post Ans. same day by d°.

* * * * *

Forbes Advertisement for Wagons, Horses, Drivers, etc.
[*Pennsylvania Gazette,* May 11, 1758]

By Order of General Forbes

Notice is hereby given, that a Number of Waggons will be wanted for His Majestys Service; That each Waggon is to be furnished with four good strong Horses, properly harnessed, the Waggon to compleat in every Thing, large and strong, having a Drag Chain, eleven Feet in Length, with a Hook

---

14 Not found.
15 Abercromby to Denny, March 15, 1758, *Pa. Col. Recs.,* VIII, 37.
16 Abercromby to Forbes, April 24, 1758, AB 189, copy.
17 Not found.
18 John Ligonier (1680-1770), later Earl Ligonier, a Huguenot emigré, who rose to highest rank in the British army. Consult the *D. N. B.*

at each End, a Knife for cutting Grass, Falling-Axe, and Shovel, two Setts of Clouts, and five Setts of Nails, and Iron Hoop to the End of every Axletree, a Linen Mangoe, a two Gallon Kegg of Tar and Oil mixed together; a Slip, Bell, Hopples, two Setts of Shoes, and four Setts of Shoe Nails for each Horse; two Setts of spare Hames, and five Setts of Hame-strings; a Bag to receive their Provisions; a spare Sett of Linch Pins, and a Hand Screw for every six Waggons. The drivers to be able bodied Men, capable of Loading and Unloading, and Assisting each other in case of Accidents. The whole to be inspected and appraised by two reputable and indifferent Persons, appointed by the Commanding Officer, and two by the Owners of the Waggons or the Persons contracting for them.

And after the Service shall be over, the Waggoners Accounts, and all Disputes and Differences, if any should arise, relating thereto, shall be adjusted and determined by the same Persons so appointed, whose Settlement and Decision shall be binding, as well on the Contractors as on the Owners of the said Waggons, Horses & c

And in case any of the said Waggons, Horses. &c shall be taken or destroyed by the Enemy, the Owners shall be paid by the Contractors, agreeable to the Appraisement and Settlement of the Persons appointed as aforesaid. The Owners to receive, for a Driver, Waggon, and four Horses, Fifteen Shillings per Day, for every Day he shall continue in the said Service, until he return to his Habitation. Empty Waggons, returning, are to drive at least 20 Miles per Day.

And for every four good strong Horses, with a Driver, for the Train of Artillery, without Harness, or any other Thing furnished, shall be paid Ten Shillings and Six-pence per Day during the Time they shall continue in the Service.

For every four Horses, after they leave the inhabited Parts of the Province, will be allowed Six Gallons of Oats per Day, or Indian Corn in Proportion, as it can be got, until they return to the same.

It is expected each Waggoner will bring his Gun along with him, for the Protection of his own Horses when they may be sent a Grazing. And All Waggoners are to have the Charge and Driving of their own Horses. The other Conditions of the Contract, not expressed here, will be explained to the Owners of the Wagons by Mr. Robert Irwin, in Philadelphia, with whom the General will contract for the Number of Waggons and Horses that are wanted and to whom the Owners of Waggons may apply.—
N.B. The other Waggons that are wanted about Carlisle, &c will be contracted for in the Back Counties.

*   *   *   *   *

*Forbes to Sharpe**
[Md.H.S. Portfolio 4. Papers and Letters No. 36. A.L.S.]

Philadelphia May 12th [1758]

Sir

I had the favour of yours[19] of the 6th and I am sorry to find that your Assembly are so late, in determining, what I believe none but themselves would have either deliberate upon, or have hesitate one moment, in complying with the just and equitable demands of their King and Country.

I understand that Sir Jn° St Clair has left Lancaster in order to go and meet you at Fort Frederick or Winchester where I have wrote[20] to Mr. Blair of Virginia to come likewise in order to settle the different demands that the provinces may have with regard to Arms Tents &c. that by some mistake or other, are not come from England as was expected. So if your 300 men are to be continued by your Assembly you will be so good as order the necessarys for them and let me know what arms you can spare in your province, as wee shall have great occasion for them, and let them be immediately putt in order.

I must likewise desire that you will order all your troops up to Fort Cumberland and make Colonel Washingtons people take up their post at Fort Frederick &c.

I hope to be able to leave this in a fortnight when I shall be glad to have the pleasure of waiting upon you being with great regard

Sir Yr most humle & most
Obt Servt
Jo: fforbes.

Govr Sharp.
[*Endorsed:*] From General Forbes May 12t, 1758

*   *   *   *   *

---

* Printed, *Md. Arch.*, IX, 176, and Stewart, *Letters of General John Forbes*, p. 17.
[19] *Md. Arch.*, IX, 176.
[20] Letter not found.

*Forbes to Pitt**
[P.R.O. C.O. 5:50, (L.C. trans.) pp. 571-577.]

Philadelphia May 19th., 1758.

Sir

I did myself the Honour of writing to you the first of this Month[21] giving you a state of the Millita^ry. affairs in the Southern Provinces at that time. There has little occurred since only I find that this Province begins to complain that the £100,000 voted for the Service of the Year is mostly expended already, owing to one half of that same being appropriated to clear the Arrears due to their Troops and other demands by which in reality they have only given £50,000 for the Service of this Year.

The striking of their Paper Money has taken up so much time that they had not got £10,000 five days ago. So you see Sir those tardy Proceedings will greatly distress our active operations; however I am still in hopes of getting about 1000 of their Men together (including those that they had on foot) by the 1st. of June; But when the rest will be got I can scarce form any Judgement.

The Maryland Assembly have as yet come to no determination, and are in the same situation that I had the honour to acquaint you off, but from some quickening letters[22] that I have lately wrote to that Province I flatter myself they will at least keep the 300 Men now on their pay for this Season and more I scarcely can expect.

The Virginians are going on slowly in compleating their Quota to the 2000 Men that they have agreed to raise, and I shall be well pleased if I get a few more than half their Number by the 1st. of June. Colonel Montgomery's Battalion is not yet come from Carolina, altho' by the last Account[23] I have reason to believe they may be embarking there by this time.

I have therefore marched the three additional Companies of that Battalion, and the 4 Companys of Col°. Stanwix's Battalion into the Back Country, to protect the frontiers until Col°. Montgomery's Battalion arrive, and the new Levies come in.

I am sorry to acquaint you that the Cherokee Indians who have been out upon several scouting party's, and with some Success, begin to weary, and languish after their own homes, complaining that they see no appearance of our Army.

---

* Printed, Kimball, *Correspondence of William Pitt*, I, 245, and Stewart, *Letters of General John Forbes*, p. 18.

[21] *Ante*, p. 76.

[22] Forbes to Sharpe, May 2, 1758, *ante*, p. 79 and 80.

[23] Not found.

Hitherto I have had the good fortune to amuse them, and keep them from returning, by promises, and presents, but how long I shall be able to continue them with us I cannot say.

But as they are by far the greatest body of Indians that we have ever ever had to join us, (they being above 700 Men) I thought it my duty to do everything in my power to continue them with us. For which reason I was obliged to purchase the necessarys for equipping of them for Warr, and for presents to them, through this, and all the other Colonies, where such goods and Arms, were to be found. I did imagine that I shou'd have had the Assistance of Sir William Johnston, and of M^r. Atkins in the Manadgement of those Indians, Being informed that those Gentlemen are solely to superintend Indian Affairs, exclusive of any other Person.

But as S^r. William continued at his Settlement 500 Miles North of this, and M^r. Atkins remained at Charleston 700 Miles to the South, I found myself obliged either to act as I have done or must have seen those Indians return to their own Country disgusted, and probably ready to join the Enemy against us. And even notwithstanding the diligence I have used in amassing those Goods, there is one Warrier and thirty of his tribe have left us, and another Warriour was actually sett out upon his return, but by sending some Intelligent people after him, have persuaded him and his followers to come back.

So you must easily see, how difficult a task it is, to keep so capricious a sett of people anyways Steady.

I have applied to this Province for their Aid and Assistance in furnishing me with Interpreters, Conductors, and such a proportion of presents for the Indians, as they should judge wou'd fall to their Share, considering that S^o. Carolina and Virginia had both contributed largely, but the Governor has been told by the provinciall Commissioners, that they had no Money, and consequently could allow nothing for that so necessary Service. So that I foresee the whole Expence of the Indians will (in spite of what I can do) fall upon the Crown. I should therefore be extreamly Happy to find what I have hitherto done approved of by His Majesty with Orders how I am to proceed and conduct myself for the future.

As the Artillery, Arms, Tents &c^a. destined for the Service in the Southern Provinces are not yet arrived, nor any Accounts of them, I have been obliged to scrape together some Guns of different Calibres from different places, with all the Ammunition—and three Royal Howbitzers that I have got cast here, in order to form a train, which, with the Assistance of an Officer and nine Men of our own train, that General Abercromby has been so good as to send me, and what I can pick out from among the Provincialls,

I hope in some Measure to be able to supply the Disappointment of the Store Ship, and Artillery Men. Having bought and borrowed a good many Firelocks, and provided 300 Tents, which in warm weather must serve them all, as every Man has a Blankett. I have now on the back Frontiers of this Province three Months Provisions for 6000 Men, and I am just entering into a contract for a sufficient number of Waggons and Packhorses for the transportation of it from one deposite to another, as soon as the Troops can be brought up and pushed forward to prepare those stockaded deposites for the reception of the provisions and stores.

I shall lose no time in getting everyting in readyness to move forward, as by that Means I may facilitate General Abercromby's operation, by preventing the West Country Indians from going to join the Canadians upon Lake George.

As I have severall people out for Intelligence I hope in a short time to inform you of the Enemy's Strength, and my Generall plan for annoying the Enemy, and shall by the first opportunity, send you a Draught of the Country,[24] with the march I intend to make.

I am S^r. with the greatest respect & regard

 Y^r. most ob^t. & hum^ble Servt.

               Jo: Forbes.

Philadelphia, May 19th 1758
[*Addressed:*] the R^t Honble Wm Pitt Esqre
[*Endorsed:*] Philadelphia, May 19th, 1758 / Brig^r Genl Forbes
  R/ July 3^d

    * * * * *

Commission of Genl. Forbes to Mordecai Thompson.*
[PA. MSS. Provincial Papers XXVI, f. 65. A.Df.]

             [Philadelphia, May 20, 1758]
By His Excellency General Forbes.

I Do hereby Appoint Mordecai Thompson of the County of Chester Deputy Waggon Master, under the Direction of Robt Irwin.[25] And Do hereby Impower the Said Mordecai Thompson, to Contract wth the Owners

---

[24] "Draught of the Country," not found, unless it be that of Potts in the Historical Society of Pennsylvania.

* Printed in *Pa. Arch.,* 1st series, III, 398.

[25] Robert Irwin, wagon master under Forbes. Cf. the advertisement of May 11, 1758, *ante,* p. 89.

of Such Waggons in the Said County as Shall Enter Into his Majesty's Servise for the Campaign, Agreeable to the Advertisement Printed by My Orders in the Pennsylvania Gazette.† And I Do hereby Promise and engage, that the Several Articles there In Mentioned, Shall, on the Behalf of His Majesty by Punctually Comply'd with as far as the nature of things will allow.

Given under my hand & Seal at Arms, Philadelphia, The 20th day of May, 1758

*   *   *   *   *

Forbes to Bouquet
[B.M., Add. MSS. 21640, f. 34, A.L.S.]

[Philadelphia, May 20, 1758.]

Sir.

As it is now time to form our Magazines, I must therefore give you the trouble to Contract for 120 Waggons to be ready to enter into the Kings pay at Carlisle by the first of June in order to transport the provisions from thence backwards to Rays town, where it will be necessary to have storehouses erected for the covering the same, and a good large spott of Ground Capable of Containing a body of troops for the protection of the Stores. For this purpose ane Engineer must choose a proper Spott of Ground for this food, and all the Carpenters belonging to the Troops may be orderd up there to gett it execute as soon as possible

Mr Rhor[26] setts out from this on Sunday to receive your commands and he has directions along with him from Mr Gordon, that you will alter as you think proper.

As I suppose you will march Col° Armstrongs[27] Reg^t to Fort Littletown and Loudoun, upon Mr Burds[28] people comming to Carlisle so I

---

† Of May 11, 1758, *ante*, p. 88.

[26] Charles Rhor, engineer, and ensign in the 60th regiment. According to Forbes, in a letter to Abercromby, October 8, 1758, he died on the expedition. He was listed as killed or missing in Grant's defeat, September 14, 1758.

[27] John Armstrong (1717-1795) historic Pennsylvanian, leader of the Kittanning expedition of 1756, senior colonel in the Pennsylvania militia, later a major-general in the War of the Revolution. Consult the *D. A. B.*

[28] Colonel James Burd (1726-1793), road builder for Braddock in 1755, colonel of a battalion of the Pennsylvania regiment in 1758, builder of Burd's Road in 1759. Consult the M. A. thesis at the University of Pittsburgh and sundry articles by Lily Lee Nixon.

fancy you will push both those reg^{ts} forward to Raes town, leaving at proper distances, escortes for the provision waggons, and carrying forward the 3 additionall Companys of Highlanders to join the 4 American Companys at Carlisle whenever any of the provincialls are able to form a body at Lancaster. By which all our route will be in safety for our Conveys and the head of ane army formed at Raes town. Coverd towards the Alegany mountain and west branch of the Susquehannah by the Cherokees, who you will Contrive to keep constantly employed sending always provincialls with them when a Scouting to keep them in Spirits, and if you want more Troops for this service, part of Col° Washingtons reg^t may be orderd to join you, and the rest orderd to Fort Cumberland.

You have 271 tents that went from this, so you may make use of a part of them for those people who must be coverd in some manner at Raes town, but as they are all the Tents we have you will deal them out with a parcimonious hand.

I have given Mr Hoops[29] all the Instructions about the Waggons that occurred to me and have settled the wages of those people who are to have the charge of the waggons.

To a Waggon Master who has charge of 40 Waggons five Shillings P day. Three if those divisions to be under the Charge of one Waggon Master to whom the other 3 Waggon masters are to report the State and Situation of their Waggons, when any accident happens, This person to have ten Shillings a Day, and therefore must be ane Intelligent Carefull Man, who can keep ane exact register of the Waggons—Horses &c with the value putt upon them at the first appreciation so that if any thing be distroyed by the ennemy, The price to be payed may be known. But all this I have spoke of fully to Mr Hoops—so shall not trouble you any more at this present writing.

Be so good as leave Directions for Mr Rhore in case you go from Carlisle before that he arrives

I need not recommend the endeavouring to get particular Intelligence of Fort duquesne, and the strength if the ennemy in those posts, and by all means to have the road reconnoitred from Raes town to the Yohageny.

I am Dr Sir with great regard Y^r most ob^t hum^le Sev^t

Jo: fforbes.

Philadelphia May 20th

Talk with Mr Hoops about Rumm and spirits for the working partys.

---

[29] Adam Hoops, Pennsylvania trader, sub-contractor for provision for Forbes expedition.

[*Addressed:*] To Colonel Bouquet Commanding His Majestys Forces at Lancaster.

[*Endorsed:*] From Genl Forbes May the 20th 1758

*   *   *   *   *

Forbes to Bouquet
[B.M., Add. MSS. 21640, f. 38. A.L.S.]

Philadelphia May 23^d 1758.

Sir

I have the pleasure of yours of the 20th[30] from Lancaster, and as I suppose Mr Hoops mett you there, do not doubt but you have settled the Waggons to be taken into the service in the back countrys, as I gave him all the necessary Instructions that I could think off.

I have a letter[31] from S^{ir} John St Clair from Winchester this morning. He says the Cherokees are Impatient and want to go home, but I hope they will with prudent manadgment be persuaded to stay.

I have told him that you was to push Col: Armstrongs and Burds Reg^{ts} forward towards Raestown in order to build the Fort and Store houses & have desired Washingtons Batⁿ, to be ready to join you after sending a reinforcement to Fort Cumberland.

Let me know what is wanted from this that it may be provided, and pray make ane Apology for me to Col^o Armstrong and Mr Young[32] for not answering their letters,[33] but I am blind writing.

I have desired S^{ir} John after settling things at Winchester to go and join you.

No fresh advice of Col^o Montgomery; nor of our Stores from New York.

Admirall Bascawen with the fleet and Army was to sail from Halifax this day senight last. I can not say when I can leave this, so shall be glad to hear from you. I am w^t great regard

Y^r most ob^t humble Servt

Jo. fforbes.

There are 271 tents sent up, so if S^{ir} Jno S^t clair want a few of them for Col: Washingtons Reg^t, you must let him have them, as I can supply you from this having orderd 200 more to be made and I think that Capt

---

[30] B.M., Add. MSS. 21640, f. 28. A.Df.   [31] Not found.
[32] James Young, Pennsylvania commissary general of muster 1756; paymaster of troops 1758.   [33] Not found.

Bosomworth after setling the Indians at Fort Littleton &c, should try and keep those at Winchester in Spirits.

Col° Bouquet

[*Endorsed:*] Letter from Gen¹ Forbes 23ᵈ May 1758.

* * * * *

Forbes to Bouquet
[B.M., Add. MSS. 21640, f. 42. L.S.]

Philadelphia 25ᵗʰ May 1758.

Sir

I Was yesterday favoured with your letter of the 22ᵈ May[34] from Lancaster, and approve of the steps you have taken in having engaged into the Service the people you think proper, I therefore shall not take upon me to give you any particular directions, as you are the properest judge, being immediately upon the Spot.

I have enclosed you a return[35] of what things were at Lancaster, and Fort Loudoun, tho, several of the Stores have been carryed away from those places since the return was given me, but I send it you as the best Information that I can give.

I likewise enclose a list of the goods[36] sent up in the Waggons under Quarter Master Oury's[37] care the Waggoners receipt I shall send to the Command^g Officer at Lancaster, with directions to endeavour to recover the Tents that are Missing in Bale N° 3.

I have ordered the Master Carpenter to sett out to morrow to join you where ever you may be, there will at the Same time leave this place a Waggon loaded with presents for the Indians, to the care of the Commanding Officer at Lancaster who will have orders to putt them in Store there or forward them to you in case the other Indian Goods are gone forward.

Your Making a provision for a Generall Hospital at Rae's Town is very right, it will in the meantime always answer for some use or other— And as you have made no demand of Garden Seeds being sent from this place, I take it for granted that you can provide yourself in the Frontiers.

The Commissioners have agreed to the expence of Horses for Expresses being fixed at Different Posts between this and Rae's Town. The executive

---

[34] B.M., Add. MSS. 21640, f. 36, copy.
[35] Not found.   [36] Not found.
[37] Lewis Ourry, lieutenant in the Royal American Regiment, the 60th. His voluminous papers are in B.M., Add. MSS. 21642 and 21643.

part rests with the Governour who is just now fixing the different Stages, so that I expect the thing will be done immediately.

Capt Hay[38] arrived here last night the ship with the Stores from New York may be expected daily as I think we may likewise do the Highlanders from S° Carolina, but since you left us we have had no accounts of them— Admiral Boscawen was to sail with the Fleet from Hallifax as last Tuesday was Sen'night, nine days ago, and by this time there is no doubt of his being before Louisbou[rg]h I am extreamly concerned to learn by my last from Sr John St Clair[39] that the anxiety and uneasiness of the Indians at Winchester continues to encrease, that sixty of them were about to sett out for their own Country—that many more were in the same disposition, and he could not promise himself any expectations of being able to detain them, notwithstanding all the encouragement he could give them, by the number of troops assembling, and the liberal presents made them. I therefore must desire that you will order Capt Bossomworth to Winchester, as I look upon his being there to be very necessary in our present desolate Situation (without Mr Atkins, or any one manadger) to dispose of the Indians to their proper destinations agreeable to the disposition fixed upon by you and me.

In two days I shall be able to send from hence 103 light fuzee's fit for Indians, and likewise 300 firelocks which will be sent to you at Carlisle, from which you will take as many of the light fuzee's as will be necessary to Arm those Indians at Carlisle who are not yet provided, the remainder you will forward with the heavy firelocks to Winchester, with proper escorts, as Sr John St Clair writes very pressingly for Arms to be sent to that place.

[*Forbes' handwriting:*] I have been out of order so could not write you myself, but save as many of the light fuzees as possible for to Content the Indians at Winchester.

I am S^{ir} with great regard Y^r very obed^t & most Hum^{le} Servt

Jo fforbes

Col: Bouquet
[*Endorsed:*] General Forbes 25th May 1758

*   *   *   *   *

---

[38] Captain Alexander Hay.
[39] Not found.

*Forbes to Sharpe**
[Md. H.S. Port Folio 4. Papers and Letters No. 36. A.L.S.]

[Philadelphia, May 25, 1758.]

Sir.

I Have the favour of Yours[40] of the 14th which I should have Acknowledged, had it come sooner to my hands.

I must Confess that your Assemblys braking up without Concurring in any way with His Majesty's Demands, is such a Piece of Presumption that Deserves a much Severer Chastisement, than I shall pretend to think of.

Your Goodness, Sir, in Attaching yourself to a few of your Militia, to go upon the Frontiers, shows well your good Inclinations to Serve the Publick in those most trying times.

I am greatly at a loss, & much Distressed how to Act with regard to the 300 Men, that you had at Fort Cumberland and Frederick in the Province pay. As you have said Nothing about them, I hope they continue as they were, untill I have the pleasure of Seeing you. At the same time, should be well pleased that they could be all got together at Fort Cumberland as by that means part of Colonel Washington's Virginia Reg^t might march to Fort Frederick, in order to Joyn the other Troops at Rays Town, but as you will See Sir John St Clair, I think those things may be easily Settled for the best.

I am Extremely obliged to Capt. Dagworthy & the officers at Fort Cumberland, and I am very Sorry that their good Endeavors to gett Intelligence, has not mett with the Desired Success.

Our Friends the Indians in those parts & the Cherokees ought to have Signals to know Each other by to prevent Mischieff.

Neither our Artillery, nor the Highland Reg^t are yet Arrived, so I cannot say when I can leave this, but am always, with real regard,

Sir

Y^r most Ob^t & most Hum^{ble} Servt

Jo. fforbes

Philadelphia May 25th 1758
Govr Sharp—
[*Endorsed:*] Copy Letter from Brig General Forbes to Governour Sharpe Dated Philad^a. 25th May 1758

*   *   *   *   *

---

* Printed *Md. Arch.* IX, 188, and Stewart, *Letters of General John Forbes,* p. 20.
40 *Md. Arch.* IX, 181.

Forbes to Bouquet
[B. M., Add. MSS. 21640, f. 48. A.L.S.]

Philad: May 29th [1758]

Sir

I have the favour of yours[41] of the 25th, and agree with you in the things you complain of, and shall do every thing in my power to relieve them, for which purpose. I have this day applyed to the Commissioners in a very peremptory manner to order all the necessary arms and accoutrements for those Campanys directly which they have complyed with, and all the Demands made from Col: Armstrong and Burds Reg^{ts} are to be forthwith sent up to the Carlisle except the Bell tents that I shall order to be provided.

The light horse to the number of 80 will sett out on Wednesday morning, under the Care of Capt Armstrong[42] with Saddles Briddles &c so you will get them mounted as soon as you please; How that Armstrongs and Burds Battalion are to be Compleated I know not, but I should think it right to Draught the new Levys to Compleat them.

Blanketts are scarcely to be gott, unless wee take a kind of French Blanketts made of owl &c Hair which wee must take rather as want—

The Arms goes of Wednesday likewise and everything that I can gett for your use or Conveniency. You certainly have heard from Sir John St clair, so need not say any thing from that quarter only I am doing everything in my power to gett the Virginia people in order as soon as possible.

You will let the Officers know that they are to provide their own tents. and that I shall try all in my power to gett their Baggage carried or Baggage money from the province.

The Hatchetts Tomahacks, & camp accoutrements are all bespoke.

I send off Mr Gordon with all the working tools on Wednesday, with 42 Barrells of powder. so there must be a store provided at Carlisle or somewhere else. I should think Shippensburgh as it is on the road to Winchester.

The Horses for the different stages are to be sent of Directly, but wee must provide the men to ride them who may be upon the footing of Guides.

I am assured Washingtons reg^t. is not yet in a Condition to march to Fort Cumberland; but I shall send them tents &c immediatly.

I hope that the Indians are now in better humour and that you will be able to persuade them to cover you at Raes town

The three companys of the Lower Countys[43] begin their march for

---

[41] B.M., Add. MSS. 21640, f. 28 A.Df.
[42] Captain George Armstrong of the Pennsylvania militia, later a major.
[43] Colonial terminology for the region of the present state of Delaware.

Lancaster to morrow, and the 2 Companys of Ashton[44] &c go from this on Wednesday, and as I shall send all the other companys up that way directly I think your chain may be Compleated from Lancaster to F; Littleton and so to Raes town.

I have spoke to the Governour about the roads & he is to give orders. but it will not be amiss that the Inhabitants be again rememberd to do their duty.

I hope your difficulty about the Waggons will be removed by M[r] Hoops —but if the people will not be convinced of what is right I would contract immediately for the number that you can employ in the transport of provisions; and I think it right that M[r] Hoops furnish provisions when wee can not get it from the province, but you must order no body to take more than one Ration.

I shall send you a letter of Creditt[45] or money by the Waggons that go from this with the arms and Ammunition on Wednesday and—I shall putt ane Advertisement[46] into the papers about deserters &c.

I do not remember to have ever spoke about Callendar[47] having the providing of Bats horses, and as I have ordered the Waggons to carry pack Saddles I think wee may use the waggon horses for that purpose so would not be in haste in engaging of Bats horses, and it is more than probable that S[ir] John may have spoke for them from some other person—

M[r] peters[48] has just shown to me a letter[49] from M[r] Shippen[50] of Lancaster by which I see that the country people have not had the 180 Waggons y[t] you want for the present transport explained to them, to be no part of the Contract. He also says that they Complain of the ten days Forrage as likewise of the great price that they are to pay for drivers, I have made M[r] Peters write to M[r] Shippen[51] and M[r] Stevenson[52] upon that head, and have desired that they would not force me into rough measures, but do their duty in procuring things easily. as I have done every thing for the ease of the Inhabitants.—

---

[44] George Ashton, captain in the third battalion of Colonel Hugh Mercer in the Pennsylvania regiment.   [45] Not found.

[46] *Pennsylvania Gazette,* June 1, 1758, *post.* p. 104.

[47] Robert Callendar, the well known fur trader, a captain in the Pennsylvania militia.

[48] Richard Peters (*c.* 1704-1776), clergyman, provincial secretary and councilor, for a generation a significant figure in Pennsylvania. Consult the *D. A. B.*

[49] Not found.

[50] Probably Edward Shippen of Lancaster, Pennsylvania.

[51] Letter not found.

[52] Letter to George Stevenson not found.

No Artillery Store ship, nor no Highlanders. Col Bird[53] is now at Winchester as I suppose with about 60 Indians and the Little Carpenter with 200 more follow him, I hope this will keep the others quiet and easy.

I send you an order Enclosed to Col° Armstrong for compleating the light troops, but as they may not know much of that, you will give the necessary orders, and Compleat those men taken from the 2 old Battalions from the new Levys. And I fancy there may be severalls in the new levys more proper for horse men, than those of the old Reg^{ts}, in which case they are to be taken.

There will be a necessity for some good guides to attend us, so if S^{ir} John has not engaged such, you will be so good as make enquiry.

I am my Dear S^{ir's} most sincerely

Y^r most ob^t humb^{le} Servt

Jo: fforbes.

Col: Bouquet

*   *   *   *   *

Forbes to Stanwix
[AB 294 A.L.S.; P.R.O. W.O. 34:35 f. 7. Copy]

Philad: May 29th. 1758.

Dear Sir

I would have wrote you last post but have been at deaths door with a severe Cholick, and my mind tormented by the most perverse generation of mortalls that ever breathed Air.

In short I meet with rubbs and hindrances in every thing depending upon the Commissioners, and they meddle, and give orders in the meerest trifles. So in spite of my blood and all the Attention I am master off. I can neither gett the old Reg^{ts} nor the new levys in to any kind of order. Want of Arms & every thing and what is worst of all is that as I have no troops up the Country. The Cherokees are now no longer to be kept with us neither by promises nor presents. And as wee have no mortall of Consequence to go among them to manadge them they begin to grow extreamly licentious, and have gone so farr as to seize the presents designd for them, and divide it among themselves according to their own Caprice, However Govr Sharp Col: Bouquet and S^{ir} Jn° S^t clair are all now at Fort Loudoun and Shippensburgh, and have quieted them a little, but that may not laste and when they leave us, wee may finish our Campaign.

─────────────

[53] Misspelling for Byrd, Colonel William Byrd, III.

It is amazing to me that neither S^{ir} William Johnston nor Mr Atkins have either come themselves, nor have they sent any one person to look after those Indians, altho repeated applications have been made to both those gentlemen. and I am told that Mr Groghan[54] was the person that Invited those very Indians last year with promises of rewards &c What the promises or rewards were, I never could learn, and consequently could never make them good.

I have this moment a letter from Col: Byrd[55] who is arrived in Bedford County in Virginia with his reinforcement of Indians, and come very *apropos* to prevent the Country people and the Cherokees that were returning home from massacring one another. He has made his Warriors write to those at Winchester Fort Loudoun &c to detain them from returning, untill they arrive, which will be off great service, as I expect that he is now at Winchester, and he writes me that the little Carpenter with 200 of their best Warrious are just behind him, So I have ordered all the Virginia and Pensylvania troops to march that way, Armed or not, or with or without Cloaths &c This I hope will amuse them some time, as I must erect a Deposite and Fort at Raes town, and open the communication betwixt that and Fort Cumberland as also to open the road across the Allegany' Mountain towards the Yohagany. This I must do directly., and be greatly on my guard, least they come from Fort due quesne to attack me, where I hear they have assembled their Indians, but are in want of provisions, So it is naturall to believe that they will make a push upon us, on purpose to keep their Indians together,

There is no Account of the Artillery & Stores from new York, nor if I had them can I make any great use of them, without Artillery men to manadge the Gunns.

Nor is there any accounts of Montgomerys Battalion. So I must do the best that I can w^t out either.

The Maryland Assembly broke up without giving one man or one Sixpence, So I do not know what to do with their 300 men who will now disband which is a pity to allow off at this criticall time. So think they ought to be kept as they are; at the Expence of the Government for the rest of this campaign considering that they must be payed to this day by the Crown, as they have been kept ever since October upon the faith of Lord Loudouns promise & order for the payment of them, which no doubt must be made

---

[54] George Croghan (d. 1782), famous Indian trader, Indian agent and land speculator. Consult Volwiler, *George Croghan and the Westward Movement.*
[55] Not found.

good, and if so it will look extreamly odd to turn them off at this time, when
wee have no men to send to Fort Cumberland for its present safety,

I shall be glad of your thoughts upon these matters, and now I think of
it, as I have not time to write Gen¹¹ Abercromby, I must beg you will send
him⁵⁶ this letter, upon which he will no doubt send me his orders, and will
certainly write to Sⁱʳ Willᵐ Johnston,⁵⁷ to send [up]† a proper person with
what orders he may think best upon this occasion. wherein no time is to be
lost, and upon which a very great deal depends.   I am

Dʳ Sⁱʳ

Your most obᵗ & very humˡᵉ Servᵗ

Jo: fforbes.

[*Note:*] I think you should send this to the Generall pʳ express—
Brigadʳ Genˡˡ Stanwix

[*Endorsed:*] Brigʳ. Forbes to Brigʳ Stanwix Philadelphia 29ᵗʰ May 1758
        Enclosed in Brigʳ Stanwix's of the 1ˢᵗ June Ans. the 4ᵗʰ
        June by the post

* * * * *

Forbes Advertisement About Deserters
[*Pennsylvania Gazette,* June 1, 1758]

Whereas information has been given to Brigadier General Forbes, His
Majesty's Commanding Officer in the Provinces to the Southward of *Delaware,* that sundry Persons have enlisted in the several Provincial Levies,
received the Bounty-money, and afterwards felonously, treacherously, and
wickedly with a View to defraud the Public, have absconded themselves:
Notice is hereby given to all such, that if they do not return to their several
Companies on or before the twelfth Day of June next, they will be proceeded
against as Deserters and tried, without Mercy, by all the Rigour of a Court-
material, whenever they are apprehended. Notice is likewise given that all
Persons, harbouring, concealing, or in any Manner aiding the Escape of
Deserters, will be prosecuted to the utmost, as the Law directs, and that
for every Article of Dress, Armour &c belonging to any Deserter, which
shall be found in their Custody, they will incur a Penalty of Five Pounds,
toties quoties. Moreover all Ferry men and Ferry-keepers, are warned, at

---

⁵⁶ This explains the present location of the original manuscript.
⁵⁷ No letter found, of Abercromby to Johnson in early June.
† Stricken out.

their Peril, not to transport or ferry over any Soldiers, Deserters or suspected Persons, without proper Passports and Credentials; and those who
cannot produce such Passports and Credentials, are to be stopped and delivered up to the nearest Magistrate, who is required to secure the Persons
so delivered up, unless they can render a satisfactory. Account of themselves, and to send immediate Notice thereof to the Commanding Officer
of the next adjacent Post. And Lastly, all Persons who shall be thus concerned in apprehending and securing any Deserter or Deserters, shall receive the Reward agreeable to Law, upon Conviction of the Person or Persons so apprehended and secured.

Given at Philadelphia, June 1, 1758, by the Brigadier Generals Command

Francis Halkett, Brigade Major

* * * * *

Forbes to Bouquet
[B.M., Add. MSS. 21640, f. 52. A.L.S.]

[Philadelphia, June 2, (1758)]

Sir.

Mr Walker[58] will deliver you this who came here from Sir Jno St clair
for a number of things wanted by the Virginians which I have endeavoured
to supply by ordering one hundred of those tents that are now on the road
to be sent forward to Winchister, and ten of the Horse tents, all of which
I will replace next week.

Whatever else they may want and that you can send them let them
have, and let me know and I will replace it.

As our Artillery is arrived, I shall send it up as fast as possible

I am Sir Yrs in haste

Jo fforbes

Philad: June 2d
Send the Enclosed[59] to Sir John.
Col: Bouquet
[*Endorsed:*] General Forbes's received the 6th June by Mr Walker

* * * * *

[58] Probably Doctor Thomas Walker (1715-1794), the famous explorer. Consult
the *D. A. B.*
[59] Not identified nor found.

Forbes to Bouquet
[B.M., Add. MSS. 21640, f. 54. Draft]

[Philadelphia, June, 1 1758.]

The great Channel of Communication to Virginia to be entirely by Carlisle and Shippensburgh without any Irruptions of the Enemy may induce Colo¹ Bouquet to alter it—and that to confirm it several Post should be made of the Provincials to secure it—at about six Miles distance.

The Road from Lancaster to be examined and put in Order as fast as possible. Parties of the Provincial Troops to be employed on that Service. The 200 Tents that are now sent up are to be forwarded to Winchester—and 100 more will be sent this Day sennight—of the 20 Horsemans Tents 10 are to be sent to Winchester and the others remain at Carlisle for the light Horse of this Province.

The light Musquets are to be disposed of by Colᵒ Boquet according as he may be advised of the Want of them from Winchester or else where. The Commissioners of Pensilvᵃ are to furnish their own Troops.

The Fusees to be delivred to the Indians.

The Waggoners carrying the Stores to be paid at the Rate of 1ˢ P. Mile.

In going along if any of the Provincials want Powder to practice to drop them a Barrel—and as soon as the Companies are compleated from Lancaster towards York or in that Neighbourhood Co¹ Boquet may order them to assemble at Carlisle when he moves from that to leave Directions with some good Officer concerning the Exercise of the new Levies in fireing at Marks—and to observe the strictest Discipline The above before the Receipt of Colo. Boquets Letter

With Regard to Waggons to take Contract Waggons if much Difficulty is in pressing if Hoops can get them, better.

Armstrong to march forward his Batt to Litletown.

The Proposed Things for the Conference approved.

The Provincials ordered in general to march towards Carlisle.

Battoemen Scheme very proper.

The Cannon at Harris's will be sent up to Fᵗ Augusta.

With Regard to the Deserters the General has nearly advertised the same.

If he thinks necessary—may march the Highlanders to Carlisle The 2 American now at Philᵃ will march the first Notice of the arrival of the Highlanders.

Two Pair of Shoes necessary—And they will be provided by sending to New York or elsewhere—1000 pair. will be sent directly.

If he pleases to march Co^lo Washington whole Reg^t to Fort Cumb. he may—Sr John ordered the Contrary in Virtue of the first Dis:agreed

A few intrenching Tools to be left at Lancaster and so on along.

[*Endorsed:*] General answers to Several things, received the 4th June by Capt Gordon. Evan-Evans 5—

* * * * *

Joseph Shippen[60] *to Capt. R. Walker*[61]
[*Pa. Arch.* 1st series, III, 409]

Philadelphia, 5th June, 1758

Sir.

It is General Forbes Orders that you immediately get your Company armed and Accoutred here, and then to march without Loss of Time to Lancaster, where you will wait to receive further Orders. I make no Doubt that you will make the greatest Dispatch possible.

I am, Sir

Your most hum. serv^t

Joseph Shippen   Brigade Major

[*Addressed:*] To Capt Richard Walker, in Bucks County.

* * * * *

Forbes to Bouquet
[B.M., Add. MSS. 21640, f. 58. L.S.]

Philad^a June 6th 1758

Sir

I had the favour of yours[62] of the 3^d last night and I thank you for your care, and the good disposition you are like to put our confused affairs in. You Shall want nothing from me that can contribute to the speedy execution of what ever is necessary. For which reason I shall send off on Thursday 200 more tents, with Canteens and Camp Kettles for the Virginians, as likewise Sadles &^c for that light troop. I shall likewise forward 40 Waggons with our Artillery stores upon Friday or Saturday, 40 more upon Monday, and the last forty with Cannon upon Tuesday. The 2 Companys of R. A.

---

[60] Major Joseph Shippen (1732-1810), second son of Edward Shippen. He rose to the rank of colonel in the Pennsylvania militia.

[61] Richard Walker, Captain in the first battalion of the Pennsylvania Regiment.

[62] In French, B.M., Add. MSS. 21640, f. 56, copy.

goes as an escorts to those Waggons, who are not to stop untill they get to Carlisle.

I shall order the 3 Companys of Highlanders to march to Carlisle from Lancaster upon Monday next. Col⁰ Montgomerys Battalion is in the river. I hope to disembark them to morrow, and shall encamp them a few days, and they shall follow up the train of Artill^y directly, so that I hope to gett the whole away from this next week. And I hope by that time to have all the provincialls in pretty great forwardness having sent Major Shippen[63] through amongst them in order to make them defile away towards Carlisle, where we must encamp them for a few days, in order to see what stuff they are made off, and to make proper detachments from them to the Forts upon Susquehanna and so to the Delaware. As to the draughting the light troop, I fancy that may be gott easily done, and the Govern^r has formed the province troops into three reg^s, but I have not got the names of the Companys that are to constitute each Reg^t, but I shall send it to you.

I shall order S^{ir} Allan McLean up to Carlisle, I shall send with the Convoy 1,000 pairs of shoes, and shall order another 1,000 to be made, and have ordered Mr Howell to send up some tuns of salt.

What you have wrote for[64] shall be taken care off.

I think S^{ir} John should come to Carlisle to superintend the Convoys, and the Estaffetts ought to be fixed at their different stages.

I agree that the Indians ought to be under the direction and manadgment of one person, and for that purpose think Col⁰ Bird[65] of Virginia would be the properest with Mr Bossomworth's[66] Assistance, as I do not yet know how farr we can trust to Mr Bossomworth, or how farr S^{ir} William Johnston will intermdele but keep this to yourself and make the best of it in the meantime. [*Continued in Forbes' handwriting:*] And tell Mr Bosomworth that I will settle some thing for him when I come up. You have done very right in Confining the French man, who deserves to be hanged, so pray let all the other french men be taken up and sent down under a Guard.

Govr Glen offers you his best wishes and believe me in haste Y^r most ob^t hum^{le} Servt

Jo: fforbes

I have not time to write to S^{ir} John St Clair
Col: Bouquet.

*   *   *   *   *

---

[63] Joseph Shippen.
[64] Bouquet to Forbes, June 3, 1758, B.M., Add. MSS. 21640, f. 56.
[65] Misspelling for Byrd.
[66] Captain Abraham Bosomworth of the 60th regiment.

Forbes to Abercromby
[AB 334 A.L.S.; P.R.O. W.O. 34:44, f. 305. Copy]

Philad: June 7ᵗʰ 1758.

Sir

I have lately been much out of order by a kind of Cholera Morbus. which prevented my writing to you, and giving you the detail of our proceedings, which has hitherto been so extreamly slow. that wee had very near lost all our Cherokees. And there was no remedying this unhappy situation. for the want of the Artillery, of the provincialls, and Montgomerys battalion, did not afford us the show of any design to attack the Enemy, or defend ourselves.

our Artillery is at length come here, and by hurrying the provinciall Commissioners out of their lives have now gott their levys in great forwardness, So that I have march'd the head of our Army from Carlisle to Raes town, where I must make my first deposite for the Army, & therefore have orderd Store houses &c to be built there, and I assemble the rest of our provincialls all along the road from Lancaster to Raes town to serve as escorts &c. to the provisions.

Col: Byrd is arrived at Winchester with 60 Cherokees, and the little Carpenter with 2 or 300 more follows him in 8 or ten days. This will be of the utmost service to us, as it will prevent the others from leaving us, which they were doing dayly, and which probably would have ended in the generall return of the whole—

I do not know how to account for the behaviour of Sⁱʳ Wᵐ Johnston and Mʳ Atkins upon so Criticall and urgent an occasion as this is, Sickness may have prevented their personall Attendance, but surely they might have sent some person versed in Indian Affairs, to have assisted in the managdment of the savages, or they might have sent their opinion in writing. how wee were to proceed. but wee have not had the scrape of a pen from either. At present I should think Sⁱʳ William Johnston could do a great deal by persuading the Senecas, if not to be our friends at least not to become our Ennemys.

I have just now fixed with the Governour to send a solemn message among the Delawares and Shawanese to beg a meeting with them where they choose to appoint, when I hope to persuade many of them at least to remain neutralls for this Campaign. This message was absolutely necessary as there has been great art used to fright those people att the Cherokees. and to incense the Senecas at our building a few houses for the Delawares at Wiomin. I send you enclosed a Copy of the Message⁶⁷ which you will be so

⁶⁷ Printed, *Pa. Col. Recs.* VIII, 129-132, June 7, 1758.

good as transmitt to S^{ir} William Johnson, who ought to have some person here as soon as possible, having no mortall that understands Indian affairs that I can confide in, so if any thing is wrong done it will be his fault not mine.

Col^o. Montgomery is this moment arrived in the River, I disembarque them to morrow, encamp them for two days, and march them and the Artillery directly up to the back country where I have [likewise]† ordered the provincialls to assemble likewise, where after seeing what they are made off, choosing out what is fitt for my purpose and leaving the Dregs for Garrisons and escortes, I shall forthwith proceed to something, both for keeping our Indians and keeping up the Spirit of the provincialls. I should therefore beg to know how farr you are ready.to begin your operations, In order that I may at least make a diversion, and facilitate your measures all that lyes in my power. Altho I find I shall be greatly retarded in my march. As I must repair and make roads build forts, and Store houses at different places, and have no mortall to oversee and direct all this but Mr Gordon. For Mr Hesse the Engineer[68] is in this place just a dying of a deep consumption, and Mr Rhor is pretty near in the same state at Lancaster, so you see my difficultys in that necessary branch of business, and you know my wants as to Artillery & Working tools having only Mr Hay and five men, So if you can assist pray let it be soon, for I declare to you that there is not, that mean capacity in the many branches that I must and should direct, that I must not see carryed into execution myself.

I beg you will let me know from time to time your intelligence from Louisburgh. or any where else that will give us pleasure. And of all things I beg that S^{ir} William Johnston may be spirited up to come or send here. for managing our Cherokees on which our whole in those parts depends.

I need not tell you the unhappiness of this Govern^t nor the difficultys that I dayly strugle with, from the mutuall jealousys of party, Nor can I tell you what step must be taken with Fort Cumberland by the Marylanders allowing their troops to disband. who indeed have very genteely offered me their service for the Campaign, which I believe I must accept off.

Complim^{ts} to Ld Howe &c and wishing you heartily a good Campaign I am with great regard & sincerity

Y^r most ob^t and
most hum^{le} Servt

Jo fforbes.

---

† Stricken out.
[68] Lieutenant Emanuel Hesse of the 60th regiment.

Generall Abercromby
[*Endorsed:*] Brig^r Forbes.
Phila^a: 7: June 1758
R the 15^t d°. by post.
Ans^d the 24th. by d°

*   *   *   *   *

Forbes to Bouquet
[B.M., Add. MSS. 21640, f. 59. A.L.S.]

[Philadelphia, June 10, 1758]

Sir.

I had the favour of yours[69] of the 7th this morning, and find that wee have all enough to do in our different departments, I assure you for my own part no Serjeant or Quarter M^r of a Regiment is oblidged to look into the small detail more than I am, and find that if I did not see the execution of things myself, we should never gett out of this town.

I have sent off forty Waggon load of artillery stores and ammunition yesterday and this day & Capt Jocelyn[70] and fifty men escortes them directly to Carlisle.

Forty more Waggon load shall follow upon Monday or Tuesday with a like detachment and I hope on Wednesday to send of the Artillery and the rest of the Stores with the remainder of your two Companys. And Col° Montgomery batt^n shall march upon Thursday and Fryday. I can not make more dispatch and perhaps will not be able to make so much.

I have been very ill used with regard to Waggons in this Country, and scarcly believe those Contracted for will be able to go further than Carlisle so I am glad to think wee have a Chance of changing them for better at Carlisle.

I should be sorry to disoblidge Hoops, and have again and again spoke to Mr Howell[71] about the Pork, and settling the rations, in place of the butter and pease, In which he promised to do everything I desired and that was reasonable. So I shall make him dispose of all that pork some other way for our men must not be poisoned. But if the flower or meal that is deliverd is fresh and wholesome, I think wee may be doing untill the Contractors can provide better.

[69] In French, B.M. Add. MSS. 21652, f. 33.
[70] Thomas Jocelyn, captain in the 60th regiment.
[71] Joshua Howell of Philadelphia, probably a sub-contractor of provisions for Baker, Kilby, and Baker of London.

I think Mr Walker[72] a proper person to be employed about the Waggons, but I think him more fitt to be employed by Hoops to assist him, and Serj^t Morton could inspect the Waggons, but this may be easily settled afterwards and some person ought to take the Direction in the mean time.

I hope you have given very strict orders to all sutlers with regard to their retailing of Spirits.

I shall endeavour to persuade some work men to follow the Army as I see that they will be needfull, and shall take some measure with regard to the stray horses, But the deserters and the French Canaille I leave you to do as you think proper.

The Cherokees are most certainly a very great plague, and I have done every thing to hasten up the troops &c to please them, but I am sorry to find you are of opinion that nothing will keep them, I wish Trents[73] method had been tryed at first and a real bargain made with them.

I am glad that you have mett with Govr Sharp and S^ir Jno and no doubt will have agreed to keep the Garrisons of Fort Cumberland & F. Frederick in our pay for the rest of the Campaign, as I shall engage for their pay from the beginning of May forward to the end of the Campaign.

I wish S^ir John was come back to Carlisle where I am sending every thing, and all the fire locks goes away on Monday for the whole provincialls except 82 which is nothing.

The bell tents will be ready Wednesday next and wee have above 400 Barrells of powder and near 40,000 flints which is surely enough.

I have gott Govr Glen[74] to write[75] to the Cherokees as he had certainly great knowledge of them, and will go up to endeavour to keep them so you may tell them this.

Pray make all your Garrisons and Camps keep a Strict look out, because there is a report that the Senecas and Shawanese are Comming down. I hope to sett out next week but am plagued w^t Cholicks. I am S^ir with sincere regard.

> Y^r most ob^t hum^le Servt
>
> Jo fforbes.

---

[72] Probably Captain Richard Walker. Cf. Shippen to Walker, June 5, 1758, *ante*, p. 107.

[73] William Trent (1715-1787), Indian trader, Indian agent, soldier, and land speculator. Consult the *D. A. B.*, but more particularly, S. E. Slick, "William Trent, Indian Trader and Land Speculator," a Ph.D. thesis at the University of Pittsburgh.

[74] James Glen (1701-1767?) governor of South Carolina, 1738-1756, a cousin of Forbes and the executor of his will.

[75] No letter of Glen to the Cherokees found.

Our Store Ship is not come but dayly expected. I rec[d] the enclosed[76] this morning.

Philad: June 10th

Col: Bouquet.

[*Addressed:*] To Colonel Bouquet Command[g] His Maj[ties] Forces at Carlisle. If not there to be sent by express to him. J: fforbes

[*Endorsed:*] from Gen[l] Forbes 10th June Answered the 16th without Copy

*　*　*　*　*

Forbes to Abercromby
[AB 356 A.L.S.]

[Philadelphia, June 15, 1758]

Sir.

Tuesday Morning our Store Ship with Artillery &c Arrived here, and I shall thereby been enabled to sett out in a few days for Carlisle where I have ordered all our Provinciall Forces to assemble and encamp. in order to separate the serviceable from the unserviceable, in which likewise I shall find difficultys, for the people of this province has not the smallest Idea (neither Officer nor Soldier) of the business they have undertaken.

I find wee shall not be able to keep the Cherokees notwithstanding all the pains and expences that they have cost us, as my last shift, I have sent up Govern[r] Glen among them, he has had great dealings and a great influence among them, if he can persuade them to stay but a very short time, I will sett out directly that is to say as soon as the roads will permitt me which at present are unpassable, and must be all made anew, So my embarras in that particular, is what I did not expect, however wee must take things as they are.

I am sorry to hear you have your own share of difficultys, and cant help thinking that M[r] Amherst[77] has come to lick the butter off both our breads, No manner of trouble; every thing ready to his hand, a weak Garrison to oppose him, and a great name to be acquired by the surrender of the place, and I suppose a Speedy passage home. This you will allow is very good luck. I hope when he has performed all this that he will send us back a few

---

[76] Not identified.

[77] Jeffery Amherst (1717-1797), professional soldier, who entered the army in 1731, served in the War of the Austrian Succession, was elevated to high rank in 1758, and commander-in-chief in America, 1758-1763. Consult the *D. N. B.*, but more particularly E. John Long's *Lord Jeffery Amherst.*

regulars, for I do assure you I have not so many as to keep my irregulars in due decency and order.

Kilby is here settling our provisions detail, His presence was very necessary and will I hope make that branch easy, altho the transport of ye provisions is attended with enormous difficultys & expence.

I can not send you any kind of return or report of our troops having hitherto had none, nor scarce possible to be gott, but I shall so soon as I gett them any ways to gether or in the smallest order.

What do you allow the men for Working, or what Rum or Spirits do you allow them, I should be much oblidged to you, if you would desire Major Spittall[78] to take out from the orders all those publick prices of manadgement, and send them to me, that I may conform.

For I see my friend S^{ir} Jno. S^t clair does not value what expence he runs into, which I must moderate as much as possible, altho at the same time I think Soldiers every where should be upon the same footing.

I shall be glad to hear your news from Louisbg^h and am.

Philadelphia June 15th D^r S^{ir}

Y^r. most ob^t & most
hum^{le} Servt.

Gen^{ll} Abercromby.   Jo: fforbes.

[*Addressed:*] On His Maj^{ties} Service
        To His Excell^{cy} [Philad 3]†
              Major Gen^{ll} Abercromby Commander in Chieff of His Maj^{ties}
              Forces in North America
                    Albany

[*Postmarked:*]   NEW YORK
[*Endorsed:*]   Brig^r Genl: Forbes.
                          Philad^a: 15^t June 1758—
                          R the 22^d by post.
                          Ans^d. the 24^t by d^o.

[*Note*   Armstrongs Battall,
in another   1200 good woodsmen,
hand:]   keeped up two years
                          Washingtons Item
                          of Virginia
                          Bouequet Detach:

                    *   *   *   *   *

---

[78] Probably Major John Spittal, earlier captain in the 47th regiment.
† Stricken out.

Forbes to Bouquet
[B.M., Add. MSS. 21640, f. 63. A.L.S.]

[Philadelphia, June 16, 1758]

Sir.

As our Store ship is now Arrived, there is Nothing that can hinder us from proceeding but the defection of the Cherokees, bad Roads and our Waggons, I have Contracted here for 120; Eight of which are already gone up to Carlisle with our Stores and the rest shall follow directly, and the beginning of next week I hope to sett out myself, as I find I must absolutely see every thing sett out before I can stirr from this.

I send of to morrow 1000 Stand of our new arms, and 200 more tents, which I hope will be more than wee will have occasion for in that way.

I suppose you have sent your orders to make all the provincialls (not immediatly employed) to assemble and encamp at Carlisle, where wee must make some regulations among them. The troops of this province are 3 Reg^ts, each Reg^t to Consist of 16 Companys.

As to the roads, I can say nothing, only I was advised by everyone to go by Raes Town, I shall be sorry if it proves impracticable—But I send of Mr Hess and Mr Dudgeon a new Engineir[79] from England to assist you —and if you think proper, I wish the road on the other side of the Allegany mountains was reconnoitred, so as to form a judgement whether we can go that way or not. I have agreed with one man, for all our Artillery horses and he has already purchased 90. I am to provide him Drivers at Carlisle from among the provincialls.

Governour Glen is so kind as to undertake a journey up to visit the Cherokees, and to endeavour at persuading them to remain some time longer w^t us, I wish heartily he may succeed in his very kind endeavours, he has had great dealings with them so hope he will if he does not, wee have done all in our power.

Govr Dobbs of North Carolina has without orders sent by sea two hundred men to Alexandria in Virginia and has ordered 100 more to march by land to Winchester, so send orders to S^ir John to gett them provisions and to march them up to Carlisle, or any other place you think more proper.

I am in hopes of bringing about a treaty with the Delawares &c by which wee may gett them to make their Brethren abandonn the Ohio, so let your Scouting partys keep to the West of the Susquehanah, and not meddle with

---

[79] In the British regimental histories the engineers are not set apart as such. If members of a regiment, they frequently held low rank, as in the case of Lieutenant Emanuel Hesse of the 60th regiment. No further data were found on Mr. Dudgeon.

our friendly Delawares, For which you will fix upon flags or marks of Distinction which ought to be made known to all Concern'd Hoops told me you was only to Contract for 120 Waggons, but I fancy it must be for two hundred and forty, which with the 120 from this will make 360 in all and that I think will be sufficient. I beg you will gett some brisk officers among the provincialls to try some scouting partys out to the Ohio at different places, at or near the same time and pretty strong partys with a good many Indians along with them, in order to gett Intelligence or prisoners, my last Intelligence was that the french there were in want of provisions as well as the Indians, that they had not been relievd this year from Canada, nor had they gott many Indians that way at present, at least no new acquisitions, and that the Indians at Loggs town were at present disobliged at the French and were removing their wives and Children up to the Lakes among the Senecas.

I am quite tyred writing so Conclude D^r S^{ir} Y^r most ob^t very hum^{ble} Servt

Philadelphia June 16th   Jo. fforbes.
Col^o Bouquet.

[*Addressed:*] On His Majestys Service To Colonel Bouquet—Commanding the Forces at Carlisle or Elsewhere in his absence to the care of the Command^g Officer to be forwarded to him. J. fforbes.

[*Endorsed:*] Rec^d at 7 Sunday Evening forwarded immediately by John S^t clair.

[*Endorsed:*] from Genl Forbes 16th June Answered the 21st Sept no Copy [*Note:*]† The 40 Waggons destine for this Service shall be sent to Philadelphia according to the Orders I received from Major Halkett. I have been this day loading them so they shall be unloaded if you want anything I can not help it.

* * * * *

Forbes to Pitt*
[P.R.O. C.O. 5:50, (L.C. tr.) pp. 577-582]

Philadelphia. June 17th . . 1758
Sir,

Col^o. Montgomery's Highland Battalion arrived here the Eight from S^o. Carolina, and I dispatch'd Capt. McIntosh^{80} the next day to Admiral

---

† Outside and crossed out.

* Printed, Kimball, *Correspondence of William Pitt*, I, 278, and Stewart, *Letters of General John Forbes,* p. 21.

^{80} Captain Alexander McIntosh, of the 77th regiment.

Boscawen. The Store Ship with Arms, Tents, Ammunition, & Artillery &c^a. arrived here the 11th, which enables me to sett out directly for the frontiers, where I have previously assembled all the new Levys of this Province and Virginia. North Carolina I am told has sent 200 Men by sea to Alexandria in Virginia, and have ordered 100 more (which is all they have) to march by the back parts of Virginia in order to join me, at Fort Cumberland, but when they will arrive I cannot tell.

The Maryland Assembly broke up without providing any one thing for the present Service, or for the pay^t. & maintenance of their troops in Fort Cumberland and Fort Frederick, since the eight of October last. By which the Crown becomes bound by the Earl of Loudoun's orders[81] to M^r. Sharpe, for the payment of those Garrisons from October last to the present time, & the necessity of keeping them there, was the preservation of those two Forts from the Enemy. As they are only 300 Men, and have been used to the Woods and the Indian Manner of fighting, I thought it would be a great loss to allow them to disband themselves, upon the province refusing them their by past pay, or continuing them during the Campaign; so have therefore made them an offer to pay them from this time during the rest of the Campaign, and to solicite for their by past pay, either from the Province, or by Virtue of the Earl of Loudoun's promise and orders to Governour Sharpe.

The Cherokee Indians are, (I am afraid) no longer to be kept with us, owing to their natural fickle disposition which is not to be got the better off by words nor presents, of both which they have had a great deal, and threats we dare not use, least they change sides, so if the seeing of our Cannon and their Cousins the Highlanders has no Effect upon their stay with us, we shall lose the best part of our strength as all the Northern Indians mostly our Enemies were kept in awe by the presence of so many Cherokees. As my offensive operations are clogged with many Difficultys, owing to the great distance & badness of the roads, through an almost impenetrable wood, uninhabited for more then 200 Miles, our back inhabitants being all drove into Carlisle. I am therefore lay'd under the Necessity of having a stockaded Camp, with a Blockhouse & cover for our Provisions, at every forty Miles distance. By which means, altho' I advance but gradually, yet I shall go more Surely by Lessening the Number, and immoderate long train of provisions Waggons &c, For I can set out with a fortnight's provisions from my first deposite, in order to make my second, which being finished in a few days, and another fortnight's provision, brought up from the first, to the second, I directly advance to make my third, and so proceed forward,

---

[81] Of November 3, 1757, *Md. Arch.* IX, 98.

by which I shall have a constant Supply security for my provisions, by moving them forward from Deposits, to Deposite as I advance, and lastly if not thought convenient to settle upon the Ohio, or in that Country, I shall have a sure retreat, leaving a road always practicable to penetrate into those back Countrys, as our Settlements advance towards them, from this side of the Allegany Mountains.

I need not point out to you, Sir, my reasons for these precautions, when you consider that had our last Attempt upon Fort Du Quesne succeeded, we must have retired directly, for want of provisions, and at that time our back Settlements were much nearer advanced to Fort Du Quesne and the Ohio, than they are at present, having properly speaking none to the Westward of Carlisle.

I have used every art and Means to get Intelligence of the strength of the French and Indians (in their Alliance) in those parts, but to little purpose, having various reports, which may indeed be true, as their Savages may be as whimsical as ours, and consequently they may have sometimes numbers and at other times few or none. But by every Account the whole of them in those parts are in a starving Condition, as there has no Provisions been sent to them this Year, either from Canada, nor by the Missippi. And this leads me to think that had those Indians who were friends, been manadged with common prudence and honesty, that they must have continued so, as we could more easily and at a Cheaper rate have supplyed them with provisions and their other necessarys. But by allowing them to be most grossly cheated and abused by the sadest of mortals called Indian traders (In place of having a fair open market under the Eye and directions of Government, and by allowing of a rage and madness in stretching out our settlements into their hunting Countries, the only resource they had for sustenance) and that without any previous Contract, or agreement with them, they have thereby been drove into the Arms of the French who with their usual chicane make them believe they do not come to drive them out, but to build Forts among them to protect them against us—But I beg pardon for this digression to you S^{ir} who knows all those sad truths from better Authority than I can pretend to. As the Store Ship was so late of Coming in, I was obliged to purchase a great many Arms, Tents &c, for the Provincialls, so shall keep the supernumerary Arms in Store, and the new Tents may serve another occasion—I have likewise been obliged to purchase every kind of thing for the Indians who came naked, having had no manner of Assistance from either off the Superintendants of Indians Affairs.

I have now above 400 Men out upon scouting partys, but as they have four or five Hundred miles in the going and returning, what Intelligence they bring is always of so old a date that there is no trusting to it.

I shall lose no Time in doing every thing in my power for the publick good to the best of my Capacity, and have the honour to be, with the greatest regard and esteem. Sir, Y^r most obed^t. & most humble Servt.

Jo: Forbes

[*Addressed:*] R^t Honble Wm Pitt Esqre
[*Endorsed:*] Philadelphia June 17, 1758 Brig^r Genl Forbes R Augt 7th

*   *   *   *   *

Forbes to Loudoun
[LO 5853 A.L.S.]

Philad: June 17th 1758

My Dear Lord.

I take the opportunity of a Ship just going for England to Salute you, and ask how your are, and how receiv'd, and whence the Storm begann, all those questions I beg you will answer, as I think myself greatly concerned, no body being more sincerely, or more disinterestedly your real Wellwisher.

I have had a most damnably spott of work to make my Affair look practicable and had brought things almost to my mind, without any assistance but to the Contrary as you well know. And by the Arrivall of Montgomerys Batt^n and the Store Ships upon the 12th Instant, resolved directly to sett out and not lose on moment, But the Cherokees who were once 800 hundred, from their naturall wavering disposition, and not seeing our troops or Artillery altho I sent up all I could scrape together to please them (being Montgomerys 3 Additionals and the 4 Companys Royall Americans,) and I borrowed old ship Gunns to amuse them, yet neither all this nor fair words, promises nor presents could prevent their going home, So I am reduced to my militia except about 100 that came with Byrd. But try I shall and that immediatly as I sett out to morrow with the last of the troops and Artillery, You know what may be expected from me, so pray let it be known—

Remember the Maryland troops at Fort Cumberland I wrote to Mr Pitt[82] this post upon that head, it will be a shame not to make your engagements good to Mr Sharp, who should have Col^o Rank for his services. The people at Fort Edward are all at six's & seven's, and are not so far advanced as your most sincere & very

hum^le Servt

Jo: fforbes.

---

[82] Forbes to Pitt, June 17, 1758, *ante*, p. 117.

In a hurry so excuse

Pray speak to S^{ir} Jno Ligonier who most certainly could serve me now
—by getting me a British reg^t at home, and I ought to have leave to come
home to save my life after the campaign—

E: of Loudoun

[*Addressed:*] To the R^t. Honb^{le} The Earl of Loudoun &c &c &c Privy
        Garden Whitehall London

[*Endorsed:*] Brigadier John Forbes Philadelphia, June 17, 1758

        His Difficulty for want of Arms and artillery

        The Cherokees all gon[e] of[f] but are a few come with
            Bird

        The[y] were once 800

        Setting out with his Troops and Provincials

        Lett it be known what may be expected from him

        Apply to Ld Ligonier to get him an English Battalion and
            leave to come home after the Campaign

        People at Fort Edward at 6 & 7

        R. August 5th 1758

*   *   *   *   *

Halkett to Bouquet
[B.M., Add. MSS. 21640, f. 65. A.L.S.]

Philadelphia, Monday 19th June 1758

Sir

    In consequence of a letter[83] from General Abercromby to Brigadier
General Forbes, accompanied with his order of the 29th of April last;[84] all
Officers whatever, are to Receive one Ration of Provisions p^r day, untill the
day of their entring into Winter Quarters—And the order of the 26 November 1757[85] for the allowance given in lieu of Provisions, is suspended.

    This order is sent to the Commanding Officer at Carlisle, to publish unto
the Troops there, as General Forbes desires that you will do to the Troops
under your Command.

    I am Sir

        Your most obedient Servant

                                Francis Halkett
                                Brigade Major

---

[83] June 4, 1758, AB 318, copy.   [84] Not located.
[85] Found in Forbes to Bouquet, December 2, 1757, *ante*, p. 20.

To Colonel Bouquet
[*Addressed:*] To Colonel Bouquet to the Care of the Command^g Officer, Carlisle.
[*Endorsed:*] 19th June Brigade Major Halkett about Rations

*   *   *   *   *

Forbes to Bouquet
[B.M., Add. MSS. 21640, f. 66. A.L.S.]

Philad: June 19th [1758]

Sir

I have yours[86] of the 14th from Fort Loudoun and I am sorry that you are oblidged to change our Route, and shall be glad to find the road proposed by Govr Sharp practicable, in which case I should think it ought to be sett about immediatly and should be glad that Mr Sharp would oversee the execution, as S^{ir} John will have business enough at Carlisle.

Mr Kilby the Contractor writes[87] by this Messenger to Govr Sharp, to make up the provision Acco^{tts} that Dr Ross[88] furnished to the Maryland troops, and Indians, and I have ordered Mr Kilby to pay them. As to the Hospitall and transport of provisions for those troops, I can give a warrant for that, when I come up the Country, and as their by past and present pay is to be thought off, I hope some Expedient may be found to content them, reserving to ourselves a Claim upon the province for any money paid to them.

I shall by to morrow's waggons send up 28 Dozen of powder Horns to Carlisle to be disposed of as you shall direct, and shall send 20 Doz: more by the end of the week.

I hope to gett all our Artillery and Stores from on board the Ships by Wednesday or Thursday at farthest, and as I send of what is necessary for us dayly, as it lands, hope to gett everything out of this town by the end of the week.

I should have been up with you myself before this time, but I find I must not leave any thing here undone.

I expect Govr Glen will be at Carlisle to morrow night, I hope he will have some Influence with the Cherokees who remain, and by dispatching Messengers to the little Carpenter, may induce him to come and join us.

---

[86] B.M., Add. MSS. 21640, f. 61, copy.

[87] June 19, 1758, *Md. Arch.* IX, 207.

[88] Doctor David Ross, of Maryland, contractor for provisions for the Maryland forces. The provision accounts were not found.

For which reason I could wish that Mr Glen and you mett, in order to concert what is best to be done.

I suppose you will reconnoitre the road across the Allegany mountains from Raes Town and if found impracticable, that the Fort Cumberland Garrison, should open the road forward towards the Crossing of the Yohagani.

They tell me there are some good brisk officers in the Armstrongs and Burds Reg^{ts}, could not they be sent upon the Scout for Intelligence while the Army assembles, and the roads are made.

Ane Express is this moment come in with your letter[89] from Fort Loudoun of the 16th I can not tell you how much I think my self, and the publick are oblidged to you, for your extream care and diligence in carrying on the service, which must be both very troublesome and disagreeable, considering the many obstacles you have to surmount, and the Inexperience of the troops under your Command.

I give you joy of your good Success with the Cherokees, and am of your opinion that 200 of them firmly attached to us, is better than three times the number wavering and unruly.

I find that wee must take nothing by report in this country, for there are many who have their own designs in representing things, so I am glad you have proceeded to Raes Town, where you will be able to judge of the roads, and act accordingly.

As Mr Kilby is here, I will settle the rations but Gen^{ll} Abercromby has fixed upon one pound of fresh beef, and one pound of Flour, to be a Sufficient ration.

I shall send up some Rumm, and Hoops has said he can gett Whiskey.

Let there be no stop putt to the roads as that is our principall Care at present.

I approve of your license[90] to Sutlers & March^{ts} with which they must Comply.

I am quite tyred so bid you farewell being sincerely Y^r most ob^t & very hum^{le} Ser^t

Jo fforbes

Col: Bouquet.
[*Addressed:*] For Col° Bouquet.
[*Endorsed:*] From General Forbes June 19th Answered the

*   *   *   *   *

---

[89] In French, B.M., Add. MSS. 21652, f. 44.
[90] B.M., Add. MSS. 21652.

*Forbes to Sharpe**
[Md.H.S. Port Folio 4. Letters and Papers No. 36. A.L.S.]

Philad: June 20th [1758]

Sir:

I Give you the trouble of this very short Letter, to Acknowledge your Favors, and the Sense I have of your Zeal for His Majesty's Service.

The Enclosed Letter[91] from Mr. Kilby, our Contractor for provisions, will show you I have taken the first opportunity of making Dr Ross easy as to what he has furnished, and I hope very soon to Enable you to make those Officers & Troops that were at F. Cumberland Easy as to the past, and I do myself Engage for the present pay, while they remain in the King's Service, during this Campaign.

I shall order Tents, Canteens, &c. for them, and send them up as soon as possible.

Colonel Bouquet[92] & Sir John St Clair[93] Writes me of the Road you propose from Fort Frederick to Cumberland; If it is thought the most Eligible, you will be very obliging in giving a look to it, and your Directions to those Employed to make it. Any Advances of money for the present to ·Clear the by past pay or Expence of the Maryland Troops, must by no means diminish, or Interfere with our Claim for the same from the Province.

I have been much out of Order, but am much

Y^r most Ob^t & most
Hum^{ble} Servt

Jo: fforbes

[*Addressed:*] His Excellency Govr Sharp.
[*Endorsed:*] Copy. Letter from Brig General Forbes to Governor Sharpe. Dated Philad^a 20th June 1758.

*   *   *   *   *

* Printed, *Md. Arch.* IX, 209, and Stewart, *Letters of General John Forbes*, p. 23.
[91] Not found.
[92] June 14, 1758, B.M., Add. MSS. 21640, f. 81, copy, and 21652, f. 40.
[93] Not found.

Forbes to Bouquet
[B.M., Add. MSS. 21640, f. 70. A.L.S.]

Philad: June 27th 1758.

Sir.

I have received yours[94] of the 21st from Juniata, I make no question of the many *embaras* that you meet with, from the Care of the Roads, to the smallest minutie, For my part I have my own Share, but *comme le vin est tiré, il faut le boire.*

As to your Scheme of getting quitt of most of the waggons for Bats horses, I have ever been of opinion that the advanced part of the Army in order to make the deposites &c, ought to have nothing else with them but than I thought that after taking post, and making of the roads that Waggons would be the most expeditious method of bringing forward the provisions, but as you are upon the spott and see the nature of the roads, you must certainly be the best judge what is properest to be done. However S^{ir} Jno S^{t}clair & Col: Armstrong are now engaging so many Pack Horses 200. and they may engage more,

I have desired S^{ir} John S^{t}clair to take care that Mr Hoops sends of the provisions, and likewise that there be rice and Indian corn, and provender for horses along the route to Raes town.

I approve of your *Etat Major* as you could not well do without them, nor do I think they could be employed at a Cheaper rate.

I hope to gett every thing out of this town by Thursday morning and shall follow the same day myself being resolved to be the last man.

Our Regstration with the Delaware Indians upon the Ohio, has come a pretty good length, being possitively assured that a number of familys came from thence back to settle upon the North Branch of the Susquehanah lately, and if so it is to be hoped that more will follow, I wish that those said to be settling at Single clamouche be not of those returning, so endeavour to be informed, and if they are not but enemy Indians, the sooner they are drove back the better—altho I could wish that wee had no rencountre with the Indians to the north of the west branch of the Susquehanah, for some days least we mistake friends for foes. But that does no ways hinder the sending scouting parties by Frankstown, and every other posts leading upon the Ohio, with very strict injunctions, that att all times and att all places, in camp or on Detachment, that they keep a Strict guard, and a look out, to prevent any kind of Surprise, for which reason I think you ought to have

[94] Letter of 21st, not found, but cf. letter of June 22, 1758, from Juniata, B.M. Add. MSS. 21652, f. 47.

some of the light horse with you, as *Avant Coureurs et pour faire la Decouverte.*

I give this caution from hearing (altho perhaps false) that Rogers[95] with a party of 50 men, had been surprised near Tunderoga, and that all were cutt off but himself mortally wounded & five more. Guarding against surprizes must be inculcated early amongst our now undisciplined troops, and the strictest orders to prevent any surprize must be dayly enjoined them.

I have been long in your opinion of equiping Numbers of our men like the Saveges and I fancy Col: Byrd of Virginia has most of his best people equipt in that manner, I could not so well send orders to others to do the same as they had gott provinciall Cloathing, but I was resolved upon getting some of the best people in every Corps to go out a Scouting in that stile for as you justly observe, the Shadow may be often taken for the reality, And I must confess in this country, wee must comply and learn the Art of Warr, from Ennemy Indians or anything else who have séen the Country and Warr carried on in itt:

For which reason I approve much of your trying to pass the Laurell Hill leaving the river Yohageny to the left, as also of knowing what can be done by the path from Franks town or even from the head of the Susquehanah. For I have all along had in view to have partys, to fall upon their Settlements about Venango and there about, while wee are pushing forward our principall Design,

As to Indian tracts I fancy you will find many of those, as no doubt they will send many partys to make discoverys what wee are about but I think they may be way laid, as most of the paths across the Allegany mountains are known, and the Carrying place upon the Susquehanah which is short may likewise be looked after. As all this may be fatiguing and requires variety of parties, yet it binds our people to their business, and keeps us quiet to continue our route and to make our Deposites and palisaded campments, & all those partys altho in generall they ought to be kept secret from every one but the officers concerned, yet that they may be distinguished and the particulars of each Commando known each party ought to have some Union Flags and the particulars Indians or Soldiers dress'd as such the Yellow Shallown or Buntin [?] upon their head or remarkable part of their body. This I have recommended to be given out among our friendly Indians in our back frontiers, so pray let your people know so much,

As soon as you can well spare them, I think no time should be lost

---

[95] Probably Robert Rogers (1731-1795) the famous ranger; in 1758 a major in command of nine companies. His career was stormy. Consult the *D. A. B.*

in taking post at Frank[s]town, as by that the Country will be explored and the Ennemys scouting partys kept at a distance, but a Communication must be kept open, whether by patronille or otherwise you will judge, but before I send of the Pensylvania provincialls, I want to see them to detatch the worst for Garrison duty, so if you order any to join you, let them be by the ten, or twenty best men of such companys, as they will not interfere with my views.

I do not see that Governour Glen can be of any great service, but when he offerd it, It was *de bon ceur, et avec le meilleure grace de monde.* And as the Indians were not then quite gone, I thought it would hurt him, and hurt myself, not to accept of such an offer from a person who has had more publick dealings with the Cherokee nation than any other man alive.

Bosomworth I am sensible has been of service but you must not believe all he says, however he must be encouraged.

I am sorry to tyre you with this long letter, but must still add, that I hope you judg[e] so well of me, as to believe that I shall look upon every suggestion for the good of the service that you please to hint to me, as a reale favour and friendship conferr'd upon me, and at the same time to believe me, with real esteem

S^r Y^r most ob^t hum^{le} Servt

Jo fforbes.

Col^o Bouquet.

[*Endorsed:*] General Forbes 27th June Received by neglegt the 14th July only

*   *   *   *   *

Forbes to Abercromby
[AB 319 A.L.S.; P.R.O. W.O. 34:44, f. 313. Copy]

Philad: June [27, 1758]

Sir,

As I had little or nothing to entertain you with of Late I have not therefore wrote and I did not choose to give you my Chapter of Grievances &c, as I fancy you have your own share of those at home.

However I thank God the last of my Artillery leaves this to morrow, as I shall be day after.

I have pushed up my head, the length of Raes town one road, and Fort Cumberland the other, at Raestown I am making store houses for the provisions &c as from thence I shall take my Departure across the Allegany Mountains. At present the troops of this province are encamped at Carlisle; except those Companys who must protect the Country betwixt the Susque-

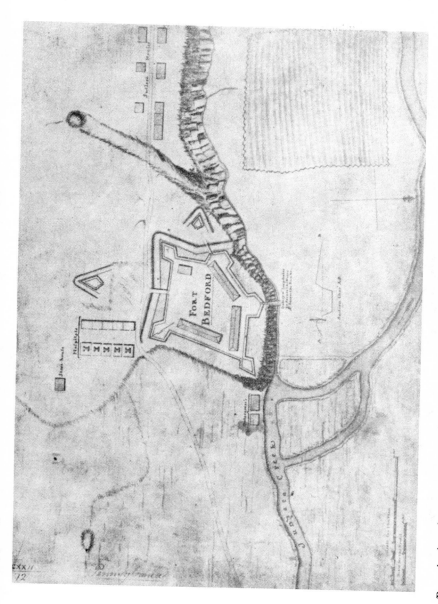

Reproduction of a map, King's CXXII, 12, described in the Catalogue of Maps and Charts in the British Museum, p. 521, as "A colored plan of Fort Bedford on the Juniata Creek. . . ."

hana & Delaware, where there is some small Scalping partys dayly, who make incirrsions into our back Settlements in their way from the Ohio to the back of the Jerseys.

I have laboured much to bring those Delawares now upon the Ohio back to their own Country, at least to come to a Conference, and I hope soon to bring this to a bearing, being well assured that twelve familys left the Ohio the fifteenth, with design to settle again on the East branch of the Susquehanah. If I can thus break the Ice, I hope more will follow altho I shall not trust much to them either. But the New Governour of the Jerseys Mr. Bernard[96] a very pretty Man) having joined in the Messages[97] sent the Indians by this province &c I am therefore in hopes that some thing may be done. particularly if S^{ir} William Johnston would second the Intentions of these provinces, with the Senacas and the Six Nations.

The Cherokees Deputed to carry Messages to the six Nations leave this to morrow on their way by new York to S^{ir} Wm Johnston &c, I fancy that this Embassy properly managed, might at least procure a Neutrality with those Savages, if not bring them to our friendship, as I hear that their Message[98] is very strong on the part of the Cherokees.—Who have now for the most part left us, and are returned home with all the presents wee made them. It is a great pity the person who spoke the Mohawk language and carried the Messages from the Cherokees, has been taken sick here and is left behind but as the rest goes forward, a great deal will depend upon S^{ir} William Johnstons getting them a speedy meeting with the chieffs of the six nations and the sending them soon back to us, and if possible to persuade them to return through the Senecas Country to the Heads of Susquehanah or Delaware of which I wish you would acquaint S^{ir} William. And as they have great Curiosity to see Your Army pray show it them and let them be civily used, as the tall man with the Hair lip is a great man in their nation, and our Strong Friend.

I have just now heard [of]† some confused tale of Rogers having been worsted and mortally wounded—I shall be very sorry if it proves true, as I take him to be too good a man in his way, to be easily spared at present.

Mr Barrow[99] has often asked me for ane order to give him to answer my warrants, So You will be so good as send him one by the first occasion.

---

[96] Francis Bernard (1712-1779), colonial governor of New Jersey, 1758-1760, and of Massachusetts, 1760-1769. On his career, consult the *D. A. B.*

[97] Of June 22, 1758, *Pa. Col. Recs.* VIII, 129-132.

[98] Of June 27, 1758, *Papers of Sir William Johnson*, II, 858, copy.

† Stricken out.

[99] Thomas Barrow, deputy paymaster general. Cf. Forbes to Barrow, September 19, 1758, *post*, p. 214.

Waggons and roads are the Devil, and cross hott headed Madmen worse,
My friend S^{ir} John having almost disoblidged the whole Virginians with
their new Governour[100] in to the bargain.

Wee have no news here of any kind. So I am S^{ir} with real regard &
esteem

Y^r most ob^t & most
hum^{ble} Servt

Jo fforbes.

Gen^{ll} Abercrombie

[*Addressed:*] on His Maj^{ties} Service
> To His Excell^{cy}
> Major General Abercrombie
> Commander in Chief of His Maj^{ties}
> Forces in North America
> Fort Edward, by New York
> Albany

[*Note:*] This to be delivered to the Postmaster of New York who is desired to forward it to the General at all Expedition
> Philadelphia June 27th

[*Postmark:*] NEW YORK

[*Endorsed:*] Brigadier General Forbes
> Philadelphia June 1758
> Replied 6 July by the post

[*Note in another hand:*] Neutrality the last thing for B. Forbes.

*   *   *   *   *

Forbes to Bouquet
[B.M., Add. MSS. 21640, f. 74. A.L.S.]

[Carlisle, July 6, 1758]

Sir

I came to this place night before last and did not find things quite so well
as I could have wished particularly the Waggons, which by mixing of Brigades and employing Waggon masters promiscuously, have fallen into the
greatest Confusion.

The provinciall troops are not much better but by making a Detachment
of 15 Men p^r Company from the 3 pensylvania Reg^{ts} I shall leave the posts

---

[100] Francis Fauquier (1704?-1768), the very able lieutenant governor of Virginia,
1758-1768. Consult the *D. A. B.*

guarded betwixt the Delaware & Susquehanah, by that detachment, as also furnish Escortes from the frontiers back as far as Lancaster.

The rest shall march up the Country directly. The 3 Additionall Comp[ys] of Montgomerys and Cap[t] M[c]Kenzies[1] of the old Batt[n] with Cap[t] M[c]Laughans[2] Company of 100 men from the Lower Countys, are all gone to Fort Littleton & the post on the Juniata with orders to send forward to you any other troops that may at present be posted there.

I expect everything here this week so shall be setting forward the beginning of next week.

I approve of your giving no money for working if you can carry it through.

M[r] Gist writes[3] that there are now at Winchester 129 Catawbas Tuscaroras & Nottaways newly arrived that he is going to march them to Fort Cumberland, so you may send what will be necessary to equip them there, or bring them to you, as you judge proper.

He has Intelligence of a large party of Indians with some white men, being discoverd in the Westermost part of Augusta County steering towards Bedford & Hallifax. Those he Supposes to be the little Carpenter, and he says that if it proves so, he will wait for him and carry him to Fort Cumberland along with him. So if Governour Glen be gone to Fort Cumberland with Col: Byrd I hope all will go well. I think Bosomworth should go to gett them equipt if he can be spared.

S[ir] John S[t]clair was the person who first advised me to go by Raes town, why he has alterd his Sentiments I do not know, or to what purpose make the road from Fort Frederick to Cumberland, as most Certainly wee shall now all go by Raes town, but I am afraid that S[ir] John is led by passions, he says he knows very well that wee shall not find a road from Raes town across the Allegany, and that to go by Raes town to F Cumberland is a great way about, but this he ought to have said two months ago or hold his peace now.

Pray examine the Country tother side of the Allegany particularly the Laurell Ridge that he says its impossible wee can pass, without going into Braddocks old road, What his views are in those Suggestions I know not, but I should be very sorry to be oblidged to alter ones schemes so late in the day, particularly as it was S[ir] Johns proper business to have foreseen and to have foretold all this, who to the Contrary was the first adviser.

---

[1] Captain McKenzie, Alexander, Hugh, or Roderick, of the 77th regiment.
[2] Captain John McClughan of the Lower Counties. Cf. his letter to Denny, *Pa. Arch.* 2nd series, II, 707.
[3] Letter not found.

Let the road to Fort Cumberland from Raes town be finished with all Diligence, because if wee must go by Fort Cumberland it must be through Raes town, as it is now too late to make use of the road by Fort Frederick and I fancy you will agree that with the Addition of those Indians now at Winchester & the little Carpenter, that there is no time to be lost. Let me hear from you how all goes &c & believe me with reale Sincerity

Y^r most hum^{le} Servt

Jo: fforbes.

Carlisle July 6th
C: Bou:
[*Addressed:*] to Col^o Bouquet Raes Town
[*Endorsed:*] General Forbes Carlisle 6th July Answered[4] the 11th as Soon as receiv'd

*   *   *   *   *

Halkett to Bouquet
[B. M., Add. MSS. 21640, f. 76. A.L.S.]

Camp at Carlisle Saturday 8th July 1758

Dear Sir

I do myselfe the pleasure of incrosing [*sic*] you an Extract of some General Orders,[5] that General Forbes has given out to the Troops Encamp'd here; and which he has directed me to inform you, he is desirous that you will publish to the Troops under your Command. I likewise transmit a Copy of them to the Commanding Officer at Fort Cumberland, which I must beg you will be so good to forward by the first opportunity. The last of the Artillery, & Highlanders, we expect here in two days, the General proposed giveing them one halting day to settle their affairs, & refresh their horses, he then intends they shall proceed to Raestown & will accompany them himselfe, at which place till I have the pleasure of seeing I remain Dear Sir

Your most obedient and most humble Servant.

Francis Halkett

Col: Bouquet.
[*Endorsed:*] From Brigade Major Halkett 11th July

*   *   *   *   *

---

[4] B.M., Add. MSS. 21652, f. 53.
[5] Not found.

*Forbes to Sharpe**
[Md.H.S. Port Folio 4, Papers and Letters No. 36. A.L.S.]

Head Quarters at Carlisle July the 8th 1758.

Sir

I have received from General Abercromby an Extract[6] of a Letter[7] to the Governour General of Canada, in relation to the Capitulation of Fort William Henry; which Extract I send your Honour inclosed with General Abercrombys order[8] in consequence of it.

I am with great Regard
Your Honours
Most obedient Humble Serv[t]
Jo: fforbes

P. S. Please forward the Inclosed by Express.
[*Addressed:*] To the Honble Horatio Sharpe Esq[r] Gov[r] of Maryland.
[*Endorsed:*] From Gen[l] Forbes 8[t] July 1758

*   *   *   *   *

*General Forbes' Instructions to Major Shippen**[9]
[H.S.P. MSS. Papers of the Shippen Family, Vol. 3, p. 225]

[Carlisle, July 8, 1758].

Major Shippen. You are to order the 2 new Levyed Companys of ——— to march without loss of time to strengthen the Garrison of Fort Augusta leaving one Officer and 30 men at Fort Hunter.

All the rest of the new levyed Companys are to march towards Lancaster and so up to Carlisle, where they will have tents provided for them.

The Arms and camp necessarys for those Companys levyed up the Country, ought to be sent to Lancaster or Carlisle, as those towns lyes most contiguous to the Companys.

You are to wait upon S[r] John St Clair if he is at Carlisle, who will give you his orders about the marching of these companys to the Camp at

---

* Printed, *Md. Arch.* IX, 219, and Stewart, *Letters of General John Forbes*, p. 23.
[6] Printed, *Pa. Col. Recs.* VIII, 140.
[7] Abercromby to Vaudreuil, June 26, 1758, *Pa. Col. Recs.* VIII, 141.
[8] Of June 25, 1758, printed, *Pa. Col. Recs.* VIII, 141.
* Printed, *Pa. Mag.* XXXIII, 90, and Stewart, *Letters of General John Forbes*, p. 33.
[9] For the probable date, cf. Halkett to Peters, July 9, 1758, *post*, p. 133.

Carlisle, From whence a Detachment equall to the Garrisons of the Forts
May be made from the whole, and the companys now there may be brought
on to join the army.

[*Endorsed:*] General Forbes Instructions

*   *   *   *   *

*To the Reverend Mr. Barton**[10]
[*Pa. Arch.,* 1st series, III, 451]

[Carlisle, July 9, 1758]

Sir,

I am sorry to find that the Troops of the Communion of the Church of
England, are not properly provided with a Clergyman of their own Profession.

In consequence therefore, of your laudable zeal for the Service of your
King & Country, & of your truly commendable inclination of discharging
your ministerial and Episcopal duty to the Troops under my command,

You are hereby invited & authorized to the Discharge of all Ministerial
functions belonging to a Clergyman of the Church of England, amongst
the Troops under my Command. And all & sundry, are hereby order'd and
requir'd, to pay all due Reverence & Respect, to you & the Reverend functions you are invested with. And be assured, Sir, that in all places & at all
times, the Clergymen, & those of the Church of England, shall always be
properly encouraged & protected.

I am, Revd Sir,
Your most obedient & Most humble Serv't.

Jo. Forbes

Carlisle, July 9th, 1758.

*   *   *   *   *

---

* Printed also in Perry, *Papers Relating to the Church in Pennsylvania,* p. 284,
and Stewart, *Letters of General John Forbes,* p. 24.

[10] Thomas Barton (1730-1780), an Anglican clergyman on the payroll of the
Soceity for the Propagation of the Gospel in Foreign Parts. Consult the *D. N. B.* and
letters, Barton to Forbes, July 8, 1758, Perry, *op. cit.* p. 284, and July 18, 1758, *Pa.
Arch.,* 1st series, III, 450.

Major Halkett to [Peters]*
[H.S.P. MSS Gratz Collection, Case 4, Box 7. A.L.S.]

Camp at Carlisle, 9th July, 1758.

Dear Sir,

You are extremely good for your long letter[11] to the General, for which everybody here joins with him in thanks, but as it has fallen upon me to acknowledge the Receipt of it, knowing how great a propensity that I have to writing long letters, I hope you do not expect that the answer is to be in proportion. I shall therefore acquaint you, that we arrived here in five days from Philadelphia, since which the General has been obliged to go through a great deal of Rideing and walking, in Reviewing and forming the Provincials, from which he has not found the least inconveniency, but on the contrary has recovered him greatly, and reistablished his health more than I have seen him since his coming to the Continent, Yesterday he made the Detachment of 15 men from each of your 48 Comp'ys, for the protection of the Frontiers, to keep the communication open to Raestown. Major Shippen has orders[12] to write to the Governor,[13] & send him a return[14] of the Disposition that General Forbes has made for their defence; they march the day after to-morrow, but how we are to get the remainder up the Country with us, is more than I can see, for several of the Companies want Kettles, Canteens, Blankets, &c. The General Reviewed the Light horse yesterday, & tho' he never expected that the Commissioners would discharge their duty to the service as they ought to have done, yet he could not have believed that they would have impos'd upon it so much as they have done, by providing such trash for the Light horse, most of their accoutrements being rendered useless already. I am in hast, Dear Peters,

Your most obedient
humble Servant,
Francis Halkett.

P.S.—The General has given the Express the Indian Collours to carry down to you.

*　　*　　*　　*　　*

---

* Printed in *Pa. Arch.*, 1st series, III, 450.
[11] Not found.
[12] Not found in the Instructions, *ante,* p. 131.
[13] No letters of Shippen to Denny in July found.
[14] Not found.

Forbes to Abercromby
[AB 428 A.L.S.]

Carlisle July 9th. 1758

Sir:

I am this moment favoured with yours of the 24th of June[15] from Fort Edward.

I am extreamly sorry to find you expressing a Surprize at my not acknowledging the receipt of your letter of the 4th of June—[16] But likewise accusing me of taking no notice of receiving any of your letters, ever since I left New York. With the further observation of the Uncommon, and extraordinary manner of Carrying on business in that way. And as you suppose no letters miscarry you refer me to the letters you have wrote; or to those of your Secretary, who has particular Instructions from Materialls and Directions left with him to answer any letters that I am write you. about the Carrying on the publick Affairs.

I do assure you S^{ir} that there has no thing happend in the Department Committed to my charge, that I have not as far as I can recollect, acquainted you of directly, Nor when Embarrassed how to proceed, that I have not asked your orders and Directions; Nor can I think any behaviour of mine with regard to you as my Commanding Officer, should draw upon me a reflection from you, for not behaving with exactness in the execution of the Duty entrusted to me.

Your letter of the 4th of June plainly evinces this, Wherein you tell me you can not advise me in the many difficultys I laboured under at that time, and leaves me to extricate myself as being acquainted with the minds of the people I had to deal with and then present upon the Spot.

I do not see in this same letter any such peremptory commands or orders, as required my acknowledging the receipt of that letter in particular. For the Highland Batt^{n} were not then arrived, and the expence of that embarkation was not known. Col: Byrd I have never as yet seen—And my transaction with Regard to the Maryland troops, & being carried on under the Eye and with the advice of Mr Kilby, and as it was intricate and tedious, I referr'd you for ane account of my proceedings in that affair to Mr Kilby. In a letter[17] that I wrote you and sent under Cover to Lieu^{t} Mclean at New York who (I was told by Brig: Stanwix) was to forward your letters when

---

[15] Not found.
[16] AB 318, copy.
[17] June 15, 1758, *ante*, p. 113.

he went away. I have since that wrote you[18] by the same Channels giving you ane account of every thing materiall, to with in a few days of my sending every person & thing from Philadelphia and the leaving it myself.

I have looked over all the letters, that you have favoured me with, since that wherein you ordered me from New York to Philadelphia,[19] And can not accuse myself of having neglected any of your Commands. I may perhaps have gone farther, or have exceeded some things, Which I shall be heartily sorry for if found fault with. But having no Directions or Instructions whatever, How to guide or carry on my Military operations, except a few Words in the Extract of M[r] Pitts letter to you,[20] and in his letter to the Southern provinces;[21] where In the one it is expected that I shall annoy and repell the Enemy in their encroachments upon the frontiers of those provinces. And in the other that I shall act offensively against his Maj[tties] Enemys. And in order to be able to fulfill those Expectations I have laboured hitherto with all the Capacity and attention that I am Capable off.

This much I thought necessary to write you as my Commanding officer, with regard to my publick transactions, and the due attention that I hitherto have paid and shall continue to pay, to all such orders as you shall please to send me.

As to private life, I flattered myself that after speaking with you at Major Robertsons, that all little jealousys or Suspicions were entirely to Subside. And that no little tattling story teller was to gain creditt. I hope it is so; For sure I am, they are neither friends to you nor to me, who attempt to sow the seeds of Dissention between us.

I have now done, and heartily wish, that I could have persuaded myself, that I was not called upon ever to begin.

The Entering upon the Affair of the Indians and Sir W[m] Johnston is too long to be soon discussed, so I shall only give you a few Anecdotes and leave you to judge.

You are under a Mistake in thinking it would have been ane Impropriety for Sir W[m] Johnston to have taken the charge and manadgement of the Cherokee Indians (believing them in M[r] Atkins department.) All Indians whatever in the province of Pennsylvania are immediately under his† [*Marginal note:*† S[ir] Will[ms]] Department and as such M[r] Croghan manadged

[18] June 27, 1758, *ante*, p. 126.
[19] Abercromby to Forbes, April 13, 1758, AB 153, copy. Forbes evidently preserved his papers.
[20] Of December 30, 1757, Kimball, *Correspondence of William Pitt*, I ,143. The extract is printed in *Pa. Arch.*, 1st series, III, 321.
[21] Printed, Kimball, *Correspondence Pitt*, II, 140.

those very Indians last year. by order[22] of S^{ir} Willm and now Mr Gist—Mr. Atkins depute—to preserve that propriety will not interfere or medle with the Indians that come over the pensylvania boundarys. as it is not in Mr Atkins department.

You must allow that this propriety, or Ceremony at this time is extreamly ill judged, and tending to the destruction of the publick concerns, and the Kings measures, particularly as those Indians came into this province [their]† at the Provinces request, enforced to them, by the E. of Loudoun.

How S^{ir} Willm was employed the 4th of June when you wrote me that letter, I do not pretend to say—But so early as the beginning of May I complained to you of the little care, that he took of the Cherokkes than at this place, and in his Department; and of the Indian affairs of this province in General. And I acquainted you likewise how Cautious wee were in medling with Indians Affairs, for fear of Giving S^{ir} W^m the handle, he now very artfully makes use off.

I am credibly informed that S^{ir} Willm [23] and Mr Atkins Commissions,[24] are no more than A Sign Manual to transact Indian Affairs, under the Direction of the Commander in Chieff, with Authority given to the Commander-in-Chieff to pay them £600 yearly for their trouble, If so, I cannot help thinking those selfish views he so much disclaims, ought to be entirely laid asside.

When you sent me a Copy of S^{ir} Williams letter to you, dated 28th of Aprile.[25] Wherein he says, "Let pensylvania go on and negotiate a peace with the Delawares &c &c.—I thereupon desired that the Governour would act, conformable to S^{ir} Williams desire—but after consulting his councill he told me, that he medled with Caution ever since he had receivd the Êarl of Loudouns Orders, and that he thought the bringing about a peace with the Indians, was, by those orders, S^{ir} Willm Johnstons own Business, and therefore did not choose to interfere. least the very gloss that S^{ir} W^m putts upon it at present, should than have been made use off—

S^{ir} W^m I believe was acquainted of this—But neither he nor any person

[22] Johnson to Croghan, November 4, 1758, *Papers of Sir William Johnson,* II, 657.
† Stricken out.
[23] Of Johnson's several commissions, the first was by Braddock, April 15, 1755, printed in *Papers of Sir William Johnson,* I, 465. For later Commissions, cf. *ibid.,* II, 434; *N.Y.C.D.,* VII, 458.
[24] Edmund Atkin's commission dated from 1756.
[25] Printed, *Papers of Sir William Johnson,* II, 830.

from him Appearing, Nor no letter of Advice or Directions from him, At the same time that the frontier Inhabitants were dayly murderd and drove from their plantations, I therefore must say that my opinion then was (as we had no troops) that every means ought to be tryed, to bring about a friendly meeting with the Indians, Altho I was at that time told by almost every person, that upon any such Invitation from pensylvania to the Indians, That S^{ir} W^m would, thereupon send a like Invitation to them to meet him, at the same time; A Sure method to frustrate the Laudable intention of the pensylvanians, which S^{ir} W^m had practiced upon them before, While at the same time he complained, that pensylvania interfered with his Commission & hurt the Indian affairs solely committed to his charge.

Self preservation is the first principle in humane nature, and the barbaratys and murders, gayly reiterated on the frontiers of this province and Jersey at last oblidged Govr Denny to send messages to the Chieffs of the Indians desiring a meeting; Copys of those Messages[26] I sent you,[27] desiring they might be transmitted to S^{ir} Wm Johnston if you thought proper. So he can not well pretend Ignorance, Nor can he say the Message was inviting the whole six Nations down to pensylvania, It being only to require a Deputation from them, or more properly from the Senecas, to send a few of their Sachems to give their Concurrence to this provinces building some houses for the Delaware Indians at Wioming, ane Article agreed to by treaty 18 Months ago, And the Not performing of which, is now given as the principall Cause, why those tribes, had retired and putt themselves under the french protection, upon the Ohio.

These Messages sent, and the building of some houses for the Delawares at Wioming, have I hope had a very good Effect. And so just and necessary were the proceedings of the Governm^t of Pennsylvania that all Sects and all parties, agreed in carrying on the Operations—And Gover^r Bernard, when at Philadelphia, was so sensible of the justice and fittness of such a message and meeting, that He and his Councill immediately dispatch'd Messengers desiring to be included in the same invitation.

The Effect of those Messages you will see by the enclosed report[28] of the Messenger that carried them—And the 50 Indians now come down to settle matters at Philadelphia, shows them sincere on their part. And I hope Gov^{rs} Denny & Bernard will be equally so on theirs, and settle the

[26] Of June 22, 1758, *Pa. Col. Recs.*, VIII, 129-132.
[27] Cf. Forbes to Abercromby, June 27, 1758, *ante*, p. 127.
[28] Printed *Pa. Col. Recs.*, VIII, 132-134, report of Charles Thompson and Frederick Post on conference of June 12, 1758.

just demands of the Indians, by which means save the lives of numbers of their Inhabitants and restore peace to their almost depopulate back Country. A thing that I have not seen S^{ir} William Johnston take any one Step to accomplish, but to the Contrary (by that extract of his letter to you of the 18th of June[29]) to give you a wrong Idea of a most absolutely necessary measure, for the salvation of those Colonys.

The Counter-working that S^{ir} W^{m} speaks off is (in my humble opinion) intirely on his part as he knows or ought to know every step taken or to be taken by the pensylvania Gover^{t}. But they were so sensible of the part S^{ir} Willm would act, that they foretold me of it upon my first arrivall among them, And Indeed I must say he has no way made them tell ane untruth—

I am sorry to be so long on this Subject, but Indian Affairs are neither so difficult nor Intricate as not to be managed but under the Auspices of Mr Wraxall[30] and Croghan, who may have views altho S^{ir} W^{m} has not—As Mr Croghan in his letter very candidly says, the Messages from these parts distracts the six Nations, and may be the means of preventing them joining your Army—where it is notorious and evident not one man is desired to go to warr with us, all required being only peace, or neutrality on their parts. I mean the Delawares and some neighbouring tribes, because as the Mohawks, Senecas, &c are Sir Will^{ms} particular care they are entirely left to his disposall, only a requisition of their friendship.

Tediuscung's giving out that the Cherokees were stopt from entering the Delaware country or passing the Susquehanah, as it was very true, was also very necessary to be made known to the Indians, because some Rascalls had maliciously propogate the Story of the Cherokees having been brought into this Country to fall upon the Delawares and the Six Nations. To remove which false Report, the Deputation from the Cherokees are now gone to S^{ir} Willm Johnston & the six nations with Belts of Friendship[31] &c and to desire the six nations to join heartily with the English in the warr against the French. I wrote you of this before[32] and beg'd if they came to your Army that you would take some Notice of a tall man among them, with a Harelip or something like it and I believe in the same letter desired your orders to Mr Barrow to answer my Warrants, Which order I have since found amongst the papers sent me by your Aid de Camp at New York.

---

[29] *Papers of Sir William Johnson,* II, 830.

[30] Pater Wraxall (d. 1759), secretary to Sir William Johnson, and historically famous for his *Abridgement of the Indian Notes.* Consult the *D. A. B.*

[31] *Papers of Sir William Johnson,* II, 858.

[32] June 27, 1758, *ante,* p. 127.

After seeing all things, and all men from Philadelphia I left it the same day June 30th, and gott here July the 4th. Where (God grant I may keep my temper) I found everything a heap of Confusion, and Sir John Stclair at Variance with every mortall, As this is most disagreeable and impedes every thing I have been employed ever since in setting the province troops to Rights, and sending detachments for the protection of their Frontier between the Susquehanah and Delaware, wch takes a great many men, and the frontier with the proper escortes to the West of Susquehanah will require so many more that I shall not have great numbers of pensylvanians left with me.

The train with the last of the Highlanders marched into Camp this Day, Tomorrow, Wednesday, & Thursday wee will all be on our march to Raestown. which without a halting day will take us nine or ten days—but as I hope to have every thing in readyness there for stores provisions &c I shall march on directly either across the Allegany and leave the Yohageny on my left, or else by Fort Cumberland and take Genll Braddocks road, which I have already opend the length of the Crossing of the Yohageny. But I find such ane *Embarras* with Waggons that I must be drove into pack horses, when I see fresh Embarassments and a great number of Inconveniences—

I wrote you before[33] that I could not send you any return of troops under my Command, our distance and dispersion is such, and our dayly changes makes the thing almost impracticable, but the moment I can gett them any way Collected I shall not fail to send you ane account of the whole.

There are 150 of the North Carolina people come to Winchester, without a scrape of a pen from Mr Dobbs, or any account of them from their Commanding officer. I do not know how they are provided, and now so farr from Philadelphia how I shall be able to supply their wants.

I have just now made a tryall of the pack sadles provided by Sir John, and they are all useless.

I have wrote to the different Governors of the southern provinces,[34] acquainting them of your having declared the Capitulation of Fort Wm Henry to be null & of no effect—

The Cherokees are all gone except about 100 with Col: Bouquet at Raestown and 60 with Colo Byrd at Fort Cumberland—But I expect dayly Capt Bullen[35] with 50 Catawbas, and its said the little Carpenter[36] is upon

[33] June 15, 1758, *ante,* p. 114.
[34] Letters not found.
[35] Probably an Indian chieftain.
[36] An Indian chieftain.

the road with 100 good men. I hope wee shall be able to keep those, as I shall not now give them time to weary—

I am glad to see you have gott over most of your difficultys, and that you will be so soon a float. I wish you most heartily a good voyage and a good and fortunate landing.

I have just now a letter[37] from Col° Bouquet acquainting me that 50 of the above 100 Indians, being Catawbas had left him so I do not believe that we shall have any left to cross the Allegany mountains with us. I wish you heartily Health and all manner of Success and am with Sincere Regard

S^{ir} y^r most ob^t hum^{le} Servt

Jo fforbes.

Camp at Carlisle July 10th

Gen^{11} Abercromby

[*Endorsed:*] Brig^r. Genl. Forbes Carlisle July 9th 1758 R the 22^d by the post Ans the 23^d

*   *   *   *   *

*Forbes to William Pitt**
[P.R.O. C.O. 5:50, (L.C. trans.) pp. 583-587.]

Carlisle Camp west of Susquehannah, July 10th. 1758.

Sir

I did myself the honour of writing to you from Philadelphia the 17th of June,[38] when I acquainted you of the Situation of the Troops under my Command. So soon as I gott the Artillery and Stores landed from on board the transports from England, and putt in some Order which was not till the 30th of June, I sett out from Philadelphia with the Highland Battal^n. of Montgomery and the train of Artillery which marches into the Camp here this day, all well and in order, altho the March was long being 120 miles in excessive hot weather, and having two great Rivers the Skulkill and Susquehannah to pass, upon Rafts and Flatts, and the last river being 1900 yards over. I halt tomorrow and shall then proceed 100 miles further to Raestown, where I have now 1500 of the Provincialls, who are building some Storehouses and stockading a piece of Ground for our Ammunition and provisions. For in Raestown there is not one single house; The place

---

[37] Not found.

* Printed, Kimball, *Correspondence of William Pitt*, I, 294, and Stewart, *Letters of General John Forbes*, p. 24.

[38] *Ante,* p. 116.

having its name from one Rae, who designed to have made a plantation there several years ago, nor indeed is there either Inhabitants or houses from this to the Ohio (except at Forts Loudoun and Lyttelton which are only two or three houses each, inclosed with a Stockade of 100 feet square) the whole being an immense Forest of 240 miles of Extent, intersected by several ranges of Mountains, impenetrable almost to any thing humane save the Indians, (if they be allowed the Appellation) who have foot paths, or tracts through those desarts, by the help of which, we make our roads.

I am in hopes of finding a better way over the Alleganey Mountains, than that from Fort Cumberland which Gen¹¹. Braddock took, if so I shall shorten both my March, and my labour of cutting the road about 40 miles, which is a great consideration. For were I to pursue Mʳ. Braddocks route, I should save but little labour, as that road is now a brushwood, by the sprouts from the old stumps, which must be cut down and made proper for Carriages, as well as any other Passage that we must attempt.

The Cherokee Indians being but bad Judges of time, came too early in the year to our Assistance, and therefore had not patience to wait our time, so that from the fickleness of their temper the greatest part of them—went home three weeks ago. You may believe, Sir, that no method was left untryed to detain them, but they are like Sheep. Where one leaps, all the rest follow.

We have still near 200 that remain, and are so much attached to us that they have given the little nothing they have into our Stores as a pledge of their Services to us during the Campaign.

This is owing in a great degree to Mr. Byrd of Virginia to whom I should do a great injustice if I was silent upon the Occasion—As he has a very large and opulent fortune in Virginia he joined the Earl of Loudoun early after his Arrival in America, Accompany'd the Army to Halifax last year, and sett a noble example to all the Gentlemen of the Continent, who had either Inclination or Abilities to serve the King and their Country.

He in the Month of February last offered his Services to the Earl of Loudoun, and embarked at New York for South Carolina, went from thence some hundreds of Miles up into the Cherokees Country, assembled their Chiefs, and by a march of near a thousand Miles conducted some of the best warriors of that Nation through both the Carolina and Virginia into this Country, and luckily arrived in time at the Army (then in Embryo) where by his Interest and the sight of His followers, their Countrymen, and Chief Sachems; The number I now have the honor to acquaint you off, remains steady to His Majesty's Service, and are now the advanced Guard of the troops under my Command: The Virginia Assembly have named him to the Command of their new raised regimᵗ, which he accepted off with pleasure, and actuated by the same spirit and Zeal for the Honour of the King and good of his Country, has I dare say at great personall expence equipt his regim^t in many necessaries not allowed of by the Virginia Assembly, and they are now all ready at Fort Cumberland.

You will pardon me Sir if I mention one other Gentleman, who tho a near relation of mine, I cannot but do his Intentions and Endeavours the Justice they deserve, I mean M^r. Glen, late Governour of S^o. Carolina, who came from thence with Montgomery's regim^t. to pay me a visit at Philadelphia, where hearing of the Defection and falling off, of the Cherokees, went off into the back Countrys directly, and as he has had formerly great dealings with them, I am persuaded his personall Interest among them, contributed greatly at this present time in making them do whatever is desired. But I am persuaded that a Message that he has sent to the little Carpenter, who is the second person of the whole Cherokee Nation will bring him and some of his Warriors to Join us before the end of the Campaign, so that, as to the point of Indians, we shall be very well if they continue steady, but that is precarious; As the least jealousy, or smallest disgust, oversetts a months Civility, and good usage at once.

In my last,[39] I had the honour to acquaint you, How that the Maryland Assembly had behaved with regard to His Majesty's Orders, communicated to them by you.

So glaring an Infraction of his Majesty's Royal Command at this critical time, draws the eye of all upon them; and their refusing all aid, and assistance, for their own protection, and repelling the Enemy, strikes all honest Men with a horrible Idea of their Ingratitude to the best of Kings

I am with the greatest regard and esteem

y^r. most ob^t. & most Hum^ble. Servt.

J^o. Forbes.

Rt. Honble. W^m. Pitt Esqre.

P. S. I am this moment informed, since writing the above, that 50 of the Catawba Indians have left us, and are gone home. Those were the tribe we placed the greatest confidence in, for their Attachment to us.

[*Endorsed:*] Carlisle Camp July 10th 1758/Brig^r. Genl. Forbes/R/ Augt. 21st

*   *   *   *   *

[39] *Ibid.*

Forbes to Bouquet
[B.M., Add. MSS. 21640, f. 79. A.L.S.]

[N. p., July 11, 1758]

My Dear Sir

Pardon a hurry of business at the same time finding every thing here in Confusion and disorder, so have employed Grant[40] and Halkett[41] to write you.

Let me hear from you how all is, and pray let some good brisk party scout forward.

Excuse me in haste no news either from Louisbourgh, or Tunderoga, only Gen¹¹ Abercromby and the troops are said to be embarked upon Lake George, so we are the last and can not help it.

I shall hurry up the troops directly so pray see for a road across the Allegany or by Fort Cumberland, which Garrison may if necessary be clearing Braddocks old road

I am Dʳ Sⁱʳ Yʳˢ most sincerely

Jo: fforbes.

Tuesday July 11ᵗʰ

I send you the last news paper from England.

Send down Major Orndt[42] directly as he is to Command all the Detachments between the Susquehanah & Delaware, he must come to me for his orders.
Jo. fforbes.

[*Addressed:*] To Col Bouquet Commanding at Raes town.
[*Endorsed:*] Gen¹ Forbes 11ᵗʰ July

*   *   *   *   *

Grant[43] to Bouquet
[B.M., Add. MSS. 21640, f. 81. A.L.S.]

[Carlisle, July 11, 1758.]

Dear Colonel.

I am directed by General Forbes, to acquaint you, that he has detached two Additionall Company's of the first Highland Battalion to Juniata, and

---

⁴⁰ Major James Grant (1720-1806) of the 77th regiment, later in command of forces defeated at Fort Duquesne. Cf. Grant to Bouquet, July 11, 1758, *post*, p. 143.

⁴¹ Cf. Halkett to Bouquet, July 23, 1758, *post*, p. 154.

⁴² Jacob Orndt, captain-major in the Pennsylvania militia, prominent in frontier warfare.   ⁴³ Major James Grant.

one Company of the Battalion with an Additionall one to Fort Loudoun the General desires that you may order those four Companys to joyn you at Raes-Town, leaving a sufficien[t] Guard at each of those Posts.

A Company of the Highlanders with four of the Provincialls march this night, with forty Waggons of Powder Provisions, Oats, Forrage &c directly to Raes-Town. Two of our Companys with Six of the Provincialls march to morrow morning as as [sic] Escort to the Artillery to Shippensburg, where they are to halt for a few days. The Gen[1] with the rest of the Army will follow in a few days. he desired that you may get as soon as possible proper places provided to receive the Baggage and Military Stores of the Army—and he begs that you may send him an Express to inform him of the state you are in, for the reception of the whole Army.

The General desires that the Road over the Allegany may be reconoitred, for he is unwilling to be put under the necessity of making any Detour,

With regard to your Prisoners[44] the Gen[1] desires that the least guilty may be immediately tryed by a Garrison Court Marshall in order to receive corporal Punishment, the others he chuses to reserve for an Example till he comes up himself.

15 men per Company of the Pensilvania Provincialls have been detached to guard the Frontiers. You may believe the best men have not been chose for that service—but we shall still have remaining of those Gentlemen about 1680, with 300 of the lower County's, 1800 Virginians, 1250 Highlanders 360 of your Corps, but making an Allowance for sickness &c with Artillerymen Waggoners, Sutlers Servants &c I imagine we shall consist of about five thousand men when we assemble at Raes-Town.

Colonel Byrds & Armstrongs Reg[ts] must share the same Fate with those here, the Gen[1] therefore desires that you may order such of the Offices as are under your Command to pitch upon the 35 best men of each Company—out of which number all detachments are to be made, the 15 or 18 remaining of each Company to be kept with you, that the Gen[1] may have it in his power to dispose of them for Escorts &c when he comes up, or when he sends you Directions for that purpose.

I came up last night with four of our Company's the Artillery Hospitall Stores, Provisions &c and in short cleared Philadelphia of everything except a small Detachment of ours, which are to remain there till relieved by the Provincialls.

───────

[44] Minutes of many court martials of Forbes' expedition are segregated in Haldimand Papers, B.M., Add. MSS. 21682.

Tis said the King of Prussia[45] is marched with fifty thousand men to Vienna. The Duke of Marlborough[46] Lord George Sackville &c with a Body of Troops and thirty Saill of the Lyne are ordered upon a secret Expedition. Gen¹ Abercromby will soon have a considerable body of Troops in Battoes on Lake George We have no accounts of Louisbourg. We shall soon meet. The Water here does not agree quite well with my Constitution. The Gen¹ Col Montgomery and all your Friends are well. I am at all times Dear Colonel

Your most obedient & most humble Servt

James Grant

Camp near Carlisle July 11th 1758
To Colonel Bouquett.
[*Addressed:*] To Colonel Bouquet Commanding his Majesty's Troops at Raes-Town
[*Endorsed:*] Major Grant for Gen¹ Forbes 11th July

*   *   *   *   *

Forbes to Bouquet
[B.M., Add. MSS. 21640, f. 93. A.L.S.]

Camp at Carlisle July 14th 1758
Sir

I had the pleasure of yours[47] of the 11th last night, and have all along thought the road from F. Frederick to Cumberland Superfluous, if we could have done with out it, which I am glad to understand wee can do by Raes town. It would have been double pleasure if thence we could have gott a good road across the Laurell hill, But by Capt Wards journall[48] I beginn to fear it would be difficult, altho' I would have you continue to make further tryalls, for I should be sorry to be oblidged to pass by Fort Cumberland. I am sensible that some foolish people[49] have made partys to drive us into that road, as well as into the road by Fort Frederick, but as I utterly detest all partys and views in military operations, so you may very well guess, how and what arguments I have had with S^{ir} John S^{t}clair upon that Subject. But I expect Governor Sharp here this night when I shall know more of this same road.

---

[45] Frederick II.
[46] Charles Spencer, Third Duke of Marlborough (1706-1738). Consult the *D. N. B.*
[47] B.M., Add. MSS. 21652, f. 53.   [48] B.M., Add. MSS. 21658, f. 16.
[49] Probably a reference to George Washington and William Byrd III, as well as to Sir John St. Clair.

I hope your second detachment across the Alleghany have been able to ascertain what route wee must take, and that consequently you are sett about clearing of it.

The Waggons have been the plague of my life, as I found them here in the greatest degree of Confusion, nor indeed had S^{ir} John taken the smallest pains, or had made the least inquiry how to sett those matters to rights. I hope however to gett to the bottom of it, when the empty wagons now at Raes town return. You will give orders that each Convoy as they arrive be examined, and those Waggons or horses found unsufficient to be marked down and turned out of the service giving them passes and marking the days that they were discharged.

Wee likewise have been and were like to be at ane Intire stop for want of provender for our horses as S^{ir} John had only made ane Imaginery provision, for in reality wee had not one pound of Hay—And all the meadows eat up five miles around us. This I have in some measure remedy'd by making provision of Rye, Cutting the Straw & grinding the grain makes both a Cheap feed & more hearty than Hay & oats, as it goes twice as farr and consequently easier transported.

As the troops are now mostly supplyed with fresh Beef, they are to receive it at the rate of seven Pound P week, And if they gett pork, they are only to have four pounds of pork, which is the rate that Gen^{ll} Abercrombie has given out in orders.

I can send you enclosed Mr Hoops Calculation of provisions[50] by which you will see, that wee have 3 months provision for Six thousand men at Raes town or upon the road from this place. So with a Continuall Supply coming in I hope this will do.

Major Jamison[51] who sett out Yesterday will acquaint you of the Detatchments that I have made from the provincialls, and where posted. The Companys are now all upon their march except six that I hope to gett away to morrow or Monday being in hourly expectation of their Necessarys from Philadelphia, which is the only thing y^t I left in trust to the provinciall Commissioners, and in which they have (as I expected) deceived me. I find such great neglects, and such slowness in everything, that I dare not venture to leave this before I sett every thing in motion, so it will at Soonest be Tuesday or Wednesday next before I sett out.

---

[50] Not found.

[51] David Jamison, major in the Pennsylvania militia, an officer in Colonel Burd's battalion.

I have sent up Major Armstrong with one Dunning[52] ane old Indian trader who has been many a time upon the road from Raes town to Fort Duquesne, and he says there is no Difficulty in the road across the Laurell Hill and that He leaves the Yohageny all the way upon his left hand about 8 miles, and that it is only 40 miles from the Laurell Hill to Fort Duquesne along the top of Chesnut ridge. I fancy he will be off Service to you, so lose no time in sending him out.

Major Armstrong has desired to have a pretty strong party to go along with this man. I would therefore give him 100 volunteers, or such a party as you shall judge proper, with provisions upon Bats horses, and some Indians, as He proposes going as farr as the Ohio and Fort Duquesne to reconoitre and to endeavour to bring of a prisoner, or gett some Intelligence, You will therefore give him your Instructions to take very great Care how he proceeds, for the Ennemy's taking any of his people prisoners would be of great use to them and to our great Detriment. So every precaution must be taken.

Send other Guides with him, who may be sent back from distance to distance to acquaint you of the route they take and agree upon some marks by which it may be found.

As the Speedy Execution of this is of great consequence you will lose no time in sending Major Armstrong away. And let the officers that goes with him be right people, who understands the woods and bush fighting.

I have just now sent orders[53] for those troops who have been working from F: Frederick to F: Cumberland to march and join you at Raes town, and I have orderd the North Carolina troops to march to Fort Loudoun to receive arms tents &c and than to join you likewise. If you want more troops you may send for them from F: Cumberland.

I have sent Compasses and Union Flags with Major Armstrong for the partys you may send out.

Upon second thoughts and if the road be found convenient across the Laurell Hill leaving the Yohageny to the left hand, why should not (upon y^t Certainty and the return of the Guides that you may send out for that purpose) a Detachment of 500 Men or more if necessary be sent directly to Laurell Hill or some where there, to take post there, and make a Stockade and place for the reception of our ammunition and provisions, but in all this

[52] Probably James Dunning, an early fur trader, for whom Dunning's Creek is named.

[53] Not found.

procedure great caution is to be used, having had Intelligence[54] from Albany, that a Number of Indians and Canadiens have been seen passing Lake Ontario supposed to have been sent to Fort Duquesne, so pray keep a good look out with your out posts and I think your piketts ought to lye au bivouac every night.

I shall send you up most of the light horse Immediatly and Second hundred of Bats horses leaves this to morrow, and a third hundred upon Tuesday. As I presume you may want Forrage, and as S^ir John has at last confessed that he had provided none but at Fort Cumberland (I suppose on purpose to drive me into that road, for what purpose I know not) If you therefore think it necessary, send Waggone to Fort Cumberland for part of it, always sending the forty waggons together, and belonging as much as possible to the same County and under the direction of the same Waggon master to prevent Confusion.

I am extremely sorry to give you the enclosed extract of Letters[55] with ane Acco^tt of Gen^ll Abercrombys landing near Tunderoga, and the untimely fate of poor Lord Howe. I do not know what to Conjecture, or how to judge, but they must have mett with a repulse or otherwise Gen^ll Stanwix would never have been so rash as to raise the Militia, and to lay ane Embargo upon the Shipping[56]—which must allarm all the Continent.

As I judge at present, this same affair of Gen^ll Abercrombys, may make me risque a forced March or two to create a Diversion.

Govern^r Sharp came here last night, but has no news only the beggary and desertion of the North Carolina Forces.

Let me hear immediately your resolution about the road and believe me
D^r S^ir

Y^r Most ob^t hum^le Servt

Jo: fforbes.

Sunday Morn^g.

Make look over all kind of Stores, and putt them in order, and gett returns of them, for in this place everything was mixed, so wee neither knew what wee had or what wee wanted.

Col: Bouquet

[*Endorsed:*] General Forbes 14th July

* * * * *

[54] Probably in two letters from John Appy, June 27, 1758, AB 393, and July 6, 1758, AB 412.

[55] Stanwix to Delancey, July 9, 1758, B.M., Add. MSS. 21640, f. 77, printed in *Pa. Col. Recs.* VIII, 146, and Delancey to Denny, July 21, 1758, B.M., Add. MSS. 21640, f. 77, printed in *Pa. Col. Recs.* VIII, 146.

[56] Stanwix to Delancey, July 12, 1758, *ibid.*

Forbes to Bouquet
[B.M., Add. MSS. 21640, f. 97. A.L.S.]

Carlisle July 17th 1758

Sir.

I wrote you yesterday[57] by Major Armstrong, but I last night received the Inclosed Conferences[58] with the Indians at Philadelphia, by which you will observe that there are hopes of bringing away the Indians from the Ohio. I am therefore affraid that our partys may fall upon those Indians returning from the Ohio to settle upon the Susquehanah &c. So you will make Armstrong proceed with great Caution, and to observe the yellow band about the head or Arms of all those who want to come in a friendly manner from the Ennemy, I having sent them word of that mark of Distinction, and sent some union Flags and some yellow Shalloon up to Fort Augusta to be given to the Messengers who might go from thence to the Ohio. Altho perhaps this may be neglected, which would occasion confusion if wee should fall in with any of them returning without those marks.

I send you enclosed a Calculation[59] for the transport of provisions for 6000 Men, by which you may judge how many Waggons & Pack Horses will be necessary to keep in the service, but so great was our Confusion, that to this present writing I can not learn how many Waggons wee have now in pay, But I have sent you up Mr Irwin of Philadelphia who has the charge of all those Waggons furnish'd down there; who will show you his books and the method that I have made him follow, which if the other Waggon masters would copy after would sett them soon to rights.

There are two hundred pack horses already sent off to you, and another hundred goes away to morrow, and I think in two days after, near 200 more. I have made Capt Stclair write you[60] as to the Distribution of so many of them among the troops, allowing three horses P Company of 50 Men, and four of those of 100.

I have sent Dunlap[61] after Ambas the Delaware Indian, and have promised Dunlap the first Commission.

The provinciall troops consist of 53 men P company out of which I keep 35 of the best men & officers for to go with us; the rest I design for detachments & escortes. The 3 Regts of this province are made equall each Regt consisting of 16 Companys. I have already Draugted and detatchd

[57] Letter not found, unless it be that of July 14, 1758, held up until Armstrong's departure.
[58] B.M., Add. MSS. 21640, f. 87, copy. Printed in *Pa. Arch.* 1st series, III, 456-459, July 6-12, 1758. [59] Not found.
[60] St. Clair to Bouquet, July 16, 1758, B.M., Add. MSS. 21639, f. 34.
[61] Robert Dunlap, an old fur trader.

Reg^t 17 Comp^{ys} that were here, and you may have the rest in your Eye, ready to be sent away, upon my Comming to Raes town. Those I have detatchd cover the Country from Delaware to Susquehanah; Garrison F: Augusta; and give 50 men here, and 50 at Shippensburgh.

All your demands as farr as possible I shall Comply with, having orderd Iron to be sent up, but Capt Bosomworths demand for the Indians, I can not help thinking extravagant, as I know (betwixt friends) that he goes half, with the merchant that furnishes them, but keep this to yourself.

I shall hurry the Troops up fast, but by what Inattention I know not, the six provinciall Comp^{ys} left here can not march, want of Kettles Canteens &c which I am informed are gone to F: Loudoun, and S^{ir} John acknowledges taking some and applying them to the use of the Virginians &c which is terrible.

Capt Sinclair[62] writes you[63] about some tents &c that go from this tomorrow or Wednesday to be sent to F: Cumberland, and some Arms, about all which you will give orders as they will be addressed to you.

You must overhawl all Sutlers, and let them know that they must lay in provisions or retire, and there must be a proportion of working tools sent to Fort Cumberland, as they Complain of want.

If you can conveniently bring Mr Glen to you, I shall be oblidged to you, and make the best Hutt you can for me, if it is not too much trouble.

I am sensible of the trouble you have by the *embarras* I have my Self.

No more news from Gen: Abercrombie nor any from Louisbourgh, which last it is hoped is ours.

I am Dr Sir very tyred but very Sincerely Y^r Most ob^t &c

Jo: fforbes.

Colo: Bouquet.

[*Endorsed:*] General Forbes 17th July.

*   *   *   *   *

Forbes to Abercrombie
[AB 452 A. L. S., P.R.O. W.O. 34; 44 f. 321. Copy]

[Philadel]† Carlisle Camp July 18 <u>1758</u>

Sir

It is impossible to express the Anxiety I feel upon the news of Poor Lord Howes untimely fate, nor the uneasiness I am under for you and the rest of the Army, as our Intelligence says little or nothing on that head. And

---

[62] Captain James Sinclair, of the 22nd regiment, A.D.Q.M.G. Cf. *post,* p. 152.

[63] Sinclair to Bouquet, July 16, and July 17, 1758, the former B.M., Add. MSS. 21639, f. 34; the latter, *ibid.,* 21643, f. 153. A.L.S.   † Stricken out.

what is mentioned is rather dark and disagreeable. So pray be so kind as make one of your Aide de Camps write us when anything happens. that wee may know the truth.

I am hurrying up the new levys as fast as possible, and hope in a short time now to have them all at Raes town & Fort Cumberland.

Most of our Cherokees have gone home, after putting us, to a very great expence and doing of nothing for it. I fancy that they have not been properly managed, but now there is no help for it—

I send you enclosed Copies of the Conferences[64] held at Philadelphia with the Delawares & Ohio Indians, which I think promises to produce some friends, if we could give them a proper time to come in, but I do not know how farr that is to be trusted to. So as to delay any of our measures for attacking the Ennemy. who I am informed are strengthening themselves dayly from the North west nations and the lower Shawanese, there having a party of those last been seen going up the Ohio in Canoes with provisions, etc and are said to be about 200—

Governour Sharp has been here some days and has laid all Lord Loudouns letters & orders[65] before me as well as those of Brigd[r] Stanwix to the officers of the Maryland Forces,[66] ordering them to remain at Fort Cumberland at their perill and assuring them of pay and provisions, as also Brigd[r] Stanwix orders[67] to Mr. Ross to carry provisions and deliver them to the troops; or Indians at Fort Cumberland—that upon these orders and assurances, to which Governour Sharp had added his own—The officers had kept the men in Garrison there, had borrowed money to give their Soldiers, in order to keep them from disbanding, and which if not repayed them must inevitably ruin them, nor can they well march. at present in obedience to my orders, as their Creditors wants security for their Debts.

These things considered I hope you will send me orders to clear those troops from October last to the first of May, from which last period I stand ingaged to them—Their demands are really so just, that I do not see there is any risque in fullfilling the Crowns engagements to them. besides Gov[r]. Sharp assures me as his real opinion, that at the first meeting of their Assembly, all that money will be made good by the Assembly, except the transportation of the provisions to Fort Cumberland—That worthy body becoming now sensible that their late behaviour might draw the Kings and nations

---

[64] Found in B.M., Add. MSS. 21640, f. 87, copy. Printed in *Pa. Arch.* 1st series, III, 456-459.

[65] Cf. *Md. Arch.* IX, *passim,* but especially Loudoun to Sharpe, November 3, 1757, *ibid.*, 98.

[66] Not found.

[67] Not found.

wrath upon them, and which I have not failed to assure them off in the strongest terms. I could write[68]

I most heartily wish and pray that this may find you safe in the possession of Teinderoga which will give life and a Spring to our actions here, which wee want prodigeously in spite of all I can do. I am S^{ir} w^t great regard

> y^r most ob^t & most
> hum^{le} Servt
> Jo: fforbes.

P:S: As we have many Indians going back and fore with messages I have been obliged to make all Friendly Indians to wear a yellow fillet or piece of Shalloon about their heads and Arms to distinguish them and prevent accidents, and when any party goes out, I make them take ane Union Flag— Gen^{ll} Abercrombie.

[*Endorsed:*] Brig^r Genl Forbes Carlisle Camp 18th July 1758 R the 1st August by Enhart Ans the 2^d d^o

*   *   *   *   *

James Sinclair to Washington*
[L.C. MSS. Papers of Washington, Vol. VIII. A.L.S.]

Carlile the 19th Juley 1758

Sir

I am desired by General Forbes to acquaint you that there is sent up to ↘Rays Town in Order to be forwarded to you at Fort Cumberland Eighty tents with Tentpoles compleat for the use of your Regiment & Colonel Byrds. This number is all we have at this place at present. I am

> Sir Your most Obedient & most
> humble Servt.
> > James Sinclair
> > A: D: Q^r. Mr Genl.

*   *   *   *   *

---

[68] Forbes to Sharpe, May 2 and May 25, 1758, *ante,* p. 79 and 99.
* Printed, Hamilton, *Letters to Washington,* II, 364.

*Forbes to Sharpe**
[Md. H.S. Port Folio 4. Papers and Letters, No. 36. A.L.S.]

Camp at Carlisle July 20th 1758.

Sir,

Having considered what you have told me concerning the Situation of Your Maryland Troops, and particularly about the Distressed Condition of the Officers, and of M^r. Ross, by whom your Forces have been Victualled (since the money which was granted by your Assembly for their Support was Expended) and being very Averse to your Troops being Disbanded at this Critical Juncture, when in all probability I shall have great occasion for their Service, I am Induced to Advance a Sum of money towards Relieving those Gentlemen in some measure from the Difficulties, wherein they are Involved by the late Extraordinary Conduct of Your Assembly, & to Encourage your Troops to keep together during the Campaign.

As I do not take upon myself to pay your Troops the Arrears that are due to them, or to Satisfy Mr Ross, but Expect that your Assembly will, out of the Supplies which they shall grant at their next, meeting; Appropriate a Sum for those purposes, I shall not Concern myself with any Accounts whatever; that I leave to your Assembly, or to such persons as you or they may Appoint, but what I Advance, I Advance upon the Credit of the Province, to be Repaid me out of the first money that your Assembly may Raise, & I Desire you will Communicate this Letter to them, that they may be thoroughly Apprised of my Intentions & Expectations.

As I Doubt not but your Assembly will notwithstanding what has lately happened be Satisfied with my keeping Your Troops together till the End of the Campaign, I shall not Scruple to Assure them that they will most certainly be paid as long as they shall Continue in the Service.

I am, with great Regard, &c   Y^r Excellencies
Most Ob^t and most Hum^{ble} Servt

Jo: fforbes.

Govr Sharp
[*Endorsed:*] Copy Letter from Brig^r. General
Forbes to Govr Sharpe
Dated Camp at Carlisle, 20th July 17[58]

*   *   *   *   *

* Printed, *Md. Arch.* IX, 235; XXI, 293; and Stewart, *Letters of General John Forbes*, p. 26.

Forbes to Bouquet
[B.M., Add. MSS. 21640, f. 99. L.S.]

Camp at Carlisle 20th July 1758.

Sir

In consiquence of the conference held with the Indians at Philadelphia, Messengers have been sent to the Ohio with invitations, and offers of peace, & accomodations for these Indians to come, and settle amongst us, the effects of which Message, is by the Messengers Instructions, to be sent by a proper person or persons immediately to me, who has orders to distinguish him or themselves, being the Messengers, & our Friends; to tye their Matchcoats to the end of a Pole, or stick, and hold it up waving it to and fro. You will therefore be so good as publish this signal to the Troops, that all Posts, out Parties, and Sentries, may be advirtised of it, to Receive him or them as our friends.

This must be publish'd at Fort Cumberland & if you can to the parties sent out up the Ohio [*Continued in Forbes' handwriting:*] And if Major Armstrong be gone out, pray let the knowledge of this Signall be sent after him. I shall leave this upon Saturday. I am Sir

Y^r most ob^t &c   Jo fforbes.

[*Note on back:*] The Express was dispatch'd from Fort Loudoun on Account of this Letter. L.O. [Lewis Ourry]

[*Addressed:*] On His Majestys Service to Colonel Bouquet Commanding at Reastown. To be forwarded Express.

[*Endorsed:*] Genl Forbes 20th July.

*   *   *   *   *

Halkett to Bouquet
[B.M., Add. MSS. 21640, f. 106, A.L.S.]

Camp at Carlisle 23^d July 1758

Sir

General Forbes is so extreamly Reduc'd & low in Spirits with the Flux, and other afflictions, that he is not able to write you, I am therefore directed to aknowledge the arrival of the Express from Reastown with your dispatches,[69] and to give you a little information of our misfortunes at Car-

---

[69] Bouquet to Forbes, July 21, 1758, B.M., Add. MSS. 21640, f. 101, A.N.S. Other letters, B. to F. of July 13 and July 14, 1758.

rilian, have enclos'd a couple of letters[70] Receiv'd from New York, which contain as full an account as any yet come to hand, General Forbes not having heard from General Abercromby since his Repulse.

Seven hundred Carrying horses are to be sent up the Country, whatever more will be necessary, can be provided in Virginia. Non [sic] but Provintials who are over & above suffitient for the protection of the different posts upon the Road to Reastown are order'd up, all the Highlanders will be detaind to the last, as an Escort to the General, being desirous of saving the consunpsion of Provisions with you, as much as possible.

The June Magazine,[71] & last News Papers[72] I have inclos'd which will give you all the intelligence that is current in these parts.

I am Dear Sir

Your most obedient humble Servant

Francis Halkett

24th July

Governor Sharp set out from hence this morning for Fort Frederick Sir John St. Clair accompanys him part of the Road in his way to Reastown.

The Camp Equipage sent up just now by the Commisioners for the Pennsylvania Troops is to set off this afternoon & likewise the' Tents for the guides with you the General haveing sent up 90 Tents in place of the 80 he formerly informed you of. The assamblage of Horses, and Cattle, that necessary must be at Reastown, will no doubt consume the Forrage greatly; upon that account the General recommends as few of them being detain'd there as possible, & when ever it is necessary to give any part of them a day, or two of rest, that they may be sent to some other part of the country, where they may be as well refresh'd, & with less inconveniency

To Colonel Bouquet

[*Endorsed:*] From Gen'l Forbes by Major Halkett 24th July Answered the 31st do[73]

* * * * *

[70] Probably Stanwix to Delancey, July 9, 1758, and Delancey to Denny, July 12, 1758, referred to *ante,* p. 148, fns. 55 and 56.
[71] Not identified.
[72] Probably the *Pennsylvania Gazette* and the *Maryland Gazette.*
[73] In French, B.M., Add. MSS. 21640, f. 112. A.C.S.

Forbes to Bouquet
[B.M., Add. MSS. 21640, f. 104, L.S.]

Carlisle July 23ᵈ. [1758]

Sir

I had the favour of yours⁷⁴ of the 21st this morning, and altho' not well in a Condition, either to write, or think, shall give you a few thoughts.

As I disclaim all parties myself, should be sorry that they were to Creep in amongst us. I therefore cannot Conceive what the Virginia folks would be att, for to me it appears to be them, and them only, that want to drive us into the road by Fort Cumberland, no doubt in opposition to the Pennsylvanians who by Raestown would have a nigher Communication (than them) to the Ohio.

Sⁱʳ John Sᵗ Clair was the first person that proposed and enforced me to take the road by Raestown, I having previous to this ordered our Army to assemble at Conegochegue which I was obliged afterwards to alter to Raestown at this Instance, altho he then declared that he nor nobody else knew any thing of the road leading from the Alleganey, over the Laurell hill, but as he has represented it of late impracticable to me, I was therefore pressing to have the Communication opened from Raestown to Fort Cumberland. Sⁱʳ John I am affraid had got a new light at Winchester, and I believe from thence proceeded to the opening the road from Fort Frederick to Fort Cumberland, I put the Question fairly to him yesterday morning, by asking him if he knew of any Intention of making me change measures and forceing me into the Fort Cumberland road, when he knew that it was at his Instance solely, that I had changed it to Raestown; I shewed him Capᵗ Ward's Journal⁷⁵ & description of the road from Raestown to the top of the Laurel Hill, telling him at the same time, that if an easy road could be found there, or made there, that I was amazed he should know nothing of it, which was evident by his telling me of late that the Laurel Hill was impracticable, he appeared nonplused, but rather than appear ignorant he said there were many Indian Traders that knew those roads very well; I stopt him short by saying if that was the case, that I was very sorry he had never found them out, or never thought it worth his while to examine them, In short he knows nothing of the matter.

Colo. Byrd in a paragraph of his letter from Fort Cumberland,⁷⁶ amongst other things writes; that he has upwards of Sixty Indians waiting my ar-

---

⁷⁴ B.M., Add. MSS. 21640, f. 101, A.N.S.
⁷⁵ B.M., Add. MSS. 21658, f. 16.   ⁷⁶ Letter not found.

rival, and ready to accompany me, but they will not follow me unless I go by Fort Cumberland. This is a new System of military Discipline truly; and shows that my Good friend Byrd is either made the Cats Foot off himself, or he little knows me, if he imagines that Sixty Scoundrells are to direct me in my measures.

As we are now so far advanced as Raestown I should look fickle in my measures, in changing, to go by Fort Cumberland, without being made thoroughly sensible of the impracticability of passing by the shortest way over the Laurell Hill to the Ohio.

The difference at present in the length of road the one way and the other stands thus—

From Raestown to Fort Cumberland 34 miles or upwards.

From Fort Cumberland to Fort Duquesne by Gen[ll] Braddocks 125 miles in all 160 to which add the passages of rivers &c and the last 8 miles not cut. The other road,

From Raestown to the top of the Laurell Hill 46 miles.

From thence to Fort Duquesne suppose 40 or 50 miles in all 90 with no rivers to obstruct you and nothing to stop you that I can see, except that Bugbear, or tremendous pass of the Laurel Hill.

If what I say is true and those two roads are compared, I dont see that I am to Hesitate one Moment which to take, unless I take a party likewise, which I hope never to do in Army Matters.

I have not told you my Opinion, and what I think of the Affairs of the road, but to Judge at such Distance, and of a Country I never saw, nor heard spoke off but in Cap[t] Wards account, I therefore can say nothing decisive, so have sent up S[ir] John S[t] Clair in order that he may explore that new road and determine the most Ellegible to be pursued, but this I think need not hinder you from proceeding upon the new road as soon as you Can Conveniently, Altho' by the letter that I made Major Halkett write you this morning[77] with the letters contained of the situation of Gen[ll] Abercrombys affairs[78] you'l see they will at least oblige me either to proceed with Coolness and circumspection; or make a hardy march according to the Certainty of Events, of which I expect a Particular account every Moment from Gen[ll] Abercromby.

The Provincialls are all gone from this, and I proposed to have left it as yesterday with the four remaining Companies of the Highlanders, but not

---

[77] *Ante*, p. 154.
[78] Stanwix to Delancey, July 9, 1758, and Delancey to Denny, July 12, 1758 referred to *ante*, p. 148 fns. 55 and 56.

to crowd you or distress you in Provender the providing of which has been most terribly neglected, the troops now shall move slowly on, and in place of allowing the Waggon Horses, and Bat horses to make their halting days of refreshment at Raestown, you will order their Waggon Masters to conduct them backwards, and you give them days of refreshment anywhere else, otherwise we might be drove to the necessity of quiting Raestown before we choose it for want of forage and Provender for our horses, I have spoke very roundly upon this subject to S^{ir} John, who was sent up the Country from Philadelphia for no other purpose than to fix the roads and provide forage, both of which I am sorry to say it, are yet to begin—but all this *entre nous* until I see you [*Continued in Forbes' handwriting:*] I have been and am still but poorly, by a Cursed flux, but shall move day after to morrow, My Complim^{ts} to My Cousin Mr Glen and I thank you for the Care you take of him. I send You enclosed a melancholly list[79] of our killed and wounded at this very very odd Affair. *porter vous bien, et ne beuver point D'eau*

I am S^{ir} Y^r Most ob^t hum^{le} Servt

Jo fforbes

This letter was begun two days ago but finished Carlisle 25th July
Col^o Bouquet
[*Endorsed:*] General Forbes 24th July 1758 answered the 31st d^o.

* * * * *

Forbes to Abercromby
[AB 474 L.S.; P.R.O. W.O. 34:44, f. 339, Copy; Extract, P.R.O. C.O.; 5: 50 (L.C. trans.) pp. 403-415]

[Carlisle, July 25, 1758]

S^{ir}.

I wrote you a letter, a few days ago[80] upon receiving an Express from Governor Denny acquainting me[81] that orders had transmitted by Gen^{ll} Stanwix to Mr Delancey[82] to raise the Militia of New York—and that he had laid an Embargo upon the shipping at Philadelphia in consequence of

---

[79] B.M., Add. MSS. 21643, f. 152. Printed in *Pa. Arch.* 1st series, III, 203, and 5th series, I, 239, and *Pa. Gazette,* July 27, 1758.
[80] July 18, 1758, *ante,* p. 150.
[81] No letter of this time, Denny to Forbes, found.
[82] Cf. *ante,* p. 148, footnotes 55 and 56.

like steps having been taken by M[r] Delancey—by the same Express I received some imperfect Accounts rather Surmises than particulars of a Repulse which a part of your Army had met with near Ticonderoga, but I was then willing to flatter myself that some of your advanced Detachments had been only concerned,—since that time I have received letters[83] with so many particulars about the killed and wounded that there is little room left to doubt of the Attacks having been pretty General at least with the Regular Troops but as things of that kind are always represented in the worst light by the Publick I am still willing to hope that your loss has not been near so considerable as it has been reported.

They talk of no less than 97 Officers with 1500 Men being killed and wounded, and that You have been obliged to repass the lake—tho they add that it is with an Intention to return when Officers are appointed and the Troops have been again put into order.

You'll I dare say do me the justice to believe that I was extremely unhappy upon receiving this sort of Information I cannot express the uneasiness and anxiety which I have been under since about you and the situation of your Army.

I am sensible of the Distress you must be under at present, if so many of Your regular Officers are rendered unfit for the service at a time when you can so ill spare them, as for the Gentlemen who have been killed I most sincerely regret them, but there is no help for misfortunes of the kind, and tis to be hoped that You'll find such resources in your numbers as to be still able to carry the service shich was projected, and I must beg of You to direct one of your Aid de Camps to give me some account of this affair 'tis the greatest favour you can do me. You'l by that means relieve me from the mellancholly state of uncertainty which I am in at present about you, your Army and our Friends.

I have already informed you[84] that I had sent Col° Bouquet to form at Post at Raystown, things are there in pretty great forwardness—Scouting partys have been sent out with the best Guides we could find, and according to the reports which some of them have made the road over the Allegany mountains and the Laurel Ridge will be found practicable for Carriages, which will be of infinite Consequence, will facilitate our matters by shortening the march about seventy miles besides the advantage of having no rivers to pass, as we shall keep the Yeogheny upon our left.

---

[83] Not found, but cf. *Pa. Arch.* 1st series, III, 472, a letter in French of July 14, 1758, from the Camp at Lake George, possibly a copy of a letter to Forbes.

[84] Probably a reference to the letter of June 27, 1758, *ante*, p. 126.

I have at last with great difficulty got the Waggons Bat Horses and provisions in to some sort of order.

I have sent Detachments to the several Forts to the Eastward of the Susquehanah to Guard the Frontiers of Pennsylvania on that side—care shall be taken of the other Posts.

The troops are all in motion from the different Posts where they have been stationed in order to be assembled at Reastown, but I have retarded the march of some of them upon the route from this place, as I am unwilling to bring them together till the route is finally determined, and till I am able to keep up constantly three months provisions at Raestown by throwing in fresh supplies according to the consumption, for with less it would not be safe or expedient to proceed.

The Artillery marched yesterday from Shippensburgh and proceeds directly to Raestown and I send of S^{ir} John St Clair tomorrow to be assisting to Col^{o} Bouquet in making the projected route over the Laurel Hill on the other side of which, about 45 miles from Raystown I intend to form another Post to open the Communication, and to have a greater facility of sending out Scouting parties Intelligence, for the Indians as well as provincials are not fond of going so far from the advanced Posts as they are obliged to do at present.

The troops have hitherto been so scattered in this Province as well as in Virginia, so many Detachments have been ordered to make roads &c that 'tis impossible to give you a state of their numbers—you well know that the Provinciall Officers are so very little exact in that matter that 'tis impossible even to depend upon their reports, when they are pleased to make them, which does not always happen.

I intend to march in a few days with the last Division of the Highland Battalion, I shall carry on the Detachments from the several posts, and Forts upon the road—and I think the whole may be assembled about the 6th of next month.

I shall inform you of our Numbers and situation, and shall be extreamly happy to receive any Commands or Directions which you are pleased to give me.

I wish you health and happiness with much Success in Your next Attack and with Sincerity & Regard

Y^{r} most ob^{t} & most hum^{ble} Servt.

Jo fforbes.

Carlisle 25th July 1758
To Gen^{ll} Abercromby

*   *   *   *   *

Halkett to Bouquet
[B.M., Add. MSS. 21640, f. 115. A.L.S.]

Camp at Carlisle 31st July 1758

Dear Sir

The General is so much indispos'd this day by taking Phisick, that he is not able to acknowledge the Receipt of your letter[85] himselfe, and as he thinks that no time should be lost in makeing of the new Road, he has directed me to inform you, that you are immediately to begin the opening of it agreable to manner he wrote to you in his last letter,[86] as he sees all the advantages he can propose by going that Route, and will avoid innumerable Inconveniencys he would encounter was he to go to the other, he is at the same time extremely surpris'd at the partial disposition that appears in those Virginia Gentlemans sentiments, as there can be no sort of Comparison between the two Routes, when you consider the situation of the Troops now at Reastown, & that there is not the least reason to expect, that we shall meet with any dificulties but what may be easily surmounted. The Alleghany mountains the General thinks is the first thing to be well look'd after as he thinks your greatest difficulty will be there. The 100 Carrying horses were all Review'd and approv'd of by Sr John St Clair before that captain Callendar sent them from hence which surprises the General fo find they are already so bad as represented.

As Captain Hay is by this time arriv'd at Reastown, you will please to order all the Men who have any knowledge of the great Gun Exercise, to practice dayly under his direction, that they may be employ'd in that service when necessary.

The Express arrivd here last night, with the letters that came to Philadelphia by the Post, but to the astonishment of the General he has not had scrape of a Pen from General Abercromby, or any of his Family since this misfortune. Captain Cunningham[87] is sent to England in the packet with the accounts to the Ministry.

Major Proby[88] (who was kill'd) commanded the Pickets who made the first attacks support'd by the Grenadiers commanded by Col: Haldimand[89]

---

[85] Of July 26, 1758, in French, B.M., Add. MSS. 21640, f. 110, A.C.S.

[86] July 23, 1758, *ante,* p. 156.

[87] Captain James Cunningham of the 45th regiment, formerly aide-de-camp to Lord Loudoun.

[88] Major Thomas Proby of the 55th regiment.

[89] Frederick Haldimand (1718-1791), colonel commandant of a battalion of the 60th regiment, later governor and commander-in-chief in Canada, 1778-1785, lieutenant-general and baronet. Consult the *D. N. B.*

(Slightly Wounded) then followed the Regulars in Corps who ought to have be [sic] Supported by the Provintials—great blame laid upon the Reconoiterers for their Reports Mr Prevost is made Brigadier General and at present acting with General Abercromby.

I am with great regard Dear Sir
Your most obedient humble Servant

Francis Halkett
Brigade Major

To Colonel Bouquet

[*Endorsed:*] from General Forbes by Brigade Major Halkett 31st July Answered[90] the 3rd Aug^t.

*   *   *   *   *

Halkett to Washington*
[L.C. MSS. Papers of Washington. Vol. VIII. A.L.S.

Camp at Carlisle 2^d August 1758

Dear Washington

I Reciived your letter,[91] & Returns[92] from Fort Cumberland.—as to my giving you my advice about the covers for your locks, I think you are the properest judge what cane be done at F. Cumberland, being immediately upon the Spot, and we can send you no assistance from hence, as many as can, I would provide, those you cannot, their is no helpe for, their Blankets will always be a greate safety to them.———

It is necessary the Troops from Virginia—should have a Brigade Major the same as Pinsylvania, and the General expects that you will be provided with one again[st] you join, it is intirely a Provintial afair, & to be of your own appointing, the recommendation General Forbes leaves to you, if it is to be Stewart,[93] he must be as Captain to your Battalion, & Brigade Major, an other Officer must be appointed Captain to the Troop, he already holds two Commissions, both as Captain in your Battalion, & of the light Troop, his haveing more would would be inconvenient.—Major Shippen has ten Shillings pr day extrordinary, allowd him by the Commissioners of Pinsylvania, for being Brigade Major.

---

[90] In French, B.M., MSS. 21640, f. 121, A.C.S.
* Printed, Hamilton, *Letters to Washington,* III, 5.
[91] Of July 21, 1758, in *Writings* (Fitzpatrick, ed.), II, 244.
[92] Found in the MSS Papers of Washington, in the Library of Congress.
[93] Probably Captain Robert Stewart.

Make my appology to Captain Stewart for not being able to write to him at this time, he will send his Return of the Troop to me, the same as he did with General Braddock, as he is a distinct Corps, the detachment that he sent down to Lancaster, are all sent to Raestown.

The General has been much afflicted with the Flux, he still is extreamly weak, but I am in hopes he will soon be able to set out for Raestown. I am Dear Washington

Your most obedient Servant
and ever well wisher
Francis Halkett

* * * * *

Halkett to Bouquet
[B.M., Add. MSS. 21640, f. 117. A.L.S.]

Camp at Carlisle 2ᵈ August 1758

Dear Sir

As the General recovers but slowley, & has frequent Returns of his most painful simptoms, he desires that you will order Lieuᵗ James Grant[94] of the Highland Regiment, whom the General has a confidence in as a surgeon, to set out immediately for this place, under an escort of the Light horse, and to wait upon Major Grant upon his coming here; to prevent any kind of allarm (which there is no Reason for) you will keep all this from Mr. Glen & the troops with you, as this is only done for the satisfaction of the General, & at the desire of Doctor Russell.[95] I am Dear Sir

Your most obedient humble Servant

Francis Halkett

P.S. You will send express back with Mʳ Grant whom you will desire to loose no time in comeing. The General has nothing to say to you, as he wrote this day[96] by Captain Callendar You will please to Furnish Mʳ Grant with whatever will be necessary to expedite him.

[*Addressed:*] To Colonel Bouquet Commanding at Reastown
[*Endorsed:*] Major Halkett 2ᵈ Aug.

* * * * *

---

[94] A common name in Scotch regiments, but probably the physician in attendance upon Forbes in his last days. Cf. Grant to Bouquet, February 20, 1759, *post*, p. 296.

[95] Doctor William Russel, Surgeon and Sub Director to the General Hospital.

[96] *Post*, p. 164.

Forbes to Bouquet
[B.M., Add. MSS. 21640, f. 119, A.L.S.]

Carlisle Augst 2^d [1758]

Sir.

Yesterday and no sooner, I receiv'd a letter[97] from Gen^{ll} Abercromby, with a tollerable confused acco^{tt} of what happened at Tienderoga the 6th and 8th Last month, without comming to the Conclusion that I wanted, which was to know what he proposed now to do, or what assistance he might want from me by way of Diversion, or what Diversion he was now to make to prevent the Ennemy, sending of reinforcements or Detachments this way, To all which he says nothing, only that he desires me to be much upon my Guard, having heard that the Enemy had already detatched this way and that some time ago.

That he had sent Brig^{dr} Gen^{ll} Stanwix with 5600 Men up the Mohawk river, with 2000 of which he is to rebuild the Fort[98] that Gen^{ll} Webb destroyed at the Oneyda Carrying place, and that Lt Col^o Bradstreet was to command the 3600 men, to endeavour to attack Fort Cataraqui[99] or prevent Mon^r Levy[100] with a large body of troops from penetrating this way or falling upon the Mohawk river, or if he could not do that to fall upon Monsr Levy in his return after perhaps having baffled me, and chaced away Mr Stanwix, This is the whole, which is really saying nothing far less doing any thing to the purpose. And as to himself he says nothing only he is encamped where Fort Willm Henry was, where I suppose he will rebuild the Fort.

In short my Dear Sir they take but very little Care about us, so wee must double our diligence, and try to do a little for ourselves. I would not be understood that as things are circumstanced, wee ought to Run the risque of meeting with a severe repulse, by any precipitate march of Comming immediatly to blows with the Ennemy, or by a tardy approach give the Ennemy the time to strengthen themselves, and so to render our attempts, Impracticable At present (I am sorry to say it) In spite of all the Endeavours

---

[97] Abercromby to Forbes, July 18, 1758, AB, 453, copy. Note also, same to same, July 23, 1758, AB, 465, copy.

[98] Fort Stanwix.

[99] This important expedition accomplished its purpose, August 26, 1758, thus rendering Forbes the greatest service. Note the Plan of Instructions of January 25, 1758, *ante*, p. 31.

[100] Francois Gaston Levis (1720-1787), prominent subordinate of General Montcalm. Consult *N.B.G.*

wee have used, Wee have not yet been able to learn almost anything with regard to Fort du Quesne or the Ennemys strength there now, or what reinforcements they expect, and at what time, so untill something of this matter can be cleared up and ascertained, Wee are, like people in the Dark, perhaps going headlong to Destruction, So for our own sakes fresh tentatives must be tryed for fresh Intilligence.

I was thoroughly convinced that our late meeting with the Indians at Philadelphia would have produced very good effects, if this unfortunate affair of Gen[ll] Abercrombys, does not make them change opinions, or make them at least delay entering into our Confederacy. Bee that as it will, wee must try to know their Intentions, by sending some small party among the Chieff men upon Beaver creek, who have lately answered[1] the messages wee sent them, by assuring us that they were heartily weary of the warr and would be very glad of a peace, and that they would willingly return to their old habitations. This was the answer of Newcoma, Kustologa Kukyusenny & Pisquitomin, the heads of the Delawares,[2] and all living upon the Beaver creek, so there can not be any danger in sending these, nor a great deal in another party above fort du quesne towards Venango, where wee might learn what reenforcements the French have lately had, & what new works or Intrenchments they have lately carried on at their Fort.

I am told that Col[o] Burd has ane Indian with him w[d] be a proper person to employ, and that there is one Ensign Crawford[3] who speaks all the Indian Languages would likewise be proper, but as I think no time should be lost in doing this and as Cap[t] Calendar[4] and M[r] Frazier[5] knows the proper people I have sent him with this up to you, and as he has bought and Contracted for the Bats horses, he will be able to answer what questions you may ask him, but I objected to both horses and saddles at first, and S[ir] John promised me to see the Saddles mended and fitted which I think ought to be done before payed for.

I made Halkett write you the other day[6] when I really was unable myself—he told you my opinion of the Laurell Hill road, and that I thought it

---

[1] *Pa. Col. Rec.*, VIII, 144-145, and cf. Orndt to Denny, July 24, 1758, *Pa. Arch.*, 1st series, III, 490.

[2] On these chiefs, consult Sipe, *Indian Chiefs.*

[3] Ensign Hugh Crawford, of the first battalion of the Pennsylvania regiment, an old fur trader.

[4] Seemingly Robert Callendar, an old fur trader, captain in the first battalion of the Pennsylvania regiment.

[5] Probably John Fraser, the famous fur trader.

[6] July 31, 1758, *ante*, p. 161.

ought to be sett about directly, as it is good to thave two strings to one Bow.

I have been in a dismall apprehension as to Forrage for horses, for which purpose I have orderd all the justices of the peace to order the parishes to send on their forrage, to be payed at the current price of the Country, & to bring it to the places upon our route most contiguous to them, I have desired M^r S^tClair^7 to transmitt Copys^8 of my letters to the Justices, to S^ir John.

As You have Scythes and Sickles might not you cause [*sic*] make Hay all arround you & along the new road as they proceed.

I have been tormented day and night these 14 Days with what they call a Flux, and what I call a Violent Constipation. I hope I shall now gett the better of it altho I neither eat nor sleep. However as my out partys has now almost brought in all the Rye and oats in this country, and that the 80 Highlanders have now joined us, I shall begin and move up the Country in 2 or 3 days at farthest, altho I dare say my presence is no ways necessary where you have the Command.

I salute my Coz: Glen, tell him not to weary, and, make the place as agreable to him as it will admitt off.

Archie^9 has gott the Flux it is a general Distemper here, owing to the Lime Water, I hope your working and scouting partys, keep you free from it. If ane hospitall is wanted Doctor McLean^10 ought to open one, for that distemper is particularly infectious, so pray make the Houses of office be filled up every other day and all kept sweet & Clean.

I am My D^r S^ir Y^r most ob^t hum^le Servt

Jo: fforbes.

Pray keep strict patronilles and a Constant good look out, nor do I suppose but your Piquets are *au Bivouac.*

C: Bouquet.

[*Endorsed:*] Genl Forbes Aug. 2^d

*   *   *   *   *

---

^7 Misspelling for Sinclair, James.

^8 Not found.

^9 Colonel Archibald Montgomery.

^10 Doctor Lau McLean, army surgeon, several of whose letters are among the Bouquet Papers.

Forbes to Abercromby
[AB 501 L.S.; P.R.O. W.O. 34:44, 317.]

Camp at Carlisle [August*] July 3ᵈ 1758

Sir

I have day before yesterday the favour of Yours[11] from Lake George but without any date, as well as my own to you[12] was. However I was glad to see it at any rate, to be freed from the many idle reports, that will keep one uneasy and in suspense spite of all your resolves to the Contrary.

I regrett extreamly your loss of officers, as that appears indeed to be the only and great one, for it is to be supposed that many of the wounded may recover, and some perhaps soon able to do duty again.

The fort at the Oneida Carrying place, I was of opinion,[13] ought to have been the first thing sett about after our arrival from Hallifax last year. And I believe nothing hindered it, but a tenderness of Lord Loudoun for General Webb. For it must strike everyone who looks into a mapp that a good large Fort is absolutely necessary there, for the Protection of all the [Mohaw]k river. I ought to rememember you that this fort ought not to be situate close to the river, but at a distance so as to Command it, with a broad ditch cut from the river up to the fort, with a sluice upon it, by which you secure all your Battoes &c under the walls of the fort, and if the Situation will allow you may have a wet ditch all round it.

Lᵗ. Colᵒ Bradstreets proposal[14] last winter, was in itself a Chimera. But might have been attended with some advantages that made my Lord agree to it in some measure.

Iˢᵗ. The winter expedition against Ticonderoga was then in Embryo, and it was thought the Building so many Battoes at Schenecady &c would draw the Eyes of the French towards the Lake Ontario &c., particularly if the Fort at the Carrying place was sett about at the same time. That if the winter Expedition failed the Battoes that were promised to be built by the 20ᵗʰ of March might then be made use of in Conveying my Lord and the troops destined against Ticonderoga early in the spring down Lake George,

---

* In spite of "July" here and at the end, it is obvious from the contents that this was an inadvertence and August the time of writing.

[11] Probably the letter of July 18, 1758, AB 453, but note the letter of July 23, 1758, AB 468.

[12] A reference to Forbes' letter of June 27, 1758, *ante,* p. 126.

[13] This thoughtful paragraph reveals Forbes as the adviser of Loudoun in 1757, and Abercromby in 1758, in regard to Fort Stanwix.

[14] This statement credits Bradstreet with the idea, however chimerical, found in the Plan of Instructions of January 25, 1758, *ante,* p. 31.

of which you have seen the necessity there was of setting early about them —Bradstreet had another argument; that from good Intelligence, The Garrison of Frontenac was weak and in want of Provisions, and at that season could not be easily supplyed and that consequently he had a fairer chance of success. But in all events, that he could not well fail of either Burning or bringing away their shipping, which lay unrigged about a mile from the Fort. Howfar these schemes or arguments may be good now, I do not know, but I am sure the Preventing of troops coming this way and the Defence of the Mohawk river are of the greatest Consequence at Present.

I remember Bradstreet had likewise Niagara in view, which indeed would be a great stroke, but how are any of those to be carryed into execution without a multitude of Battoes; and is it not too late to begin and build those now.

I should be glad to know your Intelligence about the reinforcements said to be sent this way, and about what time they should have come, for I can learn little or nothing of their state at Fort Du Quesne, notwithstanding the numberless Partys I have sent out, and the many particulars & Indian traders that I have employed to gett me Intelligence of those things.

I had great hopes last week and have still, of bringing back all the Delawares &c from the Ohio, altho I fancy the French will avail themselves of the attempt upon Ticonderoga, which may make some of those Indians change sides, But I am sure of some familys coming over immediatly from whom we may learn something otherwise I shall act in the dark, which is not rashly to be hazarded, unless our affairs were desperate, which I hope is far from being the Case.

I do not believe we shall have one Indian left, As I hear that 46 of Byrds have left him at Fort Cumberland, and Bouquet leads a dog's life with those at Raystown.

I wish S^{ir} William would send those Cherokees back that he has with him, as they appeared much our friends.

There is more trouble with the small Artillery I have than with all our Train in Flanders nor can I get them to move, altho they have the best of every tackle & horses they marched from this ten days ago and are not got to Raystown yet.

I am therefore obliged to loiter some days upon the road, to prevent us being all together at the same time, at Raystown, where want of Herbage would oblige us to separate in four days at most, S^{ir} John having served me as he did Gen^{ll} Braddock promising every thing and doing no one Individual thing in the world, except confusing what he undertakes.

There are 700 Bats horses and Bats sadles provided by him, The first days tryal of the sadles gauled all the Horses into the bone, so they must everyone be refitted & new stuffed, and when that is done, Col° Bouquet writes me[15] that the Horses can scarce carry their own weight, far less any burthen.

I have been very much out of order by what D[r]. Bassett[16] will call the flux, which is a most violent constipation attended with Inflamation in the Rectum, violent pain & total suppression of the Urine, In short I have been most miserable nor am I yet much better, but from this I can not move these 4 days, as I must now buy or take by force all the Oats and Indian Corn in this Country and send it before me, otherwise [*mutilated*] er Come, and we can no more move without provender and forage, than without Provisions.

[*In Forbes handwriting:*]

We have neither seen nor heard of any of the Enemy Indians this month by past, nor have wee had any one man either killed or Carried off. It is true wee are at a great distance and I have constantly a number of partys out.

July 4th   I am D[r] S[ir] Y[r] most ob[t] & most hum[le] Serv[t]

                                                        Jo fforbes.

Gen[ll] Abercromby.

*   *   *   *   *

Halkett to Bouquet
[B.M., Add. MSS. 21640, f. 124. A.L.S.]

                                    Carlisle 7th August 1758
Dear Sir

I have the pleasure to inform you that the General recovers daily, but from the length of his Indisposition, & eating nothing, he was greatly reduc'd & still very weak, he goes out in his Chariot every evening which does him great good, & I think will soon set him on his legs again. The other Invalides Captain Anderson[17] & Lieu[t] Wright[18] of the Artillery, are recover'd entirely, and will set out for Reastown the day after to morrow, along with Lieu[t] S[t] clair, and Serjeant Morton

---

[15] July 31, 1758, B.M., Add. MSS. 21640, f. 112, A.C.S.

[16] Doctor Bassett, one of the four surgeons attached to the medical forces of the British army.

[17] Captain Anderson, not identified. Note his employment in charging the artillery for the Delaware River forts, July 14, 1758, *Pa. Col. Recs.*, VIII, 147. Cf. Forbes to Amherst, January 26, 1759, *post*, p. 285.

[18] Lieutenant John Wright of the 45th regiment?

The General is extreamly well satisfyed with your accounts of the Road, and very glad to find that you have enterd upon the makeing of it. He has been much employ'd in ingageing of Forrage, all that is to be got in the Country he has bespoake, & thinks their is a prospect of being provided with a suffitient quantity which will be laid in here & at Fort Fredrick

Their are no news stirring here to tell you, I hope by the end of the week the General· will be upon the Road to Reastown, till that, I have the pleasure of seeing you there, I must bid you adue, assuring you that I am with great sincerity Dr Sir

Your most obedient humble Servant &c

Francis Halkett

PS—Please to present my Compliments to Mr. Glen.

[*Addressed:*] To Colonel Bouquet Commanding at Raestown
[*Endorsed:*] Major Halkett 7th August.

* * * * *

Forbes to Bouquet
[B.M., Add. MSS. 21640, f. 133. A.L.S.]

[Carlisle, Aug. 9, 1758]

My Dear Sir.

I write you those few lines, to acquaint you that I am now able to write, after 3 weeks of a most violent and tormenting Distemper, which thank God seems now much abated as to pain, but has left me as weak as a new born Infant. However I hope to have strength enough, to sett out from this upon Fryday next.

I have by this delay or rather stay here, been enabled to provide what otherwise must have created ane Intire stop to all proceedings, and that is forrage, From Raes Town to this, there was none, so no wonder Your Waggon horses fell away, and the nonsense of telling you that wee had forrage in Virginia and at Fort Cumberland was just as much to our purpose as having plenty at London.

I have sent you up some Indians with Dunlap & Hambuss,[19] I propose they should sett out Directly for Intelligence from the Ohio, M^r S^t clair will tell you my scheme for them, and Laurence Burk[20] knows all the Country about Loyall Hallan so after examining them you will give them the Directions you think proper but I think Burk ought to endeavour to

---

[19] Not otherwise identified, probably an Indian trader.
[20] Lawrence Burk, an Indian trader. Cf. Burk to Peters, July 17, 1758, *Pa. Arch.* 1st series, III, 478.

join Frederick Post,[21] who is now with the Heads of the Delawares with ane Invitation to them to return to their own Country. There names are Newcoma, Kustaloga, Pisquamin &c who have already in a manner agreed to come to us, which if they can be persuaded to do you will have every one Delaware come back to you. I suspect that they have thrown up ane Entrenchment before fort Duquesne, from the Ohio to the Monogahela but this can be easily ascertained as it may be overlooked from the high Grounds, by means of a Spying Glass.

I hope your new road advances briskly, and that from the Alegany Hill to Laurell Hill may be carrying forward by different partys, at the same Time that you are making the pass of the Allegany practicable.

By a very unguarded letter[22] of Col: Washington that Accidentally fell into my hands, I am now at the bottom, of their Scheme against this new road, a Scheme that I think was a shame for any officer to be Concerned in, but more of this at meeting. Let all out posts, advanced & working partys keep a very strikt and exact look out as no doubt the French will try something, when they come to be *Serre*. Complim[ts] to all Friends, and tell me friend Govr Glen, not to turn Indian and weary of his situation Wee shall soon make amends for the many many retardments weè have mett with, and betwixt you and I be it said, as wee are now so late, wee are yet to soon, This is a parable that I shall soon explain.

I am quite tyred but very much Y[r] most ob[t] hum[l]. Servt

Jo: fforbes.

Carlisle Aug[st] 9th

Pray let the Artillery putt all their things to rights and keep them close at it, for their dilatory doings putts me mad, Let M[r] Hay prepare some Sky Rocketts as the best signalls in those hellish woods. Adieu.

I wrote you at First that I designed Major Armstrong should have gone on from Laurell Hill, to try his fortune in getting Intelligence or a prisoner, and to have nothing to do with making the road, as I thought his Fanatick zeal would make him do the first well, and that I thought he knew nothing of making of roads.

C: Bouquet.

[*Addressed:*] To Colonel Bouquet Commanding the troops at Raestown.
[*Endorsed:*] Gen[l] Forbes 9th Aug.

* * * * *

[21] Christian Frederick Post (*c.* 1710-1785), lay missionary to the Indians, famous for journals of his negotiations with Indians. Consult the *D.A.B.*

[22] Washington to Halkett, August 2, 1758, *Writings* (Fitzpatrick, ed.), II, 260.

Halkett to Bouquet
[B.M., Add. MSS. 21640, f. 135. A.L.S.]

[Carlisle, Aug. 10, 1758]

Dear Sir

This day the General Receiv'd your letter,[23] with an account of the Revolt of 50 Cherokee Indians, who were begun their March to Fort Loudoun, to demand the presents laid up in store by the General, to have been given them at the end of the Campaign; in consiquence of which Major Grant[24] marches this afternoon with two of Highland Companys he is to continue his Route to Fort Loudoun with the utmost expedition and expects to be there to morrow afternoon, as he goes free of all Incumbrances upon that account.

In regard to the provisions, the General has fix'd that afair entirely with Mr Hoops, who writes[25] to Mr Howell Express, to morrow. The General is so much Recover'd, that he proposes to begin his March to morrow after noon, with all the Highlanders, & light horse that are here, & his arrival at Raestown will I believe be a very welcome sight to you. I wish it could have been sooner.

I am Dear Sir

Your most obedient & most humble Servant

Francis Halkett

PS I inclose the Papers I [o]ught not to call them news [for] they old but they will [Se]rve one use or another
[*Endorsed:*] Major Halkett 10th Aug:

*   *   *   *   *

Forbes to Abercromby
[AB 527. L.S.; P.R.O. W.O. 34:44; f. 343 Copy]

[Carlisle 11th August 1758]

S^ir

I received the favour of yours[26] of July the 23^d, an almost impertinent Curiosity of not only having numberless returns from each of my out posts upon the frontier, but likewise visiting them myself, Joined to a flux, at last fairly knocked me up, which is the reason I did not answer your Last much sooner—having been miserably bad.

---

[23] Of. August 8, 1758, B.M., Add. MSS. 21640, f. 126, A.C.S. and a draft of it, *ibid.*, f 130.

[24] Major James Grant of the 77th regiment.

[25] Letter not found.   [26] AB 465, copy.

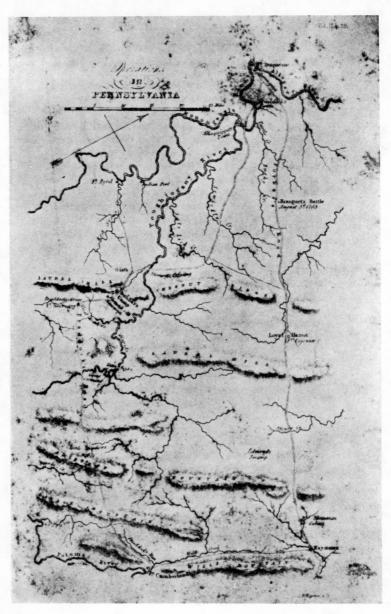

Map of Western Pennsylvania, derived from the Bouquet Papers, as reproduced in Jared Sparks, *Life and Writings of Washington* II, 38, showing Forbes Route from Fort Bedford to Fort Duquesne.

A Jealousy arising amongst the Virginians that I was to direct my march by another route, than by Fort Cumberland, came such a length as to be most Singularly Impertinent nor Could I Discover the bottom, or cause from whence this sprung untill that Col° Washington in a letter[27] to Major Halkett fairly shows the leader and adviser of their foolish suggestions upon this Head. I believe I have now got the better of the whole by letting them Very roundly know, that their Judging and determining of my actions and intentions before that I had communicated my opinion to them, was so premature, and was taking the lead in so ridiculous a way that I could by no means suffer it—

The new road from Rayston to Loyal Hanning on the other side of the Laurell Hill has been thoroughly reconnoitered and altho many bad steps, with very steep Ascents and descents at times, Yet S^{ir} John has assured me[28] that is is fully as good as the first 40 miles of General Braddock's route.

I have had these 8 or 10 days about 1200 men employed upon it so a few days more will compleat it, and when the Deposite for the Stores at Loyal Hanning is in any sort of readiness for our reception, I shall move forward from Raystown to Loyal Hanning, from whence at any time I can proceed to the Ohio, as all that Country is mostly large nut and Oak wood without any Brush below.

The Enemy has as yet given us no disturbance nor do I believe that they suspect my coming this way whereas along Mr Braddocks route from the Great meadows to the Great Crossing of the Yoghegenny, they have reconoitered every pass and Defile, and have proceded so far as already to have a *Batis de bois* where of necessity we must have passed had we been Confined to that road intirely.

I believe I wrote you[29] the distress, I was in for want of magazines of forage along my route towards Raystown, and a large magazine there to have carried forward along with us—I have done everything in my power to remedy this Evil, but not so soon, as not to feel very sensibly the Effects of that neglect; Our Waggon Horses being almost intirely wrought down for want of forage, so that they must have some days of ease to be enabled to carry up provisions and forage to Raystown, during which Interval we are still consuming of both at Raystown, notwithstanding for these 8 or 10 days by past I have put a stop to the troops marching in there, or the waggon and Baggage Horses to make any halt in that neighborhood, in order to preserve the Generall magazine.

---

[27] Of August 2, 1758, *Writings* (Fitzpatrick, ed.), II, 260.
[28] Statement not found.   [29] August 3, 1758, *ante*, p. 168.

I mentioned likewise to you[30] the jobb, or rather the Scandolous imposition of the 700 Packsadles, which after ruining a number of Horses are now useless untill I can get fresh Stuffing up from Lancaster.

M[r] Killby's Deputes M[r] Howell and M[r] Hoops may be extream good people in their way, and very proper for providing a Garrison of 100 men, but their Ideas & ways of judging of things are so narrow and Contracted, that all my Rhetorick Cannot drive it into their Heads that it is better for me to have a months provisions over, as that the Army should run a risque of being stopt for the want of one days Subsisting.

They have no notion but that live stock is to Supply every thing, and therefore for my blood I can get no Salt provisions, Altho representing to them in the strongest terms that 3 or 4 frosty mornings (which you may expect about the latter end of this month) will destroy all the pasture, and the price of Carrying up forage for their maintenance will by no means answer were it to be got, and further that a Skulking party of Enemy Indians may Hamstring their whole stock in one night, Altho kept in different parties, and a good deal asunder one from another.

I am much obliged to you for the Intelligence you send me, that the Enemy have sent reinforcements my way, as likewise for your putting me on Guard of being very watchfull upon that account.

There is scarce a day past these two months that I have not thought the knowledge of the Enemys Strength the first and principal Object of my Views, and therefore have let no moment pass during all that time of employing numbers publickly and privately to bring me some satisfactory accounts of the Enemy, which as yet I have realy not been able to accomplish to any purpose—As I get a little nigher I hope to be more fortunate, for it is a terrible thing to be Groping in the Dark.

Col[o] Byrd's Indians left him at Fort Cumberland 10 days ago, and are gone home, those Indians at Raystown are following them fast 50 of them having left Col[o] Bouquet the day before yesterday; he writes me[31] they were to come to Fort Loudoun to demand the presents designed for them and laid by there for them till the latter end of the Campaign, where if they were refused they would undoubtedly commit some outrage, and therefore advises the giving of them those Presents—As I have no mortal about me that understands Indian affairs or their Genius, I therefore immediately Detached Major Grant and 200 Highlanders to Fort Loudoun, there to represent to them in moderate terms, how Grosly they had abused and

---

[30] *Ibid.*
[31] In French, August 8, 1758, B.M., Add. MSS. 21640, f. 126, A.C.S.

imposed upon us for so many months, and now to leave us at the only time they could be of any service to us, that the Value of their presents was nothing to the King of England, and that Altho we had both the power and justice on our side to have retained those presents, yet we freely gave them in order to shew their Nation that every promise made on our part would have been fulfilled, and any services done us would over and above met with suitable rewards, he is likewise to beg if they will still stay with us, but if he finds they will not, he is to caution them against all outrage and Violence against the Inhabitants of the Countrys they may pass thro—

I have wrote upon this Head to M[r] Fauquier Governour of Virginia,[32] M[r] Dobbs[33] & M[r] Littleton,[34] but when I may have their answers[35] I do not know having wrote to M[r] Littleton & M[r] Dobbs several letters[36] since I came to Philadelphia but have never received any answers.

I propose Sending Col° Bouquet up to Loyal Hanning there to augment what he may find necessary and to follow up by Degrees with the Artillery and the rest of the Army—But the length of my route, and the number of posts that I must occupie to preserve a Communication reduces my numbers almost to nothing—Besides I must have the Appearance of troops at Fort Cumberland and of marching that way, In order to be a Blind that I may advance the easier by the other route.

We hear nothing of Louisbourg. Altho a little good news from thence might be of great service to us at present, to Counter ballance the many lies that the French have already spread among the Indians, of the advantages they gained at Lake George, which I assure you has its Effect, as our messengers Sent to reconduct the Delawares back to us, have not yet arrived, altho hourly expected with some answer.

I thank you for the kind expressions and Professions of your last, and without further discussions or altercations upon foolish Indians affairs or Indian manadgers, I accept *de bonne Ceur* your proffer of friendship and assure you that you shall always find me ready and willing of Shewing to you at all times every mark of a Grateful friendship, that shall ever fall in my way, Being with sincere Regard D[r] S[ir]

Y[r] most obed[t]. & most hum[le] Serv[t]

Jo: fforbes.

Carlisle 11th August
To His Excellency Gen[ll] Abercrombie—

---

[32] Not found.   [33] Not found.   [34] Not found.   [35] Not found.   [36] None found.

On His Maj^{ties} Service

[*Addressed:*] To His Excell^{cy}
Major Generall Abercrombie Commander
in Chieff
of His Majestys Forces in

North America
Albany &c

[*Stamped:*] NEW YORK
[*Countersigned:*] Will. Denny
[*Endorsed:*] Brig^r: Genl Forbes.
            Carlisle 11^t. August 1758

*   *   *   *   *

Halkett to Sharpe*
[Md.H.S. Portfolio No. 4, Papers and Letters. Letter No. 40. A.L.S.]

Shippinsburgh 13th August 1758.
Sir

Last night General Forbes arriv'd here where, he met with an Express[87]
from Colonel Bouquet, informing him of fifity Catawbaws and other Indians haveing come to our assistance at Winchester, they are in great want
of every thing, particularely that artikle of Blankets, in which we ourselves
are greatly distressed—The General therefore desire you will be so good
to order three hundred pairs to be bought at Baltimore, ore else where, as
they most conveniently can, and immediately be sent up to Reas town,
where they will be paid upon delivery. He begs pardon for giveing you this
trouble, but hopes the good of the service which require the most speedy
supply, will plead an excuse for the liberty that he takes. I am Sir with
great respect
                    Your most obedient humble Servant
                                        Francis Halkett
Governor Sharp.

*   *   *   *   *

* Printed, *Md. Arch.* IX, 238.
[87] Bouquet to Forbes, in French, August 11, 1758, B.M., Add. MSS. 21640, f. 137,
A.C.S.

Forbes to Bouquet
[B.M., Add. MSS. 21640, f. 139. A.L.S.]

Shippensburg 15th August 1758

Sir

I had yours of the 11th of August[38] two nights ago, and I thought to have carryed an answer and remedy to most of the disagreeable things you write of myself, but my journey here from Carlisle raised my flux & pains to so intollerable a degree Yesterday morning, that I was obliged to stop here and may not get away this day or two.

I sent Major Grant some days ago to Fort Loudoun to meet the Cherokees, where I hope he has either persuaded them to return to Raestow, or has induced them to stay till I arrive, where I should have tryed the same thing, but if all that 'would not do he was to give them their presents and they might then return home.

Col° Montgomery with the rest of the Highlanders Joins Major Grant this night or tomorrow morning at Fort Loudoun, when Major Grant will sett out with a proper Escorte to Join you at Raestown.

I Beg that Capt Bullen and those Catawbas newly arrived may be taken proper Care off but not Spoiled, that we may have at least the appearance of a few Indians amongst us.

M^r S^tClair will acquaint you what I proposed doing with Dunlap, Lawrence Burk and those Delaware Indians that went along with them if you think the scheme plausible, I beg it might be put in practise directly taking care to let Ambrose and the other Indians have proper Arms and necessaries for warr as they got nothing from us.

I have sent into Maryland[39] for 3 or 400 pair of Blanketts, when they will arrive God knows; so you must Borrow or do the best thing you can for the Catawbas.

My Intelligence[40] from S^{ir} William Johnson in the Mohawks Country is that the French have certainly sent reinforcements to Fort Duquesne, and yet I can by no means learn by where these Detachments passed or wether they be yet arrived at the Fort or not, which to us is a very material circumstance to know, because if reinforced I should think they would send Detachments out to reconnoiter us.

I have never seen any Good yet come from those small scouting parties of any Good Intelligence receiv'd from the Indians, am therefore still of

[38] In French, B.M., Add. MSS. 21640, f. 137, A.C.S.
[39] Halkett to Sharpe, August 13, 1758, *ante*, p. 176.
[40] Not found.

opinion that a Strong party such as I proposed[41] under Major Armstrong capable of supporting and bringing of itself off, and when nigh the Enemy sending small partys for Intelligence, might be of considerable Service by always taking care of having a proper retreat.

I hope the new road goes on fast and that soon we shall be able to take post at Loyal Hanning, I see nothing that can facilitate this more than by still amusing the Enemy by pushing Considerable parties along Mr Braddock's route, which parties might endeavour to try to find communications betwixt the two roads where they approach the nearest, or where most likely such passages can be found.

As it will be necessary very soon now to make a disposition of our small Army I beg you will give your thoughts a little that way, at present I think the greatest part ought to be assembled at Raestown to make our main push by that road, while Col^o Washington, or some other Officer might push along the other road, and might Join us if a Communication can be found when called upon. But this is only an Idea in <u>Embryo</u> however if we agree in this way of thinking it will be necessary to think of what officers and men are to be left at Fort Cumberland and the rest to be ready for marching at a Moments Warning. My Compliments to all with you, and if possible I will be at Fort Loudoun the day after tomorrow I am S^{ir}

Y^r most obed^t & most hum^{le} Servt

Jo: fforbes.

P:S: There is plenty of Cattle moving up, with a large escorte of waggons loaded with flou'r and Pork, and I sent off Mr Hoops from this, this morning who brings you the exact acc^t of every thing that is moving forward, which compared with that now at Fort Cumberland & at Raestow will give you a state of the whole. Pray ought not some of the stores to be sent for from fort Cumberland, as I understand that they have more there than they can have occasion for.

[*Endorsed:*] Genl Forbes 15th Aug

*   *   *   *   *

---

[41] Forbes to Bouquet, July 14, 1758, *ante*, p. 147. The repetition of this idea in mid-August possibly incited the ambitions of others, and led to Major Grant's defeat in September.

Forbes to Sharpe*
[Md.H.S. Portfolio 4. Papers and Letters. No. 36. L.S.]

[Shippensburgh, August 16th, 1758]

Dear Sir

I can not paint the misery and distress that I have been in since I had the pleasure of seeing you, by that damnd Flux, which I hope has now made its last effort by knocking me up some days ago at this blessed habitation, I now begin to mend a little, and hope in a day or two to gitt forward, where tho my presence be necessary, yet my absence creates no stop in carrying on our publick affairs, our new road advancing apace, so that in a few days I hope to have our advanced post on the other side of Laurell Hill pretty well advanced towards the Enemy.

My Gripes obliges me to make use of another Hand writing than my own which I know you have goodness enough to excuse as likewise the freedom that Major Halkett used with you two days ago[42] in desiring you would order some of your Correspondents to Buy 2 or 300 pair of Blanketts and send them directly to Raestown, by the first and readiest opportunity that can be procured.

I send you the enclos'd packett[43] and beg the favour that you will further it by Express to Williamsburg, as I really neither know the best nor nearest way of sending it, so shall leave Apolligizing any further till I have the pleasure of seeing you. Quere if I should march strait out, could you take the Garrison of Fort Cumberland under the protection of your Militia for a fortnight or so, in order that I might strengthen myself with all the Virginians that I shall other ways be obliged to leave there.

There is a talk this morning but with what foundation I know not as if Louisbourg should have been surrendered the 22d of last month but this surely cannot be true altho we are in daily expectations of good news from that quarter.

I am with real sincerity
My Dear Sir Y^r most obed^t & most hum^ble Servt

Jo: fforbes

Shippensburg 16th August 1758
[*Addressed:*]
        To Governour Sharpe.

_____
* Printed, *Md. Arch* IX, 238, and Stewart, *Letters of General John Forbes*, p. 27.
[42] Halkett to Sharpe, August 13, 1758, *ante*, p. 176.
[43] Contents of the packet, doubtless letters of August 16, 1758, to Fauquier, Dobbs, and Lyttelton, not found.

Forbes to Bouquet
[B.M., Add. MSS. 21640, f. 141. L.S.]

Shippensbourg Augst 18. [1758]

Sir

I wrote you two days ago,[44] since which there has nothing material occurred in the publick way worth acquainting you of.

A long letter[45] from Gen^{ll} Abercromby gives me A Disagreeable Idea of his Situation, and I realy think him much to be pityed, for his reflecting upon what is past, a rashness so contrary to his own Genius and temper, and his present unhappy situation putting it out of his power of redressing himself upon the Enemy must bear very hard upon him.

His regular Army all in partys and complainings about the promotions. His provincial Army ready to disband and go home officer and soldier, that there is no faith or trust to be put in them, a little of the rashness of the 8th might be very properly applied at present by shooting dead a Dozen of their cowardly Officers at the Head of the Line.

God be thanked we have nothing of this amongst us nor nothing to reproach our selves off neither in fool Hardiness nor delays and if we have gain'd no glaring advantage hitherto we are at least proceeding to deserve it by taking every step that prudence and proper precautions can suggest to us.

This same affair of the Forage has given me inifinite inquietude, and I am afraid that the Wagg[on] and Baggage Horses will give as much, if not remedied in time.

In carrying forward the new road, I think there might easily be a small road carried on at the same time, at about 100 yards to the right and left of it, and parrallel with it, by which our flanking partys might advance easier along with the line, I don't mean here to cut down any large trees, only to clear away the Brushwood and Saplins, so as the men either on foot or on horseback may pass the easier along.

I should think such a road could be easily carried along and pretty quick, if so, and that two file could march abreast, by making Collumns of Infantry march there, your line can always be formed much quicker and easier.

After many Intreigues with the Quakers, the Commissioners, the Governour &c. and with the Governour and Government of New Jersey and by

---

[44] Probably the letter of August 15, 1758, *ante*, p. 177.
[45] August 5, 1758, AB 509, copy.

the downright Bullying of S^{ir} William Johnson &c, I hope I have now brought a Convention with the Indians of whatever denomination or Tribe, pretty near to a Crissis, The Six Nations and all the Chief men of the Indians living to the eastward of the Lakes and upon the Ohio as far down as the Wabache, and Illinoi, have all accepted of our Belts of Invitation and friendship, and have promised to meet the Governours and Commissioners from all those different Provinces at East town in Pennsylvania by the 12th or midle of September, where I think nothing can prevent a solid peace being established with most of those Indian tribes, as the Indian Claims appear to me both Just and Moderate and what no man in their senses or in our situation with regard to the Indians would hesitate half an hour in granting them.

I flatter myself great good may be drawn to the publick from this meeting as I hope that private Interest and provincial Picques, will, and ought to be drove away from this meeting.

I am now considerably better of this flux being partly free from the excrutiating pain I sufferd, but still so weak that I can scarce bear Motion, but this a few days ease and sleep will soon restore.

As you must no doubt have a vast number of Cattle and Horses to provide for, I should be sorry that they should disturb us in our Motions, should they come to want, and make us change situations before we choose it.

There is near this place and I am told near F: Loudoun &c a great many of those deserted plantations where the Hay rots upon the Ground for want of Hands & Scythes to cut it down and make it, I have set this Garrison and most of the Inhabitants hereabouts a mowing and cuting down all they possibly can with the instruments they have, so that I hope to have always wherewith to feed a Convoy in case they be obliged to stop here on their march, I wish every other place where those deserted farms are, had done so, earlier, our waggoners then would not have had reason to complain that their Horses were starved, which I am afraid has been partly the case.

Mr Hoops is a good man but his Ideas and Compass of Genius for the subsistence and maintainance of an Army are all triffling and narrow, eternally Bothering upon the saving of sixpences & two pences, so must be manadged accordingly.

Be so good as order particular returns from every particular Corps, that when I come to Raestown I may know to a man what I can carry along with me.

I have proposed[46] to Govern^r Sharp to Garrison Fort Cumberland with

[46] August 16, 1758, *ante,* p. 179.

his militia when I set out, but I dont expect his Compliance as I don't think he has it in his power.

Be so good as Acquaint Capt St Clair that the German he employed to Buy oats at Lancaster has purchased a considerable quantity at a very extravag^t rate, and agrees for the transport of it to Carlisle at a more extravagant price. I therefore have been obliged to put a stop to that matter for a few days untill I can see how I shall redress myself.

It would not be amiss if he Capt St Clair has no more urgent Business upon hands If he took a step down this way to settle those magazines at the different places, for the making of Waggons carry their forage for two or three days is in reallity cheating ourselves, as they carry infinitly less provisions in proportion, by which a considerable stop is put to the support- ing of our magazi[ne] My Compliments to Govern^r Glenn who I fancy by this time is pretty weary of a military life I beg you will make it as agreeable to him as you can which I shall gratefully acknowledge in a day or two, being My Dear Sir Most Sincerely

Y^r very obed^t & most hum^{le} Servt

Jo: fforbes.

P:S: Pray exert yourself in keeping the provincials, officers and soldiers in the best temper of mind possible, that we may have no such melancholy article in our letters as those mentioned by Gen^{ll} Abercromby.

[*Endorsed:*] Genl Forbes 18th Aug

*   *   *   *   *

Halkett to Bouquet
[B.M., Add. MSS. 21640, f. 143. A.L.S.]

Shippensburgh 18th August 1758

Dear Sir

General Forbes desires that you will order the last Express you sent him from Raestown to be apprehended, and properly securd in Irons till he arrives, if you remimber I sent the News Papers, with a Note of the Pro- motions made by General Abercromby, with him, haveing likewise paid him ten Shillings currency in part of his hire, I made a Memorandum of his name which he told me, was John Mc Cotter,[47] of Captain Pattersons[48]

---

[47] John McCotter, of Captain Patterson's Company of the second battalion of the Pennsylvania regiment.

[48] Captain James Patterson of Colonel John Armstrong's battalion of the Pennsyl- vania regiment.

Provential Company, he was concerned with Mr Barrows Negro, is Stealing money from the landlord of the house.

The General is still extreamly weak, but freer from pain that he was. I am Dear Sir

Your most obedient humble Servant

Francis Halkett
Brigade Major

[*Endorsed:*] Major Halkett 18th August

*   *   *   *   *

Forbes to Sharpe*
[Md. H.S. Port Folio 4, Papers and Letters, No. 36, Copy.]

Shippensburg 23^d August 1758

Dear Sir

The Enclosed Letters[49] have given me great uneasiness, as I am sure they will do the same to you; It is Indeed greatly owing to a mistake of my own, or rather my Sickness, that prevented my Writing fully upon this Head to Mr Kilby or Mr Howell, and sending Credit for the Moneys Drawn above the 1500 £ Sterling that Mr Kilby had ordered payment for; and I really Imagined that I had not presumed upon his paying any more, except the Difference betwixt the 600 £ Sterling, & the 850 £, which I imagined would meet no Stop, having Desired Major Halkett to write so to M^r McAdam,[50] his Son in Law, and which I could have Replaced at any time. I fancy you Understood it in this Light likewise, & that the Sum Exceeding this 1750 Sterling, was rather an Advance for me, than money that I required Mr Kilby to pay, who no doubt in this Affair Behaved with great Spirit, having Advanced the 1500 £ in the frankest manner, & taking the Chances of Payment, as he Writes in his Letter.

The other Summs I certainly ought to have given Warrants for (but then, as at present Confounded by Distemper, I had not Sense to Reflect upon, or Write about them) so We must now Sett it to rights as soon as possible, to Releive Dr Ross of his punctilio, in which I do not see so much hurt, as perhaps he does, nor do I think it would have been very much blamed, had he Restored Mr Howell the Money for the Bills, untill the

---

* Printed, *Md. Arch.* IX, 240, and Stewart, *Letters of General John Forbes*, p. 28.
[49] Not found.
[50] Gilbert McAdam, son-in-law of Christopher Kilby, and aide-de-camp to Loudoun.

Affair had been Cleared up; because by that means he would have prevented the Imprisonment & have given me the time to have made all Easy.

The Case as it appeared to me, and still does, is thus—That as a Large Sum of Money was due to the Maryland Troops, for different Articles, from October last, to, I shall suppose May, Mr Kilby, upon the Acco^{tt} of the Articles concerning Provisions &c. agreed to the Advance of 1500 £ Sterling on Account; to promote the Service & to prevent a totall Stop; knowing that my hands & Inclinations were both tied up by General Abercromby's not thinking himself sufficiently Authorized to fulfill Ld Loudoun & Genl Stanwix's orders. That upon this Advance of Mr Kilby's, I should likewise give so much more Money to account, in order to Enable the people, who had been Employed, to keep their Credit, & to proceed in furnishing the Troops as formerly.

That therefore those Summs to be thus Advanced were upon the General Accompt, & not Destined to the payment of any particular Demand, as the Acco^{tts} with their Vouchers had not been properly looked over & Liquidate; and as by this means we had our Claims upon the Province for such Summs advanced for the Use of their Troops, & that to be backed by you, & the people who had furnished & Supported the Troops, particularly as they would have upon the Whole greater Summs due to them than we were to Advance.

In Consequence of this, the Bills Drawn upon Mr Howell, or Mr Kilby, has allarmed him, as perhaps he Imagined that I was to turn the whole over upon him, when in reality I Understood I was only making him pay 1750 £ Sterling in place of 1500; and that I was to Advance the rest of the money for the payment of those Bills, upon the General without Specifying the time, or the purpose for what the Money was advanced, so fancy I have no other way but to Send a Warrant upon Mr Neilson[51] of Philadelphia for the summ agreed to be paid, that Exceeds the £ 1500 pound, to be paid by Mr Kilby. But I do not well Understand Mr Ross's Letter to you,[52] wherein he says, on the 15th Mr Howell paid him £ 510 Curr^y the Bill of Exchange of £ 2976. 15. Curr^y & the order of £ 850 Sterling, in all 2770. 9.8, in full of two last orders, and a little after says, that Mr Howell Insisted on his Returning him Bills for £ 1270.9.8 & the 510 £ Curr^y All this I cannot unravel, or know how these Summs come either to be Disjoined, or linked together. As I thought the Whole money to be Advanced was a Generall one not Adequate, or appropriate to the Defraying of any particular Charge, & of which Kilby was to give Creditt for so much, and I so much more.

---

[51] Mr. Neilson, of Philadelphia, a financier.
[52] Not found.

By the Return of the Express you will be so good as Explain this to me, & point me out the Way, how that Dr Ross is to be Relieved, which I shall most readily Comply with, but be so good as to Remember that the money paid by Sir John St Clair, must be looked upon as so much money paid by me, & what I must Charge myself with.

I Thank you for yours[53] of the 21st and I am very much Obliged to you, for your offer of taking care of F^t Cumberland which will be a great help to me; but I do not think I shall want your People before the Week after next, altho' my new Road is quite ready the length of Laurell ridge, & I have Sent to take post on the other Side of it, from whence it is all good to the Ohio. But I Expect a great meeting of the Indians, when they must Determine Friends or Foes: I Fancy They'll Choose the Last, as they are now Scalping within a mile of this, and I have only 50 men with me, but I Expect 200 Highlanders this Night, so if possible shall Endeavour to way lay them, but this does not look as if they were Courting a Peace.

I am obliged to you for your Care of the Blankets, and shall send you from this an order for the money payable at Annapolis, if agreeable to you there.

I Have been very bad, but better since Yesterday, & shall sett out for Raes Town when able to bear Travelling.

I am

Dr Sir. Y^r most Ob^t

most hum^{ble} Servt

Jo: fforbes

I shall Write to you soon when your people will be wanted at Cumberland I must beg you will send me a Copy of the Enclosed Letters[54]

[*Endorsed:*] Copy / Letter from Brig[^{r} General] Forbes to Governor Sharpe.

Dated Shippensburg, 23^d Augst 1758.

* * * * *

---

[53] *Md. Arch.* IX, 240.

[54] The letters mentioned in the first line, possibly from Howell, Kilby, and Ross.

Halkett to Bouquet
[B.M., Add. MSS. 21640, f. 151. A.L.S.]

Shippensburgh 26th August 1758

Dear Sir

Tho the General goes out to take ye air daily, he still recovers but slowly, he has ordered me to inform you of the Scouting parties of the Enemy being down in these parts of the Country, and have allarm'd the Inhabitants very much, they have kill'd one man, and taken a Woman, & one of the Light horse men prisoners; 120 of the Highlanders were order'd back from Fort Loudoun upon the occasion, who with the men here have been constantly out in different parties to indeavour to fall in with them, but hitherto without suckcess, except one of the parties which was fir'd upon by the Enemy, but receiv'd no damage, our people immediate return'd the Fire, and pursued, they tracd the Indians for a Mile by the blood, but unfortunately got non of them, Major Campbell[55] is now on the North Mountains, lying upon the different passes, in expectation of intercepting them, whilst we continue to scout about the Plantations and the Country lying between them, and the foot of the Mountains, in hopes of driving them upon Major Campbells people if they are still amongst the Inhabitants, these are the propere[st] steps to be taken with ye number of people here that the General could think of, the Inhabitants are very incapable of giveing advise how to Act upon the offencive, as their views are only turn'd how to defend themselves, but from the information of what the other Scouting parties of the Enemy used to do, the General immagins, that they will take cross the north Mountains by the Heads of the West branches of the Sasquhana, that after they get upon the backs of the Mountains, they think themselves much out of danger, assemble to gether, and less upon their Guard, by which meens they may be much easier discover'd; he therefore desires that you will give directions to the party going to where the Kiskemanitas crosses the Laurell Hills, to keep a good look out, & endeavour to fall in with the Enemy as they Return, keeping proper parties constantly Patrolling cross that part of the Country to wards Venango, as it is very probable, the Enemy will strike in upon the Ohio below that place. These Patrolls should have a constant corrispondence with one an other, in order to be able to give information how the Enemy may be cut off in case the are discovered, these are a the properes[t] things he could suggest for the intercepting of the Scalping parties that now infest us, but it is in it selfe so confin'd a thing, and to so

---

[55] Major Alexander Campbell of the 77th regiment.

little purpose, that he thinks the only method will be to turn the Tables upon them, and send Strong parties to visit them in their Towns, and places of habitation, which will not only tend to the distroying more of them, but the liklies method of makeing them quit the French at Fort Duquesne. I am Dear Sir

Your most obedient humble Servant

Francis Halkett

PS. I believe I may almost venture to congratulate you upon the taking of Luisburgh, & Rogers's haveing gaind an advantage over the Enemy, when the former is once confirm'd, the General things a *Feu de Joy* will have a good effect upon the Troops, & that you ought to have one, I cannot send you the News papers, but I inclose you a private letter[56] which I Receivd this day by the express.

[*Endorsed:*] Major Halkett 26th Augt by the Genls Orders

* * * * *

Forbes to David Ross*
[H.S.P. MSS. Etting Revolutionary Papers, p. 103. L.S.]

Shippensburg 28th August 1758

Sir

I designd to have wrote you the other day when I sent Mr. Howell credit for the money paid into your hands over and above the £ 1500 Sterling allowed to be paid by Mr. Kilby, but I was so much out of order that I was not able.

I am sorry that this transaction designed almost entirely for your behoof, and the carring on of the service, should have turned out so disagreeably, nor could I have imagined that you was to conceive either Governour Sharp's honour or your own so deeply concerned as to choose to go to Prison rather than return Mr. Howell that money, when a little reflection must have suggested to you that some misunderstanding or neglect had been the cause of Mr. Howell's redemanding it, which a letter to me must have cleared up imediately.

As the neglect was mine I hope you have now got the money, I am therefore now to acquaint you in order to prevent misunderstanding betwixt Governour Sharp and me that you are not to pay away that whole sum

---

[56] Not identified.

* Printed, *Pa. Mag.* XXXIII, 86, and Stewart, *Letters of General John Forbes*, p. 30.

untill that you hear farther from Govern^r Sharp, as this money advanced by me is designed as a Generall aid to diminish the debts due by and to, the Maryland troops, and for the carrying on of the service, and not at all designed to the paying of any particular debt due in this manner, I mean transporting provisions, officers or mens pay, hospitals &c^a because, before those can be fully cleared the Accounts and the Vouchers must be properly examined and found relavant.

So therefore I would not have you use above £ 500 of the above sum untill that you hear farther from me or the Governour, and that only to stop the mouths of poor people who may be in want, the rest of the sum remaing in your hands accountable for it to me.

I hope to see the Governour in a few days when all this will be easily adjusted I am Sir

> Your most obed^t
> Most humb^{le} Servt
> Jo. fforbes.

Mr Ross
[*Endorsed:*] From General Forbes Aug 28th 1758
            Rec'd Augt. 31st by David Ross.

*   *   *   *   *

Forbes to Bouquet
[B.M., Add. MSS. 21640, f. 155. L.S.]

Shippensbourg 28th August 1758

My Dear Sir.

One must be sick to be thoroughly sensible of the affinity there is betwixt the mind and the body, whenever your Directions and orders goes smooth & easy I am all Tranquility and full of spirits, but the reverse happening disturbs my whole frame.

I am very sensible of the loss of Capt Bullen & Capt French at this period of time, altho' it is long ago since I held the Indians in the utmost Contempt except in small partys to commit murder by surprize.

We have been in chace of those scoundrells here for these 8 days and nights by past, without being able to get in with any of them, altho' two of them had the impudence to fire at the Head man of one of our partys, altho' imediately pursued they escap'd from us, unhurt, and unseen, all our partys return in to Camp tomorrow, and I will then set out for your parts if able to be carryed in any Shape.

The slow advance of the new road and the cause of it touch me to the quick, it was a thing I early foresaw and guarded again such an assistant with all the force and Energy of words that I was Master off, but being over ruled was resolved to make the most I could of wrong head,[57] but now from the ruin of our Waggon Horses, occasioned (as it is said) from our want of forage every where, and those dilatory measures in carrying on the Service projected and proposed by himself, makes me suspect the heart as well as the head.

M[r] Rhor's observations upon our second deposite appear to me, to be founded on good sense and good reasoning, the difference of 9 miles being nothing, altho I should be extreamly sorry the 300 men had any chance of being attacked there before they could throw up a proper fence or be proper[ly] sustained for which reason if that party could be strengthened for the first two or three days they might soon secure themselves and spare their supernumarys as workmen upon the roads back towards Loyal Hannon.

Your proposal of going forward yourself is what would be very satisfactory but at present as we are circumstanced I am afraid you must desist from the thoughts of it and turn the Burden of the whole upon Major Grant[58] whose parts as a Military man are inferiour to few and he has the advantage that I expect he can manadge S[ir] John and remember that one must save appearances with Col[o] Byrd who Commands Grant from his Provinciall Rank.

The Post Major Grant speaks off I think may be delayed untill we secure our head and then by working backwards and forwards at the same time the whole will be in pretty great safety and those posts or resting places can be made as we see occasion.

I have been labouring a point[59] with Govern[r] Sharp ever since you wrote me about our Numbers, and have now at last carried it by his consenting to Garrison Fort Cumberland with 250 of his militia and himself along with them, But this for the space of one whole month only, as he can no longer promise for their Stay, all I am to give them is provision and a Gill of Rum each p. Day, and he is ready to set out for the Fort Sunday next, but as this appears to me too early I think of delaying him till the 10th of September, you see this gives us all the Virginians who are able to march, and who I think might advance as far forward upon Braddocks road as to that part of it which is most contiguous to our second deposite, which I think might be about Saltlick Creek, where I here there is a spot of Ground by nature of

---

[57] A reference to Sir John St. Clair.
[58] This statement puts part of the responsibility for Grant's expedition upon both Forbes and Bouquet.　　　　[59] Consult *Md. Arch.* IX, *passim*.

very difficult access, and from whence a communication might be very easily opened to our second deposite, as I suppose it won't be above 15 or 16 miles if so much.

You will think of this, and let me know whether you would chuse their marching this way or their joining us at Raestown and their going along with us, where their converlasing people &c^a must be left along our new road by way of escortes and I could have wished that you had drafted the rest of the Pennsylvania Companies to have sent proper partys from them to Fort Loudoun, Littleton and the passage of the Juniata as Escortes by which we could have brought up 35 of Capt Sharp's[60] Comp^y from Loudoun who are by far the best woodsmen of the whole and all acquainted with the back Country towards the Alleganey.

Govern^r Sharp has just asked a favour[61] of me that I could not well refuse which was to allow him to make Capt Dagworthy a Lieu^t Colonel of the Maryland troops, and he is accordingly appointed by a Commission[62] I sent him this night. As he Commands some of the briskest people I have seen, let him with the people that will join you under Capt Sharp be directly employed with a proper mixture of others in taking care of our head or pushing forward even *al la barb* of the Enemy, which will at least restrain them from prying into what we are abo[ut], but all those partys must proceed with the greatest precautions, as a small check from the Enemy may be of bad consequence to the whole of us whereas a lucky hit to any of our partys would make us all invincible.

I have heard no more news of Louisbourg but as it is most certainly taken, I would make a *feu de joy* to put the whole Army in Spirits, which will answer the Enemy's firing at Fort Du Quesne for the repulse of Gen^{ll} Abercromby at Ticonderoga. I hope we shall hear of the Louisbourg people soon, and if they don't go up the river St Lawrence, that they'll be so kind as send me my own Reg^t and another. I received my Cousin Glens letter,[63] and am glad he is so jocular, he owns he has leggs left, mine left me 3 weeks ago. I shall send or bring him some port and claret immediately.

You must write Major Grant a Coxing letter;[64] you and [I] must keep people right if possible. Adeiu My D^r S^{ir}

Y^r most &c

                                        Jo: fforbes.

---

[60] Captain James Sharp, of the third battalion of the Pennsylvania regiment.
[61] Sharpe to Forbes, August 24, 1758, *Md. Arch.* IX, 243.
[62] Not found.
[63] Not found.   [64] Not found.

The using of Braddocks road I have always had in my head; was it only a blind—pray lose no time as that does not oblidge us to march, before wee see proper.

To Col⁰ Bouquet

[*Endorsed:*] 28ᵗʰ Aug.

*   *   *   *   *

Forbes to Peters*

[H.S.P. Peters MSS. Vol. 5, p. 52. L.S.]

Shippensburg 28 August [1758]

Sir

I wrote you by Mr Ennis the Express two days ago,⁶⁵ and have little to add, only my distemper begins to abate.

I know that your Coffee house people will make their remarks very freely why I do not proceed but they must talk; altho' I must take my own way. But the great reason is, the horrible roguery, and Rascality in the Country people, who did not at all fulfill their Contracts and agreements, neither in Carriages nor Horses. For in the place of Carrying 2000 wᵗ they never had above 14 or 1500, and in place of 12 days made 20 of their Journeys by which our magazines were dissapointed and our daily consumption at Raestown must have fallen upon them (the Magazines) had I pushed forward the troops.

Everything that depended upon the troops has succeeded to admiration, and we have got intirely the better of that impossible road, over the Alleganey mountain & Laurell ridge, so we are ready to take the very first favourable opportunity (if not with the whole) at least of visiting the Enemy with pretty large detachments. So that now my advancing will again depend upon the honesty of the Inhabitants by their furnishing proper or improper Carriages, and which I beg you will make known to every body, as the troops are in great spirits, but I must not lead them to fall a sacrafice to want of Famine, and the price I pay and the treatment the Waggoners and horses meet with, deserves a better return from the Inhabitants, than they have as yet shown, for which their Country may suffer severely in the End.

I hope we have chaced off the Enemy Indians from this neighborhood, having had 300 Highlanders with all the best woodsmen out these 3 days, night and day, but never could have the Good fourtune of falling on with any of them.

---

* Printed, *Pa. Mag.* XXXIII, 87, and Stewart, *Letters of General John Forbes,* p. 31.

⁶⁵ Not found.

Two of the Indians fired upon the Head of a party of ours of 80 men, yet notwithstanding they were Instantaneously pursued they gott away. The whole Country has been in a pannick but begin again to revive. They are a sett of helpless heartless mortalls.

Col° Byrd writes[66] me from Fort Cumberland that a large party of Ennemy Indians have been in that neighbourhood, and that Capt Bullen and Capt French who had just brought 50 Catawbas to our assistance, coming from Winchester, would go before the party when they come near Fort Cumberland, by which means they were attacked by 9 Indians, killed, and scalped within a mile of the Fort. This is a very great loss, as Bullen had proved himself a sincere friend to us.

A party of ours have returned from the Ohio with two scalps which I shall endeavour to get you, they were within a half miles of Fort Duquesne, but do not say anything extraordinary, only thinks there were about 50 Tents near the Fort and reckons there may be as many Indians there as tents, and a Garrison of 3 or 400 men.

But as this is all Conjecture, and hitherto in spite of all the partys, I have sent out, I can learn nothing that is to be depended upon, I must therefore beg that Andrew Montour[67] may be forthwith employed in getting me Intelligence of the Enemys Strength in those parts, by going himself, as likewise sending 2 or 3 trusty hands to pick up what they can learn, as to the number of the French Canadians or Indians there at present, or expected, wether they have thrown up any Entrenchments before the Fort betwixt the Ohio and Monongahela. What they have built lately either at the Fort or tother side of the river. What Guns they mount in the Fort, wether they send out partys from the Fort during the day or night to reconnoitre the Environs. How many men mount Guard daily, &c &c and the disposition of the Indians. These spies may return to our advanced post 9 miles forward from Loyall Hannon on the other side of the Chestnut ridge of Mountains and about 40 miles from Fort Du Quesne. They may make themselves known by wearing yellow Fillets about their heads and Arms, and waving their matchcoats upon a long pole.

I am in want of spying Glasses to send out with my partys so pray buy for me two or three good ones, and send up by the very first Express. Let Mr. Croghan send out people likewise with the same directions, and I shall be very glad to see him after your Congress, which I hope still goes forward and will produce something. I should be glad to know if they were Dela-

---

[66] Not found.

[67] Andrew Montour, half breed Indian, interpreter, etc. Consult Hanna, *Wilderness Trail,* I, chapter viii.

wares, that was here the other day. I dare say everything will be said to bring the Indians to see their own Interest, and to abandon the French, and I fancy any demands thay they have to make will be so moderate, as to be asily complyed with, and doubt not but many of their young men may be induced to join me, In which case Mr. Croghan would do a signall service in conducting them safe to me. Let Mr. West pruchase 50 llb. weight of Vermillion, and send it off, with the first waggons that come from Mr. Howell, with proper directions. I have broke my little Barometer, I wish you could purchase me another and send it me up safe.

Hambies[68] & Teedyuscungs son goes down to Easttown to persuade their friends to come and join me, I wish they may be sincere so pray let them be watched narrowly.

I hope the Province will make no difficulty, as to the Expence of this meeting, as it will be a most monsterous reflection upon them if they do, and they never after can either look for, or expect the favour or protection of Great Brittain.

I stand greatly in need of a few prunes by way of Laxative, if any fresh are lately arrived a few pounds will be a great blessing, or a pound 2 or 3 of such fine raisins as Mr. Allen's[69] were, as I eat nothing.

I expect all the news of Louisburgh so dont baulk me—

I am Dr Sir most sincerely yrs &c &c

Jo fforbes

[*Addressed:*] To Mr Peters
[*Endorsed:*] 28 Augt 1758
　　　　　Recd by Thos Appy

* 　 * 　 * 　 * 　 *

Forbes to Bouquet
[B.M., Add. MSS. 21640, f. 159. A.L.S.]

Shippensbourg 2^d Septem^r 1758

Sir

I really can not describe how I have suffer'd both in body and Mind of Late. And the relapsis have been worse as the dissapointment was greatter however I comfort my self in thinking that I have retarded nothing by my infirmity, as other things must necessarily have hindred me from setting directly out for the Ohio untill this time and even were wee ready now,

---

[68] Hambies or Hambus? Cf. Hambuss, in Forbes to Bouquet, August 9, 1758, *ante,* p. 170.
[69] Probably William Allen, prominent Philadelphian.

which I am sorry to say is not the Case, I think it would be Imprudent yet for some time. Because from what I can learn that the strength of the Indians at Fort du Quesne are from the Detroit and Westward of the Lakes, they are now weary and must return by the latter end of Sep^{tr} for taking care of their Hunting and for fear of the Frosts. 2do If Broadstreet has any success at Frontignac, they must recall some of their Regulars to strengthen themselves there; as Montcalm can spare none from Tienderoga and 3dly There are already above 100 Indians come to the Treaty just now to be opend at Easttown, where the Delaware and other Chieffs are dayly expected from the Ohio, Who if brought over to us will make ane Immense falling of with the other French Indians, so any stroke of ours at this criticall period, might be of very bad Consequence to us. For the French are trying every thing in their power to keep them and my Intelligence says that before the Detroit Indians return, that the French will most certainly persuade them to come in a body to attack us, at least to beat up the head of our Army at Laurell Hill. As this is a serious Consideration wee must guard against it by all means possible, For which reason my Dear S^{ir} I must beg the favour of you that without loss of time you will be so good as sett out for the head of the Army, where you can judge of the post proposed by Rhor. What numbers are sufficient to maintain themselves there untill we are able to march more troops up, which I think at present would rather be rash, considering the state of our provisions and Forrage, which at Present with the state of our Waggons, (occasiond from the want of the latter) cannot be either so soon or easily supplyed. So these things when on the Spot you will revolve in your own mind and by a proper disposition of the troops and advanced post, make it impossible for the Ennemy to march in a body without our knowledge when the troops at work may be hurryd up time enough to support the head, For which reason large out partys and advanced Guards (all extreamly allert), will be necessary, and small partys from them for Intelligence. And yet I can not think that the French will risque any thing so farr from home, except a large Scouting party, such as has harrassed us these two days by past. But of all this you will soon be able to form a judgment, and return to me directly to Raestown, for which place I shall God Willing) sett out Monday next, so you may be with me back again by the time I arrive there.

If you think this journey needless before that I get up to you, when I have many things to settle and concert with you let it alone, only send an officer to quicken all those posts, and to keep them upon their Guard and a Strict look out at all times, least of a surprise, which indeed is the only thing we have most to dread.

I have wrote you[70] of Governour Sharp's offer as to Fort Cumberland, and as I will order his people there by the 10th Septr you may be makeing disposition for the rest of the Virginia regimts.

I fired this day a *feu de Joye* for our being possessors of Louisbourg ever since the 26th July, pray let your people do the same as it will keep them in spirits and make it reach the French and Indian's Ears the sooner.

I understand that 8 men P Company, said to be detached from the French regulars for the Ohio, are sent back to Montreal and the river St Laurence, so I think we shall not have them to deal with this year, nor can I think if that be the case, how they will venture to leave their Garrison.

The Moment the treaty at East town is over Mr Croghan promises to join me with as many of the Indians as he can bring along, and I might believe that there may be a good many persuaded to come.

I send you the publick papers which is all the news.

Mr Hoops sent about 70 Bats Horses to be loaded at Littelton, but finding nothing there nor any where else indeed, they are gone down to Carlisle. There are two droves of Oxen and sheep gone thro' this town this day, and a small Convoy of Waggons, part provisions, and part forage.

The Magistrates in their different districkts all agree in the great difficulty of getting fresh Waggons or Horses, saying, the Farmers complain their Horses were starved for want of forage, so I am afraid we must make the best of what we have.

My kind Compliments to my Cousin Slender,[71] who I realy long to see, because of [*sic*] much thinner than usual he must now have become almost Invisible.

Be so good as write to Colo Washington[72] & Byrd[73] and acquaint them of my project for bringing all they can from Fort Cumerland of their troops, and the Commissary must likewise be acquainted that those Maryland Militia are to be Victualled and to have a Gill of Spirits each P. day, but I believe this last article Mr Woods[74] must settle I am Dr Sir Most Sincerely

Yr Obedt humle Servt

Jo: fforbes.

P: S:

Altho I make no doubt but all your Engineers are employed, yet I should

---

[70] August 28, 1758, *ante*, p. 189.

[71] Probably a reference to former Governor James Glen of South Carolina.

[72] Bouquet to Washington, September 4, 1758, L.C. MSS. Papers of Washington, printed, Hamilton, *Letters to Washington*, III, 82.   [73] No such letter found.

[74] Probably Draper Simon Woods, Deputy Commissary.

be very glad to talk with him who is best acquainted with Laurell Hill and forwards.

You may set the provinciall soldier that I ordered to be confined, at liberty, as his accuser acknowledged the falsity of his charge, and has since deserted.

Col° Bouquet

[*Endorsed:*] Septr the 2^d

*   *   *   *   *

*Forbes to Sharpe**

[Md. H.S. Port Folio 4. Papers and Letters No. 36 L.S.]

Shippensbourg 3^d September 1758

Sir

By a letter[75] from Mr Howell at Philadelphia dated August 30th I find Dr Ross's affair nor fully settled, altho by the return of your Express I sent Mr Howell credit for £ 1519 . . 18 . . 8 Sterling[76] to reimburse him for the money advanced to Dr Ross over and above £ 1500 sterling allowed off by Mr Kilby; This as far as I could account was the whole sum; but Mr Howell writes me that Dr Ross received from him £ 2770 . . 9 . . 8 . . Sterling in Bills of Exchange, besides £ 510 Currency, which two sums is some hundreds more than the £ 3019 . . 18 . . 8 sterling paid by Mr Kilby and me, but Mr Howell says that Mr Kilby is to be there in a day or two, who will easily set those matters to rights; So there is the less matter as Mr Ross is not, nor never was in prison, and might have prevented all this trouble by returning Mr Howell the Bills he had had from him, which I find he must do at last, as Mr Howell writes me that he believes I must send new Bills at last to prevent some losses, or some other things which I understand nothing off, such as Course of Exchange &c.

I must take notice of Dr Ross's indiscretion who when Mr Howell proposed to him to lodge the Bills and Cash in any indifferent persons Hands untill Mr Kilby or I could send our instructions about the affair, refused positively to do so, giving as his reason that as he had now got hold, he would not let go, which answer obliged Mr Howell to take the steps he did, and must of consequence oblige Mr Kilby and me to take proper receipts from Dr Ross for the money we advance upon the General account as neither

---

* Printed, *Md. Arch.* IX, 261, and Stewart, *Letters of General John Forbes*, p. 33.

[75] Not found.

[76] Letter of credit not found.

his Accts[77] nor Vouchers have been looked over by us, or properly authenticated for us to advance money upon, you will therefore be so good as write[78] the D[r] upon this subject and acquaint him that whatever money he receives now, he must be accountable for, and therefore ought to make no payments nor reimbursements without your particular allowance, as you know some of the accounts may upon examination admit of disputes unless very clearly Vouched.

I must likewise add that the sum I have ordered payment for to D[r] Ross greatly exceeds what M[r] Kilby and I at first thought necessary to be advanced, for supporting the D[rs] Credit and further carrying on the service, so it, will be necessary before you allow the D[r] to pay away that money advanced by me, that I have a Copy of the D[rs] accounts sent me, and that those articles not clearly vouched be the last that any money is paid upon.

I propose leaving this tomorrow morning in a kind of Horse litter, being so weakened by my distemper that I neither can ride nor bear the roughness of my slopwaggon. However I hope a few days will make a great change.

I have wrote[79] to Col° Bouquet of your kind agreement of Garrisoning Fort Cumberland for the first month of my absence, and that 250 of your men would be there by the 10th or 12th Instant, ordering the Commissary to furnish them with provisions and a Gill of spirits each p day during their stay in that service, If there be any thing more wanted let me know, or if when there, you find any other thing necessary you will be so good as to order it, as the Commissary shall have directions to do whatver you require. Pray let me know if you have heard of the Blanketts.

I give you joy of Louisbourg which is certainly a great Acquisition and may be of some service to me, for as I don't hear that they have reinforced Fort Du Quesne with any Regulars, I fancy their chief reliance may be upon the Western Indians from Detroit, who as M[r] Croghan writes[80] me will certainly leave them soon; this with the numbers of Delaware nations and other tribes going now to treat with us at East town prevents my hurrying measures for some days, least by a precipitate blow I might prevent the success of the treaty at East town; and the only thing I dread the French will do, is they will persuade the West country Indians in Conjunction with the shawenese to come and attack the head of my Army now taking post on the other side Laurell hill, before that the Indians return home, what are your sentiments thereupon ? wether to proceed with whole, or temporize a few days longer, untill that we see how the East town treaty turns out, where I

---

[77] Not found.   [78] Not found.
[79] August 28, 1758, *ante*, p. 189.
[80] Letter not found.

wish heartily you could have been, as you must know any Indian friendships at this critical time might prove a great dimunition to the strength of the French.

I foresee I shall be in great distress for want of waggons, the Horses of those with me being ruined as they say for want of forage, a neglect that Sir John St Clair can never answer for, who was sent from Philadelphia by me to make magazines of Forage all along the march route and to have a great Quantity in store at Raestown,

I am D^r S^{ir}

Y^r most obed^t & most hum^{le} Servt

Jo: fforbes

Govern^r Sharp

[*Endorsed:*] From Genl Forbes
Sept. 1758

*   *   *   *   *

Forbes to Bouquet
[B.M., Add. MSS. 21640, f. 161. A.L.S.]

[Shippensburg, September 4, 1748]

Sir.

Mr Hoops arrived late last night and gave me yours,[81] I am sorry you meet with so many cross accidents to vex you, and that you have such a parcell of Scoundrells as the provincialls to work with, *Mais Le Vin est firétte* you must drop a little of the Gentleman and treat them as they deserve, and pardon no remissness in duty, as few or any serve from any principles but the low sordid ones.

I fancy you will judge as I do, that the Ennemy may endeavour to surprize our advanced posts, and therefore all Care and precaution to prevent them, or indeed letting them gain any advantage over any of our out post, or Scouting partys, which with our Hero's might havd a bad effect, as by what I see they are not farr from a pannick.

My Highlanders here are vastly mended and ten times more steady and Cautious, by the Chacing of the Indians these 10 days and lying out at nights, I am thoroughly convinced [that]† had I not been here, every bitt of this town and neighbourhood had been burnt, but wee are now quite tranquille, I wish your partys could fail in with them on their return, altho you see I am

---

[81] Of August 31, 1758, B.M., Add. MSS. 21640, f. 157, Df.
† Stricken out.

at present very Cautious, untill the meeting at East town be over, as wee might break all measures, by falling on those inclined to be our Friends.

Seal and send off the enclosed express[82] to S^{ir} John by some sure hand. He is a very odd Man, and I am sorry it has been my fate to have any Concerns with him. But more of this hereafter. I agree with you that a Disposition ought to be made for marching forwards. But still that must be consider'd, as likewise the march of the Virginians as I am affraid our Army will not admitt of Divisions least one half meet with a Cheque. Therefore would consult C: Washington, altho perhaps not follow his advice, as his Behaviour about the roads, was no ways like a Soldier.

I thank my good Cousin for his letter,[83] and have only to say, that I have all my life been subject to err, but I now reform as I go to bed at 8 at night, if able to sett up so late.

Adieu My D^r S^{ir} and believe me y^{rs} most sincerely

Jo: fforbes.

I have receiv'd all your letters very safe, nor have I neglected any thing you recommended, altho perhaps I may have forgott to acquaint you.
Shippensburgh. Sepr 4th
[*Endorsed:*] Sept. the 4th
          Col: Bouquet.

*   *   *   *   *

Forbes to Abercromby
[AB. 610. L.S.; P.R.O. W.O. 34:44, f. 347. Copy.]

Shippensburg 4th September 1758

S^{ir}.

Last night I had the favour of yours of the 20th Augt[84] and am very much oblidged to you for your kind expressions with regard to my bad state of health, which realy has been in such a condition this month by past from a most violent flux, with most excruciating pains in my Bowells, and I rendered so low and weak that I had oftener than once or twice firmly resolved to have wrote you, to appoint some other person to take this Command, as I absolutely found myself incapable to proceed—But now thank God I am a great deal better, and that my sickness has never retarded my operations one single moment—I thought to have wrote you a long

---

[82] Contents of the express not found.
[83] Letter of Glen not found.
[84] AB 551, copy.

letter with regard to the seeming tardiness of my proceedings, ever since the latter end of June that I left Philad[a], however that must keep cold till next post, when I shall be in more spirits; As now the time draws nigh that we must proceed without any stop or interruption, as a great many of our material Hindrances are now remedied and that [I had]† owing to never neglecting the taking of posts and the pushing of my road forwards which greatly facilitates things now.

The many Escortes that were absolutely necessary for the Convoy of provisions and forage and the Defense of the frontiers of these provinces rob'd me of a great number of my men, nor should I have known well how to have been enabled to proceed now, had I not retained the maryland troops under promise of the Government's pay, besides 50 Voluntiers that Govern[r] Sharpe persuaded to join me, to whom I am only to give the Governm[ts] provisions and 1 pair of mohockasons apiece for their Service during the Campaign—They having the liberty to keep all the scalps they shall take to sell them to their Assembly for the promised reward of £ 50 each—They are now out upon the hunt so I wish them a good harvest Altho their hands at this present writing are a good deal tied up, least they should interfere with the Enemys Indians that we expect daily to be brought over and to join us by the ensueing treaty at East town, from whence M[r] Croghan has promised to come and join me and I am assured that I may have 50 of the Delaware Indians to join me likewise, but to say the plain truth the Cherokees behaved so infamously bad, that I dare trust none of the race of Indians, who are both perfidious and expensive, Witness Cap[t] Bullen and Cap[t] French just returned from the Catawabas with 50 of their Country men, who were shot dead going to the Fort Cumberland Camp, and it is greatly suspected that the last party of Cherokees that Left us, were the people that did it.

I have been hunting after a pretty strong party of the Enemy Indians now lurking these 10 days by past near this town and neighborhood, without being ever able to come up with any of them, notwithstanding 300 of the Highlanders have been employed night and day in their pursuit and lying in ambush for them.

I heartily give you joy of the taking of Louisburg and hope it will give your provincialls fresh spirits and enable you soon, Still to act upon the offensive, and I should be very glad either by S[ir] William Johnson's means or Bradstreet if any way nigh oswego to know what was a passing in those parts, and this might be easily done and in a very short time by proper messengers sent down thro the Indian Country directly to me.

---

† Stricken out.

If in case any of the Battalions be sent from Louisburg to strengthen your Army, I should beg you would think of me, and send me what you may think proper of regular troops, for at present I can Brag of none, notwithstanding I am very well inclin'd to think favourably, and even partially of the Highlanders and the 4 Companies of Royal Americans.

I have wrote to Governour Dobbs twice[85] upon the Subject of the N° Carolina Companies, who ought to have been 300 men but dont turn out above two, and those in such absolute want of everything that I have been oblidged to leave them in Stations by ways of Escortes. I shall write him again[86] according to your device but when that will reach him if ever God knows having changed his habitation to a Small town in Carolina near Cape Fear—Your letters to S° Carolina are equally precarious and as to any letters you write to me here in the wilderness they never will come any further than Philadelphia with any certainty no regular post being established even to Lancaster, and letters only sent by Country people who are not the most carefull althô the most curious, for which reason all your letters or any letters of consequences are always sent me by Express from Philadelphia as there is no other method to be relied upon except now and then by Escorte who take 12 Days in going or coming from whence you may Guess at the difficulty of the transport of provisions and the supplying of our magazines and our daily consumption, but more of this in my next.

I ought to acquaint you that in order to have as many of the Virginia troops with me as possible I have at length persuaded[87] Govern^r Sharp to coax his militia forward to Garrison Fort Cumberland but it is for one month only so he marches there the 10th or 12th Instant with 250 men whom I am to Give Kings provisions and a Gill of Rum p^r Diem to each while they Stay—I ought likewise to have acquainted you that when the provincialls both of Pennsylvania and Virginia were put upon the Kings allowance of provisions that the whole unanimously joined in the outcry that they were going to be starved so that Col° Bouquet who commanded at Raestown fearing a Total defection and desertion was glad to allow them the same quantitys as furnished them by their respective provinces untill that I should arrive I have ordered a second tentative which I am afraid will prove fruitless althô they have been repeatedly told that your whole Army was upon the same allowance, as what we wanted to put them to, so what I shall do, they are at present in great good humour works stoutly upon the roads without repining and very little desertion among them, so as they have

[85] Letters to Dobbs not found.   [86] Letter not found.
[87] Consult *Md. Arch.* IX, *passim.*

nothing for working but so much spirits p[r] day might not the extraordinary expence of the Ration be charged upon that fund—But this I submit, only I should be very sorry to disoblige them at this juncture.—

I must beg the favour that you will order any of your Clerks to Send me all the Excerpts and Anecdotes about Louisburg that they can pick up, for here in this immense uninhabited tract we really hear nothing—So when you Please to favour me with your future scheme of Operations and the time of your proceeding thereon it would be a sensible pleasure to me think that I am Cooperating with you at the Same time I am most Sincerely

Y[r] most obed[t] &
very hum[le] Serv[t]
Jo fforbes

P.S.

You may guess my condition when I tell you I have not Strength to ride on Horseback, nor indeed in my Body able to bear the roughness of a Waggon, and Backside (with Pardon) has been so pestered with Glisters and Stools, that I must Sally forth in a kind of Horse litter actually made by Doctor Russell and my Serv[ts].

Gen[ll] Abercromby

[*Endorsed:*] Brig[r] Gen[l] Forbes.

Shippensburg 4[t]: Sept: 1758.

R the 16[t].

*   *   *   *   *

Forbes to Pitt[*]
[P.R.O. C.O. 5:50, (L.C. trans.) pp. 589-597.]

Fort Loudoun. the 6th. September. 1758.

Sir

In my last letter[88] I had the honour to acquaint you, of my procedings in the new road across the Alleganey Mountains, and over Laurell Hill (leaving the Rivers Yohiegany and Monongahela to my left hand) strait to the Ohio, by which I have saved a great deal of way, and prevented the misfortunes that the overflowing of those rivers might occasion. I acquainted you likewise of the suspicions I had of the small trust I could repose in the Pennsylvanians in assisting of me with any one necessary, or any help in

---

*   Printed, Kimball, *Correspondence of William Pitt* . . . I, 338, Stewart, *Letters of General John Forbes,* p. 35.

88 Of July 10, 1758, *ante,* p. 140.

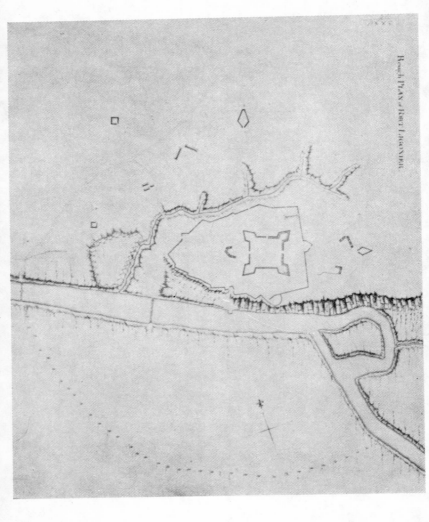

Reproduction of a map, King's XCCII, 13, described in the Catalogue of Maps and Charts in the British Museum, p. 521, as "A colored rough plan of Fort Ligonier (on the Loyal Hanon Creek), with its outworks. . . ."

furthering the Service that they did not think themselves compelled to do by the words of your letter to them.

As likewise of almost the total defection and desertion of the Southern Indians (except 80) who after the receiving of their presents &c, have all returned home not without committing egregious outrages upon the scattered Inhabitants of the Northwest parts of Virginia in their return.

I thought fit to recapitulate this least my letters dont come to hand regularly as there is no post in those parts, nor any regular one anywhere except from Philadelphia, By New York, to Boston; and even there one may be three Months in receiving a Letter, that ought to be delivered in ten days, besides my letters must now go by Merch^t. Ships, which makes the delivery very precarious. I hinted to you in my former, of my endeavouring to bring about a Treaty betwixt the Delaware Indians &c^a., neighbours to those Provinces, but of late drove into the Arms of French and removed to the Ohio, as the Indians demands were but few, and to me seemingly not unreasonable, I thought the reclaiming of those Tribes would be of very great Service to the Publick in weakening of the French Interest by setting a good example to other Western Tribes of Indians, who it is said have all the Inclination to be well with us, wanting only an Opportunity, and an Assurance of protection to declare themselves for us, or at least to remian neutralls.

This is almost brought to a Crisis, their Chief Men being hourly expected at East-town upon the Delaware, where the Govern^r. of Pennsylvania and Jersey are to meet them and settle Preliminaries; I wish it could have been done sooner, and that they could have had time to remove, because now my scene of offensive Operations must imediately be put in Execution, when it will be hard for me to distinguish betwixt our friendly disposed Indians, and our real Enemies.

My advanced post consisting of 1500 Men, are now in possession of a strong post 9 Miles on the other side of Laurell Hill, and about 40 from Fort Du Quesne, nor had the Enemy ever suspected my attempting such a road till very lately, they having been all along securing the strong passes, and fords of the rivers, upon General Braddock's route.

My greatest distress and what maybe a real hindrance to me for some days is the provisions, which altho' every care imaginable has taken by contracting for great Numbers of Waggons and Baggage horses at a very great Expence. Yet all has not been able, to supply the present consumption, and the maintaining of three Month's Provisions in store to carry along with us— This I early foresaw and acquainted the Govern^r:, and the Assembly Commissioners of my Doubts, arising from the villiany of the Inhabitants in furnishing their worst Horses at so critical a juncture,—By contract they being obliged to carry 2000 [lb]. w[t]. p Waggon, such a length of road in such a specified time, but cannot carry above 1400 at most and take up four and twenty days in place of twelve to execute it in.

I have wrote the Govern[r]. in very strong Terms[89] upon this head, beging he would shew it to their Assembly now sitting, in order that they may fall upon Methods of sending from Philadelphia, and parts adjacent, three Months provisions at once, they having Carriages in abundance, and I promising to pay so much p. hun[d]. w[t]. for everything delivered into our Generall store at Raestown Camp—This I hope is so reasonable that they will comply with it, altho' sad experience makes me dread that their dilatory Measures, and contrary factions, will so retard, so absolutely necessary a transport as to throw me, and the little Army I have the honour to command, into very great distress.

I was greatly afraid that the unfortunate stop Genl[l]. Abercrombie met with, might have enabled the French to strengthen themselves with regulars in those parts, but from every Intelligence I can possibly get, any reinforcements that have joined, or are likely to join them, are the West Country Indians, who returned from Ticonderoga, who likewise may tire at Fort Du Quesne, but of this I hope to be better informed, when still a little nigher them, by the Means of deserters of whom as yet we have not had one come in, and there is but little trust to be put in the best Spies you can find, or in the small scouting parties that you send for discovery, & no truth at all to be expected from an Indian.

The Govern[r]. of Maryland I am greatly obliged to, having personally acted with the greatest zeal for the Service, first by sending 50 Voluntiers all good Woods Men to join me, and now by marching 200 of his Militia (I believe contrary to his Assembly's inclination) to Garrison Fort Cumberland for one month or to the 12th. of October. As he stands bound for the pay and the keeping together the Maryland Troops at Fort Cumberland from the 8th. of October last, (to the beginning of May, that I retained them in the Service of the Government) by which that Fort and Country was prevented from falling into the Enemy's hands, all which he did by positive Orders from the Earl of Loudoun,[90] and the same repeated in very strong terms by Brig[r]. Gen[ll]. Stanwix[91] to him, and even to the Commanding Officers of Companys.

---

[89] No such letter found, but cf. Forbes to Denny, September 9, 1758, *post,* p. 206.

[90] Loudoun to Sharpe, November 3, 1757, *Md. Arch.* IX, 98.

[91] Not found.

This has induced me to give him to the Extent of £ 1500 Sterling, for the present support of his Credit, and the further carrying on of the Service which I Hope will meet with your Approbation, as Govern^r. Sharp assures me at the same time, that in his Opinion, the Maryland Assembly now sensible of their by past bad behaviour, will upon their first Meeting pass a Law for the payment of all those Accounts.

Govern^r. Dobbs, without previously acquainting me, did send 200 Men by Sea up to join me, and was to send 100 more by land, the first 200 are joined, but the Governour writes me[92] that having neither money nor Credit in their province, he was unable either to furnish them with Cloaths, or send pay along with them, and desires that I would furnish all those and any other Necessaries wanting, and that he would reimburse that expence, out of the first Monies paid by the Crown to that Province, hitherto they have had the King's Provisions, but as they are in want of everything, I must either give them a kind of Cloathing or get no Service from them.

I vainly at the beginning flattered myself that some very good Service might be drawn from the Virginia, & Pennsylvania Forces, but am sorry to find that a few of their principle Officers excepted, all the rest are an extream bad Collection of broken Innkeepers, Horse Jockeys, & Indian traders, and that the Men under them, are a direct copy of their Officers, nor can it well be otherwise, as they are a gathering from the scum of the worst of people, in every Country, who have wrought themselves up, into a panick at the very name of Indians who at the same time are more infamous cowards, than any other race of mankind.

If it should please God to grant Success to His Majesty's Arms in their Attempts upon the Ohio, and which I think can't well fail, I shall be greatly at a loss how to dispose of Fort Du Quesne, whether to blow it up, and destroy it and the whole Settlements thereabout, or to keep it and leave a Garrison there for the Winter, the execution of the first is as easy, as the second appears to be attended with many difficulties, all of which must naturally occur to you, from its great distance from any of the inhabited parts of those Provinces, and consequently the great difficulties of either supporting it, or supplying it with Necessaries during a long severe Winter.

I have consulted the Governours of Pennsylvania[93] and Virginia[94] upon this head, and to know what Number of Troops they could leave there in case

---

[92] Letter of Dobbs to Forbes not found.

[93] Letters not found, but cf. Forbes to Denny, September 9, 1758, *post*, p. 206.

[94] Letter of Forbes to Fauquier not found, but mentioned in *Journal of the House of Burgesses of Virginia, 1756-1758*, under date September 19, 1758.

it was thought proper to preserve it, to which I have had no positive answer, but I know the Pennsylvania troops will disband the first of December unless their Assembly makes a new Provision for their Support.

In a few days I shall have most of my Troops moved forward towards the head, there to be in readyness of seizing the first favourable Opportunity of marching to the Banks of the Ohio, which I now have in my power of doing, by a march of 48 hours, and if refused the Carriages demanded from the Pennsylvanians, or they appear too tardy, and dilatory in the execution thereof, I shall most certainly try it upon flour, and rice, with the Assistance of what live Cattle we can carry forward with us.

My health, that has been extreamly precarious these two years, has of late been very near brought to a close, by a long and severe attack of a bloody flux, which has reduced me to a state of weakness that I am obliged to travel in a Hurdle carried betwixt two Horses, but I hope the animating spirits of being able to do the smallest Service to my King and Country, will leave nothing undone on my part that can anyways contribute to the Success of so glorious a cause. I have the honour to be, with the highest esteem and regard, Sir

Y^r. most obed^t. & most hum^{ble}. Servt.

Jo: Forbes

[*Addressed:*] To Honble Willm Pitt Esqr.
[*Endorsed:*] Fort Loudoun Sept 6 1758 / B Genl Forbes / R / Nov. 14

*   *   *   *   *

*Forbes to Denny**
[*Pa. Col. Recs.* VIII, 167]

Fort Loudoun, Septem^r., 9th, 1758.

Sir:

I have the Honour of laying before you the Situation of His Majesty's Affairs under my Directions in these Southern Provinces at this Critical Juncture, and at the same time to shew you how much it depends on you and the People of this Province to assist in carrying on a Service which his Majesty has so much at Heart, or by their Neglect and Obstinacy have it in their Power to render every step that has been taken (for the safety of these Colonies) fruitless and to no Purpose, but to expend a very great Sum of Money.

---

* The original not found. Also printed, Stewart, *Letters of General John Forbes,* p. 39.

The laying in Provisions for the Support of the Army I attempted to do without even being obliged to impress any Carriages. The Quantity of Provisions to have been Collected at our principal Magazine has fallen greatly short of what I had reason to expect, because most of the Waggons were not Loaded with more than Fourteen Hundred Weight, and took a Third more time in the Carriage than they ought to have done, which obliged us to break in upon the Stock of Provisions laid in at Ray's Town, while the Troops were opening a Road over the Mountains, and Securing its Communication, which is now effectually done to within Forty Miles of the French Fort, so that if the Inhabitants who have Waggons are not obliged to furnish a Sufficient Number of them, who, in one Trip to Ray's Town, might Transport the Quantity of Provisions wanted, and where they may receive payment for the Trip at a just and equitable Price, to be fixed by Authority, in Proportion to the Quantity of Provisions so delivered and to the Length of the Journey that they make, the Expedition cannot go forward; nor can I maintain the Ground I am already Master of, but shall be Obliged to draw off my Master's Forces to the Inhabited Parts of the Country, and take Provisions and Carriages wherever they can be found. The Evil which will Attend this Procedure is, that the Innocent must Suffer with the Guilty, and the Exigence of the Case is so pressing as to admit of no delay.

I know there has been several Complaints made of the Scarcity of Forrage, and that several Waggoners has been abused by Officers. If there was any Scarcity of Forrage, it was owing to the Want of Waggons for its Transport; and no Driver ever made his Complaint but the Person who abused him was punished, so that I am induced to believe every Complaint of that kind is without foundation, and, therefore, shall not further insist on a detailed account of the Infamous Breach of Contract on the Part of Inhabitants.

I have sent to Phialdelpahia the Quarter Master General, who will explain to you fully the Situation of the Army. I should be sorry to employ him in executing any Violent Measures, which the Exigency of Affairs I am in at present must Compel me to do, if I am not relieved by a Speedy Law for the Providing the Army with Carriages, or a general Concurrence of Magistrates and People of power in those Provinces in assisting, to their utmost, to provide the Same, and that with the greatest Diligence.

Every thing is ready for the Army's Advancing, but that I cannot do unless I have a Sufficient Quantity of Provisions in the Magazines at Ray's Town. The Road that Leads from the advanced Posts to the French Fort may be opened as Fast as a Convoy can march it. Therefore my movement depends on his Majesty's Subjects entering chearfully in carrying up the necessary Provisions. The new Road has been finished without the Enemies knowing it. The Troops having not suffered the least insult in the Cutting it.

And as one Trip of the Waggons will be sufficient for carrying up Provisions to Ray's Town, they shall be paid off at that Place for the Weight they carry and discharged; When they arrive at Ray's Town I shall have nothing to do, but proceed with the Army under my Command, which hitherto have exerted themselves with the greatest Vigor and Spirit, in the great Labour they have undergone; I have done every thing in the Power of Man, to carry on this Expedition with Vigor, if any stop is made to it now, there can be no part laid to my Charge. For this stop you know I have long dreaded, as Six Weeks ago I wrote circular Letters[95] to the Different Magistrates to give all their Aid and Assistance in procuring Waggons to the Contractor's Agents for Transporting Provisions, and that nothing has been neglected that Occur to me for Expediting this so necessary Branch of the Service.

I need not repeat to you the care I have hitherto been at to prevent our Parties from falling upon the Indians, lest, by mistake, it might have fallen upon those who are any wise well disposed to us, and who are, I hope by this time at Easton to meet you, where I hope you will as soon as possible bring things to an Issue, letting the Indians know that the Regard I had for them has been the only reason why I had not long ago fallen upon their Towns, Wives and Children, but that now I could no longer Stop from putting in Execution the Orders of the King, my master, against his Enemies, and all who joined with them.

As you will see Mr. Croghan, you will be so good as to send with those who will follow up to me as soon as possible, and pray, as soon as you can form any idea how matters are likely to turn out, let me know by Express; And I beg your Sentiments as to my Proceedings, if God grants us success against the Enemy; You see the Difficulty of leaving a Garrison there, and you know how your Province have put it out of my power of leaving any of their Troops after the first of December, So I am really at a Loss what step I must take.

I have the honour to be,

Sir, your most obed*. and Hum*. Serv*.,

John Forbes

---

[95] Not found.

P. S.—As I am willing to embrace every Measure for Carrying on the Service, I have wrote[96] to Several of the Members of the Assembly, to desire their assistance in relation to Carriages, as I suppose you may think it proper to Lay my Letter before them.

*   *   *   *   *

*Halkett to Sharpe**

[Md.H.S. Gilmore Papers. Vol. II, Division I, Letter No. 8a. A.L.S.]

Camp at Reastown 16th September 1758

Dear Sir

This evening Colonel Washington arrived, who surprises the General extreamly by the account that he gives of the great scarcity of provisions at Fort Cumberland, after having wrote to Colonel Bouquet so fully upon that subject, however the General (who is greatly fatigued from the bussiness that his just coming to Reastown has oblidg'd him to go through) has order'd me to inform you, that he will send off a Convoy of provisions to morrow, the particulars of which M[r] S[t] Clair will inform you of, at the same time the bearer carryes order for all the Virginians to be ready to march immediately upon the arrival of Colonel Washington, who sets out for that purpose tomorrow morning, which will deminish the Consumpsion of Provisions at Fort Cumberland very considerably, and make it a very easy matter to support you for the future as your numbers will be so much diminish'd.

Three days ago Comissary Clerk[97] wrote to M[r] Rutherford[98] at Winchester, to supply your people with spirits, and all the other necessarys that you desir'd, which letter I hope will be in good time to answer your expectations I am Dear Sir

Your most obedient humble servant

Francis Halkett

*   *   *   *   *

---

[96] Cf. Forbes to Peters, August 28, 1758, *ante*, p. 191. Other letters not found.

* Printed, *Md. Arch.* IX, 266.

[97] Daniel Clark, earlier a lieutenant in the Augusta Regiment of Foot of Pennsylvania.

[98] Probably Thomas Rutherford, the Indian trader.

*James Sinclair to Sharpe**
[Md.H.S. Port Folio 4, Papers and Letters, Letter 41. A.L.S.]

Camp at Rays Town 16th Septemr 1758

Sir

I am desired by General Forbes to acquaint you that he is in the greatest concern to find Mr Rutherford, to whom the suplying of fort Cumberland was entirely intrusted, has not yet furnished the necessary Suplys, as the General had given such directions for that purpose, as he thought could not fail of doing it effectiualy before your arrival. There was an Express sent off yesterday to Mr Rutherford from Mr Hoops Constituent[99] at this place, to hasten things as much as possible and order him up immediately from Winchester, in the mean time, if you will be so good as let the General know your wants, they shall be suplyed from hence as well as possible, notwithstanding the great difficulty we ly under with regard to Carriages.

Sir John St Clair is returned form the Mountains, he staid here one Night, and is set out for Philadelphia and the Lower Counties to hasten up provisions & Carriages. I am with greatest Respect

Sir Your most obedient
& most humble Servant

James Sinclair

His Excellt Gover. Sharp.
[*Addressed:*] On his Majestys Service
To His Excellency Governor Sharpe
at Fort Cumberland

*   *   *   *   *

*Forbes to Washington***
[MSS. Papers of Washington. IX, 1156, A.L.S.; H.S.P.MSS. Gratz Collection. L. S.]

Raestown 16 Sept. 1758

Sir,

I have the favor of yours[100] of the 12th and I am told Mr Rutherford's complaint is occasioned by Col Bouquet's having refused some cattle of Mr Walker's, that really was not fit to be used in our way, and therefore Col B. gave orders not to purchase any more such.

---

* Printed, *Md. Arch.* IX, 269.
99 Letter of Daniel Clark to Rutherford, not found.
** Printed, Hamilton, *Letters to Washington,* III, 103, and Stewart, *Letters of General John Forbes,* p. 46.
100 *Writings of Washington* (Fitzpatrick, ed.), II, 286.

I am estreamly obliged to you for your good wishes of recovery which I now really stand in need of, being quite as feeble as a child almost—however here I am and I hope to profit daily—I am sorry to hear poor friend Col°. Byrd has been very bad. I wish he were able to come here where I should hope to prove a better physician than he will probably meet with at Fort Cumberland. They tell me here that you threaten us with a visit soon, which I should be glad of whenever it happens, being very sincerely

Yr most obed^t.

J° fforbes.

Col° Washington
[*Endorsed:*] From Honble Gene^l Forbes
16th Sept 1758

*   *   *   *   *

*Forbes to Sharpe**
[H.S.P.MSS. Dreer Collection. Letters of Officers Serving in America before the Revolution, L.S.]

Raestown 16th Septem^r 1758

Dear Sir

I received your letter[1] from Fort Cumberland at Juniata last night, and that I might answer it more exactly brought your officer on here this day, where I now find there has a transport gone from here this morning for Fort Cumberland with provisions which will serve in the meantime untill Mr. Rutherford arrives; what I was to do with regard to spirits I could not well say, imagining they could be bought as reasonable and cheap at Fort Cumberland as they could be sent from this, but now being informed of the contrary I have ordered two hogsheads to be sent off directly, which will give me time to look me for a day or two and draw Breath, being at this present moment in bed wearied like a dog.

I have the most laconic letter from Dr. Ross[2] that ever was wrote to a Gentleman where £1500. was concerned, consisting of these words. "Sir I have received yours and shall report to Govr Sharp. I am Sir"—In a day or two I hope to write you more fully upon several other things. In the meantime I am very sincerely

Yr most obed^t &
Most hum^{le} Servt

Jo fforbes

---

* Printed, *Pa. Mag.* XXXIII, 90, and Stewart, *Letters of General John Forbes,* p. 46.   [1] Of September 12, 1758, *Md. Arch.* IX, 266.
[2] Letter not found elsewhere.

P.S.—If spirits can be purchased reasonable at Fort Cumberland, I dont see why we should be obliged to send them from this. Mr. St. Clair is just now come in and informs me that the transport of provisions above mentioned, did not proceed as I have said—However as there is an Express gone to Winchester to Mr. Rutherford to hasten him up, I hope you will be able to make a shift untill that he arrives or that I can send you a fresh supply, which shall be the first thing I shall take care of when any comes to this place, and that expect tomorrow or the day after

Govr Sharp

[*Endorsed:*] from Genl Forbes to Governor Sharpe

H.S. [Horatio Sharpe]

*   *   *   *   *

Forbes to Bouquet
[B.M., Add. MSS. 21640, f. 165. L.S.]

Raes town Sepr 17th 1758.

Sir.

I got to this place night before last, and found every thing very quiet, Altho' I had a good deal of inquietude with regard to your Provisions, of which you had acquainted me in your letter[3] of the 13th but your letter[4] of the 13th and 14th that came to Col^o Mercer yesterday morning quite alarmed me, so you might believe I lost not a moments time in sending you all the assistance that I could, altho' upon enquiry Lieu^t St Clair informed me that there were provisions in plenty sent to you, which tho perhaps not then come to hand, yet your anxiety upon that head must by that time have been relieved by a letter[5] that Col^o Mercer[6] had sent you Express.

I am equaly embarrassed with regard to Fort Cumberland, where they are in great want, and intirely owing to the neglect of the Commissarys; I have run directly to Col^o Washington[7] and Govern^r Sharp[8] to quiet their minds as much as possible upon that head but I have seen with regret for this some time past a Jealousy and suspicion subsisting on the part of the

---

[3] Not found.

[4] Not found.

[5] Of September 14, 1758, B.M., Add. MSS. 21643, f. 275, A.L.S.

[6] Hugh Mercer (*c.* 1725-1777), Scotch born physician and soldier. His military services in Pennsylvania and later in the American Revolutionary War were noteworthy. Consult the *D.A.B.*, but more particularly an unpublished thesis at the University of Pittsburgh, "Hugh Mercer," by Beatrice Novak.

[7] Forbes to Washington, September 16, 1758, *ante,* p. 210.

[8] Forbes to Sharp, September 16, 1758, *ante,* p. 211.

Virginians which they can have no reason for, as I believe neither you nor I values one farthing where we get provisions from, provided we are supplyed, or Interest ourselves either with Virginia or Pennsylvania, which last I hope will be damn'd for their treatment of us with the Waggons, and every other thing where they could profit by us from their impositions, Altho' at the risque of our perdition. All this I have by letters again and again acquainted the Govern[9] The Commissioners,[10] and the principal people[11] of Philadelphia with, and notwithstanding I hear you have been told the Contrary I have wrote to Govern Denny as you desired a publick letter[12] to be shewn to the Assembly in the strongest words I could conceive, as likewise to M Isaac Norris,[13] M Israel Pemberton,[14] M Allen,[15] M Hughes,[16] and M Galway,[17] besides a flumary [sic] letter[18] along with S John to the Commissioners, all requesting their aid and assistance in procuring of Waggons, leaving the price to be paid them by us, to themselves, only beging that there might be no time lost in the execution, for in that case I had sent down S John S Clair with my possitive orders to call in the whole troops from their Eastern frontier, and to sweep the whole Country indiscriminately of every Waggon, Cart, or Horse that he could find.

This I hope by this time has had its effect, and therefore I hope we shall have no farther complaints, particularly as some quickening letters of mine to M Howell[19] and M Kilby[20] has succeeded to Admiration, M Howell writing me[21] that he has already dispatched from Philadelphia 460 Barr of the best Pork, and has 400 more ready to send off as soon as the Waggons comes in, which now as they are to be paid so much P hund Weight come in apace and of their own accord, so that I fancy by this time we have near 900 Barrels of Pork all upon the road betwixt this and Philadelphia. Flour &c I expect in proportion, and this very day I send of an Express with an open order[22] to be shewn to all Waggon Masters, and officers who command the escortes, to hasten up their Convoys with proper dilligence, so as not to ruin the Horses.

---

[9] Forbes to Denny, September 9, 1758, *ante,* p. 206.

[10] Letters not found.

[11] Cf. Forbes to Peters, August 28, 1758, *ante,* p. 206.

[12] September 9, 1758, *ante,* p. 191.

[13] Isaac Norris, Speaker of the Assembly of Pennsylvania.

[14] Israel Pemberton, prominent Pennsylvania Quaker.

[15] [William] Allen, prominent figure of Philadelphia.

[16] [John] Hughes, Provincial Commissioner.

[17] Misspelling for Galloway, Joseph, distinguished lawyer, Provincial Commissioner, later a famous loyalist.

[18] Not found.   [19] Not found.   [20] Not found.   [21] Not found.   [22] Not found.

Col⁰ Washington came here last night and goes back to Fort Cumberland this day in order to march the Virginia troops here as soon as possible.

Col⁰ Armstrong wrote me²³ desiring he might have a party of 300 men of his own Regimᵗ to go against Venango. I assure you I have had that long in view, but do not know at this time how proper it would be, as a repulse to any of our partys may be of bad consequence, I beg therefore you will examine into the practicability of such an attempt, as likewise into the difficulties that may attend it, the succeeding in such a thing would be as lucky to us as the Landing at Louisbourg was to them.

I am sorry to hear you complain of the roads, as Sⁱʳ John told me they were extreamly good, I hope therefore you will give necessary directions about them and if easily executed the cutting of the flank roads upon each side of the great road which will greatly shorten our line of March and facilitate our forming in order of Battle. I suppose I shall see you soon and we shall talk over these and several other affairs, My compliments to Major Grant and the rest of the officers and believe me Dear Sⁱʳ most sincerely

Yʳ very humˡᵉ Servᵗ &c

Jo: fforbes.

[*In Forbes' handwriting*:] C: Bradstreet has taken Cataraqui, with all their Ship's and a great booty of Furrs &c &c the particulars I have not time to write you—but I wish the French and Indians knew it, pray haste doen, but leave nothing undone, and Strict Look out for fear of a Surprize, I shall fire a *feu de joye* here to morrow.

[*Endorsed:*] General Forbes [*illegible*]

* * * * *

Forbes to Barrow
[B.M., Add. MSS. 21643, f. 200. LS.]

Reas Town, Sept. 19, 1758.

By John Forbes Esqʳ Brigadier General of his Majesty's Forces in North America, Colonel of the Seventeenth Regiment of Foot and Commanding his Majesty's Forces in the Southern Provinces of America.

You are hereby directed and required out of such Monies as are or shall come to your Hands for the Subsistence of his Majesty's Forces under my Command, to pay or cause to be paid, to Mr. James Young Paymaster to the Pennsylvania Regiments, or his Assigns, the Sum of Eight Hundred and nine Pounds, seven Shillings and nine Pence Sterling, without

---

²³ Not found.

Deduction, on account of Money advanced by him to Mr John Billings,[24] Deputy Paymaster to four Company's of the first Battalion of the Royal American Regiments for Subsistence of the said four Companies from the 25th of June 1758. And for so doing This with the Bills drawn on you by said Mr Billings to the Amount of the above Sum shall be your Sufficient Warrant and Discharge.

Given under my Hand at the Camp near Raes Town 19th September 1758.

Jo: fforbes.

[*Addressed:*] To Thomas Barrow Esqr Deputy Pay Master General at Camp near Rays Town
Ja^s Young Paymaster to the Pennsylvania Forces.
[*Endorsed:*] Mr. James Young Paymaster to the Pennsylvania Reg^t on Acc^t of Money Advanced by him to Mr Billings Pay M^r To the first Battalion of Royal Americans for Subsistence to the 25th of June 1758. Sterling £ 809..7..9

Camp Reas Town 19th Sepr 1758.

Entred

*   *   *   *   *

Forbes to Abercromby
[AB   709   L.S.]

[Reas Town, September 21, 1758]

Dear Sir

The joy of Bradstreets success at Cadiraque has been a good deal damped by a letter[25] that I received yesterday evening from Col^o Bouquet at Loyal Hannon on the other side of Laurell ridge, acquainting me of a severe check that Major Grant with [near]† above 800 men had met with at Fort Du Quesne.

He promised to send me an officer with more circumstantial accounts, but least you hear from other hands, I send you what he wrote me p^r Express, and shall acquaint you more fully when the officer arrives.

You will see by Col^o Bouquets letter that he Endeavours all in his power to apologize for this rash attempt, which was in every article directly contrary to my own opinion and my orders.[26] founded upon the best

---

[24] Lieutenant John Billings of the 6oth regiment.
[25] In French, B.M., Add. MSS. 21640, f. 167, September 17, 1758.
† Stricken out.
[26] On the validity of this claim, the earlier letters of Forbes to Bouquet throw some doubt.

information that I could possibly pick up in these parts, of the Enemys strength &c^a and to all of which I have Col^o Bouquets letters of assurances,[27] that all my direction should be faithfully complyed with which considering the situation of my little Army—was absolutely necessary, at that time, however as there is no recalling what's past, I only write the above to yourself, only I may be allowed to observe that the rashness and ambition of some people[28] brings great mischief and distress upon their friends of which you will be thoroughly sensible by the following Anecdotes.
G: Abercromby.

Early after my arrival at Philadelphia I sent S^ir John St Clair up the country to repair the roads, and lay in Provender of all kinds at every post or Stage the length of this place, where he was forced to form a large magazine for the maintenance of the horses forward, on towards the Ohio, upon assurances of this being fully executed, I then entered into Contract with the Waggons and begun the transport of my provisions in order to form my first magazine or Deposite at this place, and likewise begun to assemble my troops and new Levies in order to put them into a little form, and to serve as Escortes for the Waggons from post to post, upon the growth of the magazines here, but finding the daily consumption rather exceed what I could bring into magazine [first]† I was obliged to stop the march of the troops in order to let the magazine grow a little ahead, that so I might meet with no stop for want of provisions in going directly forward; in the mean time compleating and carrying forward my road, over the Allegheny mountain, and Laurell hill, and subsisting my whole chain upon live cattle that came in very regularly, All those necessary impediments gave me no pain or disquietude as by that means I gave the Indians full time of being sensible of their Errors and of their reconciling themselves to us at this treaty now holding at Easton, which I most earnestly laboured to bring about being thoroughly sensible of the innumerable difficulties, I must have been laid under such an immoderate length and num^r of transport, carriages, thrô so long a tract of desart and, wilderness, if I met with no forbearance or relaxation from the Indians than to a man all our Enemies.

Upon examining from time to time the state of the magazine and finding it not increased,—according to my expectation, I found the Waggons in place of carrying 2000 w^t were only able to carry 12 or 1400 w^t and that

---

[27] Bouquet's letters of assurances, August 20, 1758, and August 26, 1758, B.M., Add. MSS. 21640, f. 147 and 153 are none too specific on this matter.
[28] A reference to Major James Grant and possibly to Bouquet.
† Stricken out.

in place of making their Journeys in 12 days, they were scarce able to execute it in 20 or 24 days, this you see makes great odds in my calculations, and upon examining into the cause found that there was not a single bit of provender laid in, to the westward of Susquehanah, by which their horses were starved and rendered absolutely unfit for carrying on the Service, and consequently obliged to discharge them—to remedy this worst of evils I employed every means I possibly could contrive, and have just now about surmounted all difficulties by the help of the Assembly, and my personal friends at Philadelphia there being now on the road betwixt that and this place near 2 months salt provisions flour &c^a for 6 or 7000 men upon which foundation I could have proceeded any where or at any time what effect this unfortunate check will have with my provincialls, I do not as yet know But As the Virginians join me here tomorrow I will endeavour to find out by their countenances, what is in their hearts, and so proceed accordingly, Altho my information of the Enemys strength both as to Indians, French and Canadians and the present situation of their fort be infinitely stronger than any thing I ever could have imagined.

Mr Croghan Mr Montour and others sending me positive accounts[29] that their numbers exceed greatly 4000, in and about the Fort which altho I don't believe will yet oblige me to act with more circumspection, considering this unhappy affair of Grant's may fix some of the wavering Indians still to their Interest

I send you enclosed a list[30] of those officers said to be killed and by which you will see the necessity of sending me some reinforcement if you had it in your power; for the Detail of my Army, Guards, Garrisons, Escorts &c^a is immense in proportion to my numbers, and will leave me almost as few to act with as Major Grant had under his Command, who upon his Detachment had not made choice of the worst of Montgomery's regim^t. So you may very well imagine how I am circumstanced and what a loss I sustain in Major Grants person and Mr Rhor the Engineer which last was of more service in his way than all the rest of that Class put together.

I am sure you feel for me, and doubt not but you will send me all the good news you can get by way of comfort, and to prevent dejection of spirits we must put the best gloss upon this affair that it will bear in the mean time I beg my compliments to all with you and I thank you heartily for your good wishes. Altho I must tell you that my bodily in-

---

[29] No letters found to Forbes from Croghan and Montour, of this date.

[30] AB 659, copy. Printed, Balch, ed. *Letters and Papers* . . . p. 139, and *Pa. Arch.* 5th series, I, 253-254.

firmities are such, that had I time from the publick care, I am fitter for
a Bed and women's milk, than for the active scene that I am like to pass,
for this month to come, for Col° Bouquet excepted I am solus in every
thing even down to the triffling detail of Camp duty—

I am very unwell so can not write more or even correct this, but shall
write in a day or two—All my letters must both come and go to Philadelphia by express—there being no post regulate—

I am D^r S^{ir} Y^r most ob^t

hum^{le} Servt   Jo fforbes.

G. Abercromby.

*   *   *   *   *

*Forbes to Bouquet**
[B.M., Add. MSS. 21640, f. 173. A.L.S.]

Raestown, September 23, 1758.

Sir:—Your letter of the 17th,[31] from Loyal Hanning, I read with no
less surprise than real concern, as indeed I could not well believe that such
an attempt would have been carried into execution without my previous
knowledge and concurrence, as you well know my opinion, and dread of the
consequences of running any risque of the troops meeting with the smallest
check. As well as my fears of alienating and altering the disposition of the
Indians, at this critical time, who (tho' fickle and wavering), yet were
seemingly well disposed to embrace out alliance and protection. But I need
not recapitulate to you my good reasons against any attempt of this kind
being made at this time; nor repeat to you how happy your assurances[32]
made me, of all my orders and directions having been (and would be) complyed with. For which I rested secure, and plumed myself in our good
fortune, in having the head of our army advanced, as it were, to the beard
of the enemy, and secured in a good post well guarded and cautioned against
surprise. Our road almost completed; our provisions all upon wheels, and
all this without any loss on our side, and our small army all ready to join
and act in a collected body whenever we pleased to attack the enemy, or
that any favourable opportunity presented itself to us.

Thus the breaking in upon—not to say disappointments of—our hitherto
so fair and flattering hopes of sucess touches most sensibly. How far we

---

* Printed, Darlington, *Fort Pitt and Letters from the Frontier,* p. 71, and Stewart,
Letters of General John Forbes, p. 51.
[31] B.M., Add. MSS. 21640, f. 167.
[32] Cf. footnote 26, of the preceding document.

shall find the bad effects of it, I shall not pretent to say. At present I shall suspend judging, altho' I have languished for the officer you promised to send me down—whom I have expected hourly—and a letter from you of your present situation, with the state of the posts, and the strength at them, that the escorts may be proportioned. I acquainted you of the state of our provisions, and the hopes I have of being immediately supplied with 1,000 barrels of pork and at least 1,200 barrels of flour, all of which, by this time, is actually upon its march, and will arrive here daily. So, I shall forward it as fast as I can, altho' large convoys and escorts are very inconvenient. The description of the roads is so various and disagreeable that I do not know what to think or say. Lieutenant Evans came down here the other day, and described the Laurel Hill as, at present, impractible, but said he could mend it with the assistance of 500 men, fascines and fagots, in one days time.

Col. Stephens[33] writes[34] Col. Washington that he is told by everybody that the road from Loyal Hannon to the Ohio and the French fort is now impractible. For what reason, or why, He writes thus I do not know; but I see Col. Washington and my friend, Col. Byrd, would be rather glad this was true than otherways, seeing the other road (their favourite scheme) was not followed out. I told them plainly that, whatever they thought, yet I did aver that, in our prosecuting the present road, we had proceeded from the best intelligence that could be got for the good and convenience of the army, without any views to oblige any one province or another; and added that those two gentlemen were the only people that I had met with who had showed their weakness in their attachment to the province they belong to, by declaring so publickly in favour of one road without their knowing anything of the other, having never heard from any Pennsylvania person one word about the road; and that, as for myself, I could safely say —and believed I might answer for you—that the good of the service was the only view we had at heart, not valuing the provincial interest, jealousys, or suspicions, one single twopence, and that, therefore, I could not believe Col. Stephen's descriptions untill I has heard from you, which I hope you will very soon be able to disprove.

I fancy what I said more on this subject will cure them from coming upon this topic again. However, I beg you will cause look into the Laurell Hill, and let it be set to rights as fast as possible; and let all the different

---

[33] Adam Stephen (c. 1730-1790), officer in Virginia militia, 1754-1763, and a major-general in the American Revolution.

[34] September 9, 1758, and September 10, 1758, Hamilton, *Letters to Washington*, II, 88 and 98.

posts, and the different convoys and escorts, as they pass along, repair the bad steps, and keep the roads already made in constant order.

I have sent Mr. Basset[35] back the length of Fort Loudoun, in order to divide the troops from thence to Juniata, in small partys, all along that road, who are to set it all to rights, and keep it so; and as the partys are all encamped within five or six miles one of another, they serve as escorts to the provisions and forage that is coming up, at the same time. I am extreamly sorry for your loss of De Rhorr; nor can I well conceive what I had to do there. Mr. Gordon, who, it seems had the direction of the works here, left this without leaving the plan or sketch of this place or environs, or leaving any directions, as far as I can yet learn, either with the people employed to carry the general plan into execution, or how that they were further to proceed; and notwithstanding the multiplicity of working-tools, I am at a loss to find a sufficient number for helping the roads and clearing the stumps or other impediments about the camp; nor can I well imagine what is become of all the rest.

There are two wounded Highland officers just now arriv'd, who give so lame an account of how matters proceeded, or any kind of description of the ground, that one can draw nothing from them—only that my friend Grant had most certainly lost the *tra mon tane,* and by his thirst of fame, brought on his own perdition, and run a great risque of ours, which was far wide of the promises he made me at Carlisle, when soliciting to command a party, which I would not agree to; and, very contrary to his criticisms upon Gen. Abercromby's late affair, has fallen unhappily into the individual same error, by his inconsiderate and rash proceeding.

I understand by these officers that you have withdrawn the troops from your advanced post, which I attribute to its being too small for what you intended it, or that it did not answer the strength that you at first described it to me. I shall be glad to hear all your people are in spirits, and keep so, and that Loyal Hannon will be soon past any insult without cannon, I shall be soon afraid to crowd you with provisions, nor would I wish to crowd the troops any faster up, untill our magazines are thoroughly formed, if you have enough of troops for your own defence and compleating the roads; and I see the absolute necessity there is for my stay here some days, in order to carry on the transport of provisions and forage, which, without any constant attention, would fail directly. The road forward to the Ohio must be reconnoitered again in order to be sure of our further progress, for it would

---

[35] Lieutenant Thomas Basset of the 60th regiment. Note that according to Forbes to Abercromby, October 8, 1758, Basset was dying.

grieve me sadly that Mr. Washington or Mr. Byrd should have any reason to find fault with that, which without their knowledge they have so publickly exclaimed against. When you have settled things to your mind, I beg you will write me, and as soon as you conveniently can, come down, were it only for a day, and if Colonel Armstrong could be spared, should be glad he came along, in order to settle our further proceedings, and to sieze the first favourable opportunity of marching directly forwards. The artillery that is left here I would march in two divisions to prevent a long train of waggons, and the tearing up of the roads. The Congress at Eastown had the most favourable appearance, as there was 500 Indians already come in, but what they will now do, God knows. Pray make up a hovell or hutt for me at L. Hannon or any other of the other posts with a fire place if possible Sir John St. Clair says that if I say he was in the wrong to Colonel Stevens, he will readily acknowledge it. I do not choose meddling, but I think Colonel Stevens might act, and trust to Sir John's acknowledgment.

I am, dear sir,

Your most obedient servant,

Jo. fforbes.

* * * * *

Major Halkett to Sharpe*
Md. Arch. IX, 271. A.L.S.]

Camp at Raestown 30th September 1758.

Sir

The General being a good deal overcome with the bussiness that he has been obliged to go through, makes him unable to do himself the pleasure of writing you by this conveyance, he has therefore order'd me to acknowledge his Receiving your letter[36] this day, in which he approves greatly of every-thing you say regarding the sick at Fort Cumberland, but as it would be attended with great inconvenniency to make a Detachment from this place just now for the Garrisoning of Fort Cumberland, he is in hopes you will be able to detain the Militia now with you till the tenth of October, against (which) time he will take care to provide for its security, and in a few days he will take an opportunity to write you very fully in answer to your letter.

The Virginians make a Complaint of some of your people haveing taken up some of their horses, as stray horses & detain them, altho some of their

---

* The original can no longer be found.
[36] Sharpe to Forbes, without date, *Md. Arch.* IX, 270.

Boss men were sent over to demand them, the General therefore begs that you will be so good to examine into it, and put it to Rights, and as they have sent a party to Receive them that you will order them to be deliver'd

The General desires that you will inform Lieutenant Haze[37] of the Virginians, that it is his orders, he remain at Fort Cumberland with all the sick & recover'd men under his command til further orders.

I am Sir
Your most obedient humble serv^t
Francis Halkett.

*   *   *   *   *

Halkett to Sharpe*
[Md. H.S. Gilmore Papers. Vol. 2, Division 1, Letter 8b. A.L.S.]

Camp at Reastown 2^d October 1758

Sir

About this time we expect their will be a number of the Shannondo Waggons arriving at Fort Cumberland, with provisions from Winchester; the General therefore begs that you will be so good as to engage as many of them as possible, upon the same terms as the Pennsylvania Waggons, to go upon our Expedition, and that you will take the opportunity of their comeing here, to send over all the Buck Shott at Fort Cumberland, seven Boxes containing two hundred wight each, were lodg'd in the new store under the hill, which was sent from Fort Frederick, along with the shelles six hundred wight was likewise lodg'd in store that was blowen up, if any of that Remains undistroyed, you will send it also, and provided the Carriages can be ready time enough they may take the benefite of the officers & thirty men sent from the second Virginia Regiment for horses, to escort them. if this party marches before that the Waggons can be got Ready they must be Escorted by the Recover'd men of the Virginia Regiments.

If their are any spair Wheels or carriages for Hobtzers be pleasd to send them likewise in some of the empty Waggons, Captain Hay haveing brought no spair ones with the Train and we may come to have occasion for them I am

Sir
Your most obedient humble Servt
Francis Halkett.

---

[37] Probably Captain Andrew Hays.
* Printed, *Md. Arch.* IX, 272.

P.S. Upon showing this letter to the General, he has alter'd that part of it, for the Recovered men of the Virginians to escort the Waggons, provided the officer & 30 men be Return'd with the Horses, and desires that you will favour him with a few lines to inform him of the number you can engage, and he will order a party from this Camp to March to Fort Cumberland to Escort them hither, he hopes you will pardon his not being able to do himselfe the pleasure of writing to you, but he will take the first opportunity that offers.

[*Endorsed:*] From Major Halkett 2ᵈ Oct. 1758.

* * * * *

Forbes to Bouquet
[B.M., Add. MSS. 21640, f. 175. L.S.]

[Raystown, Oct. 5, 1758]

Sir

You are hereby required to order as many Gentlemen as you may imagine are competent Judges to hold a Court of Enquiry,[38] to examine into the affair of Captain Clayton;[39] and to acquaint me of such Report as they shall make to you

I am Sⁱʳ Yʳ most humˡᵉ Sevᵗ

Jo: fforbes.

Camp at Raystown 5ᵗʰ Octr. 1758.
To Colᵒ Bouquet.
[*Addressed:*] To Colᵒ Bouquet
[*Endorsed:*] General Forbes's orders for an Inquiry in Capᵗ Clayton's Affair 5ᵗʰ Octʳ 1758

* * * * *

Forbes to Sharpe*
[Md. H.S. Port Folio 4. Papers and Letters, No. 36. L.S.]

[Raes Camp, October 5, 1758]

Sir

I am this moment favored with yours[40] and am very much obliged to you, for the Care you have taken of our good Fort Cumberland, this will be delivered you by Mʳ Clerk,[41] whom I had sent over on purpose to settle

---

[38] Records of the Court of Inquiry, not found.
[39] Captain Asher Clayton, of the Second Battalion of the Pennsylvania Regiment.
* Printed, *Md. Arch.* IX, 274.
[40] Sharpe to Forbes, October (1758), *Md. Arch.* IX, 271.
[41] Daniel Clark. Cf. Clarke to Sharpe, October 23, 1758, *Md. Arch.* IX, 277.

matters with regard to provisions &c, So whatever you have wanted or may want he will settle with you as you shall please to direct, as to the Virginia complaint I thought it frivilous and triffling from the beginning, you can easily see I was obliged to take notice of it, on purpose to please. I shall send of an Escort tomorrow for the Waggons, but if the Escort of Coll° Byrds Reg^t is not yet come away, they may Stay and Come along with the Waggons, or escort them till they meet the Party I send off tomorrow. As there will be some empty waggons, I shall expect the Spare Wheel Carriage that Major Halket wrote about. As I understand you have some Garden Stuff such as Cabbage, &c. I beg you will be so good as ord^r some to be sent over by the Waggons. I am

My Dr Sir

Your most Obd^t humble Servt

Jo. fforbes

Raes Camp Octob^r 5th 1758.
Excuse another hand having been unable to write myself these ten days.
[*Addressed:*] To His Excellency
         Governor Sharpe
[*Endorsed:*] From Gen'l Forbes
         Oct 5th 1758

*   *   *   *   *

Forbes to Abercromby
[AB 736 L.S.]

[Rays Camp, October 8th 1758]

Dear S^{ir}

Capt McIntosh[42] got here night before last, and delivered me yours of the 7th Septem^r.[43]

I was extreamly glad to find you were all in health and spirits, and ready for a second visit to your neighbours down the Lake, I pray you God you may find less trouble in sailing twenty, than I find in advancing one mile, but to describe the many, many impediments that I meet with in this wilderness, with this hand full of men would take a Volume, and that filled with the villiany and Rascality of the Inhabitants, who to a man seem rather bent upon our ruin, and destruction, than give the smallest assistance, which if

---

[42] Probably Captain Alexander McIntosh of the 77th regiment.

[43] AB 618, copy, dated September 6, 1758. In AB 635, copy, is another letter dated September 9, 1758.

at last extorted is so infamously charged as shews the disposition of the people in its full Glare.

You heard I was very bad; no mortal could well have been worse and alive, which prevented my writing you the few things I have since learned of Major Grants affair, which to be sure no man can justify; only, a Story prevailed of the French weakness at Fort Du Quesne, which I am afraid made the major run headlong to grasp at a name, and publick applause, forgetting the inevitable mischief he was bringing upon me, and the rest of us. However it is now over and I am glad to tell you, that Grant is a prisoner and untouched, and is sent to Montreal with major Lewis[44] of the Virginians and some other officers, as you will see by the enclosed list,[45] as also the killed—I send you likewise Col.° Montgomery's recommendation[46] to the succession of Vacancies in the Reg[t] and Col° Bouquet has no body to recommend but one M[r] Hasse[47] whose character you will get from Brigadier Stanwix. as I know nothing of him. All our men are in spirits and I purposed long ere this, to have repayed M[r]. Grants reception with cost, but our Waggoners deserted by Dozens, our Magazines daily Consuming, and our Enemy daily more impudent and presuming, so that without a miracle I was at my journey's end, But by getting an act of the assembly[48] passed in my favour for the transport of provisions up this length at the small, moderate price of two and forty shillings pr hundred weight, I have got provisions up to this, but neither prayers nor entreaties, not even Money has the smallest Influence to get them one foot further, so I must compell them which makes a dreadfull piece of work.

M[r]. Gordon the Engineer has either gone off at the nail, or is turned so dilatory in every measure under his charge that it is almost impossible to get any one thing done to the purpose where he is concerned. If a triffle is to be done he makes it a labour to man and horse, and if a work of consequence makes slight of it. This is at present cruell, and now Rhorr is dead Hesse and Basset dying, I have no resource. So this branch is infinite perplexity; and the Q[r]. M[n] Gen[ll] is beyond the power of man either to change or amend. And the immense confusion of Waggons and roads are intirely S[ir] Johns creating, who by a certain dexterity has you in fresh Dilemna's

---

[44] Andrew Lewis (1720-1781), Virginia frontiersman and soldier; in the expeditions of Braddock and Forbes; in Lord Dunmore's War; and brigadier general in the War of the Revolution. Consult the *D.A.B.*

[45] Found in AB 639. Printed in Balch, *Letters and Papers* . . . p. 139.

[46] Not located.

[47] Mr. Hasse, private, first battalion, R.A.R.

[48] September 20, 1758, *Pa. Col. Recs.* VIII, 171.

every day, and with his solemn face will tell you when he has done the worst, that he really acted for the best and can justify it.

It is now ten days past, when I proposed to have marched from this, and to have marched directly for the banks of the Ohio, which would have taken eight days, having all or most of my Artillery before me within 34 miles of F. Duquesne but the provisions and Waggons put an absolute barr to that Step for a few days, and was no sooner remedied, than some excessive rains made the roads absolutely impracticable for Bats horses. So spite of all tentatives and endeavours to be of some service to the publick, for the incredible expence of so small a handfull of men, yet hitherto all my endeavours have by some fatality or other been frustrated. It is true I can account and give reasons for most of our transactions and all those dont answer the publick cry of Blood for my money.

The Indians I cannot mention to you with any manner of patience, as I look upon them, their Interpreters, their Superintendents, and every creature any ways connected or attached to them, as the most imposing Rogues that I have ever had to deal with. The manner that they have been manadged here for these twelve months by past, has absolutely put it out of our power, almost ever to have any more dealings, or trust in them. They have cost to the provinces and Crown, incredible sums of money, and except about 14 Catawbas who have behaved well at major Grants affair, no one other tribe has done any one piece of service. And they as well as the rest of the Cherokees amounting only in the whole to 100 men leaving you every day, unless retained by presents, which I do assure you they neither do nor ever can deserve, So as one may pay a great deal too dear for Gold, and that they most certainly will not stay to go to the Ohio, but carry away whatever they can get, therefore I must stop, altho it will seem odd to stop at the very critical minute, when I daily expect to come to a determination of the military operations in these desarts.

Pray my compliments to Gen.[11] Amherst if with you, I should be obliged to him if he will send me a small sprigg of his Laurells for my cursed wilderness produces nothing but briars and thorns, nor is there great hopes of vast improvement considering the labourers I must work with, who are beyond all description.

Major Derby[49] and Halkett have again spoke to me with regard to Col° Morris, As you know the affair I shall not teaze you, only I think you will oblige worthy men, and do a great deal of good to the service and Regiment.

---

[49] Major John Derby [Darby] of the 17th regiment.

As the reg^t wants a great reform and the Grenadiers almost ruined I must beg the favour that you will be so good as send me off when you can spare them and the sooner the better. One Capt. 2 Subal^s Serj^s Corporals & Drum and a pretty good recruiting party as I make no doubt but to be able to compleat the regim^t directly, from among the Virginians and Pennsylvanians having previously bespoke about 50 as fine young fellows as I ever saw, and make no doubt but I could before christmas augment the regim^t to 1000 if the Goverm^t approved, and which I thing [sic] they do not.

As this is my first letter to any person since I wrote you last[50] you must not accuse me of either neglect or forgetfullness, as I have been uncapable, and now that major Grant is gone I have no mortal belonging to my Command that I can either trust with a letter, or argue seriously about Army proceedings, Frank Halkett alone excepted, who is most diligent, I long much to hear of your proceedings and success, as I am sure it would give us all fresh Vigour, wore out with eternall labour &c. of Body and mind. Mountains, rocks, swamps, deep clay ground, Thicketts &c, with unexpected and unusuall rains are terrible to deal with, and have everything to carry. It is now fair and two days more sends me of to do something which I really cannot at present name, as the Enemys strength is in spite of all my endeavours) yet a secret. Mr. Croghan &c is possitive and makes their numbers at least 4000. This I cannot believe no more than that their whole force are not 1200 men which in their fort, could be a troublesome affair to my whole Army—however I hope soon to be able to judge myself and send you a more satisfactory account.

I am extreamly weak, having been reduced to the last extremity, and began to think that trouble and vexation is extreamly wholesome, as it operates now and then or ten times a day upon me, like the strongest Cordiall.—

I am D^r S^{ir} Y^r most ob^t &

most hum^{le} Servt

Jo: fforbes.

Rays Camp October 8th, 1758
Gen^{ll} Abercromby
[Endorsed:] Brig^r. Genl. Forbes
    Raes Camp 8: October 1758.
    R the 28th
    Ans^d... 1st November.[51]

*   *   *   *   *

[50] September 21, 1758, ante, p. 215.
[51] AB 807, copy.

Forbes to Bouquet
[B.M., Add. MSS. 21640, f. 177. L.S.]

Reastown Camp Octr 10 1758

Sir

After so many reverses I was in hopes fortune might have favoured us with a little good weather for our roads Upon which the case of our future operations depends. I am in great anxiety for the whole but particularly the Laurell hill, of which I beg youl take particular notice and consequently Dont doubt but youl soon render it very good.

I have been oblidged to press fifty waggons that came from Philadelphia who shall leave this in two days as also the Artillery of the Rains will permitt.

The Little Carpenter and King Hagler left Winchester two Days ago so I expect them here soon with sixty three of their followers, if those will join as heartily and perswade the others to return I shall take my measures so as to march the whole as soon as possible and with very few halting days move on directly so you see there is no time to be lost.

I was told this day to my great surprize that Capt Gordon was building at Loyalhanna fitt to stand a siege, you know we want nothing but a strong post So for Gods sake think of both time money and Labour and put a Stop to all superfluitys I need neither recommend your reconitring before the advanced post, nor your letting me hear from you, as also what disposition you have made for the communication betwixt this, loyalhanan and the advanced post.

I begin to mend apace for tho my time is Disagreably spent for an invalid twixt bussiness and medicines I am with Compliments to all with you Dr Sir

Your most obedient & most humble servant.

Jo fforbes

[*Addressed:*] On his Majestys service To Colonel Henry Bouquet Commanding his Majestys forces at Loyal hannan or on his march
[*Endorsed:*] General Forbes 10. Oct^r

*   *   *   *   *

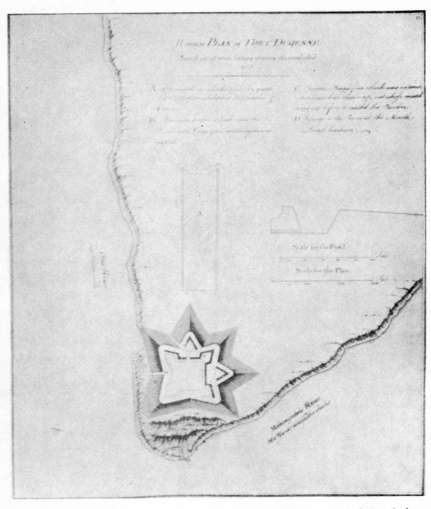

Reproduction of map, King's CXXII, 17, "Plan of Fort Duquesne, as it was before it was demolished, 1758," by J. C. Pleydell.

Forbes to Bouquet
[B.M., Add. MSS. 21640, f. 181. L.S.]

Raestown Camp Octr 15* 1758

Sir

Yesterday morning I was favoured with yours[52] of the 13th and this morning have yours[53] from Stony Creek of the 14th Upon your first letter I ordered Colonel Washingtone with his batalion consisting of two hundred men to proceed directly to reinforce Stony creek & Stopt an escort of fourty waggon load as likewise the last division of srtilery from proceeding.

I am very glad the Enemys visit[54] has turned out near as fruitless to them as ours was to us under Major Grant & hope at least that by this they will see we can fight.

I shall be very sorry, (unless they are greatly superiour in numbers) if they return unmolested which would show them their superiority over us in their fighting in the woods & give them a boldness that I would willingly crush.

Your Description of the roads peirces me to the very soul yet still my hopes are that a few Dry days would make things wear a more favourable aspect as all Clay Countrys are either good or bad for Cariages according to the wett or dry season It is true we cannot surmount impossibilitys nor prevent unforseen accidents but it must be a comfort to you and I still that we proceeded w^t Caution in the choice of this road and in the opinion of every Disinterested man, it had every advantage over the other and I am not sure but it has so still considering the Yachiogeny & Monongehela rivers—so I begg y^t you will without taking notice to any body make yourself master of the arguments for and the objections against the two roads so that upon comparison one may Judge how far we have been in the right in our Choice. Sir John Sinclair arrived here night before last and gives us a very good account both of our Waggons & provisions as the whole is in motion and by this time all betwixt this and Lancaster. I shall send you a general State of waggons baw [*sic*] horses provisions & forage[55] from which you will be able to Judge of our Situation & readiness to proceed if the

---

* An orderly book, containing numerous orders of Forbes, October 14-November 2, probably transcribed by Washington, is found in the Toner MSS. in the Library of Congress. Though not without value, these orders are omitted as too purely military.

[52] B.M., Add. MSS. 21640, f. 179.   [53] Not found.
[54] A reference to the Battle of Loyal Hannon of October 12, 1758.
[55] Not found.

weather permitts. I have sent you by this Convoy most of the things that you mention in the note you left with me of which M[r] Sinclair will send you an invoyce[56] Im affraid youl fall short both in blankits & Shoes nor could I ever remedy the scarcity of either tho I have long ago foreseen what might happen & sent the length of New York for both I have sent two hundred pair of Shoes which is all I could spare which you must take care to receive payment for. The Highlanders have Shoes coming up for themselves. I have sent two hundred pair of blankets & shall endeavour to send two hundred more by the next convoy but for Gods sake let them be given only where absolute necessity demmands because we can get no more

By Letters[57] from Easton The Congress is setting from whence I hope we will Draw some advantage altho not altogether what we expected. Their inteligence continues to be the same and the Ohio Indians have told them that the French will have in those parts near four thousand men French, Canadians, & Indians. That they have provisions in plenty as yet; That the Canadians are not all in the Fort but that they as well as the western Indians were scatered about in the Indian villages where they help the Inhabitants to build hutts & houses and were ready at a Call. That the Ohio Indians and Western Indians are at last perswaded by the French to Engage to assist them not only in Defence of their fort this fall but Drive us before winter back on this side the Alegany mountains. M[r] Crogan writes[58] me likeways that he is set out Directly to Join me with at least three score Clever fellows from Easton. This is all my news from Eastown a great part of which I cannot give too much credit to as I realy begin to think that this last trial of theirs was the making the most of the Indians before they should leave them.

Thirty Catabows from Winchester Joined the day before Yesterday as Did likeways the little Carpenter with about as many Cherokees: this gave me great hopes but those Indians under Bosomworths Direction and the others that were here who have been thoroughly spoiled by the presents already given them so as to make their Demands most insolent & most expensive have so far spoiled the rest that from the Carpenter down they appear either to be bullying us in to a mean complyance with their most sordid and avaritious demmands or they are absolutly determined to leave us and return home. This day I am to have a general meeting with them the result of which I cannot foresee altho you may be assured I will not loose them for a triffle. Yet at the same time Gold may be bought to dear

---

[56] Sinclair to Bouquet, October 18, 1758, B.M., Add. MSS. 21639, f. 68.
[57] Not found.   [58] Not found.

I can think of no more to say referring you for particulars to M Grant[59] who I have sent with this and who you will be so good as send back as soon as you well can.

You may be sure that with regard to an order of battle or fighting I will take all the care I can to make use of the most elegible and shall be cautious to whom I open my mind before you and I settle things.

I am Sir Your most obedient humble ser^t

Jo: fforbes.

N B If any party goes out after the Enemy they ought to have instructions always with regard to the roads forward as likeways ye Communication twixt Loyalha[na] and the nearest part of Mr Braddocks road which [blotted] want of all things to be reconitred in order to stop foolish mouths if it chances to prove anyways good or practicable May not such a communication be found without passing the Laurel hills.

[In Forbes's handwriting:] I do not know whether you may not have occasion to write or send to Fort du Quesne, but if you have any such occasion, you may assure the French Commander that the Famous Little Carpenter is come here, and that I will use my best endeavours to gett back Mr Belletre[60] from the Cherokees, King Higlaar of the Catawbas stay^d at Winchester, but I hope to gett him up.

[Addressed:] On his Majestys service to Colonel Bouquet Commanding his Majestys forces at Stony creek.

[Endorsed:] General Forbes. 15th October 1758

*   *   *   *   *

Forbes to Abercromby
[AB 767 L.S.; P.R.O. W.O.:34:34, f. 367. Copy.]

Rays Town Camp October 16th 1758

Sir

I wrote[61] you 8th letting you know that I was in readiness to seize the first fair moment that the weather and roads would allow us to proceed, in this situation I remained to the 13th absolutely confined by rain and the roads then Impracticable, when I received accounts[62] of the French having

---

[59] Probably Lieutenant James Grant of the 77th regiment. Cf. Halkett to Bouquet, August 2, 1758, *ante*, p. 163.

[60] Francois Mary Picoté de Belestre.   [61] *Ante*, p. 224.

[62] Bouquet to Forbes, October 13, 1758 and October 15, 1758, B.M. Add. MSS. 21640, f. 179 and 183.

attacked our advanced post at Loyall Hannon, My furthermost advanced post 10 miles nigher the Enemy having been called in ever since major Grant's affair, and not to be occupied again untill that the whole marched forward.

The 12th in the morning about eleven oclock the advanced post were alarmed by hearing some fireing about half a mile from them, which was succeeded by the Indian Halloo upon which 60 of the marylanders run towards the place whence the noise came, and when they got up, the firing became brisk—whereupon Colonel Burd of the pennsylvanians who commanded, ordered a party of the first Battalion of pennsylvanians to go and support the Marylanders, who had not marched half a mile when they met with the Enemy who were surrounding the Marylanders, and gave them their fire for some time, but upon finding them too numerous begun to retreat, a third party was ordered out, but the fire encreasing and approaching the breast work, the rest of the troops were ordered to their posts in the breast work and to line the skirts of the wood to favour the retreat of the three partys, and the alarm Guns were fired to make the Cattle and horse Guards take care themselves. In about an hour from the beginning the Enemy had drove our people into the breastwork and appeared in numbers along the edge of the wood from whence they begun afresh a very brisk fire, but our Cannon & Cohorns kept them at a distance, and certainly did execution as they were well served, however after an hours firing and finding they could make no impression they began to retire leaving only two killed and one wounded where the fire was hottest. It is said that they carried off the killed and wounded as they fell and retired in the evening to five miles distance, and next morning were seen by some of our returning scouting partys fifteen miles off. We saved all our Bullocks but they have carried off the officers horses and Batts horses but cannot learn the number.

The wounded prisoner who is since dead says that the party was above 1000 men 8 or 900 French and Canadians, the rest savages, under the Command of Capt Vitry[63] of the Marine and 2 more Cap^{ts} 8 Subalt^s. &c &c That there design was not to have attacked untill the next morning unless descovered, that they were to surprize the Outgards and our posts (of which they were very well informed, both from the prisoners that they had taken, and our deserters) and that under the Cover of our partys retreating, they were to follow in so close as to get within the breastworks and make themselves masters of the Camp and post. But that failing

---

[63] An error. M. Aubry was in command.

they were to destroy our Cattle, horses, & Carriages. He sayed that they had left 700 men in Garrison at Fort Duquesne, and that since they had come away, they had received accounts of a reinforcement having just arrived up the Mississippi and Ohio, of 500 regular Troops and 60 large Battoes loaded with provisions of which they had for some time been in great scarcity. That the Fort was all pallisaded and had a good coverd way and mounted 15 pieces of Cannon.

I send you enclosed the list[64] of killed &cᵃ in this great Action of which (I beg you keep my secret) I must make the best, but I am apt to believe that the Enemy were not so strong as call'd, and that we had above 1500 effective men within men our breast work exclusive of sick and yet neither made one Sortie or followed them half a yard, but shamefully allowed them to bury the few they had killed, Carry off their wounded with some Prisoners and all our horses, [nor did we follow or pursue them one inch.]†

But as the difficultys in roads and rains, provisions for man and horse had sunk the Spirits of every living annimall a Victory with a critical arrival of near 200 Waggons loaded from Philadelphia Coming in was necessary so I puffed up everything and ordered a General *Feu de Joy,* which great surprized the remaining few of the Indians, who by this time had all to a man prepared to leave us next morning. But they were now quite astonished for in the middle of this General joy, The famous Cherokee warrior (The Little Carpenter) with about 60 of the best warriors of the nation came into Camp from Winchester. He is as great a Rascal to the full as any of his companions in place of going out to War with me or persuading those were with me to stay, he has strengthened them in their extravegant demands, by making his own more unreasonable than the others, and has made me four or five stupid speeches all of which I have answered,[65] he gives me his finall answer tomorrow on which depends whether I shall have one Indian with me or not, If I have any they will cost dear, and yet should any thing fail the Cause may be attributed to the want of Indians who's presence I have lost for Saving a few hundred pounds, after foolishly having spent several thousands upon them, It is hard how to judge or to choose the best how to act for the good of the Publick, but I know one thing certain, that a little good luck and success often justifies the worst of measures and stupidest of actions.

I beg our defence of Loyal Hannon and the repulse and retreat of the

---

[64] Found in AB 749 and P.R.O. W.O. 34:44, f. 365. Printed, Balch, *Letters and Papers . . .*p. 142.

† Stricken out.

[65] Answers not found. They may not have been recorded.

enemy may meet with as little dimunition as possible, as it has made all the Waggoners, horse drivers &c^a. here and on the road as brave as Lyons, so if our list of killed and wounded was sunk for a little it would not be amiss. I hope soon to make a real *feu de joye* for your Success and am Sincerely

Sir

Y^r most obed^t & most hum^{le} Servt

Jo: fforbes—

P.S. I hope in God you will lose no time in endeavouring to get back Maj^r. Grant from Montreal, [for altho]† As he was my only plight anchor, and support, I can expect no assistance this Campaign but without him the Reg^t is undone as they can do nothing Officer or Soldier, being equally ignorant of almost every part of military duty, nor can it well be expected otherwise, as they are quite young and unacquainted—Another year with Grant would make them a find Battalion.

I have heard nothing from the treaty of Easton[66] from whence I expected great things, which unless monstrously mismanadged must have happened—if I could have brought it about a little earlier, but now I am afraid it is too late.

I am ruined and undone by Rain, So pray God send us a few fair days— At present can not move one yard————

Gen^{ll} Abercrombie

[*Endorsed, W. O.:*] Brigadier General Forbes

Rays Town Camp 16th October

1758 Rec^d the 28th

Ans^r 1st Novem^r.[67]

*   *   *   *   *

*Forbes to Peters**

[H.S.P. Peters MSS.; Vol. 5, p. 55. A.L.S.]

[Raystown Camp, October 16, 1758]

Sir

I have been of late but a bad correspondent as I could only write of multiplicity of grievances crowding upon the back of one another, all dismall to look at, yet by patience and perseverance, to be in some measure

---

† Stricken out.

[66] October 6-26, 1758, *Pa. Col. Res.* VIII, 175-223.

[67] Not found, but possibly Bouquet to Forbes, October 28, 1758, B.M. Add. MSS. 21640, f. 193, A.C., was posted late.

* Printed *Pa. Mag.* XXXIII, 91, and Stewart, *Letters of General John Forbes,* p. 57.

surmounted or alleviate. This I hope in God I have done, and trust greatly that from the same principles I shall be able to accomplish what yet remains.

I wish sincerely your treaty could have been brought about a little earlier, from whence wee might have drawn some powerfull helps this very Campaign, but I never repine at what cannot be remedyed, and I am this moment flattering myself that from the joint endeavours of all with you, the dropping of foolish trifles, some measures will be taken with those originale Inhabitants as to strengthen ourselves and diminish our Ennemys Influence with them in those parts for if it is as I see things giving up sometimes a little in the beginning will procure you a great deal in the end.

Frederick Post has been here some time, I think he has execute the Commission he was sent upon, wth ability and Fidelity, and deserves a proper reward. The two people who reconducted him here, deserve likewise of any Government, but I think if what he says of Daniell[68] be true that he deserves no countenance. I do not know whether the province will defray those charges, but they certainly ought as they may reap the profitts, I have no kind of judgment what Post deserves. I have ordered him fifteen pounds in the mean time I send him to you by this Express, that he and his two Conductors may be sent directly back with proper Messages (as the Governor shall direct) to the Ohio Indians to retire directly, as the season will admit of no delay.

Pray make my excuse to Mr. Croghan for not answering his letter,[69] but I approve of his measures and proposall of joining me, which I wish he would do without the loss of one moment of time, as now that I have everything in readyness at Loyall Hannon, I only want a few dry days to carry me to the Ohio Banks, where I hope our operations will not be long, so send me back the express that carrys this, with all diligence and let Mr. Croghan write me[70] the day that he intends setting out, with his route, and when I may expect him here, with the number that he expects to accompany him, Dispatch at present is absolutely necessary, so I should think he can dispense without seeing the end of your Congress.

Most of the Indians that have been preying upon us all year, have after getting all they possibly could expect, left us, and the few remaining were just agoing home in spite of every kind of means used to prevent them, when the little Carpenter arrived at this Camp with about 60 good Warriors, But he is as consummate a Dog as any of them, only seeing our distress, has made him exceed all the others in his most avaricious demands, There is no

---

[68] Shamokin Daniel, Delaware Indian, who accompanied Post.
[69] Not found.   [70] Not found.

help for those criticall minutes, and after foolishly laying out many thousands of pounds, I judged it would be wrong policy to lose him and all the rest for a few hundreds more.

Upon the 12th in the morning the French from Fort Du Quesne having a mind to repay Major Grants visit came to drive us away from our advanced post at Loyall Hannon destroy our Magazin, Bullocks, Carriages, &ce. They consisted of a body of 900 French and Canadians and two Hundred of those Friends, you are now treating with, they had gott within five miles of the post, and proposed attacking all the out post and Guards next morning, but being discovered they resolutely attempted to storm the Breast work thrown up about the Camp—accordingly fell a firing and Hallooing in order to bring out detachments, by which they proposed entering the Brestwork pell mell with them when routed. The 60 Maryland Volunteers went out and attacked them with vigour and Courage, but overpowered, Col. Burd who commanded sent a strong detachment of the 1st Pennsylvania Reg^t to sustain them, but they being likewise repulsed a third detachment of the Virginians &c, went out to bring the other off, which they did by retreating to the Breastwork. The Enemy followed closs to the edge of the Wood where they were stopt by the Grape shot from our Cannon and the shells of the Coehorns and Howbitzers, however they continued fireing upon the breast work from eleven to three in the afternoon without any Considerable loss on our side, they retreated a little, and carried away their dead and wounded in which they were favoured by the lying of the Ground, and then marched five miles off. Wee saved all our live Cattle, but the officers horses are either carried away or a missing. Two Maryland officers are killed and about 60 of our men are missing altho wee cannot believe them killed having only found six bodys, one officer of the Train wounded, wch is all our loss. That of the Ennemy wee cannot ascertain, altho it must neads be Considerable considering the advantages wee fought with against them, a Breast work & Cannon—I fancy they will not visit soon again and it has put all the Waggoners in such spirits that a single waggon will go now without one escorte, but these cursed Rains upon our new roads in clay soils and everything upon wheels, has at present renderd the Laurell Hill quite unpassable so wee must wait some dry days to be able to go forward. God grant them soon—

I think Mr. Croghan might send a trusty man or two or three towards Venango, in a direct Road from you, who by coming down the Ohio might come over and join us at Loyal Hannon with what intelligence of the Reinforcements lately gone to the French they could pick up, and what tribes of Indians are still with them which sure can not be many now as I am sure they are scarce of provisions. Pray make my apology to Govr Denny for not writing him, being still extreamly bad that is to say, weak, and my Complim^{ts} to him and Govr Bernard, to whose negotiations, I sincerely wish success, and hope they cannot fail, send me all your news by the express and believe me Sir very sincerely

Y^r most ob^t hum^{le} Servt

Jo fforbes

Raystown Camp
October 16th

Pray heartily for fair weather and dispatch of Business—But what absurd mortall made your Assembly settle the price of transporting provisions this length and no further—This length the Waggons do come & finer horses and Waggons I never saw, each bringing at least 2000 Weight with ease, but one foot further they will not move, so I am drove to the necessity of persuading them to move forward in the military way, but still paying them in proportion, or leaving the price to their Assembly—I am quite tyred. Adieu. I have sent home your books.
Mr Peters
[*Endorsed:*] General Forbes

*   *   *   *   *

Forbes to Pitt*
[P.R.O. C.O. 5:50, (L.C. Trans.) pp. 599-606]

Raes Town Camp. 20th Octob^r. 1758.

Sir

I have done myself the honour of acquainting you from to time of any material Circumstances that have happened to the small Body of troops under my Command. But the variety of chances against any letters going safe that is entrusted to a post Office in this Country, more particularly in these Uninhabited Wilds, makes me afraid my letters do not reach you in due time, or indeed miscarries, as we are also obliged to trust to Merchant Ships, for the sending them home. I acquainted[71] you of Major Grant of Col^o. Montgomery's Battalion with a strong detachment of 900 men, having gone to Fort Du Quesne in order to reconnoitre the roads & Fort, to check the Enemy's scouting partys and to endeavour to make some Prisoners in order to get some Intelligence of the Enemy's Strength, &c^a., which,

---

* Printed, Kimball, *Correspondence of William Pitt* . . . I, 370, and Stewart, *Letters of General John Forbes*, p. 59.
[71] Letter not found.

in spite of all my Endeavours to learn, by every Means That I could devize we are still in the dark off, as to certainty of their Numbers.

Major Grant trusting to false reports of their strength, divided his troops in order to bring them into an ambuscade, and at break of Day, beat his Drums and discovered himself to the Fort, who immediately poured out a large Body of Men, attacked his divided troops one after another, never allowing him time to get them together, and consequently had no difficult task in totally dispersing of him.

The Majors Grant and Lewis of the Virginia Provincialls were mad prisoners with 4 more officers, seven officers killed and 270 Private Men. This was a most terrible check to my small Army, at that time (the 14 September) just got in readiness to have marched to the Enemy, as to our Men, had the roads, provisions for man and horse, and the other absolute necessarys corresponded, as it raised the Enemy's Spirits and depressed our's, and at that Critical time was of great consequence, as it run a risque of rivetting the Indians to their Interest, who were then fluctuating betwixt the sides that they were to choose, and who I then verily believed were upon the point of returning to their old habitations upon the Susquehannah, and declaring for us.

For which reason I had Some time before that, suspended all military Operations against them and their villages, in hopes of gaining them entirely to our Interest, which I hope is now in a great Measure done, in a sollemn meeting with their Chieffs at Easton upon the Dellaware, where we have gott the Governours of Pennsylvania and Jersey to attend them, but as yet I do not know the result of their deliberations.

Since then nothing has happened, except that upon the 12th. . Inst^t. a Body of 900 French & Canadians, came to repay Major Grant's visit, and to attack our furthest advanced post at Loyal Hannon, which if they did not carry, they were to destroy our Baggage Horses and the live Cattle for our Subsistance. They attacked the Post for three hours, with little damage on either side, as our men were both more numerous, covered with a good Breastwork, and had two small Redoubts, and five piece of Cannon and Cohorns that played upon the Enemy.

They retreated in the Evening after burying their killed except a very few, and carrying off their wounded, so I do not know their loss, ours were two Maryland officers, and about 60 Men killed and missing, of which last severals have come in since, having been lost in the woods.

They carried off all the Baggage Horses belonging to that post, but we saved all our Oxen, I was extreamly angry to find our people had not pursued and attacked their rear in their retreat, from which we might have made reprizalls, but as our troops were mostly provincialls, I was obliged to attribute it to their ignorance, for to do justice I must commend the spirit of some of the provincialls, particularly the Maryland troops, who I retained in the Service, after being left to disband by their province, and therefore I was obliged to keep them together on our pay, and have been necesitated to advance them from time to time, money for their support, and cloathing, to enable them to carry on the Service, and without which they must have left us, as they had no manner of cloathing but one bad blankett each, which will not do in these cold evenings and mornings, no shoes stockings or Breeches, or any one necessary against the Inclemency of the Weather.

The Cherokee and other Southern Indians who came last winter, and so early in the Spring to join us, after having by every Art they were Masters off, gott every thing they could expect from us, left us without any remorse when they found they were not likely to get any more presents for retaining them, so that I have not now left with me above fifty, and I am now upon my march to the Ohio, as the Season will not admitt of one Moments delay, and I wish most sincerely I could have proceeded sooner, as I have no alternative left me now, but a bold push at last, to which I have been absolutely drove by a Multiplicity of Cross Events, too long to trouble you with at present; but the principal reasons that retarded us after gathering our troops together, was the Waggon-Horses failing in bringing up our provisions, neither making proper journeys, nor carrying the stipulated weight, by which the Magazines (upon the faith and strength of which I was to have proceeded) diminished daily, nor is it easy to replenish them, or support the daily Consumption of an Army, 300 miles distance, and that all land Carriage. The 2ᵈ. was the roads, first over the Alleganey Mountains, and then over the Laurell Hills, that are worse. The whole an immense uninhabited Wilderness overgrown every where with trees and underbrush, so that no where can anyone see twenty yards those roads during the hott and dry Seasons were made practicable for carriages, and I was assured by every one, and made believe that the Months of October and November were the two best Months in the year for an Expedition, because of the trees losing their leaves, by which one can see a little thro' the woods, and prevent the Enemy's surprizes, which is their only strength, and likewise, that in those two Months the Indians leave the French as it is their chief hunting Season, in which they provide for their familys during the winter.

This last was of great consequence to me, as the Enemy's Numbers had all along been represented to me, not only equall, but even to exceed what I could carry against them, so it was absolutely necessary that I should take precautions by having posts along my route, which I have done from a project that I took from *Turpin's Essay Sur la Guerre.* Last Chaptre 4th. Book. Intitled *Principe Sur Lequel on peut etabler un project de Campagne,* if you will take the trouble of looking into his Book, you will see the Generall principles upon which I have proceeded.

I am this Moment in the greatest distress, occasioned by unusuall rains at this Season, which joined to our Number of Carriages have rendered the clay roads absolutely impracticable to our Artillery and Waggons. As the Horses are a good deal wore out, I still hope a few days will make a change and enable me to proceed; If the Weather does not favour, I shall be absolutely locked up in the Mountains, nor do I scarce see a possibility of recrossing the Alleganey Mountains. This I could not forsee, nor prevent, as it is quite uncommon here.

I have therefore sent to Virginia,[72] Pennsylvania,[73] and Maryland,[74] begging to know what Troops they will furnish me, during the Winter, for the Protection of their Frontiers & Garrisoning the posts and footing we have got so nigh the Enemy, representing to them the small number of regulars I have (not above 1200 Men) and how unequal to such a task. But as all their troops are only engaged to the beginning of December, I dread the dilatory procedure of their Assemblys will not answer my peremptory Demands of their Aid, at this perplexing juncture for me.

I cannot form any judgement, how I am to extricate myself, as every thing depends upon the Weather, which snows and rains frightfully, but I shall do myself the honour of writing you every step I take, which to the Utmost of weak abilities shall be for the best. I have this Moment an Express[75] from the treaty with the Ohio Indians at Easton, who, have promised to join us, but require time, a thing at present so precious to me, that I have none to spare, and must in a day or two choose either to risque every thing, and march to the Enemy's Fort, retreat across the Alleganey if the provincialls leave me, or maintain myself where I am to the Spring.

I have the honour to be with the greatest regard & Esteem Sir

Yr most Obedt. & most humle. Servt.

Jo: Forbes.

Camp Top of the Alleganey Mountains. October 27th.

---

[72] Letter, Forbes to Fauquier not found, but mentioned in the *Journal of the House of Burgesses of Virginia,* 1756-1758, p. 50

[73] Forbes to Denny, September 9, 1758, *ante,* p. 206.

[74] No letters to this effect found.

[75] Contents of the express not found.

Most of the above letter was wrote some days ago, but finding the weather did not mend, I thought it necessary to march forward, to be ready to embrace the first opportunity.

R^t Honb^{le} Wm Pitt Esqr

[*Endorsed:*] Raes Town Octr 20th 1758

Brig^r Genl Forbes/R Jan^{ry} 19th

*   *   *   *   *

Forbes to Bouquet

[B.M., Add. MSS. 21640, f. 190. L.S.]

[Raystown, October 21, 1758.]

Sir

I have waited with Impatience either for a Letter from you or the return of Mr Grant ever since I had last the pleasure of hearing from you as from thence I thought I could have formed a full Judgement of the Circumstances of your Situation and of the Roads; as now the Weather has been extremely fine I doubt nothing but you are all in the best Order I could expect, or that the Circumstances of things will admit, and as we have now plenty of provision betwixt this and Loyal Hannon for forty days, besides five hundred Pack horses on the Road from Carlile with Provender &c and the Season of the year pressing hard upon us, I have therefore ordered the whole to march upon Monday next with a design to make very few halting days, untill that we see the Enemy, besides having engaged the Little Carpenter with upwards of Eighty of the very best of the Indians to accompany us to whose Capricious disposition delays might prove dangerous.

As I shall leave nothing behind me but barely sufficient for Escorts and a Common deffence I beg you will make your Disposition accordingly that we march as strong as possible. I have thought and thought again on an Order of Battle and a Line of march, but can not yet satisfy myself what is right or what is wrong, as I am afraid most People are prepossessed in their own way of thinking, therefore, pray be so good as have something cut and dry to propose that one may not be to seek.

What with Disorder, Indians, Waggons, Provisions & Provendor my Life has been a perfect Burthen to me ever since I saw you so am now oblige to beg the favour of Mr Sinclair to write for me, I think of setting out Monday myself, but perhaps it may be Tuesday, so you will guess the time when I will see you at Loyal Hannon. I don't know whether to advise taking possession again of the advance Post, leaving that to yourself as you know both the danger and profit to us in it. I do not think I have any more to say at Present, but rest

Your most Obed^t Servant

Camp at Rays Town 21st Oc^t 1758

Jo fforbes.

To Col° Bouquet
[*Endorsed:*] General Forbes 21st Oct^r

*   *   *   *   *

*Forbes to Denny**
[*Pa. Col. Recs.* VIII, 224]

Raystown Camp, October 22d, 1758.

Sir:

The Heavy Rains that have fallen of late has rendered the Roads almost Impassable for Carriages; these few Days past of dry Weather have given things a more favourable Aspect, and every thing is in Motion, the last Division being to March from hence to-morrow.

My State of Health continues precarious, but not so bad as to occasion any stop to our Operations, which must now come to a speedy Conclusion on account of the Advanced Season of the year.

Whatever the Fate of the Army may be it is impossible to foresee, but whether we are sucessful or not it is necessary for me to leave as large and extensive a Barrier as possible to cover the Province of Pennsylvania.

The Number of the King's Troops that I have under my Command does not exceed Twelve Hundred Men, the greatest part of which I must send down to the Inhabited Parts of the Country to recruit and fit themselves out for the ensuing Campaign; for were I to leave the whole during the Winter in the uninhabited parts of the Country, these Corps would not be a Condition to march on Service early in the Spring.

I shall lay before you the Posts that are proposed to be kept up, which are now in possession of us, leaving it to you and the Assembly of your Province to judge of their Importance to them, and to know how far they can contribute in Men and Expences for the Supporting of these Posts, and making the Soldiers' Lives comfortable, without which no real Service can be expected from them.

I have received no Answer from you relating to Fort Duquesne, if it should please God to grant Success; but whether that Fort is taken or not, the Forts of Loyal Hannon, Cumberland, Raystown, Juniata, Littleton,

---

*Original not found. Printed, also, in Stewart, *Letters of General John Forbes,*.
p. 62.

Loudoun, Frederick, Shippensburgh and Carlisle, ought to be Garrisoned, beside those on the other Side of the Susquehannah. I have wrote to Mr. Fouquiere[76] to know what assistance I may have from the Colony of Virginia, which I do not expect will be very great, not even to Garrison Fort Cumberland, their Frontiers are so extensive that Augusta County will require Two Hundred Men to Garrison its Forts; Winchester, with the south Branch of Potomack, Three Hundred Men more, to which Colonel Washington's Regiment will not amount at the End of the Campaign. I have nothing to expect from Maryland, as I am told they have abandoned Fort Cumberland and Fort Frederick.

It will easily occur to you the Things that will be necessary for making the Soldiers' Lives Comfortable in this severe Climate during the Winter. The most necessary are, a second Blanket in lieu of a bed, a Flannel Jacket, a new pair of Breeches, two Pair of Stockings, a pair of Shoes.

I should be glad to know, without the Loss of Time, how far your Assembly will go in putting it in my power to maintain the Ground that is Gained. If they do nothing for the Safety of the Province, I am certain it is not in my Power to defend them during the Winter with the strength that I shall have left and which I must expect will daily diminish.

To Cover the Country between Susquehannah and Potomack, and to secure the Communication to the advanced Posts will require, in my Opinion, Twelve Hundred Men, stationed in the following manner, Viz[t]:

At Loyal Hannon	300
At Ray's Town	200
At Fort Cumberland	200
At Fort Frederick	100
At Juniata	100
At Littleton	100
At Loudoun	100
At Shippensburg and Carlisle	100
	1200 Men

I must intreat you to return me an Answer[77] to this Letter as soon as possible, as it is a Matter of the greatest Consequence to the Colonies.

I am, with the greatest Regard, Sir,

Your most Obedient and Hume, Servant,

John Forbes.

---

[76] Francis Fauquier, Lieutenant-Governor of Virginia. The letters, not found, are mentioned in the *Journals of the House of Burgesses of Virginia, 1756-1758,* p. co.

[77] Answer not found.

Forbes to Abercromby
[AB 788 L.S.; P.R.O. W.O. :34;44, f. 373. Copy.]

Raestown October 24th 1758

S^{ir}.

I wrote[78] you the 16th acquainting you of the state of our affairs then, since which nothing material has happened, except that most of my Embarrassments had taken a favourable turn, and every thing two days ago wore a promising face.

S^{ir} John St Clair who went down the Country, used such diligence and application, that in a short time fresh Waggons came up with our provisions, which Mr Howell the Contractor for Kilby had greatly neglected, So that I am now Master of provisions to the 20th November—And the provender for horses in which S^{ir} John had been dissapointed and which raised all the clamour, he has now got put upon a better footing, altho not sufficient, to satisfie the Clamour of the Waggoners, however we are every way so much mended in the Q^r Mr Generals Department that I beg leave to retract my reflections upon that Branch.

Our roads were become so good that I dreaded no more impediment on that score, and the Virginians were at last convinced and acknowledged, that I (as a disinterested person to their Provincial politicks) had made a much better choice, that by Gen^{ll} Braddock's route, being 50 miles nearer and no ways subjected to the floods of the Monongahela, which has not been three times fordable this year.

Our Indians I have at lenght brought to reason by treating them as they always ought to be, with the greatest signs of scorning indifference and disdain, that I could decently employ, So the Little Carpenter with 100 good Indians, all well fitted for war are gone to our advanced post of Loyal Hannon, ready to act as desired.

The flux and Bilous fever has been, and is very severe upon us, as we have or will be obliged to leave 500 men behind, either sick or Convalescent, this with the Garrisons for Escorts &c leaves me but a small Body either to make conquests, or maintain myself where I am, if it is true as I am assured from all hands, that the French are more numerous than I could ever have believed them, and that lately they have received supplys from the Mississippi by 50 large Battoes. The Battoes our scouting partys have actually seen, but do not know their contents

---

[78] *Ante,* p. 231.

All this considered makes me very uncertain how to form any judgement of success, if I should get to the Fort without a Battle, or if succedding in the fight whether I shall be able to take it when I get before it.

I write you that our roads are very passable in fair weather, but I ought likewise to acquaint you, that two days rain with carriages upon a deep clay soil, renders them impracticable to Cannon, &c even the Baggage horses are so weakly animalls, that they cannot get along. This with the daily advancing season gives me many a thoughtfull hour, nor can common prudence well govern you, as I can not form a judgement, how much is expected from me, or how far any rash attempt, would find favour in case of Failure.

I wrote you some time ago[79] desiring your Instructions and directions, as also acquainting you,[80] that I had wrote to the southern Provinces upon the same head, which was supposing I should be so lucky as to become Master of Fort duquesne, whether the place was to be destroyed or preserved, and I have since wrote to the Governors of Pennsylvania[81] and Virginia[82] upon the same head, letting them know the state of the Regular troops under my Command, and desiring them to give me a definitive answer to what number of men they would maintain for the Defence of their Frontiers which were very extensive, and how they were to be provided in Victualls and necessarys during the winter, but to those I have had no answer so I am in a terrible plight—For my 1200 or 1400 regulars cannot remain in those Wilds later than the latter end of Nover. without incredible cost & destruction to them, having no fewer than eight Garrisons or Forts from the Susquehanah to the out post at Loyal Hannon, to which no waggon can either go or return after the 20th of Novr. So Sir I beg your immediate orders how I should behave myself for as I understand things I shall have no answer from the provinces untill out of time. And if not imposed upon the provinciall troops are engaged only to the first of December or during the Campaign; I shall construe it to be to the first of January, and garrison these Frontiers and Forts, is the Crown to be at all the charge of provisions &c.

As I am so far (by inevitable chances that were neither unforeseen, nor every means tryed to guard against) laid in, as to carry my Artillery to

---

[79] July 25, 1758, *ante,* p. 158.

[80] No such letter found.

[81] Forbes to Denny, October 24, 1758, *ante,* p. 242.

[82] Letters not found, but mentioned, *Journal of the House of Burgesses of Virginia, 1756-1758,* p. 50.

Fort Du Quesne, I begin to see the impossibility of being able to bring it back this winter over the Laurell hill, and the Allegany Mountain, as this is a serous consideration; I beg to know your opinion of the risque I run, in stretching further than I can well retire, or indeed in case of a check of undoing the small army, losing my Artillery, and disabling myself from protecting the Frontiers of the provinces.

As this present time every post is in such order as not to run any risque without Cannon brought against it, and as far as I can judge the chain of posts have been well chose for the protection of the Country, as none almost of the Enemy Indians have ventured within them this Campaign, at least to do but small damage, which in part answers Mr Pitt's instructions;[83] If seasons, climate, situation and strength of the Enemy prevent, a farther distress upon them it ought not to be attributed to dilatoriness or loss of one moments time, unless that the facts are glaring and obvious, which I thank God is not the Case with us, having improven every moment of opportunity of getting forward, that possibly could be devized.

There is one Lieu^t. Ray of the first Batt^n of Royal Americans dead, I therefore take the liberty of recommending to you in the strongest manner Capt Stewart[84] of the Virginia light horse, as one every way qualified and deserving a much better recompense, having to my knowledge spent five hundred pounds of his own money in the service without any reward. And this would be a certain kind of bread, he is from Argyle shire and his story deserves being taken notice of—As he is a Highlander and speaks the language I do not think it would do any hurt to the Service to make him a Lieutenant in Montgomerys, as really and truly they want some good Officers as well as their neighbours.

The above was wrote four days ago, but as I found the necessity of marching forward the troops immediately, I postponed finishing it untill I could say something of the roads, which were much worse than they were described, and even so bad as the horses cannot carry back the empty Waggons.

This confounds and destroys one intirely; as I am told that it is impossible unless assisted by a miracle to proceed, and whatever provision or Cannon passes Laurell Hill now, must there remain, this is so contrary to the Description and advice given by every Individual, of October & November being the finest months for our Expedition, and that the Extraordi-

---

[83] Pitt to Abercromby, December 30, 1757, Kimball, *Correspondence of William Pitt,* . . . I, 143.

[84] Captain Robert Stewart.

nary rains are quite unexpected & unusuall, so that I have nothing to say, as I cannot stop the continued floods, nor repair the roads anew.

I am now upon the very top of the Alleganey mountains. and altho the best made road of the whole, The Waggons have taken one whole day to proceed 3 Miles and must halt a Day to refresh.

I proceed to Loyal Hannon Day after to morrow, from whence I shall send you the state of my present Circumstances, which at best are most disagreeable and comfortless, notwithstanding all the small endeavours in my power, and if my Intentions are rendered abortive I confess my sanguine hopes of success are sunk to the lowest depths of distress, nor is it possible for me to Stop the vulgar Clamour that must destroy more power, Capacity, and Intergrity, than perhaps I can boast off althô I must both say and think, that in the present situation of my health, I have done as much and ventured as far as any man ever did, nor can I reproach my self of any one neglect in the service from any dilatoriness of mine, whatever may have happened under Gentlemens directions belonging to my Command.

I am S^{ir} with great truth and sincerity most Sincerely
Your most obedent
Humble Servt

Jo: fforbes.

Camp top of the Allegany Moun^{tns}.
Octob^r.
[*Addressed:*] On His Maj^{ties} Service.
To His Excellen^{cy}
Major Gen^{ll} Abercrombie Commander
in Chief of His Majestys Forces in North America Albany
To be forwarded by Express from New York

Jo. fforbes

[*Endorsed:*] Brig^r Genl Forbes
Raestown October 24^t
1758. Rec^d. 13^t November

*   *   *   *   *

Forbes to Bouquet
[B.M., Add. MSS. 21640, f. 191. A.L.S.]

Raes town October 25th

Sir

I had the favour of yours[85] of the 20th by Mr Grant and am glad to find that your new road over the Laurell Hill is so easy, and join with you in thinking no time is to be lost in falling upon some method of returning. For us our affairs are so precarious no means must be left untried to prevent mischieffs, that will be extreamly difficult to remove, if they were to happen.

The few days of fine weather last week raised my spirits and fluttered my hopes that every thing would go easy and well, and my Success in persuading the little Carpenter and all the Indians to join us was more than I could have ixpected, but now all those flattering Fancys are in a manner blown in the Air, for I dread that these four last days perpetuall rain have entirely putt the roads past all hopes of recovery for this season, and I have just now seen letters from the Govr of Jamaica[86] desiring that the little Carpenter might be sent down directly to conciliate a peace betwixt the Cherokees & Virgininians as the former had actually begunn scalping the white people. How to manadge here, I scarcely know; for to acquaint the Carpenter of this and send him away, is directly strengthening the arguments he made use of to me for returning home, and if he leaves us we shall not have one Indian that will stay with us—and I hear no accounts from Eastown of their proceedings there, nor of Mr Croghan and his Indians that were to have joined us about this time.

Col. Montgomery and Byrd marchd day before yesterday and Capt Hay with the remainder of the artillery march'd from this, this morning but so incessant a Rain has made me make the whole Halt at the Shawnese Cabins, as such a train of waggons in rainy weather would hurt the roads more in one hour than wee could repair in a week. So wee have nothing for it but patience, and hopes, that att last wee may meet with some favorable moment, to show the world that there neither good will nor Inclination was wanting in us, to do all, or more, that could well be expected from our small force, attended by such a Multiplicity of Embarrassments. But neither you nor I nor no mortall can either foresee of foretell what the weather may prove.

---

[85] B.M., Add. MSS. 21640, f. 184, f. 186, f. 189, A.C.S.
[86] Possibly a reference to Governor Lyttelton of South Carolina, later governor of Jamaica. Henry Moore was lieutenant governor of Jamaica in 1758.

I have wrote long ago and lately to the Govern^rs of Virginia,[87] Pensylvania[88] &c desiring ane immediate answer, to what numbers of men they will maintain as frontier Garrisons this winter at Loy^ll Hannon &c back to Carlisle, declaring y^t our regulars were neither in a Condition, nor numerous enough for their protection, and begging their speedy resolutions upon so necessary a measure but have not as yet had one word of answer, so if the provincialls disband and return the latter end of Novr what can wee do?, I really do not know, I therefore have wrote twice upon the same Subject to Gen^ll Abercromby[89] desiring his orders and directions, but I have not had one scrape of a pen from hime since the beginning of Sep^r, so it looks as if wee were either forgott or left to our own good or bad fate and manadgment, For my own part I am soon determined and that is to do all in my power that prudence can suggest for the good of the service, nor do I think that in the Criticall way things stand, one is any ways flatterd to run the risque of ruin, in a rash pursuit of a military glory, But more of this betwixt you and I When wee meet, which I thought might have been about this time had not these rains quite oversett all my schemes, however at all events I leave this Fryday morning. I hope Col. Burds partys will bring you some good Intelligence and pray recommend making a prisoner.

The road to the Advanced post ought to be sett about or indeed whatever is thought proper to be done. The Catawbas marchd Monday with some Cherokees do not let them be idle, as they are in good humour

I do not know what to say to the Carpenter but I believe he will Come with me.

Whatever you and I may suffer in our minds pray let us putt the best face upon matters, and keep every body in Spirits. I expect Col^o Mercer with all the rest of the Waggons and Bats horses, and a great Convoy of Cattle, in here to morrow, I shall make them instantly defile off. The Waggon teams are extreamly good and I hope to be able to send up sufficient provender to feed the horses and keep the Waggoners in good humour.

This is all that occurrs at present but I am Dr S^ir Y^r Most ob^t hum^le Servt

Jo: fforbes/

---

[87] Letters not found, but mentioned in the *Journal of the House of Burgesses of Virginia, 1758-1761,* p. 11 and p. 50, the latter specifically mentioning a letter Forbes to Fauquier, October 22, 1758.

[88] Letter, Forbes to Denny, September 9, 1758, and October 22, 1758, *ante,* p. 206, and p. 242.

[89] October 16, 1758, and October 24, 1758, *ante,* p. 231, and p. 244.

Col: Bouquet.

Pray make my Complim^{ts} to Col° Washington who's letter[90] I receiv'd, and who's desire should have been Complyed with—as Major Steuart will tell him[91] who writes by this conveyance to him upon that head, having at present no time myself, for which I shall apologize at meeting.

[*Endorsed:*] General Forbes [25th Oct] 1758

*　*　*　*　*

Forbes to Bouquet
[B.M., Add. MSS. 21640, f. 194. A.L.S.]

Stonycreek Octob^r 30th [1758]

Dear Sir

I arrived here this afternoon from the top of the Allegany, where I pass'd a Day accompanyed by the artillery, and Col: Montgomerys and Byrds Battalions, they lye this night at Edmunds swamp, with the help of forty of the best horses taken from those waggons, that I mett going down the Country.

The Allegany Mountain is broke to peices from down right neglect, I have left 100 men to work upon it but had not tools enough to employ them. A thing strange to me.

The road this day is frightfull and I think it repairable, but I shall employ Mr Bassett & Col: Mercers people for some days upon it.

I shall stay here to morrow and shall lye at the foot of the Laurell Hill Wednesday so should be glad to see you there or early on Thursday morning. Be so good as order a hundred men over to the foot of the Hill as ane escorte to me if you can spare y^m as I hear you have marchd 1000 to the advanced post.

I have orderd sixty oxen to sett of from this to morrow and there still remains here 180, besides what is comeing up with the Last of the Waggons &c that Col° Mercer with his detachment brings up, I have ordered every thing up directly particularly provision for horses, but shall not croud you untill I see you. My Comp^{ts} to Washington &c, and send Mr Gordon or any Engenier that has been with you to meet me Wednesday early at the foot of Laurell Hill where I would rather wish to see you, than on Thursday, as time is precious.

I am S^{ir} Y^r most devoted hum^{le} Servt

Jo: fforbes.

---

[90] Washington to Forbes, October 8, 1758, *Writings* (Fitzpatrick, ed.), II, 295.

[91] Robert Stewart to Washington, Hamilton, *Letters to Washington*, II, 123. Forbes seems to have confused Robert Stewart with Walter Steuart.

[*Addressed:*] To Col⁰ Bouquet Command^g His Maj^{ties} Forces at Loyall
Hannon. or to the Command^g officer Jo fforbes
[*Endorsed:*] General Forbes October the 30th

* * * * *

Forbes to Bouquet
[B.M., Add. MSS. 21640, f. 196. L.S.]

Camp at Stoney Creek 31st October 1758

Dear Sir

I this morning Receiv'd your letter,⁹² as likewise one from Colonel
Washington,⁹³ inclosing the General Court Martial⁹⁴ of which he was
president.

I wrote to you last night,⁹⁵ but in case the Messenger should be dilatery
upon the Road, I dispatch this to inform you, that I am to March from
hence to morrow morning, and will be at the foot of Laurel Hill by two
oClock in the after noon at furthest, when I shall expect to see you, as I
have a great deal of different affairs to talke to you upon, which requires an
interview as soon as possible.

I am very sensible that your prudent behaviour, will get the better of
all darke under hand Intrigues. I am Dear Sir
Your most obedient humble Servant
Jo fforbes

[*Addressed:*] To Colonel Bouquet Commanding at Loyalhannon
[*Endorsed:*] General Forbes Octr the 31st

* * * * *

Forbes to the Shawanese and Delawares on the Ohio*
[H.S.P. Penn Manuscripts, Indian Affairs, IX, 61]

[November 9, 1758]

Brethren, I embrace this opportunity by our brother, Pesquitomen⁹⁶
who is Now on his Return home wth some of your Uncles, the Six Nations,
from the Treaty of Easton, of giving you Joy of the happy Conclusion of

---

⁹² Of October 28, 1758, B.M., Add. MSS. 21640, f. 193, A.C.   ⁹³ Letter not found.
⁹⁴ Records of the Court Martial of October 30, 1758 in the Library of Congress, in
MSS. Papers of Washington, IX, 1165. For those of October 26, 1758 consult the
orderly book in the Toner MSS., *ibid.,* and P.R.O.W.O. 71, 131.
⁹⁵ *Ante,* p. 250.
* Printed, seemingly from a different copy, in Craig, *Olden Time,* I, 161, and
Stewart, *Letters of General John Forbes,* p. 64.
⁹⁶ Consult C. Hale Sipe, *Indian Chiefs.*

that great Council, wch is perfectly agreable to me; as it is for the mutual advantage of Y^r Brothers, the Indians, as well as the English nation.

I am glad to find that all past Disputes and Animosities are now finally settled, & amicably adjusted; & I hope they will be forever buried in Oblivion, and that you will now again be firmly united in the Interest of your brethren, the English. As I am now advancing, at the Head of a large Army, against his Majesty's Enemies, the French, on the Ohio, I must strongly recomend to you to send immediate Notice to any of your People, who may be at the French fort, to return forthwith to your Towns; where you may sit by y^r Fires, wth y^r Wives and Children, quiet and undisturbed, and smoke your Pipes in safety. Let the French fight their own Battles, as they were the first Cause of the War, and occasion of the long difference, wch hath subsisted between you & your Brethren, the English; but I must entreat you to restrain y^r young Men from Crossing the Ohio, as it will be impossible for me to distinguish them from our Enemies; wch I expect you will comply with, without Delay; lest, by your neglect thereof, I should be the innocent Cause of some of your Brethren's Death. This Advice take and keep in your own Breasts, and suffer it not to reach the Ears of the French.

As a proof of the Truth and Sincerity of what I say, and to confirm the tender Regard I have for Lives and Welfare of our Brethren, on the Ohio, I send you this String of Wampum.

I am, Brethren and Warriors,
Y^r Friend & Brother,
Camp at Loyalhannon   Jn° Forbes.

*   *   *   *   *

Forbes to Kings Beaver and Shingas*
[H.S.P. Penn Manuscripts, Indian Affairs, IX, 61]

[November 9, 1758]

Brethren, King Beaver & Shingas,[97] & all the warriors, who join with you:

The many Acts of Hostility, committed by the ffrench against the British Subjects, made it necessary for The King to take up Arms, in their Defence, and to redress their Wrongs, which have been done 'em; Heaven hath favoured the justice of the Cause, and given Success to his fleets and Armies, in different Parts of the World. I have received his comands, with

---

* Printed, seemingly from a different copy, in Craig, *Olden Time,* I, 162, and Stewart, *Letters of General John Forbes,* p. 64.
[97] On these Indian chiefs, consult C. Hale Sipe, *Indian Chiefs.*

regard to what is to be done on the Ohio, & shall endeavour to act like a Soldier by driving the ffrench from thence, or destroying them.

It is a particular Pleasure to me to learn, the Indians, who inhabit near that River, have lately concluded a Treaty of Peace wth the English; by which the antient Friendship is renewed with their Brethren, and Fixed on a firmer foundation than ever. May it be lasting unmoveable as the Mountains. I make no doubt but it gives you equal Satisfaction, and that you will unite your Endeavours wth mine, and all the Governors of these Provinces, to strengthen it the Clouds that, for some time, hang'd over the English, and their Friends, the Indians on the Ohio, and kept them both in Darkness, are now dispers'd & the chearful Light now again shines upon Us, and warms us both. May it continue to do so, while the Sun and Moon give Light.

Your people, who were sent to us, were rec'd by us wth open Arms; they were kindly entertain'd, while they were here, and I have taken Care that they shall return safe to you, with them come trusty Messengers, whom I earnestly recommend to your protection; They have several matters in Charge and I desire you may give Credit to what they say; in particular, they have a large Belt of Wampum, & by this belt we let you know, that it is agreed by me, & all the Governors, that there shall be an everlasting Peace with all the Indians, established as sure as the Mountains, between the English Nation and the Indians, all over, from the Sun rising to the Sun setting: and as your Influence on them is great, so you will make it known to all the different Nations, that want to be in ffriendship with the English & I hope, by your Means and persuasions, many will lay hold on this Belt and immediately withdraw from the French; this will be greatly to their own Interest and your Honor, and I shall not fail to acquaint the Great King of it.

I sincerely wish it, for their good; for it will fill me with Concern, to find any of you join'd with the French, as in that Case you must be sensible I must treat them as Enemies however, I once more repeat, that there is no time to be lost; for I intend to march with the Army very soon; and I hope to enjoy the pleasure of thanking you for your Zeal, & of entertaining you in the Fort ere long. In the mean time I wish Happiness and Prosperity to you, your Women and children.

I write to you as a Warrior should, that is, with Candour and Love, and I recommend Secrecy and Dispatch.

  Kings Beaver & Shingas & Brother Warriors,
    Your Assured Friend and Brother,
              Jo Forbes

From my Camp at Loyalhannon,
Novr 9th 1758.

    * * * * *

*Bouquet to Washington**
[L.C. MSS. Papers of Washington Vol. IX. D.S.]

Camp at Loyal Hannan 16th Novr 1758

Dear Sir

I am directed by the General to inform you that he had receiv'd your letter,[98] and Sends you 42 falling axes, which could not be collected Sooner.

The General thinks that Col. Armstrong is not upon the good Road. Therefore desires that you Send Capt. Shelby[99] to blaze the Road before you and bring Col. Armstrong's Party in it.

The distance of his last Encampment being only 16 miles from here, does not answer our Purpose and the General wishes that you could join him, (in cutting the Road) to day, and march together or his Detach^t. before you as you may think best, and mark out an Incamp^t at about 20, or 22 miles from here, as we had agreed where you are to Stay intrenching your Camp, untill Col Montgomery joins you;

You will then take the necessary Tools and march wth a sufficient force to the heads of Turtle Creek where you [mutilated] Camp—leaving to Col. Montgomery's Brigade the Road to cut to you;

The Beeves for your four days meat go wth Col. Montgomery's Brigade, and I shall bring wth me a Supply for Col. Armstrongs Party, whose men are to join their respective Corps as they come up.

I hope to be wth you as Soon as Col. Montg^y tho' I Sett out only to morrow.
I am   D^r S^r

Your most obed^t
h^{ble} Servant
H. Bouquet

P:S: as the Troops behind you have no Tools, The General desires that nothing be left undone upon the Road, of what you judge necessary; & begs you would get a Chimney built for him in each of the extreme [mutilated] Camps.

[*Addressed:*] On his Majesty's Service
To Colonel Washington
Commanding the Troops to ye Westward

---

* Printed, Hamilton, *Letters to Washington*, III, 128.
98 Of November 15, 1758, *Writings* (Fitzpatrick, ed.), II, 301.
99 Captain Evan Shelby, an officer in the Maryland militia in 1758, but earlier in Pennsylvania service.

Forbes to Abercrombie
[AB 824 A.L.S.; P.R.O. W.O. 34:44, f. 381. Copy.]

Loyall Hanning Novr 17th 1758

Dear Sir.

I am extreamly sorry that the distance between us deprives me not only of your Correspondence, but of your advice and orders in the manadgement of this small body of people, who from circumstances require more care to provide; than ten times their numbers in any part of Europe, and, I may safely say that in spite of everything in my power they cost the Government ten times the money. God Grant they answer the purpose, but as my advanced post is only 20 miles distant from their fort, so a few days determines their fate or mine.

You may believe wee have frequent skirmishes and allarms, None of great Consequence, yet we are thereby kept extreamly allert. As my numbers do not at all answer to the immense tract of Country I must protect, nor to the multiplicity of Convoys and escortts that I must have; through a Barren uninhabited Wilderness 2 or 300 Miles.

Two hundred of the ennemy came to attack our live Cattle and horses on the 12th—I sent 500 men to give them chace with as many more to Surround them, there were some killed on both sides, but unfortunately our partys fired upon each other in the dark by which we lost two officers and 38 private kill'd or missing. Wee made three prisoners from whom wee have had the only Intelligence of the Enemys strength, and which if true gives me great hopes, I shall in spite of every cross perverse accident still be able to give a good account of them But I am in the greatest anxiety how to proceed in case of Success for you know S^{ir} I have no Instructions or orders whatever, and altho I have applyed every where for either or both I have hitherto received none.

I wrote you in my Last[100] that Col° Morris and the Majors Darby and Halkett, were very pressing with me that I should use my good Offices with you; to get their affair brought to a Conclusion, Now S^{ir} as it hurts nor interferes with any person whatever, that this change goes forward, which is for the real advantage of the service and doing of pleasure to so worthy particulars I flatter myself you will order the Commissions to be made out as soon as possible I have therefore wrote[1] to the Reg^t What I have wrote you, in order that Col° Morris if necessary may write you upon the occasion

---

[100] An error. This item was in the earlier letter of October 8, 1758, *ante*, p. 226.
[1] Letter not found.

desiring leave to retire. I can say no more upon this subject unless acknowledging that your Complyance will very much oblige me.—

one of the Officers kill'd is Lieut Evans[2] of the Royall Americans, So as
two are Vacant I beg to recommend most ardently Mr MacDougall,[3] a
Cousin of Col: Mac Dougalls[4] for ane Ensigncy, he carries arms now in
Col: Montgomerys Battalion.

I just hear of another Officer of the provincials with four private being
cutt off, but those things will happen—

I beg Cap[t] Steuart[5] of the Light horse may be remember'd I will write
in two days a much longer and more circumstantial letter about many
things. In the mean time I beg to be believed D[r] Sir

Y[r] most ob[t] & most
humb[le] Serv[t]
Jo fforbes

Loyall Hanning Novem[r] 17
[*Endorsed:*] Brigad[r] General Forbes
    Loyall Hannon Nov[r] 7th
    Rec[d] Decem[r] the 6th

*   *   *   *   *

*Forbes to Burd**
[H.S.P. MSS. Papers of the Shippen Family, Vol. 3, p. 219, A.L.S.]

New Camp, 20 miles west of Loyal Hannan,
November 19th, 1758

Sir:—

[mutilated] astonished and amazed upon [mutilated]
[mutilated] and villainous desertion of [mutilated]
[mutilated] of the methods he had used [mutilated]
[mutilated] from our assistance at so very critical a time

He has often told us in public that his nation were going to make war
against the virginians & His Majesty's Subjects. I therefore thought him a
good pledge in our hands to prevent that, and consequently the whole of them

---

[2] Lieutenant John Evans of the 60th regiment.
[3] John MacDougal of the 77th regiment.
[4] Colonel MacDougal was not in service in America.
[5] Captain Robert Stewart, of Virginia.
* Printed Balch, Letters and Papers, p. 148; *Pa. Mag.* XXXIII, 95; and Stewart,
Letters of General John Forbes, p. 66.

were indulged in every extravagant, avaricious demand they made; but seeing that those who have thus deserted, and abandoned us, with all the aggravating circumstances attending their desertion, now preludes to what we may expect from them, I therefore desire, that upon receipt of this, you will instantly dispatch an express to the commanding officer at Rays town, who is to send one to Winchester & Fort Cumberland, in case that he, the Carpenter & his Followers, should have already past Raystown, and notice ought to be sent to fort Loudoun likewise with my orders, which are that having under the Cloak of Friendship robbed us these several months, but that now having discovered themselves our private Ennemies, and having turned the Arms, put in their hands by us, against His Majesty's Subjects, which the Former parties have already done, That, therefore prudence and self preservation obliged us, to require of them the returning of their Arms & ammunition directly, as likewise the horses that were furnished to them to accompany us to war; that as their Blankets, shirts, silver truck, &c., are not of that consequence, therefore the peremptory stripping them need not be [mutilated] upon, But I insist upon the inhabitants [mutilated] chester making them d [mutilated] and horses, which is but [mutilated] fellow subjects of the parts of Virginia [mutilated] borough, where no doubt they would commit all sorts of outrage, so that it will be necessary to send a Sufficient escort along with them, allowing of them a Sufficiency of provisions and no more, so that the Cherokee nation may see plainly they will have nothing to complain off but the baseness and perfidy of those, whom they have sent amongst us as friends for these seven months past.

The Garrison of Fort Cumberland is strong enough to compel them to deliver up their Arms, so let a Copy of this my letter be sent to the Commanding officer, who is to make use of all the fair means in his power before He takes their Arms from them,

At Raystown they are to do the same.

But as the garrison of Fort Loudoun is perhaps too weak either to refuse them their presents, or make them deliver up their Arms, I desire, therefore, that in case they take that way, that Major Wells marches directly himself with a Sufficient force from Raystown to Fort Loudoun to execute this, which you and all Concerned, are always first to try by gentle methods, before that rougher ones be made use off; As it is impossible any of your Garrison can overtake them before they reach Rays town, I therefore desire no time may lost in sending copies of my letter and directions to Rays town, to be forthwith transmitted by express to Fort Loudon, Cumberland and Winchester by expresses [mutilated] they take [mutilated] at Fort Loudon was [mutilated] Campaign Mr. Smith the interpreter[6] ought to be sent after them to serve to explain matters, and to prevent as far as can be, the bad consequences of their going home through Virginia and North Carolina, armed, for which purpose this letter is wrote, as Virginia has always suffered.

> I am, S^{ir}
> Y^r most ob^t, hum ser^t,
> Jo fforbes

Col° Burd

*   *   *   *   *

Halket to Byrd [Burd]*
[H.S.P. MSS. Papers of the Shippen Family, Vol. 3, p. 219]

> New Camp Monday morning six o'clock
> 20th November 1758

Sir

It is General Forbes orders that you immediately Detach two hundred of your best men, with a proper proportion of officers, to take post at this Camp, in order to strengthen Convoys of Provisions &c coming to the Army, and keep the Communication open.

They are to be serv'd with eight days provisions at Loyal Hannon and remain upon this duty till it is expended, & not to break in upon any of the provisions coming up to the Troops. This Camp I compute to be about 22 miles from Loyalhannon, by nature extreamly strong, and fortifyed with four Reduts, so they cannot be at a loss for the Post. I am

> Sir
> Your most obedient humble Servant
> Francis Halkett
> Brigade Major

[*Addressed:*] To The Honble Col° Byrd

*   *   *   *   *

---

[6] Not otherwise identified than as Richard, interpreter for the Cherokees with Forbes army. Cf. Forbes to Abercromby, May 4, 1758, *ante,* p. 86.

* From the location of this manuscript, it was considered as addressed to Colonel James Burd, left behind by Forbes, at Loyal Hannon.

Forbes to [Washington] *
[B.M., Add. MSS. 21640, f. 198. A.L.S.]

[November 20, 1758.]
From the Camp where they are building
the Redoubts just arrived 2 a Clock
afternoon.

Sir

The Catawbas & those Indians that came with Croghan, I have persuaded to march forward and join you were it never so late this night, the Cherokees are not come up. I know nothing of how far you go this night or where you make your last stop, so as by this time Col° Bouquet must have joined you I suppose all that is settled. Be therefore so good, as send me back with a fresh Horse, where you are, this night, where you go to morrow, what orders Col° Montgomery has, and as far as you have learned, the distances of the places before you as well as those distances from this forward to you, Turtle Creek &c and where you intend to push for, that wee may assemble and proceed togather I have sent forward 30 head of cattle from the 90 that came from Loy[11] Hanning with the last Division (and I understand that Col° Bouquet has ordered forward 15 more) they have orders to make no stop untill they reach you. I shall order Col: Montgomery to strengthen their escorts I never doubted of the ennemys scouting partys discovering us, but I think it highly necessary that wee discover them likewise, as also the sure knowledge, if ever they send out any force from their fort capable of attacking us I could not well join Montgomery this night, but shall if possible to morrow, for which reason if he is not absolutely necessary up with you his making a short march to morrow will give me ane opportunity of joining him to morrow night, and wee can join you next day.

The Stillgards &c were sent you P express 2 days ago, I have sent another express back to hasten up the Carpenter.

I have ordered 40 of the Waggon horses that arrived yesterday at Loy[11] Hanning (which are very fine) to be directly sent off with light loads of Flour in order to make the train quite easy—And as there are a great number of Bats horses loaded with flour I should think the men ought to be putt again to their old Allowance, for otherwise our Cattle will not do and wee have flour enough.

Croghan has sent off 3 of his Indians toward the Ohio for Intelligence,

_____

* By internal analysis this letter must have been written to Washington but turned over to Bouquet.

and Jacob Lewis[7] that Col° Armstrong sent out last Thursday is just come in without having done, or learning any one thing

If Col: Bouquet chooses that Col° Montgomery should halt ane hour or two for me to morrow morning, let him send him back orders by the return of this express to night or order him a short march & I can join him and bring Cattle Artillery and all in with us.

This must serve as ane answer to Col° Bouquet[8] and your letters[9] I received this morning, wrote in my litter so excuse

Y^r most obseq^t &c

Jo: fforbes.

[*Endorsed:*] 20th Nov.

*   *   *   *   *

*Halkett to Washington**
[L.C. MSS. Papers of Washington, Vol. IX, A.L.S.]

Washingtons Camp 21st November 1758

Sir

In consiquence of your letter,[10] the General has orderd out a Working, & covering party from Col: Bouquets Brigade, who are to begin at the Camp, and open the Road upon Capt Shilbeys Blazes till they meet your party. The Commissary has orders to have the provisions for the men of your Brigade ready to deliver immediately upon your Returning to Camp, and to set it a part by Corps, which will make as little delay as it is possible, the numbers he Calculates by the Return[11] you sent back to the General when on his March, so any errors as they must be small, can easily be recti-fyed upon your coming in The General desires that you will Reconoitre the length of the old Path, & begin to open the Road as near to it as you think you may venture to do so that the two parties may finish it this day & send him an account by the Light Horse man of the nature of the Country—Fifty Felling axes which are all that are good ones, with a proportion of shovels, & Pick axes are given to this Party I am Sir

Your most obedient humble Servant

Francis Halkett

Brigade Major

---

[7] Probably a Pennsylvania civilian.   [8] Letter of Bouquet not found.
[9] Washington to Forbes, November 18, 1758, *Writings* (Fitzpatrick, ed.), II, 306.
* Printed, Hamilton, *Letters to Washington*, III, 130.
[10] Washington to Forbes, November 18, 1758, *Writings* (Fitzpatrick, ed.), II, 306.
[11] Several such returns are in the MSS. Papers of Washington in the Library of Congress.

[*Addressed:*] On His Majestys Service
          To Brigadier Washington on his
          March
[*Endorsed:*] Gen¹ Forbes—by Brigade Majʳ Halket. 21ᵗʰ Nov 1758

*   *   *   *   *

Forbes to Bouquet
[B.M., Add. MSS. 21640, f. 199. A.L.S.]

[November 22, 1758]

Dʳ Sir

I have had the pleasure of yours[12] by Capᵗ Callender just as I had taken the resolution to halt the two Brigades here for this night, as indeed it seemed to me impossible to proceed, for it was a quarter of hour past four and rather dark, I had no reason either to expect that the road was better, or better open'd that what I had come, which was so monstrously and Carelessly done that I lost all manner of patience, and was oblidged to employ the artillery guard to make Bridges & Openings to let them pass, This made it impossible for the artillery to have gott one bitt of Ground further than this to night, as it is now seven o Clock and the rear is not yet come in. I therefore ordered Col: Montgomerys working party and advanced Guard, amounting to near 300 men to march forward to join & strengthen you, which will be sufficient.

If your post pleases you altho I do not know the distance to F Duquesne I would begin early to morrow morning and putt it in a posture of Defence, You may employ the tools that Montgomerys working partys has with them for that purpose, and if you want any others let me know by a message this night and I will send them forward to you by break of Day. As it will take all to morrow to settle our matters for next days operations I beg that the Indians be sent forward to morrow for Intelligence, with orders to lye out all next night and watch any force that the Ennemy may either send to attack us or bring to their fort, and for the same purpose some of the very best of your Scouters ought to be sent out, with the like orders but to send of to acquaint us from time to time of whatever happens. I think some of the light horse might now be very usefully employed, particularly in gaining all the heights and reconnoitring the Grounds on the flanks, and in bringing quick intelligence of what ever happens, all this is so materiall I need not recommend the sending off all those by day break.

---

¹² Not found.

Mr Croghans 3 Indians joined us on our march, and I suppose have gone forward to you, as I could not well understand them I know not what discoverys they have made, but I fancy no great ones

I hear nothing worth acquainting you. Capt Callender says that if there was 3 miles cutt forward from your camp that all the rest of the road is easy to the fort, I think this might be tryed to morrow if possible.

Let me hear from you and believe me

Y^r most ob^t humb^le Servt

Jo fforbes

I have sent the light horse to pass the night upon the tops of the Hills all round. Wednesday 22^d past seven at night.

[*Note on Back:*] I shall send off a Waggon load of Entrenching tools by break of day to morrow.

[*Addressed:*] To Col° Bouquet at the Advanced Camp.

[*Endorsed:*] Genl Forbes 22^d Nov^r

*   *   *   *   *

Forbes to Abercromby and Amherst
[P. R. O. C. O. 5:54 (L.C. trans.) pp. 5-8; P.R.O. W.O. 34:44, f. 385. Copy.]

Fort Duquesne now Pittsbourg 26th Novem^r. 1758

Sir

I have the pleasure of acquainting you with signall success of His Majesties Arms over all His Enemies on the Ohio, by having obliged them to burn, and abandon their Fort Duquesne, which they effectuated upon the 24th Ins^t; and of which I took possesion with my light troops the same Evening, and with my little Army the next day—The Enemy having made their escape down the River, part in Boats, and part by land to their Forts and Settlements upon the Mississippi, being abandoned, or at least not seconded by their friends the Indians, whom we had previously engaged to act a neutrall part, after thoroughly convincing them in severall skirmishes, that all their attempts upon our advanced posts, in order to cut of our Communication, were vain, and to no purpose, so they now seem all willing, and well disposed to Embrace His Majesties most Gracious protection.

Give me leave therefore to congratulate you upon this important Event, of having expelled the French from Fort Duquesne, and this prodigious

Forbes marker on Penn Avenue, Pittsburgh, Pennsylvania.

tract of fine rich Country, and of having in a Manner reconciled the various tribes, and Nations of Indians inhabiting it, to His Majesties Government.

You may remember S^{ir} that I applyed to for your orders,[13] and instructions, how I was to behave myself in case I was so fortunate as to bring this affair to a happy crissis, acquainting you at the same time, that I had wrote to the different Governours concerned, beging of them their advice, and councill, but never had an answer to any of my repeated applications from any one person being left entirely to act upon my own weak foundation, I must now therefore beg, that as soon as possible, I may have your direction with regard to what strength I am to leave here for the protection of the Country, and for whom I must build a Blockhouse to cover them from the severity of the Season.

The Pennsylvania, Maryland, Virginia, and North Carolina troops, may all disband tomorrow, as their provinces will pay them no longer, however I have used the freedom to detain 250 of them here, which indeed is more than I think I can possibly mantain during the Winter, considering 400 miles of land carriage thrô an immense Wilderness, and the worst roads in the world.

So far I had wrote you the 26th, but being seized with an inflammation in my stomach, Midriff and Liver, the sharpest and most severe of all distempers, I could proceed no farther, and as I have a thousand things to say, have ordered Major Halkett down the Country in order to explain the motives upon which I proceeded, and the various, and almost insurmountable difficulties I had to grapple with.

I have ordered him to proceed directly for England, which I hope you will approve off, and forthwith order a Packett to sail with him, as I cannot put pen to paper myself, and as he is the only person with me, in whom I could place the smallest confidence, or from whom I have met with the smallest assistance, Col°. Bouquet alone excepted.

I shall leave this as soon as I am able to stand, but God knows when, or if I ever reach Philadelphia.

I expect the heads of all the Indians in here tomorrow,[14] when I hope very soon to finish with them what I have laboured hard at these 6 months, and which tho in the end has turned out as I foresaw it would, yet I had so many different Interests to reconcile, that I almost despaired of Success.

Our men had neither Tents, cloaths, shoes, or stockings, and provisions

[13] In letters of October 24 and November 17, 1758, *ante,* p. 245 and p. 255.

[14] Since this part of the letter was written on November 30, 1758, the Indians were expected on December 1, 1758.

-only from day to day, so you may believe it is high time for me to Seperate. I am D^r. S^{ir}

With great regard and esteem

Y^r. Most obedt.

Most humble Servt.

Jo: fforbes

30th November

[*Endorsed:*] Brigadier General Forbess's Letter of the 26th & 30th Novr. 1758 in M. G. Amherst's of Decr. 18th 1758

* * * * *

Forbes to Denny*
[*Pa. Col. Recs.* VIII, 232.]

Fourt Duquesne, or now Pittsburgh, the 26 Nov^r., 1758

Sir:

I have the Pleasure and Honour of Acquainting you with the Signal Success of his Majesty's Troops over all his Enemys on the Ohio, by having obliged them to Burn and abandon their Fort, Duquesne, which they effectuated upon the 24th Instant, And of which I took Possession with my little Army the next Day,—The Enemy having made their escape down the River, part in boats and part by Land, to their Forts, and Settlements on the Mississippi being abandoned, or at least not seconded by their Friends, the Indians, whom we had previously engaged to act a neutral part, And who now seem all willing and ready to Embrace His Majesty's Most gracious Protection.

So give me leave to congratulate you upon this publick event of having totally expelled the French from this Fort and this prodigious tract of fine Country, and of having in a manner reconciled the various Tribes of Indians inhabiting it to His Majesty's Government.

I have not time to give you a detail of our proceedings and approaches towards the Enemy, or of the Hardships and Difficulties that we necessarily met with; all that will soon came out, but I assure you, after receiving the Ground & Fort, I have great reason to be most thankful for the part that the French have acted.

---

* Also printed *Pa. Arch.* 2nd series VI, 432; and Stewart, *Letters of General John Forbes,* p. 69. Varying copies of this document exist, in H.S.P. Penn Papers, Official Correspondence; P.R.O. C.O. 5:54, pp. 49-50; and elsewhere. Since the content is the same, the matter of determining the relation of the copies to each other is not carried out.

As the Conquest of this Country is of the greatest Consequence to the adjacent Provinces, by securing the Indians, our real Friends, for their own Advantages, I have therefore sent for their Head People to come to me, when I think in few Words and few Days to make every thing easy; I shall then set out to kiss your Hands, if I have the Strength enough left to carry me through the Journey.

I shall be obliged to leave about Two Hundred Men of your Provincial Troops to join a proportion of Virginia and Marylanders, in order to protect this Country during Winter, by which Time I hope the Province will be so sensible of the great Benifit of this new Acquisition, as to enable me to fix this noble, fine Country, to all Perpetuity, under the Dominion of Great Britain.

I beg the Barracks may be put in good repair, and proper Lodging for the Officers, and that you will send me, with the greatest Dispatch, your opinion how I am to dispose of the rest of your Provincial Troops for the ease and Convenience of the Province and the Inhabitants.

You may also remember that Colonel Montgomery's Battalion of Thirteen Hundred Men, and Four Companies of Royal Americans, are after so long and tedious a Campaign, to be taken care of in some Comfortable Winter Quarters.

I kiss all your Hands, and flatter myself that if I get to Philadelphia, under your Cares and good Companys, I shall yet run a good Chance of reestablishing a Health that I run the risque of ruining to give your Province all the Satisfaction in the Power of my weak Abilities.

I am, Sir, with great Esteem and regard,
      Your most Obedient and Hum^{le}. Servant,
Governor Denny
                                Jo. Forbes.

[*Endorsed:*] Copy A Letter from Gen. Forbes to Govr Denny Nov. 26th 1758 in M. G. Amrherst of Jan^{ry} 18th 1759

P.S.—I must beg that you will recommend to your Assembly the building of a Block House and Saw Mill upon the Kisskaminities, near Loyal Hannon, as a thing of the utmost Consequence to their Province, if they have any intention of profiting by this Acquisition.

I send the New Levies to Carlisle, so beg you will loose no time in sending up Mr. Young, the Commissary, to clear them.

                *   *   *   *   *

Forbes to ————*
[Hazard's *Register of Pennsylvania*, VII, p. 125.]

Fort Du Quesne, Nov. 26th, 1758.

Sir,—Our march has been attended with innumerable difficulties, a country wild and desolate, through and across mountains, where civilized man had not before trod, by Indian paths almost impracticable and harrassed at every step by merciless savages who hidden from our view would pour forth their deadly shot with impunity. As we approached the Fort the danger of a surprise became greater; the recollection of the defeat of Braddock made us cautious; I ordered Major Grant who was in the advance to guard against ambuscades.—That officer with three hundred men approached the Fort on the supposition that the French had withdrawn, when suddenly the hostile Indians rose on each side and poured forth a destructive fire and the Garrison numerous and strong rallied out and made a fierce and violent attack; the attack was on every side but Grant ordered a retreat, the men formed a compact band and awed the assailants by a resolute and determined combat. Many were killed, many were taken prisoners, but the success of the enemy met with a powerful check, for they came in contact with the body of the army being led on with skill and circumspection; met them boldly and compelled them to give up their attempts; the retreat of Grant was the last success of the enemy, they were convinced that all hopes of saving the Fort were fruitless; they withdrew to the Fort, destroyed most of the works, and went down the Ohio, in number exceeding five hundred men. On the twenty fourth the English flag waved triumphantly over Fort Du Quesne. In the third year after the commencement of hostilities about that fortification, it fell into our hands after having kindled so fierce a flame in so destructive a war. With the change of masters it has assumed the name of Fort Pitt, and Pittsburgh the propriety of which is too evident to require a justification of the change; two plans of operation have been judicious, extensive, vigorous and successful.

My health is still delicate.

With sentiments of respect

I remain yours, &c.

Forbes.[15]

*   *   *   *   *

* Also printed, Stewart, *Letters of General John Forbes*, p. 71.

[15] The original of this letter was not found. Hazard says it was communicated for publication. To whom it may have been addressed is unknown. It does not resemble other letters of Forbes. It may be a forgery.

Forbes to William Pitt*
[P.R.O. C.O. 5:50, (L.C. Trans.) pp. 607-613]

Pittsburgh, 27th Novem^r. 1758
and
[Philadelphia 21st, January 1759]

Sir,

I do myself the Honour of acquainting you that it has pleased God to crown His Majesty's Arms with Success over all His Enemies upon the Ohio, by my having obliged the Enemy to burn and abandon Fort Du Quesne, which they effectuated on the 25 th:, and of which I took possession next day, the Enemy having made their Escape down the River towards the Mississippi in their Boats, being abandoned by their Indians, whom I had previously engaged to leave them, and who now seem all willing and ready to implore His Majesty's most Gracious Protection. So give me leave to congratulate you upon this great Event, of having totally expelled the French from this prodigious tract of Country, and of having reconciled the various tribes of Indians inhabiting it to His Majesty's Government.

It would be too tedious for a Letter to enter into detail how this affair has been brought to a conclusion, I have therefore thought it proper and necessary to send over to you Brigade Major Halkett whose serving with me all this Campaign, and knowing from whence Events arose will be able to give you a true and succinct Account of the whole Affair from the beginning. I beg to recommend that Gentleman to your Protection, whose Zeal and abilities in the Service have been particularly distinguished, not only in this but every preceding Campaign from the beginning of the war in this Country, and whose Father S^r. Peter Halkett,[16] lost his life at the Monongahela under Gen¹ Braddock.

I should have carried the troops up the River to the Lake Erie, and destroyed the French posts at Venango and Presque Isle, but the Season of the Year, and the Scarcity of my Provisions, does by no Means admitt of it, this last inconveniance (being obliged to carry every bit of my Provisions for Men and horse for betwixt 3 & 400 Miles thro' almost impracticable roads and Mountains) renders it extreamly difficult for me to leave a sufficient Garrison here for the Protection of this Country, as all Manner of Communication with the inhabited parts of the provinces will be cut off during the Winter for at least four Months, notwithstanding that I

---

* Printed, Kimball, *Correspondence of William Pitt* . . . I, 406, and Stewart, *Letters of General John Forbes*, p. 72.

[16] Locally famous for the dramatic manner of his death on the battlefield.

have built Forts, and erected Posts at proper distances, to have kept the Communication open if possible.

Altho' that I have made frequent Applications[17] not only to the Commander in Chief of His Majesty's Forces for his Orders, and instructions who indeed very rightly told me that as I was upon the spot I therefore might be the best judge of what was to be done and indeed judging at 5 or 600 miles distance or keeping up a Correspondence was difficult but likewise to the Governours of the adjacent colonies and Provinces for their Advice and Councill how I was to behave myself in case that I was so fortunate as to render myself Master of Fort DuQuesne, and the Country of the Ohio, yet I have never been favoured with any of their Sentiments upon that subject, except in one letter from the Lieut. Govern^r.[18] of Virginia, wherein he tells me that his Assembly and Councill would not venture to give any opinion, but at the same time acquaints me that they had addressed him to recall their troops by the first day of decem^r., therefore having been left to act intirely from my own judgment hitherto, I must beg His Majesties Indulgence that He would be graciously pleased to attribute my faults or ommisons that I may have made, to my want of greater abilities and not to want of Zeal for His Majesty's Service, which I shall ever think my duty to exert to the utmost of my power. As thus you see S^{ir}., that I am without advice or Orders, and that I very soon run a risque of being without troops if Pennsilvania recalled theirs as well as Virginia, I shall soon be greatly difficulted how to maintain our new conquest should the Enemy return, as I will have only 4 Companies of the Royal Americans and Col^o. Montgomery's young battalion to depend upon, both greatly impaired as to Numbers by their frequent skirmishes with the Enemy during the Campaign.

This far I wrote at Fort Du Quesne upon the 27th: Novem^r. since which time I have never, either been able to write, or capable to dictate a letter; but as General Amherst acquainted me[19] that he had sent to you my letter[20] with the Accounts of my taking the place, I was the less anxious of sending Major Halkett, but now dreading my silence may have some wrong construction put upon it when the true cause is unknown it will very well bear, I now send you the Major who must give you the best Accounts he can, untill I am able to write more circumstantially, which I hope will be

---

[17] Found in some cases in the letters herein published. In other cases the letters were not found.

[18] No letter, Fauquier to Forbes found.

[19] Not found.

[20] Forbes to Abercromby, November 26, 1758, *ante,* p. 262.

by the first Packett altho' my Physicians and all our Hospital People unaimously agree that I must go directly for England for to save my life, I must therefore beg it as the greatest favour that you will be so good as to move His Majesty to be graciously pleased to give me His leave of returning home as soon as I possibly can in order to re-establish my health, which at present renders me incapable of any service, or doing any duty whatever.

I must likewise take the boldness, to beg your Countenance & Protection with His Majesty of having me restored to my Rank which is one day antecedant to Gen[1]: Amherst as Lieut. Col[o]. .—Had I ever committed any fault, or been guilty of any misdeameanor in the Service, I should be now ashamed of making this Application to you, but the having so many people put over my head, without my being sensible of any *faux pas* committed, has made and still makes the deepest impression on my mind. If Lord Ligonier pleases to let you know the hardness of my case, I flatter myself with the protection and Service of M[r]. Pitt, to restore me to Peace of mind.

I have used the freedom of giving your name to Fort DuQuesne, as I hope it was in some measure the being actuated by your spirits that now makes us Masters of the place. Nor could I help using the same freedom in the naming of two other Forts that I built (Plans of which I send you) the one Fort Ligonier[21] & the other Bedford.[22] I hope the name Fathers will take them under their Protection, In which case these dreary deserts will soon be the richest and most fertile of any possest by the British in N[o]. America. I have the honour to be with great regard and Esteem, Sir,

Your most obed[t]. .& most hum[le]. serv[t].

Jo: Forbes

Philadelphia 21st. January 1759.
R[t] Honb[le] Wm. Pitt
[*Endorsed:*] Pittsburgh Nov. 27 and Jan. 21st. 1759
Gen[1] Forbes   R[23]   March 11th

*   *   *   *   *

---

[21] Plan of Fort Ligonier, *ante,* p. 203.
[22] Plan of Fort Sedford, *ante,* p. 173.
[23] Received, ironically enough, on the day of the death of Forbes in Philadelphia.

Forbes to Bouquet
[B.M., Add. MSS. 21640, f. 201. A.L.S.]

Bouquet Camp Decr 4th 7 at night.

Dr Sir

After a very long march[24] wee gott here at six this evening, so you may well allow the 12 miles were at least sixteen.

Wee mett with the provisions and I have orderd three days to be taken here and the rest of the Cattle are to proceed with all diligence to you, But as I thought that Halkett or St Clair would probably know the Number of troops that you had ordered to march as this day or to morrow, but finding them both ignorant, I desired they would settle the affair with Hoop's Commissary and to write you[25] a Circumstantiall Account of what they do, so by the remainder you may judge [wha]t will be wanting for the Garrison, which must [abso]lutely be left let the Difficultys and expence of prov[idi]ng for them cost what it pleases.

I send you a Curious performance of two noble personages that I received this afternoon, I shall take no more notice of their letter,[26] untill they find their names and orders in the Brigade Majors Books for I find some people can bear no sort of Indulgence, but what they forgett them selves, and run into intollerable impertenence.

I hope with your address, you will soon gett quitt of the Indians as I really pity you as much as I detest them. However hope you will be able to make them easy, with regard to our just and Hon^{le} Intentions towards them.

I am My Dr S^{ir} Y^r Most Devoted &c &c

Jo fforbes.

Keep the enclosed[27] untill you can send it to me.

If you gott any money from Barrow for the Garrison of Pittsburgh, be cautious how it is given, lest wee are really putt to the necessity of recalling them, In which case any advance would be lost.

I think a great part of the undergrowth strubby bushes ought to be burnt after the march of the Artillery—but do in that as you pleas[e] Y^{rs}

J F

*   *   *   *   *

---

[24] Forbes left Pittsburgh, December 4, 1758, on the day of the Indian Conferences, which he was too ill to attend.

[25] No such letters found. Cf. Hoops to Bouquet, December 14, 1758, B.M., Add. MSS. 21643, f. 261, and Clark to St. Clair, December 15, 1758, *ibid.*, 21658.

[26] Not identified. Probably Sir John St. Clair was one of the noble personages.

[27] Probably the letter mentioned, in the third paragraph.

Halkett to Bouquet
[B.M., Add. MSS. 21640, f. 202. A.L.S.]

Tomhach Camp 28 December 1758

Dear Sir

How great was our disappointment upon coming to this ground last night, to find that the Chimney was unclay'd, no fire made, or any Wood cut that would burn, this you may imagine distress'd the General to the greatest degree, by obliding him after his long journey, to sit above two hours without any Fire expos'd to a snow storm, which had realy very near distroy'd him intirely, but with great dificulty by the assistance of some Cordials, and other applications he was brought to, & is now thank God tollerably well again. A number of things concur'd at the same time to ruffle his temper, & distress his mind much, & not the least, is all the Waggon horses being almost knock'd up for want of Corn, of which they have not one grain, an Express was dispatched last night to Stony Creek, to see if any was to be got from thence, but I fear the worst.

Rissety the Indian is at Fort Augusta, & comeing up with a party to Reastown, that fellows fidelity will be rewarded.

The Captain Provost[28] I suppose has been a little pressing with you, to know what is to be done for him. The General promises that he shall not be forgott but paid punctually for his services last campaign. We proceed this day to Stoney Creek, where Mr Basset is stopt till the Generals arrival. I am Dear Sir

.Your most obedient Humble Servt

Francis Halkett

[*Endorsed:*] Major Halkett 28th Decr 1758.

*   *   *   *   *

Halkett to Bouquet
[B.M., Add. MSS. 21640, f. 203. A.L.S.]

Camp at the foot of the East Side of the
Alleganey 29th December 1758

Dear Sir

We have now thank God surmounted the two great obstakles, and hope in like manner will do all other deficulties, a small supply of Forrage haveing come this night for the Waggon horses, & the General in tollerable spirits.

---

* Not identified. There was a Captain Marcus Provost in the army, but the reference may be to a staff officer.

The inclos'd letter[29] was met upon the Road this day, and as the General saw it was upon His Majestys Service, and from Colonel Armstrong he open'd it, when he was extreamly surpris'd to find that all the Regular Troops were march'd from Reas town so contrary to his inclination, but this mistake he will Remidy as soon as in his power, by sending Orders express for the Highlanders to Return, and march immediately up the Country, which opportunity he will make use of, to send likewise, all the Carrying Horses that can be got, loaded. The steps taken by Colonel Armstrong, are very different from what the General and you settl'd at Fort Ligonier, but it will be put to Rights upon the Generals getting down to Fort Bedford, when he will write you what he has done.

The General is inform'd from Captain Paris,[30] that the Marylanders are deserting in great numbers from F Cumberland, and at the same time acquaints him, that their assembly has made no provision for their mentainance, but this he can say nothing to, as he has not heard from Governor Sharp for this Month past, tho it is very contrary to what he then inform'd him and which you may easily imagine occasions great surprise, I am Dear Sir

Your most obedient humble Servt

Francis Halkett

[Addressed:] On His Majestys Service To Colonel Bouquet Fort Ligonier.
[Endorsed:] Major Halkett 29th Dec^r
[Note on back:] Mr Sinclair[31] got to Reas Town yesterday and immediately Colonel Armstrong sent off orders[32] to stop the Highlanders, the first Division had past Littleton and the Second to Juniata

By a letter[33] from Hoops the following Provisions at Lancaster, Carlisle Fort Loudoun, & Fort Littleton, is ready to be sent up whenever their are Carriages or Horses provided

1075 Barrels ⎫
    38 Baggs   ⎬ Flour
40,000 lb Bulk ⎭
182 Barrels of Pork
14 Barrels of Beef

---

[29] Armstrong to Bouquet, December 27, 1758, B.M., Add. MSS. 21643, f. 277, A.L.S.
[30] Captain Richard Pearis, of the Virginia troops, an old fur trader. The information may have been given orally.
[31] Probably Lieutenant James Sinclair of the 22nd regiment, A.D.Q.M.G.
[32] Orders not found.
[33] Not found.

25,000 Pounds of Beef at Carlisle
18 Barrels of Rice
Hoggs upon the Road from Winchester to the amount of 50,000 lb.

*   *   *   *   *

Halkett to Bouquet
[B.M., Add. MSS. 21640, f. 205, A.L.S.]

Fort Bedford 31 December 1758

Dear Sir

The General was extreamly well pleased to learn by your letter[34] which I was favoured with last night by the return Express, that the Troops at Fort Ligonier are all put under cover.

Two hundred Highlanders, and fifty of the Royal Americans, with a proper proportion of Officers, are order'd to march back immediately to this place, where if they meet with no orders, or directions from you, they are to proceed upon their March to Fort Ligonier, where they are to be dispos'd of as you shall think necessary.

I Need to say nothing of Provisions, or the Hoggs that came this day from Virginia, as Mr Ourry writes[35] you fully upon that Subject by this Convayence.

The General stands his Travling tollerably well, and proposes continuing his journey downward to morrow, the Weather promises well, & I doubt not but he will be able to go through with it. No letters are yet come from General Amherst. Sr John has been sick at Carlisle of a Cold, & pain in his Breast, so I don't expect he will meet us, & I even doubt if we shall overtake him. Lieu^t Sinclair set out for the Inhabitants the day after he came to this place. I am Dear Sir Your most obedient humble [Servant]

Francis Halkett

[*Addressed:*] On His Majestys Service To Colonel Bouquet at Fort Ligonier.

[*Endorsed:*] Major Halkett 31st Decr 1758

[*Note at top of letter:*] 100 Pennsylvanians of this Garrison are to march the day after to morrow for Fort Ligonier.

*   *   *   *   *

---

[34] Not found.
[35] Lewis Ourry to Bouquet, January 1, 1759, B.M., Add. MSS. 21643.

Halkett to Bouquet
[B.M., Add. MSS. 21640, f. 207. A.L.S.]

Fort Loudoun 4th January 1759

Dear Sir

Thus far we have got through both good, and bad Weather, the General continuing in a very tollerable way, and sets out this day for Chambers's[36]. He has yet neither seen Sr John St Clair, or heard of Captain McPherson,[37] how they are imploy'd nobody can imagine, but the General is determind that non of them shall be Idle whenever he sees Sr John at Carlisle, & as the great defitiencies at the Forts up the Country will be in the Artikle of Flower, all hands are to be employ'd in forwarding that particular, the number of Hoggs already come from Virginia, with the others upon the Road, makes a good provision for the meat.

Seven hundred & fifty men are ordered for the Forts Ligonier, and Pittsburgh, to be proportioned to the particulars as you shall think necessary, 100 of the Provintials were ordered up from Fort Bedford, 80 of the Highlanders we met yesterday between this and F. Littleton, the Remaining 120 are expected with the 50 Royal Americans, as soon as the nature of things will permit, from Carlisle.

The General Receiv'd a letter[38] from Mr Amherst yesterday, with very little assistance by way of Instructions, but approving of the plan he had form'd himselfe, the General has therefore ordered Major Campbell[39] with the Highlanders here to March down to Carelisle, and intends to dispose of them for this Winter on the Frontiers at Carlisle, Lancaster, and Readen, as he does the Royal Americans from Canogochigue, to York.

Captain Mc Kenzey[40] who Commanded the 80 Highlanders, had directions from the General, to take some of the Blanketts out of the Kings Stores, to Cloath those men who are quite naked, and an account of the particular men are to be keepd; that the price of them, and payment be settld afterwards. I am

Dear Sir
Your most obedient humble Servt
Francis Halkett

---

[36] Chambersburg of later times.
[37] Probably Captain Robert McPherson of the third battalion of the Pennsylvania Regiment, acting as assistant deputy quarter-master general to Sir John St. Clair.
[38] Amherst to Forbes, December 25, 1758, P.R.O. C.O., 5:54 (LC. tr.), p. 67.
[39] Major Alexander Campbell of the 77th regiment.
[40] Alexander, Hugh and Robert McKenzie were captains in the 77th regiment.

[*Addressed:*] On His Majestys Service to Colonel Bouquet at Fort Ligonier

[*Endorsed:*] Major Halkett 4th Jan[y]

*   *   *   *   *

Forbes to Amherst
[P.R.O. W.O. 34: 44, f. 389. L.S.]

Shippensburgh 6th January 1759

Sir

I had the pleasure, and favour of Receiving your Letter[41] from New York of the [blank] Instant, I thank you most heartily for thinking my weak endeavours to serve the King, and Country, merited the suckcess they met with, I assure you, had you known the dificulties, and perplexing imbarrasments that so small a Body of Men have cost me, you would have pityd me several times during the Campaign, God be thank'd it's over, altho many things are left at sixes, and sevens and many of those of a delicate nature, particularly the Indians, which absolutely requires your immediate personal presence at Philadelphia, where the Governors of Virginia & Maryland, ought to attend you, in order to put a finishing stroke to that most material affair for the safety, and welfare of these Provinces, Peace with the Indians, which at presence a few days may settle, and which if neglected, perhaps may not be so easily recover'd.

You judg'd very right in thinking me extreamly out of order in not sending away Major Halkett, but I assure you I have never been able to write one scrape by him till this present moment however I hope in a day or two at farthest, he goes down the Country: when he will Receive your Commands, and satisfy you as to my Embacill state of Health, which by this convayence has oblidg'd me to solicit Doctor Hucks presence at Philadelphia, who I therefore beg you will send as soon as possible.

In a day, or two I hope to write you a more circumstantial Epistle, as I now begin to Breath an other Air in the Inhabited Country, excuse therefore my making use of an other hand and belive me to be with great regard, and sincerity Sir

Your most obedient humble Servant

Jo fforbes

His Excellency Gen[l]. Amherst

*   *   *   *   *

---

[41] Of December 25, 1758, P.R.O. C.O., 5:54 (L.C. tr.), p. 67.

Forbes to [*Bouquet*]
[B.M., Add. MSS. 21640, f. 209, L.S.]

Carlisle 8th January 1759

Dear Sir.

I arriv'd here last night, but find that things are neither in that for-wardness I wish'd or expected.

Captains Mᶜ Ferson,[42] & Callender, with other people, are employd still in Raising Horses for the service in the different Counties, & to en-courage those people who will not enter into the service, to carry Flower upon their own accounts, which service they shall be continued in till a suffitient number are engag'd, but as I was very apprehensive that this method alone would not Establish a sufftient Store of Provisions so early as I intend, I have order'd Sʳ John St Clair to publish Advertisements[43] in the Counties of Lancaster, York, Cumberland, Frederick, upon the South Branch, & the districk of Winchester, proposing to the Inhabitants in these parts, the Scheme that we talk'd of & offering £ 4 Pennsylvania currency for every hundred weight of Flower deliver'd by them at Pittsburgh, which shall be paid by principal men (nam'd in the Advertisements) residing in their different districts, upon their producing Certificates from either the Commissary, or Òfficer Commanding at Pittsburgh.

By the calculation we have made 80000 lbˢ will be sufficient to serve 800 men for four months, with the Forrage to support the horses that carrys it, will employ 684 horses.

We allow 42 days for the Horses to go from Carlisle, to Pittsburgh, and return again.

The expences that attends Engaging of Horses into the service to carry Flower, including the hire of the Horses, Horse Masters, and drivers, with their provisions, and the prise of the Flower, the Sadles, and other Artikles about the horses, amounts to 4322£..16ˢ..00ᵈ. by which means their will be a saveing of 1122£ 16ˢ.00 at the allowence of four pounds Pennsylvania currency pʳ Hundred wight deliver'd at Pittsburgh by the Inhabitants.

But as the makeing certain of a suffitient quantity of Provisions is the principal concern, and not the expence, I have put every Iron in the Fire that I think will tend to that effect, and Sʳ John has wrote to Lancaster, and the lower Counties to engage Waggons to carry Flower to Fort Bed-

---

⁴²Probably Captain Robert McPherson of the Pennsylvania militia.
⁴³Not found.

ford, in order to replace what is forwarded to the uper Posts upon Pack Horses.

One hundred and twenty horses set out from hence to morrow loaded with oats, of which there are 1500 Bushells in Store, and more daily comeing in from the Country, these horses are two thirds to be loaded at Fort Bedford with Flower, and the rest with Oats for their support, and I shall take care that the horses as they come in here are directly sent off with Flower, or Oats, as the demand at the Posts up the Country are most pressing.

All the Hay that can be got about Fort Frederick, and Canogochigue, is order'd to be laid in at Fort Loudoun; a considerable quantity is already laid in at Shippensburgh, and this place and as much more as can be procur'd is orderd to be sent in likewise.

Last night I receiv'd the Commissions[44] for the Vacancies in the Corps under my Command, Blaine is made a Lieutenant, and McDugal the Voluntier suckceeds him, I do ashure you, I made no alterations in the Recommendations for your Vacancies, but I find by General Abercromby's letter,[45] that Mr Stanwix has interfeerd, and carry'd it by which poor Hydler[46] is not yet provided for.

The Commissioners[47] of this Providence have sent up £800 worth of Indian goods under the care of Mr Tuckness,[48] if their are no part of them to be allow'd by the Commissioners, to be given in presents to the Chief Men, as I think it may be a necessary act at this time, let Colonel Mercer make a proper present out of the Indian goods in the Kings Store to the leading Men that ought to have them, as much depends upon our behaviour to them at present, or till things are fix'd in a more certain way.

I have order'd your people to march to York Town, Reserving Frederick town for those who are to Return down the Country, or as occasion may require.

Since writing the preceding part of this letter, one hundred more horses are come in that will likewise be loaded with Oats to Fort Bedford, and then with Flower as the former. I am with real esteem & regard Dear Sir
Your most obedient humble Servant

Jo fforbes

[44] Not found.   [45] Of December 25, 1758, AB 845, copy.

[46] [Martin] Hydler, probably a private in the army.

[47] Joseph Galloway, John Hughes, Jos. Fox, William Masters. Cf. Pa. Arch. 1st series, III, 498.

[48] Robert Tuckness, trader and merchant, agent of Pennsylvania at Pittsburgh, 1759. The agency's account book, the oldest extensive Pittsburgh business ledger, is in the Darlington Collection of the University of Pittsburgh Library.

P. S. In case that non of the Indian goods are sent up the Country from Fort Bedford, you will order what proportion you think necessary to be immediately forwarded to Pittsburgh to the care of Colonel Mercer, and as the Season of the Year is very severe upon upon [sic] those men who are badly Cloathd I think your very well intitl'd to make free with the Blankets, to cover those men who are naked who are ordered up the Country.

I have granted a warrant[49] for 700£ to Captain Harden upon account Subsistence for the Royal Americans

[Endorsed:] Gen¹ Forbes 8th Janʸ

*   *   *   *   *

Forbes to Amherst
[P.R.O. W.O. 34:44, f. 391. L.S.]

Lancaster Janʳʸ 13th 1759

Sir

I wrote you some days ago[50] which I hope has come to your hands & in which I endeavoured to perswade you of the Urgent necessity of your presence at Philadelphia which Dayly I see more and more necessary so therefor beg that you will, give me hopes of seeing you soon.

Colonel Morris is now at New York soliciting I suppose the sale of his Commission as his Story and the Gentlemen concerned is so fair and tending so much to the good of the service I dare swear it will meet with no Stop on Your part as General Abercrombie can recount to you all the different transactions that have passed in it.

There is likeways another commission to be Disposed of in my Regiment in which I must solicit you with all the instance I am master of, that is Captain Vaughan[51] who has served fourty Years in the service being quite wore out and incapable of any Duty wants to retire as there is no subaltern that will content him I must beg that Sir Hary Setton[52] now a Captain in Frazers may have leave to satisfy him for his commission and that he may retire where he pleases and Sir Hary now at New York be made Captain in his room—

---

* Cf. Abstract of Warrents, *post*, p. 294, payment to Captain Ralph Harding of the 60th regiment.

⁵⁰ January 6, 1759, *ante*, p. 275.

⁵¹ Captain Thomas Vaughan of the 45th regiment.

* Sir Hary Setton, i.e. Sir Henry Seton, of Abercorn and Culbeg, a captain in the 78th regiment.

Major Halket will be at new York in two or three Days to receive your commands—I hope you was so good as to send Doctor Huck altho by the time I reach Philadelphia I dont know whether he will be of any service to me or not As I am weaker than a child and recover no Strength, I am

Sir with great sincerity and truth

Your most obedient humble Servant

Jo fforbes.

N.B. I set out for Philadelphia tomorrow morning.

*   *   *   *   *

Forbes to Bouquet
[B.M., Add. MSS. 21640, f. 213, L.S.]

[January 14, 1759]

Sir.

Had my abilities been equal to my will, you would have heard from me several times since I parted with you at Ligonier, altho' in the mean I must confess I am greatly mended.

I made Halkett write[53] you any material things that I had done for to procure a speedy suply of provisions, to be forthwith transmitted to Pittsbourg & Ligonier, which I hope will have its effect, but that does not hinder my proceeding by every measure I can devise, to get as many Baggage horses as will transport all we possibly want untill the Spring, and as they come in, and are dispatcht, I have ordered M[r] Sinclair[54] to acquaint you regularly.

As to the quartering of the troops I did not think it worth while to send the Americans to Reding, because, upon my meeting with Gen[ll] Amherst, I propose carrying down the Highlanders, and Royal Americans, to the neighbourhood of Philadelphia.

The weather has been so favourable, that I durst not risque the losing of one day loitering upon the road, so I am got this length thank God, and proceed tomorrow, hoping to arrive at Philadelphia Wednesday night.

I think it vastly wrong that Raestown should continue without a Field Officer, but that Garrison as well as all the rest down this way I left you the trouble to settle as the moment I leave the Army you Command with the same power that I do and therefore hope you will settle all those places

---

[53] January 4, 1759, *ante,* p. 274.
[54] James Sinclair to Bouquet, January 9, 1759, January 17, 1759, and January 27, 1759, in B.M. Add. MSS. 21639 f. 70, 21643, f. 12, and 30.

to your liking which I assure you will please me, and meet with my approbation.

Halket left me yesterday at Lancaster on his way to England, I grant
you it is a little late but I could not force distemper.

I hope to have the pleasure of seeing you soon at Philadelphia, where I
should be glad you were, when Mr Amherst is present, as betwixt us we
could let him know things he has no notion of. I am D^r S^{ir} with real sincerity and truth

Y^r Most obed^t & Most humb^{le} serv^t

Jo fforbes.

The Halt, 14th January 1759

P:S. There was a tent and Markee of mine forgot in the stores as likewise
a barrell of Hams—Mr Sinclair promised that they should be sent safe
down the country but as I dread his performance, be so good as speak to
Ourry about them, to whom my compliments.

Col° Bouquett.

[*Endorsed:*] General Forbes 14th Jany 1759

*   *   *   *   *

Forbes to Lords Commissioners of His Majesty's Treasury
[P.R.O. T. I. Bundle 389. f. 88]

[Philadelphia, January 18, 1759]

To The Right Honourable the Lords Commissioners of
His Majesty's Treasury.
The Memorial of Brigadier Forbes Commander in Chief
on the Expedition to the Ohio, and Fort du Quesne Anno 1758
Humbly Sheweth

That in consequence of His Majesty's instructions, Your Memorialist
on the 13th April 1758, had the Honour to receive orders[55] to take upon
him the above Command; the Troops destined for this Service were, a
Detachment of 400 Men, under Colonel Bouquet from the Royal Americans; Montgomerie's newly raised Battalion of Highlanders, a Body of
Provincials, and a few friendly Indians.

That your Memorialist immediately repaired to Philadelphia the place of

---

[55] Pitt to Abercromby, December 30, 1757, Kimball, *Correspondence of William
Pitt* . . . I, 143.

Rendezvouze, and with the Utmost Expedition Assembled his Troops; But had the Mortification to discover disagreement, constant jarring and animosity among the Troops of the differing Provinces, and Coolness and Dispondency in the Indians; He first Applied himself to remove these difficulties, by reconciling his Men to one another, and to the Service they were going on: For this purpose he took a house, and kept open Table at Philadelphia; he had the leading Men of the different Provinces constantly with him; he made them Acquainted with one another; and by degrees had the good fortune to induce Harmony and Unanimity amongst them; The Indians he took immediately under his own Care; they were always with or about him, and everything was done to encourage and Attach them to His Majesty's Government.—At the same time the Memorialist was busy in providing necessarys for a March of several hundred leagues thro an unfrequented Wilderness; the Expence of doing which was immense, as every thing for defence, for Accommodation, and even for Subsistence during the whole time of the Expedition, were purchased, as well as Horses and Carriages for transporting them.

That after Struggling with many difficulties, Your Memorialist had the Satisfaction to leave Philadelphia, at the head of his Little Army Unanimous, determined, and well provided, The difficulties they encountered and Surmounted in the March are known; The Memorialist lost his Horses, and was Obliged to send to Philadelphia to replace them.

That after accomplishing the great Object of the Expedition Your Memorialist next applied to and succeeded in executing the second part of his instructions, by reconciling and renewing the Treaties with the Hostile Indians on the Banks of the Ohio; he had recourse to the common Method of entertainment and present, and in these Negotiations he found the benefit of his Care and Attention to the friendly Indians their Report of which to the others greatly facilitated the Treaties.

That at the end of Nine Months Your Memorialist returned to Philadelphia, having first accomplished all the purposes of his Command.

That the extra expence Attending these services Amounted upwards of £2,000; and as your Memorialist is a Soldier of Fortune, and had no Money of his own, he was obliged to pay the same out of the Publick Money, and it now stands a Charge against him.

That your Memorialist does not desire to put any Money in his Pocket by this Command, all he wished for is to be indemnified, and he flatters himself it will not be thought an unreasonable request in him to pay for the same Appointments, that his predecessor in the same Command General

Bradock had, to Wit, 1,000 for Equipage, and such other indemnification as Your Lordships shall seem Meet.[56]

*   *   *   *   *

Forbes to Amherst
[P.R.O. W.O. 34:44, f. 393. L.S.]

Philadelphia Jan[ry] 18th 1759

D[r]. Sir

I arrived here last night I wish I could say in perfect health—

I received your letter[57] by Captain Garth the Engineer & Should have answered your request then in giving you Distances & Strength of every one of my posts from Pittsburgh down to Carlisle but upon reflection that bare Description was not at all satisfactory without plans &c attending it I chose to Let it alone considering I flattered myself with soon having the pleasure of seeing you

Your hint about the Highlanders I had long ago made use off So that the way our Garrisons stand at present pretty near as to Strength Is as follows —Pittsburgh 350, and 50 more when we can Supply them w[t] provisions; Fort Ligonier 400; Stony creek 30, Fort Bedford 300, Fort Juniata 50, Fort Littletone 50, Fort Loudon 50, Shipenburgh 30, In Carlisle I design to have one hundred Thus you see the Chain who have orders to support one another & to forward all Convoys with proper Escorts. I am thinking that if your time would admitt of it That it would be very necessary for you to Require M[r]. Fauquier[58] & Governour Sharp[59] to meet you here as there are a great many things to be settled with those two provinces particularly the last who by a fatality has embarked me to advance a large sum of money for the support of these troops but absolutely necessary for carrying on the Service—

I beg you let me know soon as possible how soon I may expect you here and that you will be so good as order one of your Aid de camps to signify to

---

[56] In the same Bundle is the unfavorable reply of the Lords Commissioners, rejecting the petition.

[57] Of January 9, 1759, P.R.O. C.O. 5:54, f. 71.

[58] Amherst had other important matters on hand. The letter, Amherst to Fauquier, March 30, 1759, P.R.O. C.O. 5:54, f. 330, deals with other matters.

[59] No such letter in *Md. Arch.* IX, but Amherst wrote to Sharpe, February 7, 1759, according to B.M. Add. MSS. 21634 f. 3.

Captain Forbes[60] of Murrays Regiment whether you will allow him come and pass a month with me as I have great occasion for him

I am D[r]. Sir with great sincerity

Your most obedient humble servant

Jo fforbes

P.S. As to Indians and Indian affairs I Did everything that lay in my power to settle them as well as time & circumstances would admit off But they will require a thorough search and a just and equitable settlement to fix them our friends as long as we please to keep them—

*   *   *   *   *

Forbes to Amherst

[P.R.O. W.O. 34:44, f. 395. L.S.]

Philadelphia Jan[ry] 26th 1759

D[r]. Sir

I received yours of the 19th of Jan[ry61] which I would have answered sooner had I been able; and make no doubt but your multiplicity of business with General Abercrombie has been very interesting, but I Assure you my Dear Sir that if I dont misjudge greatly, you have business here of fully as great consequence to look into, and give your orders about as any in North America.

For first the Jealousy subisiting betwixt the Virginians & Pensilvanians is as much to be paried & reconciled as possible in order to Draw service from one of the Provinces, and as both are aiming at engrossing the commerce and Barter with the Indians, and of settling and appropriating the immense tract of fine country to be under the direction of their own province by fixing of the roads & the prices of the goods they exchange against the furrs: These things I dare venture to say you will think highly necessary to have settled on some solid footing, as the preservation of the Indians, and that Country, Depends upon it.

Therefor as I hinted to you before,[62] it will be highly necessary to require Governour Fauquier & Governour Sharp to meet you here at this place, And that; if I may be allowed to offer my advice to be as soon as possible. For my intelligence from Pittsburgh & the west[63] admitts of few

---

[60] Captain William Forbes of the 45th regiment.   [61] Not found.

[62] January 18, 1759, *ante*, p. 282.

[63] Hugh Mercer to Forbes, January 8, 1759, P.R.O. W.O. 34:44, f. 403; Bouquet to Forbes, January 13, 1759 and January 15, 1759, B.M., Add. MSS. 21640, f. 211, A.C.S. and f. 215, A.C.S.

Delays in securing to our interest or loosing a Capricious avaritious barbarous priest rid people—And the French who are still amongst them are availing themselves of every neglect of ours. So that I shall not be surprized when Monsieur Delinerie[64] who is still at Venango & Preskill make those Canadians that went Down the river join him at Pittsburgh and attack us assisted by all the Young people of Indians who are naturally fond of Change and of the Tinsil Raiments the French makes them presents off; none of which we have ever found openess of heart to give away:

I shall say no more upon this interesting & extensive subject, But that your presence or some Bodys presence is absolutely necessary. Nor shall I mention the necessity of your orders and Directions about the liquidating and ascertaining the various expence of this most expensive little body of troops.

I propose that it should be done by Neutral Commissarys appointed by the Army and the Inhabitants but this youl be able to Judge of when present:

The Sums advanced for the subsisting ye Maryland troops and Defraying in part Lord Loudons & Brigadier Stanwix's engagements[65] as also the General Behaviour of that province with regard to his Majestys affairs will require your particular and immediate consideration, as their assembly may meet soon and for want of being told properly your opinion of their Behaviour may therefor proceed in their error so I cannot help thinking that you would find it greatly to your satisfaction to have all those Governours as well as New York and New Jersey here together during the vaccancy of their assemblys.

I must own that what you wrote me about Colonel Morris surprized me very much having at that very time his memorial & resignation[66] in my pocket ready to be transmitted to you, which as I thought it wanted no further recommendation and that you would order the commissions out directly, I was the less anxious of forwarding it—But send it herewith enclosed not att all doubting but it will meet with your approbation as all partys are agreed—

Your proposal of keeping Major Halket from going to Brittain I must confess hurt me not a little for you my Dear Sir must be very sensible how far to Blame I have been in not Dispatching him from the first momment, nor have I left me any way of setting myself to rights and of wiping off that

---

[64] M. Francois de Marchand de Ligneris, born 1704, commandant at Fort Duquesne, 1756-1758, killed at Niagara in 1759.

[65] Loudoun to Sharpe, November 3, 1758, *Md. Arch.* IX, 98.

[66] LO 5226; P.R.O. W.O. 34:44, f. 399.

Stain that may be justly laid to my Door of neglecting to Do, what I could have no other excuse for, but the real one of being incapacitate by infirmity & Distemper: Nor had I any person that could be employed upon this message proper to acquaint the ministry with matters of fact but Major Halket who alone was the only person I had to trust But who Im affraid will make but a bad puff of an Ambassador at home—however I hope he is gone, as Likeways Capt Anderson[67] of the Train, who by the means of his access to Lord George Sackville & Lord Ligonier the ministry might been informed of a great many of my very extensive manuvers that other-ways they must remain in ignorance off.

I beg if Halket missed General Abercrombie that you will be so good as to order him away by the very first conveyance that possibly can be procured for Love or money as I shall scruple no expence rather as lay under the imputation of Dilatoryness or neglect where the Kings business is concerned.

I have a great Deal to say to you with regard to those provincial troops and the fixing and supporting of our Different posts in the back Countrys, which is a consideration of very great momment considering the immensity of the expence—however at present I have them free from all insult having now a garrison of 450 at Pittsburgh and having of late Discovered[68] the Enemys cannon thrown into the river, which I had ordered Diligent search to be made after, and which I have now directed to be got out soon as possible and placed upon the fort.

You see My Dear Sir that I wrote you without either Ceremony or Disguise as we have known one another a long time and were pretty much bred under the same masters.

I should therefore think myself unpardonable If I did not contribute as much as in me lay, to your success in managing the great affairs the King has entrusted you with as I really am your sincere well wisher & Friend—

Jo fforbes

General Amherst
[*Endorsed:*] B^r General Forbes
Jany 26th 59
Recd 29th Jan^y

* * * * *

[67] Note previous reference, Halkett to Bouquet, August 7, 1758, *ante,* p. 169. The Artillery, or Train, appears to have had separate organization.
[68] Source of information not found.

Forbes to Amherst
[P.R.O. W.O. 34:44, f. 401. L.S.]

Philadelphia Jan^ry 28th 1759

Dr Sir

By a letter[69] I have received this momment from Major Halket, I find that he has missed of his passage in the Kinington Man of war; an addition to the neglect that I have already been guilty off, which occasioned me the greatest confusion and pain: as my Dispatches home[70] contain nothing but General observations, referring myself entirely to what questions the Ministers might think proper to ask of Major Halkets knowledge of my operations; I am therefor Sir at this critical period to beg of you all the assistance in your power in getting Major Halket Dispatched for England instantly without one momments loss of time. I shall not pretend to argue how far it is convenient for you to Dispatch the packet directly with him as the Nightingale will still remain in port to carry any pressing Dispatches you may have:—But if that cannot be complyed with which would be the greatest relief in the World to my uneasy mind, I must then beg that the first Ship that to be met with in harbour may be hired on purpose to carry him over.—You may easily see my uneasiness impatience &c by my taking no notice of your thinking Major Halkets journey to England unnecessary But as I am positive of the Consequence it is off to me I hope therfor My Dear Sir You will pardon and pass over any of my inadvertencys or blunders and in place of retaining Halket make me exceeding happy in contributing to send him of Directly: I shall apologise for all this when I have the pleasure to meet you.

I take the opportunity of Sir John Sinclairs going to New York to send this to you altho in my last dated two Days[71] ago I have wrote pretty fully on the same subject, in which perhaps I Did not explain fully the evident necessity of your presence in the Southern Colonys where without a meeting of the Governours of Virginia, Maryland, Pennsylvania, Jersey, and New York, and that Directly the Indian affairs to the Northward and westward must necessarily fall into the greatest confusion, and The Indians themselves tho now well Disposed to us and easily secured fall again under the French Direction—It is impossible by letter to Describe to you the many ruises and Doublins I have been obliged to make use off,—Halket can

---

[69] Not found.
[70] Probably a reference to the Memorial, *ante,* p. 280.
[71] January 26, 1759, *ante,* p. 283.

acquaint you of a few but previous to your talk with the Different Governours it will be necessary I acquaint you off the whole.

There are arrived in this place last night an Embassy from the Chiefs and head Warriors of the Alegany and Ohio Indians with belts and messages[72] for me, they keep the purport of their Embassy extremly private— I Dont know when my health will permitt me to see them—nor indeed Do I know without your approbation what answers I can make to any of their Demands.—The settling of the Frontier Garisons, and the Levys of these provinces likeways Demmand your orders & Directions ;—

I shall not enumerate a multiplicity of things that I think of great consequence to be lookt after, only As I am incapable of business myself It would give great pleasure to see one here who is   I am

My Dear Sir

Your most obedient &c &c &c

Jo: fforbes

N.B. I send enclosed Copys of a Letter from Colonel Mercer[73] Commanding officer at Pittsburgh as also a Conference[74] held there with some Indian chiefs, Some which are arrived in Philadelphia, whose business is to enforce the Contents of the Conference

General Amherst

*   *   *   *   *

Forbes to Amherst

[P.R.O. W.O. 34:44, f. 405. L.S.]

Philadelphia Jan^{ry}. 30th 1759

D^r. Sir

I Dare say youl think I have taken a rage to write you letters, which by the by, I must tell you is the plague and Bane of my life—

Sir John Sinclair being gone to York will attack you upon a subject upon which I must put you on your guard—He has taken it in his Noble mind, that as Quarter master General he commands in the army wherever he comes, outposts, Detachments &c are instantaneously to obey his sovereighn will, and even Garrisons have been threatened with pains & penaltys for not attending him immediately on his arrival and receiving the parole & report of the State of their Garrison.

---

[72] *Pa. Col. Recs.* VIII, 264-269.

[73] Of January 8, 1759, P.R.O. W.O. 34:44, f. 403.

[74] Minutes of conference, December 4-5, 1758; B.M., Add. MSS. 21655, f. 19. Printed in *Pa. Arch.* 1st series, III, 571-573.

This fancy tho never so absurd is not to be removed by me altho I told him that I had a longer experience than him in that office of quarter-master general, and never lookt upon myself in the active military Capacity, But only as a person employed to take care of the Police of the Army—
This has not hindered him from interfering with military command, & putting several field officers in arrest for not complying w^t. his immediate orders: producing some rediculous orders Given out by the Commanders in chief on purpose to give him a little sway where perhaps there were nobody to serve but Provincials—

I beg if he talk to you, that you will set him right as to this affair, and let him know that an Overslaw for him in the army Dispenses with him from all military Duty nor can he either act, or be obeyed in the military capacity till the overslaw is removed in the publick orders.—

Mr Halket can tell you a great Deal about this and of Sir Johns be-haviour. He has likeways conceived a new krotchet, that the providing of bagage horses, Waggons for the transport of provisions & in short the General police of the army is not his Department but ought to be the care of some pimping purveyors belonging to the provision Contractors,

This he has only given out of late tho his actions might have long Declared his Sentiments of which Halket can fully inform you from the beginning to the present time.

I have Nothing new to add but thought it necessary you should know this: so I am

My Dear Sir

General Amherst   Your most obedient humble servant

Jo: fforbes

* * * * *

Forbes to Amherst
[P.R.O., W.O. 34:44, f. 407. L.S.]

Philadelphia Febry 7th 1759—

Dr Sir

As this is to be a letter of sincerity, I therefor throw of all Ceremony By begging leave to assure Mr Dear Jeffrey that there is no one man in north America more sensible of the Civilitys and favours he has latly received than John Forbes.

I shall not enumerate my account of them, yet I cannot pass over in silence the real sense I have of your allowing Halket to go so readily, without any stop and the procuring of him a Ship.

This moment yours[75] of the 4th designed to have come by Sir John Sinclair (who has fallen and broke his face by the way) is come to hand, and the alternative of the packet for the hired ship for carrying over Major Halket has happened very luckily.

Your argument about the propriety or necessity of Halkets going over would have satisfyed me at any other time but the present but I was put upon my guard to call to mind The rock Loudon hurt himself upon God knows what I had to say was very immaterial as I neither entered into a Detail of one thing or another, and imagine I had a sufficient excuse considering I have not been able to write one letter wt my own hands these two months.

I forgot to acquaint you, which I hope youl excuse that in giving Mr Pitt an account of my bad State of health[76] I likewise gave him the opinion of my Doctors, which in a few words is, That I cannot be fitt for service this Campaign, nor can I live in the Country to the Autumn, But as I must make application to you more fully upon this chapter, I say no more at present, Doctor Huck being able to inform you better than me.

I am certainly obliged to you, in your thinking the small services I may have Done the publick, will speak for themselves but my Dear Jeff: you and I both know the world enough, to have seen Wrong lights, and faint shades thrown upon very good intentions, which I hope with your good assistance will not be the case with me.

The State of the Indians all along the Ohio Shawnese and Delawares, is Im affraid not generally understood, of if understood, perverted to purposes serving particular ends, Nor can I conceal from you my opinion, That I have all along thought, that the publick measures and the private interested views of Sir William Johnstone and his Myrmidons have never once coincided in my time, nor can I at present conceive, why I am honoured with one of Sir Willm Johnstones people at this place, when During the summer when there were nine Hundred Indians at one time to be taken care off, I could not get a single person to look after them, from Sir William, altho Pensilvania was entirely his District:—

I Delayed hearing what those Indians had to say who came lately down still flattering myself I might have the pleasure of seeing you soon, and imagining that the consideration of Indian affairs and the fixing and settling those Scoundrals to be of more consequence to those Colonys in the neighborhood than you seem at present to be aware off:—I agree with you

---

[75] Not found.
[76] Forbes to Pitt, November 27, 1758, *ante*, p. 268.

that they always will incline to the Strongest which has not been our fate in those parts for some time by past, and now that we have the ball at our foot I think it is not be neglected by any means, by which I fancy The French will be a great time of recovering their lost ground, But this requires a long and serious Confab to discuss; only I beg in the mean time that you will not think trifflingly of the Indians or their friendship; when I venture to assure you that twenty Indians are capable of laying half this province waste, of which I have been an eye witness.

I am sorry to acquaint you that I dont find[77] we have found all the French cannon, altho in Dayly expectations, as some of their Young ones, are willing to blab, for that God of theirs, Rum.

I wish from my heart you had some news from great Brittain as from thence you could Determine your motions, which if not soon set about in spite of all Your Dilegence and care, you will find at the long run very tardy

I should be glad to know what answer Sir John Sinclair had with regard to his Commanding as Deputy Quartermaster General as I am pretty sure that that was one of his principal errands at New York.

I send you inclosed a letter[78] I received two Days ago from Governour Sharp—He tells me he has offered to send you a Detail of his whole affair w^t Copys of My Lord Loudons & General Stanwixs orders to him & his officiers by which you will see a clear State of that matter, which I fancy you will think requires to be lookt into.

Doctor Huck who carries this will give you all the history of those parts, which is not very interesting——

If the weather was a little milder I believe I should be Desperate ineough to come and see you were it but for two or three Days as I think always your presence here w^t the Governours is indispensably necessary—

I should be glad of any news that came by the Rose Man of war old British News papers or magazines are noveltys to us.

This is a long letter to little purpose, but I know youl excuse me & hope youl believe me will great sincerity.

> My Dear Sir
>
> > Your most obedient humble servant
> >
> > > Jo: fforbes.

---

[77] Source of information not located.
[78] Sharpe to Forbes, January 26, 1759, *Md. Arch.* IX, 319.

WRITINGS OF GENERAL JOHN FORBES

PS If not too much trouble I beg my service to your Brother,[79] and Roger[80] whose letter Im not able to answer.
General Amherst.

*   *   *   *   *

Forbes to Bouquet
[B.M., Add. MSS. 21640, f. 224. L.S.]

Philadelphia Feb^ry 8th 1759

Dr Sir

You may be very well assured that I neither would have been so long of writting to you nor of answering your last,[81] had I not waited from time to time for Mr Amhersts joining me here, But as he Does not chuse quitting of New York before the packet arrives, from whence he is to Learn the measures to be pursued, I therefor remain as ignorant of anything to be Done, as I was the Day I came here.

As our Governour is now returned from holding his Assembly in the Lower Countys I therefor design to see that Deputation of Indians to-morrow[82] and to hear what they have to say, which from their talk to Mercer leaves me in Doubt what credit they ought to meet with. If it is to stirr up Jealousies & bred Dissensions twixt us and our new friends, I think by all means that is to be prevented altho I would not Discredit them entirely, but have an eye upon the Delawares and Shawnese untill that by some firmer tye, than what has hitherto been touched upon They be secured entirely to our interest. And that I am sorry to say will meet with more rubs and hinderances than I could have thought off all owing to the Delatoryness of the provinces themselves.

I have had some people from the south branch with me who had De-livered provisions at Pittsburgh and who have received Colonel Mercer's orders,[83] to be payed, by the Contractors at the highest rate they gave for provisions, which I think was but fair and right, But they had not remained above twelve hours in town before it was whispered them they ought to ask so much for the carriage of provisions over and above the price; this

---

[79] William Amherst (1732-1781). Consult John Clarence Webster, *Journal of William Amherst.*

[80] Possibly an aide-de-camp, either Lieutenant Roger Kellet of the 44th regiment, or Ensign Roger Pomeroy Gilbert of the 15th regiment.

[81] Of January 23, 1759, B.M., Add. MSS. 21640, f. 218.

[82] Note the anticipated date of the Indian Conference. Forbes was too ill to attend and was represented by his surgeon, Lieutenant James Grant.

[83] Not found.

you may be sure did not go down as it was their own private venture. However I coxed them and sent them of well pleased with a promise of being paid ready money if required, and have accordingly this Day by Mr Speirs[84] sent six hundred pounds to Colonel Mercer to supply any wants he may have occasion for.

I understand my friend Halket sailed in the packet for Brittain on Monday last from what motives I will not pretend to say but I found that both our old, and New Commanders in chief were a little averse to his going home. He writes me from New York,[85] That Sir John Sinclair has been there with General Amherst where he left not a Stone unturned to perswade him that as Quartermaster General he ought to Command the army, I Dont know his answer but understand he gives it out, it was in his favours entirely without hesitation, altho Halket writes me diametricaly conterary from Amhersts own mouth.

I heard Sir John has been extremly liberal in his criticisms, remarks and observations upon all our Doings up the Country, gainsaying with great additions what he had often repeated to me while with the army, and Im sorry to say that he has endeavoured as much as possible to Diminish the small share of merit we had on reducing of Fort Duquesne, and is not ashamed of creticising almost every one of our actions, altho one and all of them under his Department, I therfor beg you would throw your loese thoughts together[86] of his General behaviour & the General care he has taken of supplying the Army wt forage &c. during the Campaign, as likeways the indefatigable care he took of the only bitt of the roads passable or well made from Fort Bedford to Pittsburgh, In short I am sorry to say it, But his late behaviour has now confirmed me in an opinion I was loath to give way to.

I hope your winter quarters is to your mind, but that you are not so riveted, as not to come and pay us a visit which I could wish were some time before Mr Amherst arrived here, in order that we should be uniform in our Discourse, as Im sure we are in our Sentiments.

I could wish you wrote Mercer[87] that this Six hundred pounds is to Strengthen his hands so as that he may not be Distressed at particular occasions, and as the Indian goods from Pensilvania and Virginia are not yet arrived at Pittsburgh where the Indians are in want of traffick, I see no reason why that the rest of the Kings Stores left at Fort Bedford ought not

---

[84] William Spears, cf. the warrant, *post,* p. 299.
[85] Halkett to Forbes, February 5, 1759, B.M., Add. MSS. 21640, f. 220, copy.
[86] Bouquet to Forbes, February 14, 1759, B.M., Add. MSS. 21640, f. 228, A.C.S.
[87] No such letter found.

be sent immediately to Pittsburgh and there bartered w^t the Indians for the Governments behooff at moderate prices; for to say sincerly I thought there were too many of them to make them all in presents unless to serve particular ends. I wish Mercer would send us, a true State, where, and of what Numbers the French are.

Im affraid the scheme of beating up their quarters is broke upon by accident, One Paterson[88] of the Pensilvanians a Lieu^t having set out from Fort Augusta with Sixteen Delawares Warriors, the 19th of last month, unknown to any body, in order to beat up the French quarters at Venango, Preskill Bukalone & Wherever they could find them on the upper parts of the Ohio, or even to push further according to their success. This youl acquaint Mercer of,[89] so that we may learn if they make any noise in those parts.

I am Dr Sir Your most Obedient humble servant.

Jo: fforbes.

Colonel Bouquet.

[*Addressed:*] On His Majestys service to Colonel Bouquet of the Royal American Reg^t at York Town in Pensilvania p^r favour of Mr Speirs
[*Endorsed:*] from Genl Forbes 8th Febr^y answered[90] the 14th d^o by Express.

*   *   *   *   *

Abstract of Warrants Granted by the Late Brig^r General Forbes, during the Campaign 1758, on Account of the following Services.
[P.R.O. W.O. 34:44, f. 411]

Ord'nance

1758

		£	Sh	d
May 19th...	To Capt. Harry Gordon on Acco^t. of the paym^t. of Engineers, & other Expenses of the Ordinance, without Deduction..	√ 100....		
29.....	To Capt. Lieut: David Hay, on Acco^t. of Various Expenses incurr'd in the Service of the Ordnance, without Deduction	√ 500....		
30.....	To Capt Harry Gordon, on Acco^t. of Expenses in the Service of the Ordnance, without Deduction...	√ 60....		
June 9th....	To Capt. Lieut David Hay, for purchas-			

---

[88] Lieutenant Paterson, not identified.
[89] No such letter found.
[90] B.M., Add. MSS. 21640, f. 228, A.C.S.

ing One Eight Inch Howitser &ca, without Deduction...   √127 16   1

12.....To Lieut: James St Clair A D Q M G
for various Expenses in the Service of
the Ordnance, without Deduction ... √1455 17   6

20:....To Capt Lieut: Hay on Acco^t of purchasing Howitsers, Howitser Carriages
& ca., without Deduction...   √380.... 10

Subsistence

1758
June 12th...To the Honble Col. Arch^d Montgomery,
on Acco^t of Subsist^{ce} for the 1st Batt. of
Highlanders, from the 25th March to
the 24th June, Inclusive, without Deduction...   √1947....

Octr. 25....To Capt John Gordon of the first High- £   Sh   d
land Battalion, on Acco^t of Subsistence
for said Battalion from the 25th June
1758, without Deduction...   √1700   8   6

Jan^{ry} 8th...To Capt. Ralph Harding, on Acco^t, of
Subsistence of four Companys of Royal
Americans from the 25th June 1758,
without Deduction...   √700....

Hospital

1758
July 22....To William Russel Esqr Sub Director of
the General Hospital, on Acco^t of Expenses of the Hospital, without Deduction...   √124   8   10½

Sepr 29....To Mr John Munro,[91] Surgeon's Mate
to the General Hospital, Messrs Robt
Bass[92] & Wm Baines,[93] Apothecaries
Mates, On Acco^t of their pay from the
25th March 1759 to the 24th June Inclusive. . .   √ 63 12   9

Feb^{ry} 13...To William Russel Esqr Surgeon to the

[91] John Monro, not otherwise identified.
[92] Robert Bass, not on regimental basis.
[93] Will Bains (Baines), later surgeon in 95th regiment.

General Hospital, on Acco[t]. of his pay
as Sub Director to the Hospital, with-
out Deduction...   √ 144. . . .
...To Ditto...on Acco[t]. of Extraord[y]. Ex-
penses of the Hospital, without Deduc-
tion...   √ 150. . . .

For the Use of the Indians

1758

May 29....To William West,[94] on Acco[t] of purchasing Goods for the Indians, without
Deduction...   √ 1284   5   3¾

June 29....To Andrew Elliot[95] Esq.[r] on Acco[t] of
Shoes for the Cherokee Indians, with-
out Deduction...   √ 218   17   4

July 22....To M[r] Draper Simon Wood,[96] Dep.
Commissary, on Acco[t]. of Provisions
purchased for the Indians, & ca., without
Deduction...   √ 171   15   3½

Dec[r] 11....To Mr. Geo. Gibson[97] for Sundry
Goods furnished by him for the Indians
at Pittsburgh, without Deduction...   √   18   14   11½

Carried forward   9214—17   04½
Bro[t]. forward ....£...9214. 17   ¼

Secret Services

1758

June 7th...To Capt: M[c]. Intosh, On Acco[t]. of Secret Service, without Deduction ...   √   50. . . .

July 25....To Rich[d]: Peters Esq[r]. Secretary to the
Proprietor & Gov[r]. of Pensylvania, On
Acco[t]. of Secret Service, without De-
duction...   √ 311   2   2½

1759

Feb[y]. 13...To Capt: Alex[r]. M[c]. Intosh, on Acct.
of Secret Service, without Deduction...√   24   2   2

---

[94] William West, Indian trader, member of Pennsylvania Assembly.
[95] Andrew Elliot, merchant and trader.
[96] Draper Simon Wood, not otherwise identified.
[97] George Gibson, Indian trader and Western Pennsylvania Revolutionary figure.

Waggonage, & ca.

1758

June 30th... To Conrade Snyder, on acco^t. of a Waggon & Cart &ca, without deduction... √   58   15   8¼

July 13.... To M^r. Adam Hoops for the Hire of
Waggons for transporting Provisions, &
other Contingent Expences of the
Troops, without Deduction...   √ 1000....

.... To M^r. Ja^s Coultis, on Acco^t of the
Hire of Waggons & Horses for the Artillery, &ca; without Deduction...   √ 2056   10   9

17.... To Adam Hoops, on Acco^t. of the hire
of Waggons for transporting Provisions
&ca, without Deduction...   √ 500....

19.... To M^r. Joseph Pugh, on Acco^t. of the
hire of Waggons for Transporting Provisions, without Deduction...   √ 567....

hire of Waggons for Transporting Pro-

Sir John St Clair's Departm^t: as D.Q^r. M^r. G.

1758

June 8th... To M^r. Thos. Willing, for the Use of
Sir John S^t. Clair, on Acco^t. of Various
Contingent Expences in his Department,
without deduction...   √ 3000....

July 11.... To Sir John S^t. Clair D.Q.M.G. on
Acco^t. of Various Contingent Expences
of the Troops, without Deduction...   √ 1000....

19th.... To Ditto ... on Acco^t. of Ditto, without
Deduction...   √ 1000....

Augst: 9... To Lt James S^t. Clair A.D.Q.M.G. on
Acco^t. of purchasing Forrage for the
Service of the Troops, without deduction...   √ 700....

Sep^r: 8.... To Sir John S^t. Clair, D Q M G, on
Acco^t. of the hire of Waggons, without
Deduction...   √ 1600....

20.... To L^t. James St Clair, A D Q M G. on
Acco^t. of Various Contingent Expences
of the Troops in his Department, without Deduction...   √ 300....

Octo^r. 6....To Ditto . . . on Acco^t. of Ditto without Deduction... √ 655 2 2½

22....To Sir John S^t. Clair, D Q M G. on
Acco^t. of Ditto, without Deduction... √1000....

Novr. 9....To Ditto . . . on Acco^t. of Forrage &
other Contingent Expences of the
Troops in his Department, without Deduction... √ 700....

Decr. 21...To Lieut. S^t. Clair, A D Q M G. on
Acco^t. of Various Contingent Expences
of the Troops, without Deduction... √ 400....

26....To Ditto . . . on Acco^t. of Ditto, without
Deduction... √ 600....

1759
Jan^{ry} 1st...To Lieut. Lewis Ourry, A D.Q.M.G.
on Acco^t. of Various Expences of the
Troops in his Department, without Deduction... √ 186 13 4

23....To St. John S^t. Clair D.Q.M.G. on
Acco^t. of Ditto, without Deduction... √1000....

Contingencies

1758
May 22^d...To John Malcolm, for paym^t. of Waggon Cloths, without Deduction... √ 936 8 10½

....To Ditto. for Tents & Tent Poles, & ca,
without Deduction... √ 44 3 6½

31....To M^r. Andrew Elliott, On Acco^t. of
Ditto, without Deduction... √ 292 16 6¾

June 1st...To Captain Harry Gordon, for the Use
of Col^o. Bouquet, on Acco^t. of Contingent Expences of the Troops, without
Deduction... √1000....

Carried forward £28187 12 4¼
Brought forward £28187 12 4¼

Contingencies

1758
June 12th...To The Honble: Col: Arch^d Montgomery, on Acco^t. of transporting the first
Battⁿ. of Highlanders from Charlestown
to philadelphia, without deduction... √1392.... 10¾

13.... To Major Francis Halkett, on Acco^t. of
Various Current Contingent Expences of
the Troops, & ca, without deduction... √ 300....

19.... To Major James Grant, on Acco^t. of
transporting the first Battalion of Highlanders to Philadelphia, without Deduction... √3315   8   3¾

20th.... To M^r. Andrew Elliot, on Acco^t. of
Tents, Belles & ca Armes & ca, for the
Province Troops, without Deduction... √ 395   7   8

.... To Ditto ... on Acco^t. of Tents, Kettles, & ca, for the Provincials without
Deduction... √ 532   12   7

Augst. 11th.. To M^r. John Ingles, on Acco^t. of Various Contingent Expences of the Troops,
without Deduction... √ 100....

26.... To M^r. Joshua Howell, on Acco^t. of
Various Contingent Expences of the
Troops, without Deduction... √1519   10   8

30.... To Francis Halket Esqr. Major of Brigade, on Acco^t. of various Contingent
Expences of the Troops, without Deduction... √ 100....

Sep^r: 8th... To John Cary, on Acco^t. of Blankets &
Sundrys purchased by him for the Use
of the Troops, without Deduction... √ 205   14   9

Octr. 11th... To Colonel Dagworth of the Maryland
Troops for the Cloathing & Support of
Four Companys of said Troops, without
Deduction... √ 715   15   11¾

.... To Major Hugh Waddle of the North
Carolina Troops, for the Cloathing &
Support of three Companys of the said
Troops, with Deduction... √ 538   15   10½

25.... To M^r. John Ingles, on Acco^t. of Expences incurred by him for the Service
of the Troops, without Deduction... √ 62   4   5

Decr. 1.... To Capt: Evan Shelby of the Maryland
Comp^y: of Voluntiers, on Acco^t. of their

Service, during the Campaign, without
Deduction... √ 84 3 1¼
18....To Colonel Hugh Mercer, on Acco^t. of
Various Contingent Expences of the
Troops at Pittsburgh, without Deduc-
tion... √ 50....
....To Ditto ... on Acco^t. of Ditto, without
Deduction... √ 155 11 1
....To Capt: Gordon Engineer, to be paid
by him to the officers who Contracted
to Build a Fort at Pittsburgh, without
Deduction... √ 124 13 2
1759
Feby 7.....To M^r W^m. Spears, to be paid to Col:
Mercer, or the Officer Commanding at
Pittsburgh, on Acco^t. for purchasing
Provisions & ca., without Deduction...√ 372 6 8
13....To M^r. W^m. Scrogie, on Acco^t. of Vari-
ous Contingent Expences of the Troops,
without Deduction... √ 1000....
Totall £39,152 17 6¼

* * * * *

The Last Will and Testament of Forbes
[Photostat in Society Collection of Photostats of Hist. Soc. of Pa. of MS copy from
the original in the Registry of Wills. Df.S.]

[Philadelphia February 13, 1759]

In the Name of God. Amen. I John Forbes Brigadier General of His
Majesties Forces in America and Colonel of the Seventeenth Regiment of
Foot, being at present weak in body, but of sound and disposing Mind,
Memory and Understanding, do make this my last will and Testament, as
follows, to wit my just debts being paid, I give demise and bequeath, all
Real and Personal Estate whatsoever and wheresoever, to my two Brothers
Arthur[98] and Hugh[99] Forbes, and their Heirs for ever, to be equally divided
betwixt them share and share alike. And I appoint my cousin James Glen

[98] Cf. John Forbes to Hugh Forbes, Portsmouth, April, 1757, *ante,* p. 4.
[99] Hugh Forbes, of Edinburgh, Scotland. Note the data in the third and fourth
letters of this edition.

Esquire late Governor of Carolina Executor of this my last Will and
Testament which I have executed at Philadelphia this thirteenth Day of
February in the Year of our Lord One Thousand Seven Hundred and
Fifty Nine.

Jo fforbes

Signed, Sealed, published, pronounced and declared by the Testator as
his last Will and Testament in the presence of

Richard Peters abt[r]

W[m] Russell Jur[r]

James Grant Jur[r]

5 + P. Jus[r] 24 March 1759

*   *   *   *   *

James Grant to Bouquet

[B.M., Add. MSS. 21643, f. 57, f. 59; Shippen MSS. L.C.]

Phila. 20 Feb. 1759

General Forbes highly sensible of the many fatigues and hardships you
and your Officers and the Troops in General under his Command have un-
derwent during the course of this most extraordinary Campaign that has happened in this or any other Country, and willing at the same time to give
Some publick testimony of his approbation to the Gentlemen under his
command, has ordered me to acquaint you and the Commanding Officers
of corps that he has directed a Gold medal to be struck to the following
purpose which he hereby Authorizes the officers of his Army to wear as an
honorary reward for their faithful services and as soon as opportunity offers
he intends to inform his Majesty of it. In the mean time your Officers &
Colonel Montgomery's may be provided in Town.

The Medal has on one side the representation of a Road cut thro an immense Forrest, over Rocks, and mountains. The motto Per tot Discrimina—
on the other side are represented the confluences of the Ohio and Monongahela rivers, a Fort in Flames in the forks of the Rivers at the approach of
General Forbes carried in a Litter, followed with the Army marching in
Columns with Cannon. The motto Ohio Brittannica Consilio manuque.
This is to be wore round the neck with a dark blew ribbon—by the Genl[s]
comand

Grant

N.B. General Forbes is of oppinion that Such of your officers as chuse to
provide themselves with the above Medal should have a Copy of this letter
Signed & attested by you as a warrant for thus wearing it

J.G.

Obituary of General John Forbes*
[Pennsylvania Gazette, March 15, 1759]

On Sunday last died, of a tedious illness, John Forbes, Esq., in the forty-ninth year of his age, son to ———— Forbes, of Petincrief, Esq.; in the shire of Fife in Scotland, Brigadier General, Colonel of the Seventeenth Regiment of Foot, and Commander of his Majesty's troops in the South Provinces of North America; a gentleman generally known and esteemed, and most sincerely and universally regretted. In his younger days he was bred to the profession of physic, but early ambitious of the military character, he purchased into the regiment of Scots Grey Dragoons, where by repeated purchases, and faithful services, he arrived to the rank of Lieutenant-Colonel.

His superior abilities soon recommended him to the protection of General Campbell, the Earl of Stair, Duke of Bedford, Lord Ligonier, and other distinguished characters in the army; with some of them he served as aide-de-camp, and with the rest in the familiarity of a family man. During the last war he had the honour to be employed in the character of Quarter Master General to the army under His Royal Highness the Duke; which duty he discharged with accuracy, dignity, and dispatch.

His services in America are well known. By a steady pursuit of well concerted measures, in defiance of disease, and numberless obstructions, he brought to a happy issue a most extraordinary campaign, and made a willing sacrifice of his own life to what he valued more, the interest of his King and Country. As a man he was just and without prejudice, brave without ostentation, uncommonly warm in his friendship and incapable of flattery; acquainted with the world and mankind; he was well bred, but absolutely impatient of formality and affection. Eminently possessed of the sociable virtues, he indulged a cheerful gratification; but quick in sense of honour and duty, so mixed the agreeable gentleman and man of business together as to shine alike (though truly uncommon) in both characters without the giddiness attendant on the one, or the sourness of the other. As an officer he was quick to discern useful men, and useful measures, generally seeing both at first view, according to their real qualities, steady in his measures, but open to information and council; in command he had dignity without superciliousness, and though perfectly master of the forms, never hesitated to drop them when the spirit, and more essential parts of the service required it. Yesterday he was interred in the chancel of Christ Church in this City.

* Printed, also, *Olden Time,* I, 189; *Pennsylvania Magazine of History and Biography,* XI (1887), 120.

The form and order of march at his funeral was as follows.

I. The Pioneers.
II. The Seventeenth Regiment, and two companies of Colonel Mont-gomery's Regiment, the colours with crapes; the drums covered with black; and the officers with crapes on their arms.
III. Two pieces of cannon, with Commanding Officers of artillery.
IV. The Engineers
V. The Staff
VI. The servants, in mourning, uncovered, two and two.
VII. A led horse, covered with black, conducted by a groom.
VIII. The Surgeons.
IX. The Physicians
X. The Clergy and Chaplains of the army
XI. The Corpse and the pall held by six field officers.
XII. The mourners.
XIII. The Governor, the Councill, the Speaker, and members of the As-sembly, the Judges, the magistrates, and gentlemen of the Province and city, two by two.
XIV. The Officers from the different garrisons, two and two.

N.B. The minute guns were fired from the time the corpse was brought out untill the interment was over; and the whole ended by a triple discharge of the small arms.

March 15, 1759

Memorial Tablet to Brigadier General John Forbes on the
north wall of Christ Church, Philadelphia, Pennsylvania.

Index

The First American Frontier

AN ARNO PRESS/NEW YORK TIMES COLLECTION

Agnew, Daniel.
A History of the Region of Pennsylvania North of the Allegheny River. 1887.

Alden, George H.
New Government West of the Alleghenies Before 1780. 1897.

Barrett, Jay Amos.
Evolution of the Ordinance of 1787. 1891.

Billon, Frederick.
Annals of St. Louis in its Early Days Under the French and Spanish Dominations. 1886.

Billon, Frederick.
Annals of St. Louis in its Territorial Days, 1804-1821. 1888.

Littel, William.
Political Transactions in and Concerning Kentucky. 1926.

Bowles, William Augustus.
Authentic Memoirs of William Augustus Bowles. 1916.

Bradley, A. G.
The Fight with France for North America. 1900.

Brannan, John, ed.
Official Letters of the Military and Naval Officers of the War, 1812-1815. 1823.

Brown, John P.
Old Frontiers. 1938.

Brown, Samuel R.
The Western Gazetteer. 1817.

Cist, Charles.
Cincinnati Miscellany of Antiquities of the West and Pioneer History. (2 volumes in one). 1845-6.

Claiborne, Nathaniel Herbert.
Notes on the War in the South with Biographical Sketches of the Lives of Montgomery, Jackson, Sevier, and Others. 1819.

Clark, Daniel.
Proofs of the Corruption of Gen. James Wilkinson. 1809.

Clark, George Rogers.
Colonel George Rogers Clark's Sketch of His Campaign in the Illinois in 1778-9. 1869.

Collins, Lewis.
Historical Sketches of Kentucky. 1847.

Cruikshank, Ernest, ed,
Documents Relating to Invasion of Canada and the Surrender of Detroit. 1912.

Cruikshank, Ernest, ed,
The Documentary History of the Campaign on the Niagara Frontier, 1812-1814. (4 volumes). 1896-1909.

Cutler, Jervis.
A Topographical Description of the State of Ohio, Indian Territory, and Louisiana. 1812.

Cutler, Julia P.
The Life and Times of Ephraim Cutler. 1890.

Darlington, Mary C.
History of Col. Henry Bouquet and the Western Frontiers of Pennsylvania. 1920.

Darlington, Mary C.
Fort Pitt and Letters From the Frontier. 1892.

De Schweinitz, Edmund.
The Life and Times of David Zeisberger. 1870.

Dillon, John B.
History of Indiana. 1859.

Eaton, John Henry.
Life of Andrew Jackson. 1824.

English, William Hayden.
Conquest of the Country Northwest of the Ohio. (2 volumes in one). 1896.

Flint, Timothy.
Indian Wars of the West. 1833.

Forbes, John.
Writings of General John Forbes Relating to His Service in North America. 1938.

Forman, Samuel S.
Narrative of a Journey Down the Ohio and Mississippi in 1789-90. 1888.

Haywood, John.
Civil and Political History of the State of Tennessee to 1796. 1823.

Heckewelder, John.
History, Manners and Customs of the Indian Nations. 1876.

Heckewelder, John.
Narrative of the Mission of the United Brethren. 1820.

Hildreth, Samuel P.
Pioneer History. 1848.

Houck, Louis.
The Boundaries of the Louisiana Purchase: A Historical Study. 1901.

Houck, Louis.
History of Missouri. (3 volumes in one). 1908.

Houck, Louis.
The Spanish Regime in Missouri. (2 volumes in one). 1909.

Jacob, John J.
A Biographical Sketch of the Life of the Late Capt. Michael Cresap. 1826.

Jones, David.
A Journal of Two Visits Made to Some Nations of Indians on the West Side of the River Ohio, in the Years 1772 and 1773. 1774.

Kenton, Edna.
Simon Kenton. 1930.

Loudon, Archibald.
Selection of Some of the Most Interesting Narratives of Outrages. (2 volumes in one). 1808-1811.

Monette, J. W.
History, Discovery and Settlement of the Mississippi Valley. (2 volumes in one). 1846.

Morse, Jedediah.
American Gazetteer. 1797.

Pickett, Albert James.
History of Alabama. (2 volumes in one). 1851.

Pope, John.
A Tour Through the Southern and Western Territories. 1792.

Putnam, Albigence Waldo.
History of Middle Tennessee. 1859.

Ramsey, James G. M.
Annals of Tennessee. 1853.

Ranck, George W.
Boonesborough. 1901.

Robertson, James Rood, ed.
Petitions of the Early Inhabitants of Kentucky to the Gen. Assembly of Virginia. 1914.

Royce, Charles.
Indian Land Cessions. 1899.

Rupp, I. Daniel.
History of Northampton, Lehigh, Monroe, Carbon and Schuykill Counties. 1845.

Safford, William H.
The Blennerhasset Papers. 1864.

St. Clair, Arthur.
A Narrative of the Manner in which the Campaign Against the Indians, in the Year 1791 was Conducted. 1812.

Sargent, Winthrop, ed.
A History of an Expedition Against Fort DuQuesne in 1755. 1855.

Severance, Frank H.
An Old Frontier of France. (2 volumes in one). 1917.

Sipe, C. Hale.
Fort Ligonier and Its Times. 1932.

Stevens, Henry N.
Lewis Evans: His Map of the Middle British Colonies in America. 1920.

Timberlake, Henry.
The Memoirs of Lieut. Henry Timberlake. 1927.

Tome, Philip.
Pioneer Life: Or Thirty Years a Hunter. 1854.

Trent, William.
Journal of Captain William Trent From Logstown to Pickawillany. 1871.

Walton, Joseph S.
Conrad Weiser and the Indian Policy of Colonial Pennsylvania. 1900.

Withers, Alexander Scott.
Chronicles of Border Warfare. 1895.